AMERICAN INSANITY

How The Biden-Harris Administration
Attempted
to Destroy Our Constitutional Republic
LEROY E. COSSETTE

American Insanity
Copyright © 2025 by LeRoy E. Cossette

ISBN: 979-8894790947 (sc)
ISBN: 979-8894790954 (e)

All rights reserved. No part of this publication may be reproduced, distributed, or transmitted in any form or by any means, including photocopying, recording, or other electronic or mechanical methods, without the prior written permission of the publisher and/or the author, except in the case of brief quotations embodied in critical reviews and other noncommercial uses permitted by copyright law.

The views expressed in this book are solely those of the author and do not necessarily reflect the views of the publisher, and the publisher hereby disclaims any responsibility for them.

The Reading Glass Books
1-888-420-3050
www.readingglassbooks.com
fulfillment@readingglassbooks.com

Table of Contents

PROLOGUE v
Chapter 1: Where Am I 1
Chapter 2: Political Conversion 17
Chapter 3: Constitutional Republic 30
Chapter 4: Incompetent Federal Government 86
Chapter 5: Democrat Party 329
Chapter 6: Republican Party 337
Chapter 7: Donald J. Trump 348
Chapter 8: First Amendment 366
Chapter 9: Harsh Political Realities 371
Chapter 10: America's Shift 377
Chapter 11: Who Should Decide 386
Chapter 12: American Frustration 392
Chapter 13: The Biden's 404
Chapter 14: The Swamp 420
Chapter 15: Soros And Globalism 427
Chapter 16: Marxist-Communist 436
Chapter 17: Bankrupting America 446
Chapter 18: Retirement Woes 462
Chapter 19: Insurrection That Wasn't 465
Chapter 20: Social Insanity 485
Chapter 21: Chinese Dominance 507
Chapter 22: Is America a Failed Experiment? 516
Chapter 23: Election Integrity 524
Chapter 24: Article V - Convention of States 533

PROLOGUE

This book is a testament to my profound concern for the future of the United States. The political insanity that has overtaken our nation, fueled by the apathy of American citizens and their failure to keep a vigilant eye on our governing politicians, is leading to the loss of the America I grew up in. My grandchildren, great-grandchildren, and future generations will never experience this reality. We are living in a time of political insanity, witnessing the rapid transformation of our Constitutional Republic into a Marxist-Communist Nation.

I offer a critique of our bloated and corrupt federal bureaucracy and our two-party political system that has failed to support and protect our Judeo-Christian and conservative values. The parties have lost their moral compass, strength, and courage to stand against those who would see our Constitutional Republic fall. This has allowed ushering in a non-representative governing system due to elected officials lacking the leadership, statesmanship, and moral character to unify America and save our Constitutional form of government and our Judeo-Christian values. I highlight the lack of government leaders with the will, strength, and courage to serve "We the People" with honor and integrity.

"American Insanity" addresses the depth of corruption and treasonous acts to which our once-trusted elected officials have descended. It dissects a lawless, inefficient, ineffective, out-of-control, and bloated bureaucracy that governs beyond the people's consent. "American Insanity" addresses the unconstitutional and illegal activities of a government determined to strip the American citizenry of their rights and freedoms and fundamentally transform our Constitutional Republic into a Marxist-Communist third-world Nation.

LeRoy E. Cossette

What is presented in this book are not just opinions but my deeply held personal views, interpretations, and opinions. They are not meant to reflect or represent anyone else's views or feelings regarding any subject matter I address unless otherwise quoted as being another's insight or information. It must also be pointed out that any reference to "Marxist-Communist Democrat Party" is intended to refer to the Party leadership and radical elements of the Democrat Party and not individual Democrat voters personally. Further, any reference to American conservatism means support of Christian values, moral absolutism, traditional family values, and American exceptionalism while opposing abortion, euthanasia, same-sex marriage, and transgender rights.

Chapter 1
Where Am I

I have just awoken in the Twilight Zone, a dysfunctional junction in time and space. In this place, absurdity overwhelms common sense, and individuals have become nothing more than hateful and intolerable human beings incapable of interacting with one another or discussing each other's beliefs and values without disdain toward those with different points of view or opinions.

I find myself in the land of the brave, where the brave can no longer find the courage and strength to stand against radical, woke malcontents determined to bring chaos and uncertainty to our lives. No matter which way I turn, I see political clowns to one side and woke jokers to the other side, and standing with me between them is fear for the future of our children and our Nation.

Where am I that so much apathy exists among people living in a country that provides so much freedom and opportunities, who have lost their faith in God and their faith in a Nation founded upon Judeo-Christian values? Are there really that many willing to worship at the altar of Marxi tenth of the casualties sustained, and maybe, just maybe, we would st-Communism, believing that their salvation rests in the hands of a godless and evil government willing to make slaves of them? I am mentally unable to grasp the reality of this place because this is not the United States of America of my youth. Instead, this is a place being consumed by an evil that is Marxist-Communism.

I am dumbfounded that there are so many American citizens who truly believe that life under Marxist-Communism would be euphoria while life under a Constitutional Republic is oppressive; that being a subject of a Marxist-Communism form of government under one-party rule will provide for a more free and prosperous life than would a Constitutional Republic form of government subject to the will of "We the People" and does not treat its citizens as subject but instead places the rights of its citizens above the rights of the government. Are there so many so ready to give up their God-given rights under a constitution that guarantees each of its citizens freedoms found nowhere else in the world? Can this still be the United States of America, whose past generations were capable of setting aside their differences and were able to find the strength, courage, and determination to confront and defeat the evil of Nazism, Fascism, and Communism?

Could we have lived in a land of freedom for so long that our citizens now assume they are entitled to these freedoms and privileges with no obligation to protect and fight to retain them? What happened to the greatest and strongest God-fearing nation on earth? This is not the America I grew up in, so what happened to the land of the brave and the home of the free? What happened to the land of diversity in which every citizen had God-given rights, talents, and skills that contributed to achieving their dreams and, by extension, the prosperity of our great Nation if only they were willing to make the necessary sacrifices to achieve those dreams? Is this not still the United States of America in which each one of us was so privileged to be born? Have any one of us ever wished to live anywhere else, including the anti-American malcontents?

Where am I that so many citizens have come to care so little about what is occurring within their government and seem to not care about the real possibility that their children and grandchildren will never know the America of their grandparents and great-grandparents? How is it that so much has changed so rapidly, or is it more conceivable that these changes have been slowly occurring over time, but we have been so preoccupied with worldly achievements that we have failed to recognize what has been happening all about us? I struggle to believe that I am still in the country which was founded and fought for by a rag-tag army of brave men and women to gain their freedom from tyranny and oppression. Men and women with the courage and conviction to fight against England, the most powerful military force in the world in their time.

I am no longer in the country that those brave individuals fought for, risking their fortunes and their very lives for a dream of freedom from tyranny and oppression. Men with the courage and wisdom to form a new Nation governed by a constitution that grants every citizen God-given rights to the blessings of Life, Liberty, and the Pursuit of Happiness. Has America reached that point in its history, which Benjamin Franklin warned about in his statement that "We have a Republic if we can keep it," that a constitution written to withstand the passage of time has failed to do so? Have so many citizens of these United States become so addicted to free benefits and entitlements that they are willing to allow the entire Nation to be sucked into an abyss of slavery by the government?

Where am I that the leadership of some of the world's largest and most successful corporations has been so easily driven to fear by intellectually irrational "Woke" fools? It is inconceivable that individuals and companies with the ability to become so successful in a highly competitive world could so easily be brought to their knees by such a small number of woke agitators, causing them to capitulate to their woke nonsense. Are they not among the brave of the United States, and if so, where are they, and why do they not have the courage to stand up against these despots and say, "NO" this is not acceptable!" Bravery and courage are lost among the leadership of these giant corporations. Why else would those with the intellectual ability and courage to take the risks necessary to become so successful not realize that becoming involved with purely political agendas will only result in their demise? Their place is to ensure that their products meet the expectations of their customers and a profit margin acceptable to their shareholders and not to become involved in the latest politically correct trend.

We have become so morally weak in mind and spirit that God may very well have given up on our once truly Judeo-Christian nation, or perhaps God is merely testing our faith in him and in our Constitutional Republic. Will the faithful find the strength to endure and banish the evil that is Marxist-Communism, or will we suffer the same demise of so many other promising nations throughout history and fall into the clutches of this evil that is Marxist-Communism? Is the anti-Christ present among us instilling hatred and disdain for one another when, not so long ago, we all stood united in our Christian values and heritage?

Have we become so addicted to self-satisfaction and self-gratification that America has become no more than a second Sodom and Gomorrah, slowly being destroyed by God for our wickedness? Has a diabolical movement taken control of a once patriotic John F. Kennedy Democrat Party and turned that Party into a stronghold of evil?

Americans are confused and disorientated as a result of all the caustic political rhetoric being thrown at them, causing great concern in our country's ability to find a path out of this hollow hell and return to being the home of freedom, liberty, and security. Corrupt sociopathic minions from hell are elected to government positions only to turn around and use those positions to destroy our Constitutional Republic and "We the People" without shame or remorse. To destroy the one country in the world that remains a Judeo-Christian Constitutional Republic under God's guidance. I wonder where I am that no matter how I vote, how I participate, what I say, or how much I pray, Satan's grip on our Nation's elected officials seems beyond salvation; where elected officials, who once were believed to be trustworthy and honorable, and as such, in whom we entrusted our faith to protect our Constitution and "We the People," but rather have abandoned us. Trust obviously misplaced! We are in a strange dimension of the universe wherein the America we so loved and many have fought for has been consumed by wickedness. An evil wickedness determined to turn our Judeo-Christian Constitutional Republic into a malicious abyss. An abyss of chaos, riots, hate, distrust, corruption, and divisiveness.

Where am I that the Constitutional right to speak freely regarding one's thoughts and opinions or to practice one's religious doctrine without fear of government retribution has suddenly vanished? Are not those with conservative viewpoints still citizens of the United States of America? Innocent and vulnerable citizens can no longer live safely, families struggle to feed their children, young couples can no longer afford to buy their first homes, and citizens struggle to put gas in their vehicles to go travel to work.

Where are we that children can no longer expect to receive an education that will prepare them for a successful life without their being indoctrinated to values and beliefs not held by their parents? Where radical teachers are allowed to brainwash our children to be racist, subject them to age-inappropriate sexual material, subject them to drag queen reading hour or sexually explicit performances, encourage students as young as five and six years old to believe that they were born in the wrong body and, therefore, should be provided with school resources to assist them in transitioning? All without the explicit permission of the parents.

I struggle to grasp the possibility that I am still in the America I so loved, with so much disdain all around me. Once trusted leaders are no more than evil and deceitful minions of the devil, willingly and knowingly committing treasonous acts against America's Constitution, laws, and its citizens. In this place, the devil has brought together the most incompetent, corrupt, and heartless individuals to lead America, all of whom are systematically attacking, intimidating, and destroying the lives of American citizens much in the same manner Stalin did to gain control of the citizens of the Soviet Union. Citizens who must be brought under control or eliminated because they proudly subscribe to the ideology of conservatism and refer to themselves as Christians or

MEGA followers of a previous President. A previous President who was fraudulently and criminally denied reelection to his rightful position as the President of the United States.

Where am I that if a biological male pretends to be a female, I am obligated to accept their mentally ill delusion and pretend along with them; that allows biological males who self-identify as females to unfairly compete in female sports, shower in female locker rooms, or utilize female bathrooms in our federally funded schools; that foreign nations influencing our elections is bad, but illegal immigrants voting in our elections is good; or that people who never owned slaves should pay reparations to people who have never been slaves.

Where am I that illegal immigrants are provided free housing, education, food, and medical care at taxpayer expense while veterans who served honorably in our military forces to protect our constitutional Republic are sleeping in the street and America's poor are going hungry, where illegal immigrants with tuberculosis or polio are welcomed, but you had better be able to prove your dog is vaccinated?

In this foreign place, it is not the terrorist from the Middle East coming over our open border that is America's greatest threat; it is not the unvetted Afghanistan citizens who were flown out of Afghanistan to America and may have intentions of harming our citizens that are America's greatest threat; it is not Antifa or Black Lives Matter, who have maliciously destroyed small business, burned down law enforcement buildings, murdered police officers and innocent citizens, and rioted in the streets of our cities across the country that are America's greatest threat; nor is it fentanyl and other deadly drugs smuggled across our open border killing tens of thousands of our young children and adults that are America's greatest threat. It is none of these, according to the corrupt Marxist-Communist politicians and their Washington elitist allies. To these morally deprived agents of evil, it is law-abiding citizens who refuse to accept their Marxist-Communist ideologies, who refuse to accept the radical transition of our Constitutional Republic into a nation of chaos, hate, and division that are America's greatest threat. It is those with the courage to stand up and fight against this evil who are the terrorists and the most significant threat to America.

Irish doctors and German engineers who want to immigrate to the United States must undergo years of rigorous vetting. Still, malicious, illiterate gang bangers, traffickers, drug smugglers, and terrorists who illegally enter our country are welcomed with open arms without the need to wait their turn or to be subjected to any vetting.

Where am I that $5 billion for border security is too expensive, but billions of dollars to anti-American nations to secure their borders is not; where if you are caught cheating or lying to gain admission to a college, you are rejected and villainized, but if you cheat or lie to get into our country, you go to college for free; or, those who commit election fraud are not held accountable, but those who can provide substantial evidence of that fraud or the mathematical improbability of the election results are persecuted and prosecuted?

Is it even conceivable that the land of the free and the brave is now the land of despair and hopelessness because Marxist-Communist puppets have led American citizens to believe that all white American citizens are racist from birth and must, therefore, be punished for atrocities they had no part in? That all people of color are born oppressed with no hope of achieving the American dream or must be paid retribution for wrongs they never experienced? Would it not be the faithless and Godless people who pretend to serve the American people from within our government be America's greatest threat? How is it possible that the Marxist-Communist puppets, who have no problem weaponizing the Department of Justice (DOJ), the Federal Bureau of Investigation (FBI), and the Internal Revenue Service (IRS) against their political rivals and "We the People" not be America's greatest threat? Should it not be those who despise our freedoms and belief in a God who has provided us our earthly rights be the villains and shunned by the people?

Where am I that a Marxist-Communist movement will insist that there is no such thing as gender but, within the same breath, demand a female President be elected; where history documents that Marxist-Communist governed countries always collapse, but somehow Marxist-Communism seems like an excellent idea for the United States; where dangerous criminals are caught-and-released back into our communities by George Soros bought-off District Attorneys, only to harm more people, but attempting to stop them while they are committing a crime is a violation of their civil rights?

Where am I that soulless minions of the Marxist-Communist movement can, without fear of retribution, attack, threaten, and intimidate every freedom-loving conservative citizen into accepting an ideology they do not believe in; into thinking that there is no God or God-given rights but only rights given by the government; where every MAGA conservative, every parent of school-age children who dares confront school boards regarding a school's curriculum, and every citizen who owns a weapon are considered domestic terrorists?

Where am I that law-abiding citizens are intimidated if they fail to accept and comply with an ideology against their moral values? Where those who dare exercise their God-given rights under America's constitution are intimidated, harassed, publicly humiliated, hunted down, and jailed because they dared to speak out against an evil and corrupt government and the corrupt politicians within that government. Are these people really the greatest threat to America, or are they the greatest threat to the elitist status of corrupt Washington political hacks?

Have the Marxist-Communist elements in Washington, D.C., rescinded the Constitution, allowing them to provide funding to the U.S. Postal Service (USPS), not to improve a failed mail delivery system but rather to establish a unit to spy on American citizens and to fund the IRS with an additional $82 billion to hire and support 80,000 new Gestapo agents willing to carry firearms and shoot their fellow American citizens? Would not the USPS or the IRS, an already feared agency, turned into a Russian-style KGB unit to hunt down American citizens who dare defy the evil Marxist-Communist ideology, be America's greatest threat? How can this still possibly be the United States of America if federal departments and agencies, which once served the people, can so easily be politicized and weaponized into an army against its law-abiding citizens? How can this still possibly be the United States of America if a president is allowed to circumvent Congress and legislate by passing Executive Orders depriving Americans of their freedoms during a pandemic? Is it truly America if health officials can cancel rental contracts or declare loan payments in suspension? Must we look forward to the future closing of mom-and-pop stores, the engine of the American economy, declaring it illegal for them to sell flowers or shoes during quarantine but not so for Walmart or Target? Is this what American citizens can now expect any time the federal government determines it advantageous to declare a medical emergency to quarantine the masses in order to control them?

Where am I that the government can create a government Ministry of Truth agency? Whose truths will be determined appropriate or inappropriate, and by whom? Will there be an objective manual available to the Ministry of Truth to make these determinations, or will these determinations be subjective based on the ideology of the ruling regime? Just one more sign out of many that our freedom of speech and expression is soon to be made illegal by a rogue Marxist-Communist federal government. A government that feels free to either intimidate or bribe big tech social media to monitor conservative conversations and cancel any that do not meet the Marxist-Communist Democrat Party's standards. It has become physically dangerous to speak the truth on a university or college campus where the objective is to provide students a platform to debate different viewpoints and ideas.

Can this be the America in which so many brave men and women have sacrificed their lives to defend our right to be safe in our homes and our person, while brain-dead woke followers call for the defunding of our law enforcement units, leaving American citizens unsafe and open to violent crimes propagated by individuals who have little to no regard for our laws; where destructive and violent criminals are not being held accountable for destroying the lives of innocent people, but rather are given inappropriately minimum to no punishment for their crimes by an injustice legal system? At the same time, the immense power of the federal government is arrayed against those whose only crime is dissent and protest, as allowed under our Constitution, against these unjust and lawless actions,

Can I possibly still be in the free America I grew up in if what I observe is a police state in which citizens with opposing ideologies are being intimidated, harassed, and arrested for expressing political views that do not fit the Marxist-Communist narrative? In this place, law has been turned from a shield to protect the innocent into a sword to conquer the people.

Where am I *that a Speaker of the House would, with impunity, so disrespectfully tear up the State of the Union address on national television because she hates the person who delivered that speech? Hated for his solid Christian conservative views and his strength and courage to take on the Washington bureaucracy.*

Where am I that the FBI has the right to subvert the campaign of such a candidate because it disagrees with that person's ideology? Was it suddenly made legal for one presidential candidate to hire a foreign ex-spy to subvert the campaign of their rival through the creation of a fake dossier? If not, then why is such behavior going unpunished? What happened to our once honorable legal system?

In this strange place, there are no borders but rather a place open to every other country's criminal element: drug dealers, traffickers of young children and girls, the mentally ill, the poor, and their freeloaders. America is nothing more than an extension of the corrupt and dysfunctional countries of Central America and beyond. The place I now find myself is rapidly spiraling out of control from a once prosperous, safe, and free Nation into a land of historical deterioration. This once prosperous Nation now faces record-high crime rates, record-high inflation, record-high fuel prices, record-high food prices, dependency on foreign countries for energy supplies, and the control of its citizens through unconstitutional mandates. A place where citizens have been pushed into a world of unemployment, welfare, and need for financial and housing assistance from the government in a strategic Marxist-Communist move to enslave our citizens to a corrupt government. This is not the land for which so many proudly served in combat to protect.

Where am I that our legal system can abruptly decide that theft is not a crime, assault not a felony, where thieves can walk out of stores with bags of stolen goods without fear of the law because of Soros-funded District Attorneys; where District Attorneys who have taken an oath to uphold the law are no better than the criminals who terrorize our streets; or, where District Attorney's elections are being allowed to be financed by evil and corrupt out-of-state billionaires determined to foster chaos within our legal system? Is it not the intention of the election process to be conducted, in all aspects, by those who reside in that state and to whom that District Attorney represents and answers to and not wealthy billionaires from out of state to whom that elected District Attorney then owes his allegiance? How can citizens of that state receive unbiased legal justice if that District Attorney's loyalty is to an outside influencer and not the citizens of the state they were elected to provide legal justice?

When did "We the People" decide that seventy percent of voters are incapable of casting their ballots on Election Day, allowing for the Marxist-Communist movement to ignore their State Constitution and laws, allowing for days, if not weeks, to perform this civic duty; provides for the use of unsecured ballot drop-boxes which were are so easily stuffed with phony ballots to sway an election? Who determined that members of minority groups were intellectually incapable of obtaining a photo identification card to vote, yet those same people must have a photo identification card to purchase certain medications, enter certain facilities, or drive their vehicles? What an insult to our minority citizens. Were these revolutionary changes to our election processes the subject of state or national debate by elected representatives?

Where am I that voter returns cannot be counted and election results made public by the end of election day? It was only a short time ago that this was how our elections were conducted. Did the fact that our government turned to electronic ballots and computerized tallies make it that difficult to tabulate votes? If so, is this not a clear justification for returning to the traditional one-vote, one-day, paper ballot policy?

Where am I that a once trusted FBI allows its directors to mislead or outright lie to Congress, deceive judges with concocted tales from fake dossiers and doctored documents, and do so without repercussion? Did Congress pass a law that leadership within the FBI or Central Intelligence Agency (CIA) could lie with impunity under oath without consequences? Meanwhile, average citizens face heavy fines and jail time for the same act. In light of everything we know today about how the corrupt FBI and the Department of Justice (DOJ) conduct their business, perhaps it is time to revisit the tragedy of Waco and Ruby Ridge. Maybe the narratives we were initially given were manufactured by the FBI and the DOJ, much like what comes out of those agencies today.

Who proclaimed that the Chairman of the Joint Chiefs of Staff had the authority to call his Chinese Communist counterpart to warn him if a supposedly unstable American president was planning an attack and do so without fear of facing charges of treason? Is this not treason? If such an act is treason, why has there been no accountability held against the Chairman of the Joint Chiefs of Staff for doing so?

Has it always been true that retired generals routinely labeled their former commander-in-chief as a Nazi, a Mussolini, or an adherent advocate of the tools of Auschwitz? If such comments by former prominent military leaders are held to be protected by the First Amendment, then why are American citizens who question face masks, untested vaccines, or quarantines being subjected to cancellation on social media at the direction of our federal legal system, or worse yet harassed, intimidated, and threatened with legal action by our federal legal system? Who within our federal government or military has been approving retired senior military personnel to enter into contracts with foreign countries, some of which are or potentially may be enemies of our country, to provide and train those foreign entities with our military tactics and strategies? Is this not treason?

It would seem that it is no longer against federal law to swarm the homes of Supreme Court justices to picket their homes to intimidate Justice's families in efforts to affect a judge's rulings. If this is not the case and it is still against federal law to do so, how then, with impunity, were the stupidest of our society allowed to surround the homes of our Supreme Court Justices, furious over a Supreme Court decision? A decision that did not rescind any woman's right to abort their unborn child but merely followed the Constitution and returned legal decisions regarding abortion restrictions back to the sovereign states where those decisions have always belonged. How could these mobs of irrational radicals so easily swarm our justices' homes without any action or interference from our law enforcement agencies?

Is this not a constitutional republic that provides its citizens unequaled levels of freedom and liberties? If so, how is it that there are citizens who believe our Constitutional Republic is so evil that it needs to be abolished and replaced with an authoritarian form of governance?

Was it really a virus that resulted in the cancellation of many of our Constitutional rights, forced the mandatory lockdown of our schools and small businesses, and robbed us of our collective sanity, or was it the Washington Marxist-Communist Elitist who merely utilized the virus as a means to test their ability to control the population? Who or what allowed brain-dead disciples of "Wokism" to cause hysteria and ignite insanity within our businesses, corporations, entertainment institutions, and institutions of learning and allowed for the imprisonment of fellow citizens who refused to believe in these falsehoods and ideologies and exercised their Constitutional right to protest and express their grievances and frustrations against a corrupt federal government and election results. Wasn't America once a land in which its citizens were allowed to hold and express opposing views and beliefs but had the strength to tolerate one another's viewpoints while remaining united in the hands of God? This is not the United States of America of my youth, so then where am I?

Are we all lost in some surreal reality where those elected to go to Washington to represent "We the People" are so quick and willing to sell their souls to the temptations of power, status, and wealth? Are we now at the point where it is a genuine possibility that all that has been accomplished over the past two hundred and thirty-two years may be lost because of evil and corrupt political leaders who, without care or remorse, openly disrespect, ignore, or purposely misinterpret our laws and the most significant governing document ever penned by man, the Constitution of the United States of America? Done so in order for the Marxist-Communist Washington elitists to gain control of the population, turning a once proud people into obedient sheep. It is undoubtedly conceivable because that is what happened during the COVID-19 pandemic. We were directed to wear masks, and we complied; we were directed to maintain a six-foot distance between each other when standing in line, and we complied; businesses were directed to close down, and we complied; we were directed to stay in our homes unless we were essential employees and we complied; we were directed to get untested vaccine shots, and we complied.

The Marxist-Communist Washington elitists view clean-burning, cheap, and abundant natural gas as the equivalent to dirty coal and view prized natural gas, which had made America energy self-sufficiency and a world supplier, reduced pollution, and provided inexpensive electricity, a fuel whose extraction was a war against nature. Which lawmakers, laws, and votes by the people declared natural gas development and pipelines criminal? Are we still not a nation of representative governance, and if so, how can our representatives enact these actions when well over half of our eligible voting citizens do not agree with such dramatic actions?

Could I possibly be awake, and the United States of America is the nightmare? Is it possible that this once prosperous and united country has become a divided hell on earth controlled by a small group of wealthy and evil Marxist-Communist elitists determined to change a once free citizenry into nothing more than obedient servants? Can I possibly be awake in a world of nightmares led by corrupt politicians who have never lived a day of their lives as a humane, hardworking American citizen? Individuals so evil, it is difficult, at best, to fathom that we have not descended into hell itself. Is it even conceivable that these cognitively wanting representatives can wreak so much evil without Marxist-Communist puppeteers pulling their strings in the background? If so, who then within the Washington swamp is the devil using to manipulate these corrupt elected officials who are conspiring to destroy a Nation of hope and dreams?

Nightmare or reality, the place I now find myself is a place being led by Marxist-Communist advocates who have no honor or integrity. In this place, corrupt politicians have long since sold their souls and become willing puppets of evil, determined to destroy a Judeo-Christian nation that believes in God, not government—sold their souls for earthly and Godless gifts and disguising themselves as Christians while systematically profoundly, and shamelessly transform the greatest Judeo-Christian Constitutional Republic in the world into nothing more than another tyrannical Godless third world country. Nothing makes sense anymore: no values, morals, or civility.

This is an upside-down world where right is wrong and wrong is right, where moral is immoral and immoral is moral, where good is evil and evil is good, where killing murderers is terrible, but killing unborn babies is okay. America, once the greatest Nation on earth, the Shining Light of the World, has been taken over and consumed by inconceivable levels of evil and is fast spiraling into the abyss of hell from which we may never escape.

Chapter 2
Political Conversion

I grew up in a staunch Catholic Democrat family. My parents and my grandparents, who legally migrated to the United States from Canada, firmly believed in the Democrat Party as the party of the working people. One of my uncles, who served honorably in the Korean War, was a Democrat party official at the State level in North Dakota and strongly advocated for the party's platform and values. My family passionately believed that elected Democratic officials and the Democrat party would always do the right thing to preserve our Judeo-Christian values, defend our Constitutional Republic, and honor their oath to serve and protect the people of this great Nation. They were all members of the John F. Kennedy era Democrat Party and not the Democrat Party that it has evolved into over the past six decades. Sadly, many members of my family have failed to recognize the evolution of their Democrat Party into a profoundly Marxist Communist-leaning Party. Should they ever come to realize that the current Democrat Party no longer supports their Christian core values and beliefs, they would never maintain their membership in the Democrat Party. They were right in their belief in and support of the Democrat Party until Lyndon B. Johnson became President of the United States. Although the Democrat Party's shift to the left took a foothold with the 1932 Roosevelt administration, with the assassination of President John F. Kennedy and the inauguration of President Lyndon B. Johnson, the Democrat Party was placed on an accelerated path to self-destruction as a Marxist-Communist ideological party with the Johnson Administration. Unfortunately, many Republicans who ascribed to Marxism followed Johnson's lead and voted with the Democrats on Johnson's Marxist-Communist legislative proposals referred to as the "Great New Deal."

Along with President Johnson's passage of the "Great New Deal," President Johnson also escalated the civil war in Viet Nam by injecting American military forces into that civil war between a corrupt, inept, democratically elected South Vietnam government and the South Vietnam Communist (VC) guerrilla forces, which the North Vietnam Communist government of Ho Chi Minh heavily supported. This support to the South Vietnam guerrillas by North Vietnam was the justification used by the Johnson Administration to send American destroyers into the Gulf of Tonkin in 1964 to conduct surveillance and intercept North Vietnamese communications in support of the South Vietnamese civil war efforts.

On August 2, 1964, the United States destroyer USS Maddox was off the coast of North Vietnam in support of a South Vietnam military covert operation in the coastal region of North Vietnam. In response to this operation off their coast, three North Vietnam People's Navy torpedo boats attacked the USS Maddox. There were no United States casualties, and the USS Maddox was unscathed except for a single bullet hole from a Vietnamese machine gun round. President Johnson claimed that this attack on a United States destroyer was unprovoked even though the destroyer was in that area in direct support of a South Vietnam military operation. President Johnson used this incident to persuade Congress on August 5th, 1964, to allow him to significantly escalate the United States' involvement in the Vietnam War with the injection of hundreds of thousands of American military personnel.

President Lyndon Johnson and his administration led the American people to believe that not injecting military forces into South Vietnam to defeat Ho Chi Minh's communist Viet Minh forces would result in a domino effect, leading to the spreading of communism throughout Southeast Asia. The domino theory was a Cold War policy that suggested a communist government in one nation would quickly lead to a communist takeover of neighboring countries, each falling like a row of dominos. In Southeast Asia, the United States government used this discredited domino theory to justify our involvement in Vietnam. In fact, America's failure to prevent a communist victory in Vietnam had much less of an impact than had been assumed by proponents of the domino theory. Except for Laos and Cambodia, communism has failed to spread throughout Southeast Asia.

The Johnson Administration made a seriously wrong calculation that led to one out of every ten Americans who served in Vietnam becoming a casualty. Out of 2.7 million men and women who served in Vietnam, 58,148 were killed in action (KIA), never to return home to their loved ones, and well over 304,000 were wounded, many so severely that a life without pain, suffering, and nightmares would become a daily mental, emotional, and physical struggle. I was one of those 2.7 million American men who served in Vietnam. For years following my return home and following the daily news regarding our increasing losses with no end in sight and no reasonable justification for those losses, I began to lose trust in our federal government. Their lies, which led to the injection of our country into the concerns of a foreign country's civil war, have led to a life of suffering from severe anxiety, panic attacks, depression, drug dependency, nightmares, flashbacks, aggression, and high suicide rates for veterans who fought in that and subsequent wars. These problems, later to be diagnosed as Post Traumatic Stress Disorder (PTSD), have led too many combat veterans to fail in their relationships with their spouses, families, and friends, and tragically, many to commit suicide.

I am a personal testament to the results of our country's unjustified injection into the civil war of another country. Since my return from Vietnam, my life has been one of many difficult periods, suffering from extreme anxiety, depression, and the failure of two marriages, all as a direct result of Post-Traumatic Stress Disorder (PTSD). The shadow of combat in Vietnam is a never-ending dominant force within my mind. These forces have led me to question and challenge government authority and author articles regarding our elected officials and the Washington Swamps' failure to follow the laws and Constitution of our country. This Post-Traumatic Stress Disorder cross that I bear has been the motivation for my activism in politics and to author political articles addressing the egregious acts being perpetrated against the American people by the politicians we have elected to represent us and our Christian values. I author these articles and now this book in the hope that I may, in some small way, contribute to informing our citizens of what is indeed occurring in the government of the United States. Information that our corrupt Marxist-Communist corporate news media outlets refuse to report and are suppressing our Constitutional right to be informed. I am a political activist attempting to help save our Constitutional Republic from the increasingly determined attacks on our Constitutional Republic by Marxist-Communist elements of our federal government and citizenry.

After eighteen years of a childhood growing up in an environment much akin to that of "Tom Sawyer" and "Huckleberry Finn," my happy life abruptly ended with my landing on the beaches of Vietnam on June 6th of 1965, at the age of nineteen. This landing occurred after two fantastic years at the Camp Pendleton Marine Corps Base in California, where I had made many good friends. Before our assault onto the beaches of Vietnam, we were gathered on the decks of the ship transporting us to this war-torn world and told that we were going to Vietnam to stop the spread of communism throughout Asia and eventually from coming to America. Unlike children who are going through our current public school system, we were taught about the evil of Communism and the destructive nature of such a governing system. As one would expect of eighteen- and nineteen-year-olds who feel invincible, we were ready and willing to confront and stop this evil.

I, those who landed with me, and those who were to follow, had no idea what the cost would be for a failed ending to America's involvement in that civil war. I spent twelve traumatic months in Vietnam serving with the 1st Battalion, 9th Marines, whose sole mission was to search for and destroy the enemy. To that end, my Battalion fought for months at a very heavy cost of Marine lives, suffering our first Killed-In-Action (KIA) the very next day following our arrival to South Vietnam.

We were able to stop the spread of communism in Europe and Asia but failed miserably in Vietnam. Communist Vietnam defeated the greatest armed force in the world. How could that possibly happen? It happened because a Marxist-Communist Democrat President refused to allow the military to manage the war and do what was necessary to win. Johnson was a Marxist-Communist Democrat President who chose to micro-manage the war personally. President Johnson's belief in his superior knowledge of military strategy and tactics failed miserably. Perhaps he should have allowed his military Generals to manage the war and not allowed hippie protesters, Marxist-Communist news media, and his senior war advisor, news anchor Walter Cronkite, to dictate his strategic decisions. Then, America would have won that war in a relatively brief period, with a tenth of the casualties sustained, and maybe, just maybe, we would not be fighting communism here in America today.

The 1st Battalion, 9th Marines, with which I proudly served in Vietnam:

- Endured the *Longest Sustained Period of Combat* and suffered the *Highest Killed in Action (KIA)* rate in Marine Corps history.
- They were constantly engaged in battle during the entire time in Vietnam.
- Sustained KIA every single week we were in Vietnam.

- The Vietnam Memorial Wall in Washington honors the supreme sacrifice of 618 Marines from the 1st Battalion, 9th Marines.

- Ho Chi Minh, the President of the North Vietnamese Enemy Forces, labeled the First Battalion, 9th Marines, Di Bo Chet (The Walking Dead) following the death of his nephew at the hands of the 1st Battalion, 9th Marines during a combat engagement with a North Vietnam Regular Army unit of which he was a part.

<u>Sources & Additional Information</u>: *(https://www.wearethemighty.com/mighty-history/this-is-how-the-1 Bt-9th-marines-became-the-walking-dead/) (https://en.wikipedia.org/wiki/1st_Battalion,_9th_Marines) (*

Ho Chi Minh, the communist leader of North Vietnam, vowed to wipe out our Battalion in revenge for his nephew's death, and until then, we were Walking Dead. Although he failed to destroy our battalion, his directing his forces to accomplish this threat caused an extremely high number of casualties for the battalion. Ho Chi Minh's forces' attempt to carry out his threat failed to succeed, and it came at an exceedingly high cost for Ho Chi Minh's forces.

The 1st Battalion, 9th Marines, was awarded the United States Presidential Unit Citation, the Navy-Marine Corps Unit Commendation, and two Navy-Marine Corps Meritorious Unit Commendations and began to be referred to as "The Walking Dead." Unlike far too many, I survived those twelve months in Vietnam, but to this day, I endure flashbacks that bring back the indescribable fear I felt while there.

After serving in Vietnam at our country's call, you would think that returning home would have drawn some joyful attention from someone. For Vietnam veterans, this was not the case. Unlike those who served in World War II, Iraq, Afghanistan, and the Korean War, Vietnam veterans came home with no fanfare and no public reception to honor our service or welcome us home. No news media, no crowds of people, no nothing. We just offloaded from the ship and got on trucks that took us to the Marine Corps base in San Diego for processing and orders for our next assignment. Life just went on as if we had merely been on another training exercise and not returning from a deadly war in Vietnam. What we did have were hippy protesters calling us baby killers and murderers who seemed to take pleasure in getting in the faces of Vietnam veterans' and spouting profanity. This made the proudly wearing of military uniforms off base miserable, so no more uniforms off base.

Following my three and a half years with the Marine Corps, I continued serving the citizens of America, both as an employee and as a volunteer in different facets of government. I served three years with the United States Postal Service, thirty-two years with the Department of Veterans Affairs (VA), three years with an Army Reserve MASH Unit, and two two-year terms as a Township Council member. My time with the Army Reserves and as a Council member was concurrent with my career with the Department of Veterans Affairs. These years were followed by eleven years as a volunteer firefighter and Emergency Medical Technician (EMT), six election cycles as a poll worker and one election as a poll observer, a District Captain and Content Writer for the Convention of States Action movement, and as an active volunteer for my County Republican Party.

During my thirty-two years with Veterans Affairs, I worked at seven different Veterans Administration Medical Centers (VAMC) nationwide as a Healthcare Administrator. This position required me to interact with various veteran organizations and state and federal elected officials who represented the Medical Center's jurisdiction. At forty-two, I transferred to the Veterans Affairs (VA) Headquarters in Washington, D.C., first serving as the Chief of Operations, then after a reorganization, as Chief of Policies and Operations. During the last two years of my career, I served as VA Acting Director of the Headquarters' Health

Administration Service. During those eleven years at the VA Headquarters, I worked closely with Congress and White House staff members regarding veterans' healthcare matters and issues.

I met with elected members of Congress to outline which issues, in my opinion, were ambiguous and required legislation to clarify or what new legislation was needed to help keep our promises to our veterans, especially our severely disabled combat veterans and former Prisoners of War (POW). In the case of clearly needed legislation to better serve our veterans, congressional members would campaign on the promise to propose and push through Congress those required laws to fulfill those needs. However, once elected, nothing would happen. Just more empty promises to America's heroes. Why the failed promises? Was it the fear of failing to appease their party leaders, re-election donors, unions, or woke corporations? The answer is probably all of the above.

So, who really governs the United States? Your answer would likely be "Congress,." Who interprets the laws passed by Congress when laws are unclear? You would be surprised to learn that only a small portion of laws are ever interpreted by "the courts." Over the years, these responsibilities have fallen into the hands of the individual federal Departments and Agencies. It is *regulations* that carry the same weight as any law passed by Congress, authored and issued by unelected officials representing federal departments or agencies that dictate the benefits to be provided by that department or agency. When Congress fails to carry out its legislative responsibilities, then bureaucrats gladly step in and issue regulations imposing crushing burdens on our businesses and citizens.

This was my role with the Department of Veterans Affairs. My staff authored regulations based on our understanding of the laws passed by Congress. When no law existed covering an operational aspect of the Department's mission, we unelected officials would create regulations to support our operational needs. It was all done without any oversight by Congress or any element of

Congress. The reality of a "representative" government, "for, by, and of the people," has become nothing more than a memory as Congress has long since surrendered its constitutional obligations to millions of bureaucrats within the Washington swamp. The American is, in reality, a country of unelected administrative rulers. The move from Congressional legislating to Department and Agencies' regulating had slowly evolved until the Supreme Court's 1984 decision in Chevron versus Natural Resources Defense Council. In that case, the Supreme Court held that whenever a law is ambiguous, a federal agency is free to interpret the scope and content of that ambiguity any way it likes, limited only by the requirement that its interpretation be "reasonable."

The Supreme Court's 1984 decision in Chevron versus Natural Resources Defense Council empowered the bureaucracy at the expense of the people's will and the Framers' vision as articulated in the Constitution. This Supreme Court decision has played an enormous role in expanding the Washington bureaucracy. It has resulted in the American people being subjected to the tyranny of the bureaucracy, over which they have extraordinarily little control or ability to demand accountability. Under this decision, the Supreme Court made a remarkable amount of deference to federal agency interpretations of law, even when those agency interpretations are not mandated by the statute that Congress passed, and the president signed. The Chevron deference insulates bureaucrats who make the rules and regulations Americans must live by, creating perverse protection for people who make life worse for everyday citizens. Far too many of the bureaucrats, quite frankly, do not give a damn about what the voters think. One of the reasons why you see so many regulations affecting businesses and citizens is precisely because elected officials do not have to pay the price for those decisions. This protects elected officials because they can merely blame bureaucrats. The Chevron decision by the Supreme Court undermines Congress' legislative power by allowing federal agencies to make their own rules, and it undermines judicial review. Not surprisingly, agencies have exploited this authority to expand their power since its passage. "Reasonable" has become a term defined by the very individuals who want to impose further constrictions on America or provide exceptions to friendly entities.

While working with Congressional members of both parties, in both chambers of Congress, I became aware that most members of Congress were there for their own personal benefit and interests and not for the benefit of the people they were elected to represent. It is my opinion that far too many of these representatives and senators were sociopaths who had no business being in Congress representing anyone, as they did not have the moral or ethical capacity to represent anyone other than themselves. These morally ill individuals are governing beyond the consent of the people and are pushing America towards bankruptcy, oppression, divisiveness, and taking unconstitutional control of "We the People," much like one would find in a tyrannical Marxist-Communist nation. These Marxist-Communist elitist members of Congress do not ascribe to the ideology of the John F. Kennedy Democrat Party, which has long since died. Instead, the Marxist-Communist Democrat Party and like-minded Republicans are leading the charge towards a dictatorial Stalinist regime representing only themselves, the Washington elites, and America's wealthiest citizens.

As a writer, I am constantly watching the ongoing soap opera in the Washington Swamp, which stars well-known actors within all four branches of government. Yes, I said all four branches of government: the Executive Branch, the Legislative Branch, the Judicial Branch, and the unelected Washington Bureaucracy Branch. Four branches of inept, dysfunctional, discriminatory, corrupt, and self-serving officials happily spending away our hard-earned tax dollars. After all, it is not coming out of their pockets, so they continue spending as if they were royalty. Few of these actors have any moral code, honor, or integrity. Then we have the infamous supporting actors referred to as swamp creatures who are so deeply embedded within the Washington governing system that cleaning out that swamp of rats will be no easy undertaking. Our congressional representatives and these creatures of the swamp have created the most toxic political environment in American history. These individuals, who purport to represent the people, are demonstratively morally weak, corrupt, and evil creatures of the Washington swamp. They led me to author articles addressing the insanity of our government, our politicians, and the bureaucrats within our government. Politicians and bureaucrats who seem hell-bent on destroying our Nation. I author Articles addressing the misdeeds of both Democrats and Republicans, which has gotten me into no end of trouble with the leadership of both Parties, banned from several media platforms, and demonized for daring to express my views and opinions.

In early January of 2021, my wife and I drove to Washington, D.C., to attend the infamous January 6th, 2021, protest rally (aka insurrection). This rally in support of President Trump took place in an already divided and destructive political environment that had gone into overdrive as a result of President Trump's loss to Joe Biden. A man who campaigned from the basement of his New Jersey home and, in my opinion, spent his entire adult life as a congressman had never introduced any major impactful legislation, been wrong on every foreign policy initiative, was a known pathological liar, and was corrupt to the core. To this day, it is still my opinion and belief that the 2020 elections were indeed compromised through incompetency, fraud, and criminal activity. This election of Joe Biden brought in President Obama's third term and the resuming of President Obama's promise to forever fundamentally change America from a Constitutional Republic into a Marxist-Communist Nation.

With the election of Joe Biden and his selection of far-left radical Marxist-Communist-minded individuals to head his Cabinet positions, based solely on equity and not on expertise, President

Obama's vision of destroying our Constitutional Republic was put into motion. The Marxist-Communist elements of Washington, D.C. began an all-out campaign ramping up their rhetoric about conservatives being anti-American, anti-black, anti-LGBTQ, anti-social programs, anti-abortion, anti-justice for minorities, and of being inherently white supremacists. This rhetoric was followed by destructive and deadly riots in many of our Marxist-Communist governed cities following the shooting death of a black individual by a white police officer. Riots were supported and funded by Marxist-Communist billionaires, big tech, members of Congress, and Vice President Kamala Harris, who personally paid the bail for individuals arrested for criminal acts while participating in those anti-American destructive and deadly riots. Riots were instigated and justified by rare incidents of deaths of African Americans at the hands of police officers while resisting arrest. Deaths which occurred when individuals being arrested failed to comply with police orders.

It was clear to me that I could no longer stand on the sidelines just watching America turn into another Venezuela. I could no longer stand by as radical Marxist-Communists destroyed our Constitutional Republic—destruction being orchestrated by the Soros and Obama puppet Joe Biden. A man deeply compromised and indebted to the Chinese Communist Party. Biden did not act alone; he was assisted in his agenda to destroy our Constitutional Republic by like-minded Marxist-Communist Democrat and Republican members of Congress. Evidently, the freedoms and safety my wife and I had enjoyed up to this point in our lives were rapidly deteriorating. Even the community we had chosen to spend the remainder of our lives in was beginning to turn into a drug- and homeless-infested area.

As a result of this deterioration of our federal government as a Constitutionally representative government, the increasing levels of riots and crime, and out of fear for our safety and freedom, we made two decisions. The first was to become more active in politics, hoping to help in whatever capacity was available to us to save our constitutional government, and the second was to purchase firearms and obtain concealed carry permits to protect our lives against the ever-increasing crime levels. Our first decision to become more involved with politics began in September of 2021 when our new neighbor invited us to join her at a Republican-sponsored event at the County Republican Party Headquarters. At this time, we learned about the County Republican Party's monthly meetings, which were open to the general public. In keeping with our commitment to becoming more active in politics, we began attending these monthly meetings to become better informed about the Republican Party, the actions they were taking to protect our God-given rights, protect the Constitution of the United States of America, and the restoration of America back to the Constitutional Republic as intended by our Founding Fathers.

I had been involved in politics for the better part of my adult life but had stepped back from that world several years before our moving to western North Carolina. Upon moving to Western North Carolina, I became highly active with the County Republican Party. I volunteered to man Republican information booths at various events and served as a Precinct Chair and a member of the Board of Executives. During the 2024 election campaign season, I was asked by the County Republican Party Chairman to serve as the Election Integrity Director to coordinate the recruiting of volunteers to serve as Poll Workers, Poll Observers, and Poll Greeters.

Chapter 3
Constitutional Republic

To be respected members of the international community, all nations must ensure that their nation and the citizens therein are subject to moral and honorable laws. Nations that adhere to those laws will mean the continued survival of that nation, while rejection will lead to the death of that nation. Liberty and equal justice under the law can survive or perish during times of peace as well as periods of war, as can now be observed in the United States under a Marxist-Communist-controlled bureaucracy. In the United States, the need for constant vigilance by the citizenry has been inadequate, leaving our Nation seated on a weak foundation. It is critical to a nation's survival that its citizens are constantly willing to stand up and speak out if the government fails to respect and implement those laws intended to maintain stability within a nation. This is where the citizens of America have failed. Americans have become apathetic and complacent. Instead of taking the time from their busy life to confirm, identify, and seek resolutions to governing problems and their causes, they have merely sat back and assumed that whatever the situation, the next Administration will magically step in and correct course. The Marxist-Communist elements have taken this mindset as an opportunity to push forward its anti-American, anti-constitutional agenda. After years of apathy towards our Constitution and our Republic, America has been severally infected by the Marxist-Communist ideology, which many believe has placed our Constitutional Republic on its deathbed.

Source & Additional Information: (https://www.ohchr.org/)

The vicious Marxist-Communist constant attacks are causing instability within our constitutional republic and threatening its very existence. They may very well end in their victory to destroy our Constitutional Republic. However, this need not be true so long as "We the People" refuse to surrender to the radical Marxist-Communists and give up on our Constitutional Republic. Remember that the conflict between good and evil is never-ending; instead, it is a daily battle that we must find the strength and courage to combat; otherwise, all is lost. The dark temptations placed at the feet of every citizen are inviting and sometimes difficult to resist. This reality is within each of us, but for those elected to protect our Constitution and "We the People," the temptations placed at their feet can be overwhelming: power, influence, wealth, and status in a community of evil. Be assured that we are in the midst of powerful and unrelenting forces struggling to bring our constitutional Republic to its knees. Each of us must commit to one side or the other of this political war. Each one of us is either submissive, unwilling to stand for what is right, or courageous and willing to combat menacing assaults upon our nation's Constitutions and its citizens. It may very well be said that truth during peace may be worse than the dangers of war, which is uniquely valid for our country today.

Our Constitutional form of government is complex, with its multiple branches intended to keep each other in check. There are significant advantages to such a complex form of governance. Still, such a complex government is more prone to disruption than simple forms of democracies, monarchies, or autocracies. Suppose we are to retain these advantages and prevent dangerous disruptions in our Constitutional form of governance. In that case, we must jealously guard the distinctive characteristics of this form of governing against the tendency of corrupt and power-hungry men willing to destroy and eliminate any trace of that governing system. Today, we are in a battle against the evil of Marxist-Communism, a form of autocratic government that is the worst form of governance in that it creates a centralized government with all power placed in the hands of one person.

Due to the failure of our federally funded school system, polls indicate that fully one-third of American college students approve of communism over capitalism. Our young are no more than ignorant fools being taught by Marxist-Communist indoctrinators. Our children should be taught that you can foolishly vote yourself into communism, but you have to shoot your way out of it. Marxist-Communist leaders live a life of luxury, while their subjects live a life of misery. Marxist-Communist leaders do not want to give up their power easily and will fight, even kill, to keep it. Far too many of our college professors are intellectual malcontent misfits who are the products of the 1960s anti-American radical hippie movement who are now brainwashing our children rather than educating them in the skills and knowledge that will allow them to thrive in a competitive world.

Source & Additional Information: (victimsofcommunism.org)

Over the past few decades, the balance of power within our federal government, as well as between the sovereign states and the federal government, has come under ever-increasing attacks by Marxist-Communist advocates in Washington, D.C., as well as Marxist-Communists who govern states and cities, all willing to disregard the Constitution and State's power under that Constitution. As citizens of this great nation, we must be willing to become involved with the political activities of our government to guard against the dangerous encroachment against our Constitutional form of government. We must be willing to sacrifice our time and talents to this end in honor of those who have given their lives or suffered horrendous injuries in times of war to protect our Republic. We must be willing to stand courageously and persistently to defend our God-given rights and the Constitution of the United States. If our Constitutional form of governance is to survive, it must be maintained as written by the Founding Fathers or modified by Amendments to the Constitution. It must always be a life priority of "We the People," those elected to represent us, those within our judicial system, and those within our executive branch to stand united to assure the perseverance of our unique form of government: for the people, by the people, and of the people. Remember, wise men establish governments, brave men defend and die for governments, and weak, corrupt, and ambitious men destroy governments.

The strength and power of our Nation does not rest upon the fact that we are a federation of States but that we are a Union of States based upon a Constitution devised by the people, adopted by the people, defended by the people, and preserved by the people. No objective is so important that we should ever sacrifice the very nature and glory of our system of government. It is critical for the survival of our Constitution that any attempt to destroy it must be quickly and sternly rebuked. Elected, as well as unelected government officials, who, through motives of cowardly expediency, weakness of moral or mental character, or for other seditious reasons, have failed to stand courageously together with honor and integrity to protect our God-given rights and must be stopped and eliminated.

Source & Additional Information: (https://clausewitzstudies.org/readings/OnWar1873/BK1ch01.html)

Today, our Constitutional Republic is being seriously threatened by perverted and corrupt Marxist-Communist-created anarchy. Anarchy is the means utilized by the wicked, malicious, and envious among our citizenry to gain control over the citizenry. Our Nation's peril is currently in the hands of such treacherous elected and unelected officials. Officials who so easily fall to misleading demands for change in our established and tried governing system are sometimes made under the pretense of reform and sometimes masquerading as justice. Therefore, the highest and most patriotic goal is to understand the fundamental principles of our Constitutional heritage and defend and protect them with our very lives. Defend them against those who would narrowly restrict our God-given Constitutional rights and those who would destructively expand them.

Not since the Civil War have we faced such a great force bound and determined to bring down our way of life, to divide and separate "We the People" to destroy our Constitutional Republic, and to marshal in a Marxist-Communist form of governing. There is a path forward, but it requires us to look back to the framers who rightly insisted on preserving the prominent governing role of the State legislatures as a crucial mechanism to contain the power of the federal government. In fact, other than the limited specified powers granted to the federal government within our Constitution, the States retain for themselves complete governing authority as articulated in the Ten Amendment: "Those powers not delegated to the United States by the Constitution, nor prohibited by it to the States, are reserved to the States respectively, or to the people." Article V of the Constitution expressly grants "We the People" through our state legislators' significant authority to rebalance the constitutional structure to restore our founding principles should the federal government shed its limitations, abandon its original purpose, and grow too powerful, as is now the case. It must be understood by the citizens of this great Nation that we are at war against the attempted takeover of our Constitutional Republic by the Marxist-Communist elements of our governing system. It is no longer acceptable for any citizen of this country not to acknowledge this reality and join in the battle to save our republic.

Today, more than ever, we desperately need to Convene a "Convention of States" under the authority of Article V of the Constitution to add Amendments to the Constitution to halt the Marxist-Communist movement from their consistent and determined path to destroying our Constitutional Republic and enslave "We the People" to their evil dictates. It is far past time that the legislators of every state called for the Convening of a "Convention of States" under Article V of the Constitution to rein in our corrupt and out-of-control federal government, which has exceeded the people's will. A Convention of States focused on addressing three critical subjects:" 1) Term Limits; 2) Fiscal Responsibility; and 3) Restricted Federal Jurisdiction and Overreach. State legislators must realize that their State is sovereign and not under the federal government's rule. Our founding fathers provide state legislators, within the Constitution, the power to act as a firewall between the state and federal government to reject any attempt by the federal government to diminish either the State's or citizen's rights under the Constitution. *(Convention of States defined in Chapter 24)*

What I present in the coming chapters is information supporting my opinion that the United States of America is rapidly turning from being the shining star of the world, with freedoms and liberties found nowhere else in the world, to an oppressive and destructive Marxist-Communist governed nation. I speak of a transformed citizenry that has become so complacent that they no longer feel any obligation, responsibility, or willingness to keep themselves politically informed or actively involved in the governance of our country, in particular, our election processes. The citizens of this country have become so addicted to government entitlements, benefits, and rewards that they are willing to sacrifice their constitutional rights to maintain these unconstitutional perks and benefits. Citizens who are all too willing to take for granted the freedoms and liberties they enjoy believing that those freedoms and liberties will remain intact under a centralized Marxist-Communist government. It is this complacency caused by our citizens that has led our Constitutional Republic to be controlled by sociopaths who are so corrupt and callous that they are willing to systematically and maliciously destroy our Nation for their self-serving interests. America's failure to maintain vigilance over a fragile form of governance has allowed for the rise of an inept, corrupt, and uncontrollable federal government led by elected and unelected traitors to our Constitution and our nations. A government that no longer believes that it is the servant of the people but the ruler of the people.

As an active Convention of States Action member, I man a booth at our county's monthly flea market to obtain petition signatures to support convening a Convention of States under Article V of the Constitution. I attempt to engage with individuals shopping at the flea market to discuss the need for term limits, restrict federal government spending, and restrict the federal government's overreach into state affairs. It is both astonishing and depressing to hear so many American citizens tell me that they are not interested in signing the petition because they don't care how long congressional members stay in power; they don't get involved in politics; they agree with the need for term limits and fiscal responsibility but are too busy shopping to take two minutes to sign the petition; signing the petition won't change anything so why bother; or, they are perfectly happy with the way things are going in the Washington swamp. Far too many American citizens are unwilling to take the two minutes it would take to sign the petition to support changing our government's out-of-control attitude toward their constituents and our country. It is listening to the apathy shown by so many people that I begin to understand why our Constitutional Republic is in such a dire situation and being so easily assaulted by Marxist-Communist elements of our government and citizenry.

In my day-to-day interactions, I'm struck by the number of people who lack knowledge about the history of our Constitution, its contents, and the significance of living in a Constitutional Republic. To bridge this gap and foster a deeper understanding, I present the history of our Constitution in this chapter. Understanding this history is crucial to appreciating the rights enshrined in our Constitution, which are rapidly slipping away. A small but important portion of that history follows:

"The Continental Congress adopted the Articles of Confederation on November 15, 1777. This document served as the United States' first constitution. It was in force from March 1, 1781, until 1789, when the Constitution was enacted.

Following the pivotal Lee Resolution that proposed independence for the American colonies, the Second Continental Congress took a momentous step. On June 11, 1776, it appointed three committees, one of which was tasked with determining the form of the confederation of the colonies. This committee, comprising a representative from each colony, was led by John Dickinson, a delegate from Delaware.

The Dickinson Draft of the Articles of Confederation named the confederation "the United States of America." After considerable debate and revision, the Second Continental Congress adopted the Articles of Confederation on November 15, 1777.

Originally called to amend the Articles of Confederation, our nation's first written constitution, the delegates engaged in protracted and often contentious debates over states' rights, representation, and slavery. These debates, ultimately leading to the birth of the U.S. Constitution, were a significant and weighty moment in our nation's history.

The Constitution of the United States of America is the fundamental law of the United States system of government. It is a landmark document in the Western world and the oldest written national constitution. The Constitution defines the principal structure of our government, its jurisdictions, and the fundamental rights of citizens.

The Constitution, a testament to our nation's resilience and adaptability, was crafted in Philadelphia, Pennsylvania, in the summer of 1787. It was the collective effort of 55 delegates, each with their unique perspectives and convictions, who convened at the Constitutional Convention. This event, showcasing the unity and diversity of our nation, is a source of great national pride.

The creation of the Constitution was not without its challenges. Delegates from small and large states engaged in heated debates over the issue of representation in the new federal legislature. The question of whether each state should have the same number of representatives, as under the Articles of Confederation (1781–1789), or if representation should be based on a state's population, as proposed in the New Jersey Plan sparked intense and contentious discussions, underscoring the intensity of the historical moment and the fervor of the debates. and Virginia Plan.

Source & Additional Information: (https://www.britannica.com/topic/Articles-of-Confederation) (https://www.britannica.com/topic/New-Jersey-Plan) (https://www.britannica.com/topic/Virginia-plan)

In addition, some delegates from Northern states sought to abolish slavery or, failing that, to make representation dependent on the size of a state's free population. At the same time, some Southern delegates threatened to abandon the convention if their demands to keep slavery and the slave trade legal and to count slaves for representation purposes were not met.

Ultimately, the framers found common ground by embracing a proposal from the Connecticut delegation. This proposal, known as the Great Compromise, was a turning point in the debates. It led to the creation of a two-house legislature, with a Senate where all states would be equally represented and a House of Representatives where representation would be based on a state's free population plus three-fifths of its enslaved population. Another significant compromise on slavery was the prohibition of Congress from banning the importation of enslaved people until 1808 (Article I, Section 9).

Source & Additional Information: (https://www.britannica.com/topic/Connecticut-Compromise)

After all the disagreements were bridged, the new Constitution was signed by 39 delegates on September 17, 1787, and it was submitted for ratification to the 13 states on September 28.

In 1787–88, Alexander Hamilton, John Jay, and James Madison published a series of essays on the Constitution and Republican government in New York newspapers to persuade New York to ratify the Constitution. Their work, written under the pseudonym

"Publius" and collected and published in book form, became a classic exposition and defense of the Constitution.

In June 1788, after nine states had ratified the Constitution (as required by Article VII), Congress set March 4, 1789, as the date for the new government to commence proceedings (the first elections under the Constitution were held late in 1788).

Because ratification in many states was contingent on the promised addition of a Bill of Rights, Congress proposed 12 amendments in September 1789; the states ratified ten, and their adoption was certified on December 15, 1791. *The Federalist* (1788).

Source & Additional Information: (https://www.britannica.com/topic/Federalist-papers) (Bill of Rights, https://www.britannica.com/topic/Bill-of-Rights-United-States-Constitution)

Preamble

We, the People of the United States, in Order to form a more perfect Union, establish Justice, ensure domestic Tranquility, provide for the common defense, promote the general Welfare, and secure the Blessings of Liberty to ourselves and our Posterity, do ordain and establish this Constitution for the United States of America.

Article I

Section 1: Congress

All legislative Powers herein granted shall be vested in a Congress of the United States, which shall consist of a Senate and House of Representatives.

Section 2: The House of Representatives

The House of Representatives shall be composed of Members chosen every second Year by the People of the several States, and the Electors in each State shall have the Qualifications requisite for Electors of the most numerous Branch of the State Legislature.

No Person shall be a Representative who shall not have attained to the Age of twenty-five Years and been seven Years a Citizen of the United States, and who shall not, when elected, be an Inhabitant of that State in which he shall be chosen.

Representatives and direct Taxes shall be apportioned among the several States which may be included within this Union, according to their respective Numbers, which shall be determined by adding to the whole Number of free Persons, including those bound to Service for a Term of Years, and excluding Indians not taxed, three-fifths of all other Persons.

The actual Enumeration shall be made within three Years after the first Meeting of the Congress of the United States and within every subsequent Term of ten Years, in such Manner as they shall by Law direct. The number of Representatives shall not exceed one for every thirty Thousand, but each State shall have at Least one Representative; and until such enumeration shall be made, the State of New Hampshire shall be entitled to chuse three, Massachusetts eight, Rhode Island and Providence Plantations one, Connecticut five, New-York six, New Jersey four, Pennsylvania eight, Delaware one, Maryland six, Virginia ten, North Carolina five, South Carolina five, and Georgia three.

When vacancies happen in the Representation from any State, the Executive Authority thereof shall issue Writs of Election to fill such Vacancies.

The House of Representatives shall chuse their Speaker and other Officers; and shall have the sole Power of Impeachment.

Section 3: The Senate
The Senate of the United States shall be composed of two Senators from each State, chosen by the Legislature thereof, for six Years; and each Senator shall have one Vote.

Immediately after they shall be assembled in Consequence of the first Election, they shall be divided as equally as may be into three Classes. The Seats of the Senators of the first Class shall be vacated at the Expiration of the second Year, of the second Class at the Expiration of the fourth Year, and of the third Class at the Expiration of the sixth Year, so that one third may be chosen every second Year; and if Vacancies happen by Resignation, or otherwise, during the Recess of the Legislature of any State, the Executive thereof may make temporary Appointments until the next Meeting of the Legislature, which shall then fill such Vacancies.

No Person shall be a Senator who shall not have attained to the Age of thirty Years and been nine Years a Citizen of the United States, and who shall not, when elected, be an Inhabitant of that State for which he shall be chosen.

The Vice President of the United States shall be President of the Senate, but shall have no Vote, unless they be equally divided.

The Senate shall chuse their other Officers, and also a President pro tempore, in the Absence of the Vice President, or when he shall exercise the Office of President of the United States.

The Senate shall have the sole Power to try all Impeachments. When sitting for that Purpose, they shall be on Oath or Affirmation. When the President of the United States is tried, the Chief Justice shall preside: And no Person shall be convicted without the Concurrence of two-thirds of the Members present.

Judgment in Cases of Impeachment shall not extend further than to removal from Office, and disqualification to hold and enjoy any Office of honor, Trust, or Profit under the United States: but the Party convicted shall nevertheless be liable and subject to Indictment, Trial, Judgment and Punishment, according to Law.

Section 4: Elections
The Times, Places and Manner of holding Elections for Senators and Representatives, shall be prescribed in each State by the Legislature thereof; but the Congress may at any time by Law make or alter such Regulations, except as to the Places of choosing Senators.

The Congress shall assemble at least once in every Year, and such Meeting shall be on the first Monday in December, unless they shall by Law appoint a different Day.

Section 5: Powers and Duties of Congress
Each House shall be the Judge of the Elections, Returns and Qualifications of its own Members, and a Majority of each shall

constitute a Quorum to do Business; but a smaller Number may adjourn from day to day, and may be authorized to compel the Attendance of absent Members, in such Manner, and under such Penalties as each House may provide.

Each House may determine the Rules of its Proceedings, punish its members for disorderly Behavior, and, with the Concurrence of two-thirds, expel a member.

Each House shall keep a Journal of its Proceedings, and from time to time publish the same, excepting such Parts as may in their Judgment require Secrecy; and the Yeas and Nays of the Members of either House on any question shall, at the Desire of one-fifth of those Present, be entered on the Journal.

Neither House, during the Session of Congress, shall, without the Consent of the other, adjourn for more than three days, nor to any other Place than that in which the two Houses shall be sitting.

Section 6: Rights and Disabilities of Members
The Senators and Representatives shall receive a Compensation for their Services, to be ascertained by Law, and paid out of the Treasury of the United States. They shall in all Cases, except Treason, Felony and Breach of the Peace, be privileged from Arrest during their Attendance at the Session of their respective Houses, and in going to and returning from the same; and for any Speech or Debate in either House, they shall not be questioned in any other Place.

No Senator or Representative shall, during the Time for which he was elected, be appointed to any civil Office under the Authority of the United States, which shall have been created, or the Emoluments whereof shall have been encreased during such time; and no Person holding any Office under the United States, shall be a Member of either House during his Continuance in Office.

Section 7: Legislative Process
All Bills for raising Revenue shall originate in the House of Representatives; but the Senate may propose or concur with Amendments as on other Bills.

Every Bill which shall have passed the House of Representatives and the Senate, shall, before it become a Law, be presented to the President of the United States; If he approve he shall sign it, but if not he shall return it, with his Objections to that House in which it shall have originated, who shall enter the Objections at large on their Journal, and proceed to reconsider it. If after such Reconsideration two-thirds of that House shall agree to pass the Bill, it shall be sent, together with the Objections, to the other House, by which it shall likewise be reconsidered, and if approved by two-thirds of that House, it shall become a Law. But in all such Cases the Votes of both Houses shall be determined by Yeas and Nays, and the Names of the Persons voting for and against the Bill shall be entered on the Journal of each House, respectively. If any Bill shall not be returned by the President within ten Days (Sundays excepted) after it shall have been presented to him, the Same shall be a Law, in like Manner as if he had signed it, unless the Congress by their Adjournment prevent its Return, in which Case it shall not be a Law.

Every Order, Resolution, or Vote to which the Concurrence of the Senate and House of Representatives may be necessary (except on a question of Adjournment) shall be presented to the President of the United States; and before the Same shall take Effect, shall be approved by him, or being disapproved by him, shall be repassed by two-thirds of the Senate and House of Representatives, according to the Rules and Limitations prescribed in the Case of a Bill.

Section 8: Powers of Congress
The Congress shall have Power To lay and collect Taxes, Duties, Imposts and Excises, to pay the Debts and provide for the common Defence and general Welfare of the United States; but

all Duties, Imposts and Excises shall be uniform throughout the United States;

To borrow Money on the credit of the United States;

To regulate Commerce with foreign Nations, and among the several States, and with the Indian Tribes;

To establish a uniform Rule of Naturalization, and uniform Laws on the subject of Bankruptcies throughout the United States;

To coin Money, regulate the Value thereof, and of foreign Coin, and fix the Standard of Weights and Measures;

To provide for the Punishment of counterfeiting the Securities and current Coin of the United States;

To establish Post Offices and post Roads;

To promote the Progress of Science and useful Arts, by securing for limited Times to Authors and Inventors the exclusive Right to their respective Writings and Discoveries;

To constitute Tribunals inferior to the supreme Court; To define and Piracies and Felonies committed on the high Seas, and Offenses against the Law of Nations;

To declare War, grant Letters of Marque and Reprisal, and make Rules concerning Captures on Land and Water;

To raise and support Armies, but no Appropriation of Money to that Use shall be for a longer Term than two Years;

To provide and maintain a Navy;

To make Rules for the Government and Regulation of the land and naval Forces;

To provide for calling forth the Militia to execute the Laws of the Union, suppress Insurrections and repel Invasions;

To provide for organizing, arming, and disciplining the Militia, and for governing such Part of them as may be employed in the Service of the United States, reserving to the States respectively, the Appointment of the Officers, and the Authority of training the Militia according to the discipline prescribed by Congress;

To exercise exclusive Legislation in all Cases whatsoever, over such District (not exceeding ten Miles square) as may, by Cession of particular States and the Acceptance of Congress, become the Seat of the Government of the United States, and to exercise like Authority over all Places purchased by the Consent of the Legislature of the State in which the Same shall be, for the Erection of Forts, Magazines, Arsenals, dockyards and other needful Buildings;-And

To make all Laws which shall be necessary and proper for carrying into Execution the foregoing Powers, and all other Powers vested by this Constitution in the Government of the United States, or in any Department or Officer thereof.

Section 9: Powers Denied Congress
The Migration or Importation of such Persons as any of the States now existing shall think proper to admit, shall not be prohibited by the Congress prior to the Year on thousand eight hundred and eight, but a Tax or duty may be imposed on such Importation, not exceeding ten dollars for each Person.

The Privilege of the Writ of Habeas Corpus shall not be suspended, unless when in Cases of Rebellion or Invasion the public Safety may require it.

No Bill of Attainder or ex post facto Law shall be passed.

No Capitation, or other direct, Tax shall be laid, unless in Proportion to the Census or Enumeration herein before directed to be taken.

No Tax or Duty shall be laid on Articles exported from any State.

No Preference shall be given by any Regulation of Commerce or Revenue to the Ports of one State over those of another: nor shall Vessels bound to, or from, one State, be obliged to enter, clear, or pay Duties in another.

No Money shall be drawn from the Treasury, but in Consequence of Appropriations made by Law; and a regular Statement and Account of the Receipts and Expenditures of all public Money shall be published from time to time.

No Title of Nobility shall be granted by the United States: And no Person holding any Office of Profit or Trust under them, shall, without the Consent of the Congress, accept of any present, Emolument, Office, or Title, of any kind whatever, from any King, Prince, or foreign State.

Section 10: Powers Denied to the States
No State shall enter into any Treaty, Alliance, or Confederation; grant Letters of Marque and Reprisal; coin Money; emit Bills of Credit; make any Thing but gold and silver Coin a Tender in Payment of Debts; pass any Bill of Attainder, ex post facto Law, or Law impairing the Obligation of Contracts, or grant any Title of Nobility.

No State shall, without the Consent of the Congress, lay any Imposts or Duties on Imports or Exports, except what may be absolutely necessary for executing it is inspection Laws: and the net Produce of all Duties and Imposts, laid by any State on Imports or Exports, shall be for the Use of the Treasury of the United States; and all such Laws shall be subject to the Revision and Control of the Congress.

No State shall, without the Consent of Congress, lay any Duty of Tonnage, keep Troops, or Ships of War in time of Peace, enter into any Agreement or Compact with another State, or with a foreign Power, or engage in War, unless actually invaded, or in such imminent Danger as will not admit of delay.

Article II

Section 1
The executive Power shall be vested in a President of the United States of America.

He shall hold his Office during the Term of four Years, and, together with the Vice President, chosen for the same Term, be elected, as follows:

Each State shall appoint, in such Manner as the Legislature thereof may direct, a Number of Electors, equal to the whole Number of Senators and Representatives to which the State may be entitled in the Congress: but no Senator or Representative, or Person holding an Office of Trust or Profit under the United States, shall be appointed an Elector.

The Electors shall meet in their respective States, and vote by Ballot for two Persons, of whom one at least shall not be an Inhabitant of the same State with themselves. And they shall make a List of all the Persons voted for, and of the Number of Votes for each; which List they shall sign, certify, and transmit sealed to the Seat of the Government of the United States, directed to the President of the Senate.

The President of the Senate shall, in the Presence of the Senate and House of Representatives, open all the Certificates, and the Votes shall then be counted. The Person having the greatest Number of Votes shall be the President, if such Number be a Majority of the whole Number of Electors appointed; and if there be more than one who have such Majority, and have an equal Number of Votes, then the House of Representatives shall immediately chuse by Ballot on of them for President; and if no Person have a Majority, then from the five highest on the List the said House shall in like Manner chuse the President. But in chusing the President, the Votes shall be taken by States, the Representation from each State having one Vote;

A quorum for this Purpose shall consist of a Member or Members from two thirds of the States, and a Majority of all the States shall be necessary to a Choice. In every Case, after the Choice of the President, the Person having the greatest Number of Votes of the Electors shall be the Vice President. But if there should remain two or more who have equal Votes, the Senate shall chuse from them by Ballot the Vice President.

The Congress may determine the Time of chusing the Electors, and the Day on which they shall give their Votes; which Day shall be the same throughout the United States.

No Person except a natural born Citizen, or a Citizen of the United States, at the time of the Adoption of this Constitution, shall be eligible to the Office of President; neither shall any person be eligible to that Office who shall not have attained to the Age of thirty-five Years, and been fourteen Years a Resident within the United States.

I Case of the Removal of the President from Office, or of this Death, Resignation, or Inability to discharge the Powers and Duties of the said Office, the Same shall devolve on the Vice President, and the Congress may by Law provide for the Case of Removal, Death, Resignation, or Inability, both of the President and Vice President, declaring what Officer shall then act as President, and such Officer shall act accordingly, until the Disability be removed, or a President shall be elected.

The President shall, at stated Times, receive for his Services, a Compensation, which shall neither be increased nor diminished during the Period for which he shall have been elected, and he shall not receive within that Period any other Emolument from the United States, or any of them.

Before he enter on the Execution of his Office, he shall take the following Oath or Affirmation: "I do solemnly swear (or affirm) that I will faithfully execute the Office of President of the United States, and will to the best of my Ability, preserve, protect and defend the Constitution of the United States."

Section 2
The President shall be Commander in Chief of the Army and Navy of the United States, and of the Militia of the several States, when called into the actual Service of the United States; he may require the Opinion, in writing, of the principal Officer in each of the executive Departments, upon any Subject relating to the Duties of their respective Offices, and he shall have Power to grant Reprieves and Pardons for Offenses against the United States, except in Cases of Impeachment.

He shall have Power, by and with the Advice and Consent of the Senate, to make Treaties, provided two thirds of the Senators present concur; and he shall nominate, and by and with the Advice and Consent of the Senate, shall appoint Ambassadors, other public Ministers and Consuls, Judges of the supreme Court, and all other Officers of the United States, whose Appointments are not herein otherwise provided for, and which shall be established by Law: but the Congress may by Law vest the Appointment of such inferior Officers, as they think proper, in the President alone, in the Courts of Law, or in the Heads of Departments.

The President shall have Power to fill up all Vacancies that may happen during the Recess of the Senate, by granting Commissions which shall expire at the End of their next Session.

Section 3
He shall from time to time give to the Congress Information of the State of the Union, and recommend to their Consideration such Measures as he shall judge necessary and expedient; he may, on extraordinary Occasions, convene both Houses, or either of

them, and in Case of Disagreement between them, with Respect to the Time of Adjournment, he may adjourn them to such Time as he shall think proper; he shall receive Ambassadors and other public Ministers; he shall take Care that the Laws be faithfully executed, and shall Commission all the Officers of the United States.

Section 4
The President, Vice President and all civil Officers of the United States, shall be removed from Office on Impeachment for, and Conviction of, Treason, Bribery, or other high Crimes and Misdemeanors.

Article III

Section 1
The judicial Power of the United States shall be vested in one supreme Court, and in such inferior Courts as the Congress may from time to time ordain and establish. The Judges, both of the supreme and inferior Courts, shall hold their Offices during good Behaviour, and shall, at stated Times, receive for their Services, a Compensation, which shall not be diminished during their Continuance in Office.

Section 2
The judicial Power shall extend to all Cases, in Law and Equity, arising under this Constitution, the Laws of the United States, and Treaties made, or which shall be made, under their Authority;-- to all Cases affecting Ambassadors, other public Ministers and Consuls;--to all Cases of admiralty and maritime Jurisdiction;--to Controversies to which the United States shall be a Party;-- to Controversies between two or mor States;--between a State and Citizens of another State;--between Citizens of different States;-- between Citizens of the same State claiming Lands under Grants

of different States, and between a State, or the Citizens thereof, and foreign States, Citizens or Subjects.

In all Cases affecting Ambassadors, other public Ministers, and Consuls, and those in which a State shall be Party, the supreme Court shall have original Jurisdiction. In all the other Cases before mentioned, the supreme Court shall have appellate Jurisdiction, both as to Law and Fact, with such Exceptions, and under such Regulations as the Congress shall make.

The Trial of all Crimes, except in Cases of Impeachment; shall be by Jury; and such Trial shall be held in the State where the said Crimes shall have been committed; but when not committed within any State, the Trial shall be at such Place or Places as the Congress may by Law have directed.

Section 3
Treason against the United States shall consist only in levying War against them, or in adhering to their Enemies, giving them Aid and Comfort. No Person shall be convicted of Treason unless on the Testimony of two Witnesses to the same overt Act, or on Confession in open Court.

The Congress shall have Power to declare the Punishment of Treason, but no Attainder of Treason shall work Corruption of Blood, or Forfeiture except during the Life of the Person attained.

Article IV

Section 1
Full Faith and Credit shall be given in each State to the public Acts, Records, and judicial Proceedings of every other State. And the Congress may by general Laws prescribe the Manner in which such Acts, Records and Proceedings shall be proved, and the Effect thereof.

Section 2
The Citizens of each State shall be entitled to all Privileges and Immunities of Citizens in the several States.

A Person charged in any State with Treason, Felony, or other Crime, who shall flee from Justice, and be found in another State, shall on Demand of the executive Authority of the State from which he fled, be delivered up, to be removed to the State having Jurisdiction of the Crime.

No Person held to Service or Labour in one State, under the Laws thereof, escaping into another, shall, in Consequence of any Law or Regulation therein, be discharged from such Service or Labour, but shall be delivered up on Claim of the Party to whom such Service or Labour may be due.

Section 3
New States may be admitted by the Congress into this Union; but no new State shall be formed or erected within the Jurisdiction of any other State; nor any State be formed by the Junction of two or more States, or Parts of States, without the Consent of the Legislatures of the States concerned as well as of the Congress.

The Congress shall have Power to dispose of and make all needful Rules and Regulations respecting the Territory or other Property belonging to the United States; and nothing in this Constitution shall be so construed as to Prejudice any Claims of the United States, or of any particular State.

Section 4
The United States shall guarantee to every State in this Union a Republican Form of Government and shall protect each of them against Invasion; and on Application of the Legislature, or of the Executive (when the Legislature cannot be convened) against domestic Violence.

Article V

The Congress, whenever two thirds of both Houses shall deem it necessary, shall propose Amendments to this Constitution, or, on the Application of the Legislatures of two thirds of the several States, shall call a Convention for proposing Amendments, which, in either Case, shall be valid to all Intents and Purposes, as Part of this Constitution, when ratified by the Legislatures of three fourths of the several States, or by Conventions in three fourths thereof, as the one or the other Mode of Ratification may be proposed by the Congress; Provided that no Amendment which may be made prior to the Year One thousand eight hundred and eight shall in any Manner affect the first and fourth Clauses in the Ninth Section of the first Article; and that no State, without its Consent, shall be deprived of its equal Suffrage in the Senate.

Article VI

All Debts contracted and Engagements entered into, before the Adoption of this Constitution, shall be as valid against the United States under this Constitution, as under the Confederation.

This Constitution, and the Laws of the United States which shall be made in Pursuance thereof; and all Treaties made, or which shall be made, under the Authority of the United States, shall be the supreme Law of the Land; and the Judges in every State shall be bound thereby, any Thing in the Constitution or Laws of any State to the Contrary notwithstanding.

The Senators and Representatives before mentioned, and the Members of the several State Legislatures, and all executive and judicial Officers, both of the United States and of the several States, shall be bound by Oath or Affirmation, to support this

Constitution; but no religious Test shall ever be required as a Qualification to any Office or public Trust under the United States.

Article VII

The Ratification of the Conventions of nine States shall be sufficient for the Establishment of this Constitution between the States so ratifying the Same.

The Amendments to the Constitution

First Amendment
Congress shall make no law respecting an establishment of religion or prohibiting the free exercise thereof; or abridging the freedom of speech, or of the press; or the right of the people peaceably to assemble, and to petition the Government for a redress of grievances.

Second Amendment
A well-regulated Militia, being necessary to the security of a free State, the right of the people to keep and bear Arms, shall not be infringed.

Third Amendment
No Soldier shall, in time of peace, be quartered in any house, without the consent of the Owner, nor in time of war, but in a manner to be prescribed by law.

Fourth Amendment

The right of the people to be secure in their persons, houses, papers, and effects, against unreasonable searches and seizures, shall not be violated, and no Warrants shall issue, but upon probable cause, supported by Oath or affirmation, and particularly describing the place to be searched, and the persons or things to be seized.

Fifth Amendment

No person shall be held to answer for a capital, or otherwise infamous crime, unless on a presentment or indictment of a Grand Jury, except in cases arising in the land or naval forces, or in the Militia, when in actual service in time of War or public danger; nor shall any person be subject for the same offence to be twice put in jeopardy of life or limb; nor shall be compelled in any criminal case to be a witness against himself, nor be deprived of life, liberty, or property, without due process of law; nor shall private property be taken for public use, without just compensation.

Sixth Amendment

In all criminal prosecutions, the accused shall enjoy the right to a speedy and public trial, by an impartial jury of the State and district wherein the crime shall have been committed, which district shall have been previously ascertained by law, and to be informed of the nature and cause of the accusation; to be confronted with the witnesses against him; to have compulsory process for obtaining witnesses in his favor, and to have the Assistance of Counsel for his defence.

Seventh Amendment

In Suits at common law, where the value in controversy shall exceed twenty dollars, the right of trial by jury shall be preserved, and no fact tried by a jury, shall be otherwise reexamined in any Court of the United States, than according to the rules of the common law.

Eighth Amendment
Excessive bail shall not be required, nor excessive fines imposed, nor cruel and unusual punishments inflicted.

Ninth Amendment
The enumeration in the Constitution of certain rights shall not be construed to deny or disparage others retained by the people.

10th Amendment
The powers not delegated to the United States by the Constitution, nor prohibited by it to the States, are reserved to the States respectively, or to the people.

11th Amendment
The Judicial power of the United States shall not be construed to extend to any suit in law or equity, commenced or prosecuted against one of the United States by Citizens of another State, or by Citizens or Subjects of any Foreign State.

The Judicial power of the United States shall not be construed to extend to any suit in law or equity, commenced or prosecuted against one of the United States by Citizens of another State, or by Citizens or Subjects of any Foreign State.

12th Amendment

The Electors shall meet in their respective states and vote by ballot for President and Vice-President, one of whom, at least, shall not be an inhabitant of the same state with themselves; they shall name in their ballots the person voted for as President, and in distinct ballots the person voted for as Vice-President, and they shall make distinct lists of all persons voted for as President, and of all persons voted for as Vice-President, and of the number of votes for each, which lists they shall sign and certify, and transmit sealed to the seat of the government of the United States, directed to the President of the Senate; --

The President of the Senate shall, in the presence of the Senate and House of Representatives, open all the certificates and the votes shall then be counted; --

The person having the greatest number of votes for President, shall be the President, if such number be a majority of the whole number of Electors appointed; and if no person have such majority, then from the persons having the highest numbers not exceeding three on the list of those voted for as President, the House of Representatives shall choose immediately, by ballot, the President.

But in choosing the President, the votes shall be taken by states, the representation from each state having one vote; a quorum for this purpose shall consist of a member or members from two-thirds of the states, and a majority of all the states shall be necessary to a choice.

And if the House of Representatives shall not choose a President whenever the right of choice shall devolve upon them, before the fourth day of March next following, then the Vice-President shall act as President, as in case of the death of other constitutional disability of the President.

The person having the greatest number of votes as Vice-President, shall be the Vice-President, if such number be a majority of the whole number of Electors appointed, and if no person have a majority, then from the two highest numbers on the list, the Senate shall choose the Vice-President; a quorum for the purpose shall consist of two-thirds of the whole number of Senators, and a majority of the whole number shall be necessary to a choice.

But no person constitutionally ineligible to the office of President shall be eligible to that of Vice-President of the United States.

13th Amendment
Section 1
Neither slavery nor involuntary servitude, except as a punishment for crime whereof the party shall have been duly convicted, shall exist within the United States, or any place subject to their jurisdiction.

Section 2
Congress shall have power to enforce this article by appropriate legislation.

14th Amendment
Section 1
All persons born or naturalized in the United States, and subject to the jurisdiction thereof, are citizens of the United States and of the State wherein they reside.

No State shall make or enforce any law which shall abridge the privileges or immunities of citizens of the United States; nor shall any State deprive any person of life, liberty, or property, without due process of law; nor deny to any person within its jurisdiction the equal protection of the laws.

Section 2

Representatives shall be apportioned among the several States according to their respective numbers, counting the whole number of persons in each State, excluding Indians not taxed. But when the right to vote at any election for the choice of electors for President and Vice-President of the United States, Representatives in Congress, the Executive and Judicial officers of a State, or the members of the Legislature thereof, is denied to any of the male inhabitants of such State, being twenty-one years of age, and citizens of the United States, or in any way abridged, except for participation in rebellion, or other crime, the basis of representation therein shall be reduced in the proportion which the number of such male citizens shall bear to the whole number of male citizens twenty-one years of age in such State.

Section 3

No person shall be a Senator or Representative in Congress, or elector of President and Vice-President, or hold any office, civil or military, under the United States, or under any State, who, having previously taken an oath, as a member of Congress, or as an officer of the United States, or as a member of any State legislature, or as an executive or judicial officer of any State, to support the Constitution of the United States, shall have engaged in insurrection or rebellion against the same, or given aid or comfort to the enemies thereof. But Congress may by a vote of two-thirds of each House, remove such disability.

Section 4

The validity of the public debt of the United States, authorized by law, including debts incurred for payment of pensions and bounties for services in suppressing insurrection or rebellion, shall not be questioned. But neither the United States nor any State shall assume or pay any debt or obligation incurred in aid of insurrection or rebellion against the United States, or any claim for the loss or emancipation of any slave; but all such debts, obligations and claims shall be held illegal and void.

Section 5
The Congress shall have the power to enforce, by appropriate legislation, the provisions of this article.

15th Amendment
Section 1
The right of citizens of the United States to vote shall not be denied or abridged by the United States or by any State on account of race, color, or previous condition of servitude.

Section 2
The Congress shall have the power to enforce this article by appropriate legislation.

16th Amendment
The Congress shall have power to lay and collect taxes on incomes, from whatever source derived, without apportionment among the several States, and without regard to any census or enumeration.

17th Amendment
The Senate of the United States shall be composed of two Senators from each State, elected by the people thereof, for six years; and each Senator shall have one vote. The electors in each State shall have the qualifications requisite for electors of the most numerous branches of the State legislatures.

When vacancies happen in the representation of any State in the Senate, the executive authority of such State shall issue writs of election to fill such vacancies: Provided, That the legislature of any State may empower the executive thereof to make temporary appointments until the people fill the vacancies by election as the legislature may direct.

This amendment shall not be so construed as to affect the election or term of any Senator chosen before it becomes valid as part of the Constitution.

18th Amendment
Section 1
After one year from the ratification of this article the manufacture, sale, or transportation of intoxicating liquors within, the importation thereof into, or the exportation thereof from the United States and all territory subject to the jurisdiction thereof for beverage purposes is hereby prohibited.

Section 2
The Congress and the several States shall have concurrent power to enforce this article by appropriate legislation.

Section 3
This article shall be inoperative unless it shall have been ratified as an amendment to the Constitution by the legislatures of the several States, as provided in the Constitution, within seven years from the date of the submission hereof to the States by the Congress.

19th Amendment
The right of citizens of the United States to vote shall not be denied or abridged by the United States or by any State on account of sex.

Congress shall have power to enforce this article by appropriate legislation.

20th Amendment
Section 1
The terms of the President and the Vice President shall end at noon on the 20th day of January, and the terms of Senators and

Representatives at noon on the 3d day of January, of the years in which such terms would have ended if this article had not been ratified; and the terms of their successors shall then begin.

Section 2
The Congress shall assemble at least once in every year, and such meeting shall begin at noon on the 3d day of January, unless they shall by law appoint a different day.

Section 3
If, at the time fixed for the beginning of the term of the President, the President elect shall have died, the Vice President elect shall become President. If a President shall not have been chosen before the time fixed for the beginning of his term, or if the President elect shall have failed to qualify, then the Vice President elect shall act as President until a President shall have qualified; and the Congress may by law provide for the case wherein neither a President elect nor a Vice President shall have qualified, declaring who shall then act as President, or the manner in which one who is to act shall be selected, and such person shall act accordingly until a President or Vice President shall have qualified.

Section 4
The Congress may by law provide for the case of the death of any of the persons from whom the House of Representatives may choose a President whenever the right of choice shall have devolved upon them, and for the case of the death of any of the persons from whom the Senate may choose a Vice President whenever the right of choice shall have devolved upon them.

Section 5
Sections 1 and 2 shall take effect on the 15th day of October following the ratification of this article.

Section 6
This article shall be inoperative unless it shall have been ratified as an amendment to the Constitution by the legislatures of three-

fourths of the several States within seven years from the date of its submission.

21st Amendment
Section 1
The eighteenth article of amendment to the Constitution of the United States is hereby repealed.

Section 2
The transportation or importation into any State, Territory, or Possession of the United States for delivery or use therein of intoxicating liquors, in violation of the laws thereof, is hereby prohibited.

Section 3
This article shall be inoperative unless it shall have been ratified as an amendment to the Constitution by conventions in the several States, as provided in the Constitution, within seven years from the date of the submission hereof to the States by the Congress.

22nd Amendment
Section 1
No person shall be elected to the office of the President more than twice, and no person who has held the office of President, or acted as President, for more than two years of a term to which some other person was elected President shall be elected to the office of President more than once.

But this Article shall not apply to any person holding the office of President when this Article was proposed by Congress and shall not prevent any person who may be holding the office of President, or acting as President, during the term within which this Article becomes operative from holding the office of President or acting as President during the remainder of such term.

Section 2
This article shall be inoperative unless it shall have been ratified as an amendment to the Constitution by the legislatures of three-fourths of the several States within seven years from the date of its submission to the States by the Congress.

23rd Amendment
Section 1
The District constituting the seat of Government of the United States shall appoint in such manner as Congress may direct: A number of electors of President and Vice President equal to the whole number of Senators and Representatives in Congress to which the District would be entitled if it were a State, but in no event more than the least populous State; they shall be in addition to those appointed by the States, but they shall be considered, for the purposes of the election of President and Vice President, to be electors appointed by a State; and they shall meet in the District and perform such duties as provided by the twelfth article of amendment.

Section 2
The Congress shall have power to enforce this article by appropriate legislation.

24th Amendment
Section 1
The right of citizens of the United States to vote in any primary or other election for President or Vice President, for electors for President or Vice President, or for Senator or Representative in Congress, shall not be denied or abridged by the United States or any State by reason of failure to pay poll tax or other tax.

Section 2
The Congress shall have power to enforce this article by appropriate legislation.

25th Amendment
Section 1
In case of the removal of the President from office or of his death or resignation, the Vice President shall become President.

Section 2
Whenever there is a vacancy in the office of the Vice President, the President shall nominate a Vice President who shall take office upon confirmation by a majority vote of both Houses of Congress.

Section 3
Whenever the President transmits to the President pro tempore of the Senate and the Speaker of the House of Representatives his written declaration that he is unable to discharge the powers and duties of his office, and until he transmits to them a written declaration to the contrary, such powers and duties shall be discharged by the Vice President as Acting President.

Section 4
Whenever the Vice President and a majority of either the principal officers of the executive departments or of such other body as Congress may by law provide, transmit to the President pro tempore of the Senate and the Speaker of the House of Representatives their written declaration that the President is unable to discharge the powers and duties of his office, the Vice President shall immediately assume the powers and duties of the office as Acting President.

Thereafter, when the President transmits to the President pro tempore of the Senate and the Speaker of the House of Representatives his written declaration that no inability exists, he shall resume the powers and duties of his office unless the Vice President and a majority of either the principal officers of the executive department or of such other body as Congress may by law provide, transmit within four days to the President pro tempore of the Senate and the Speaker of the House of Representatives their written declaration that the President is unable to discharge the powers and duties of his office. Thereupon Congress shall decide the issue, assembling within forty-eight hours for that purpose if not in session.

If the Congress, within twenty-one days after receipt of the latter written declaration, or, if Congress is not in session, within twenty-one days after Congress is required to assemble, determines by two-thirds vote of both Houses that the President is unable to discharge the powers and duties of his office, the Vice President shall continue to discharge the same as Acting President; otherwise, the President shall resume the powers and duties of his office.

26th Amendment
Section 1
The right of citizens of the United States, who are eighteen years of age or older, to vote shall not be denied or abridged by the United States or by any State on account of age.

Section 2
The Congress shall have power to enforce this article by appropriate legislation.

27th Amendment
No law, varying the compensation for the services of the Senators and Representatives, shall take effect, until an election of representatives shall have intervened.

This unique document was signed on September 17, 1787, by thirty-nine delegates to the Constitutional Convention. It is a day worthy of every citizen of the United States to pause to celebrate and recognize its impact on "We the People" and the world in general. This day is celebrated every year on the 17th day of September. Sadly, few Americans know about this day of recognition and celebration because of our failed federally funded school system. If there is no change to our school system's curriculum requiring the teaching of our children about the United States Constitution and this day of celebration for its creation, it will soon be forgotten.

What were the Founding Fathers attempting to achieve when they created this unprecedented document? The answer rests in the Preamble to the Constitution. "We, the people of the United States, in order to form a more perfect Union." "To form a more perfect union" is the first goal and intention of the Constitution. This goal comes first in the Preamble because the "United States" is meant to be an example to the world of what people can achieve with the help and guidance of God: A Constitution based on Judeo-Christian values and a shining star to every foreign government in the world that a country governed by, for, and of the people is possible.

The Constitution of the United States of America is a unique self-governing idea that recognizes that people's rights are granted by God and not by the government. America's Constitution further acknowledges that "We the People" and the sovereign States grant limited authority to the federal government to protect and serve the several States. Ideals, which, after nearly two hundred and fifty years, are being turned upside down by power-hungry Marxist-Communist elitists who have gained control of our federal government, corrupting its purpose and intent. Far too many politicians and bureaucrats have become corrupted by their hunger for power, influence, and wealth. Politicians who do not have the honor and integrity needed to withstand the temptations leading to our constitutional form of government's desecration knowingly and willingly turn a blind eye to its desecration for a price.

Our Founding Fathers formulated our Constitution to make America a Nation free of oppression and tyranny, which our Founding Fathers had endured in England under the rule of a king. This Constitution was intended not only to protect America's God-given rights to life, liberty, and the pursuit of happiness but to radiate hope to all other peoples of the world. These noble intentions of our Constitution are struggling to hold any semblance to what the Founding Fathers had envisioned for the United States. Under the agenda of the Marxist-Communist elitists, these noble intentions are evaporating as they push the United States ever deeper into a Marxist-Communist Nation of oppressed people. The Constitution of the United States, as written by the Founding Fathers, once represented our Judeo-Christian values and great American culture and heritage. The Constitution has now become an instrument no longer being adhered to by Washington's Marxist-Communist politicians, causing it to rapidly lose its place as the legal means by which "We the People" are guaranteed our God-given rights to life, liberty, and the pursuit of happiness without infringement by our government. It is being replaced by the dictums of a small group of Marxist-Communist elitists and billionaires who are advocates of globalism.

Benjamin Franklin acknowledged the fragility of our Constitutional Republic following the Constitutional Convention in 1787, when Elizabeth Willing Powel, a prominent society figure and the wife of Philadelphia Mayor Samuel Powel, asked, "Doctor, what have we got? A republic or a monarchy?" to which Franklin reportedly responded, "A republic if you can keep it." Another of Benjamin Franklin's famous quotes from that era comes after George Washington was elected the first president. Franklin stated, "The first man put at the helm will be a good one. Nobody knows what sort may come afterward." But that is not the full quote. He continued, "The executive will be always increasing here, as elsewhere, till it ends in a monarchy."

In 1967, Ronald Reagan delivered one of the most memorable lines of his career: "Freedom is never more than one generation away from extinction. It must be fought for, protected, and handed on for our children to do the same." The truth of this statement appears to be raising its ugly head in light of the violent turmoil spreading across our nation. Turmoil being injected into American society by a generation of misled, misinformed, and indoctrinated malcontents who are encouraged and funded by those who wish to see America brought down to its knees. "Freedom is never more than one generation away from extinction." Has America reached that junction in American history where those warnings are becoming our reality? It is hard not to wonder if our generation is allowing for the ending of our God-given rights under the Constitution, America's position as the greatest nation in the world, and as the last great hope for self-governance by, for, and of the people.

Constitutional Denigration: Ever-increasing Marxist-Communist influence over our Constitutional Republic has placed a tremendous amount of pressure on our Constitutional Republic by both Democrats and Republicans alike. With a governing system that has become so prone to wokism and Marxist-Communist ideology, fears for our Constitutional Republic's ability to survive have dramatically grown in just the past two decades. Our representative system of government is no longer composed of ethical, honorable men and women dedicated to protecting our Constitution and the legal citizens of the United States. If our federal government officials were always honorable, there would be no need for checks and balances or congressional oversight. The Founding Fathers understood this, so they designed a governing system that protected minority points of view, to protect us from leaders inclined to lie, cheat, and steal, and to protect the majority against minorities determined to subvert the Constitution. But will the Founding Father's protective measures hold true? Under President Trump's leadership and willingness to take on the Washington bureaucracy, enormous pressure was being placed on Congress, the Courts, and the bureaucracy to correct course and return to constitutional mandates and the rule of law. With the Biden-

Harris Administration, our government institutions became politicized, weaponized, and significantly weakened, making them more vulnerable to efforts to subvert their original purposes. There is no guarantee that our constitutional Republic will survive the sustained and organized assault being directed against it by the Marxist-Communist Democrats and fellow Marxist-Communist Republicans.

Today, more than ever, our Constitution is being denigrated and feloniously ignored by our elected officials, federal departments, federal agencies, federal commissions, and the federal bureaucracy as a whole. We have political Partys infiltrated by Marxist-Communist members, charged with providing oversight over the various departments and agencies but who are openly ignoring Constitutional mandates and allowing bureaucratic entities to regulate outside of their constitutional authority. These unconstitutionally established departments and agencies are systematically and blatantly stripping away our Constitutional rights. These unconstitutionally established entities are rapidly diminishing the sovereignty of our States by confiscating state responsibilities and rights, allowing the invasion of the United States through our southern border, stripping away our right to self-determination, infringing upon our right to free speech and religious freedoms, and infringing upon our Second Amendment rights to own and bear arms. Under Marxist-Communist Administrations, State governors, and city mayors, drugs, murders, rioting, homelessness, and the malicious destruction of property are running rampant.

Enormous amounts of money (trillions) are being spent on state, county, and local projects and initiatives through unconstitutional federal grants and entitlements, none of which the federal government has the Constitutional authority to authorize. Billions of dollars are being given to corrupt foreign countries who despise the United States, much of which ends up in the pockets of those countries' corrupt officials and not spent on humanitarian initiatives as intended. Members of Congress authorizing bills providing our tax dollars to these entities know that corrupt officials are siphoning much of this money. Yet, they continue to pour ever more money down these drains, all of which have our country teetering on the verge of bankruptcy and being withheld from assisting American citizens in need.

The United States Supreme Court is the final appellate court of the United States judicial system. It has the power to review and overturn the decisions of lower courts. The Supreme Court also has original jurisdiction in certain cases involving public officials, ambassadors, or state disputes. The Supreme Court's constitutional responsibility is to decide if laws are constitutional, not to legislate. Our Supreme Court Judges are not constitutionally authorized to legislate from the bench or interpret the Constitution to fit a political point of view. Over the years, however, our Supreme Court Judges have been rewriting our Constitution with politically motivated Marxist-Communist misinterpretation of the Constitution. Currently, the Court is controlled by a majority of conservative-leaning Judges who are beginning to review and, where appropriate, overturn previous Supreme Court decisions that are determined unconstitutional. Hundreds of rulings need to be revisited by this constitutionally conservative-minded court.

Today, we have two Constitutions; the original Constitution drafted by delegates to the Constitutional Convention during the summer of 1787, is an approximately seven-page document signed on September 17, 1787, establishing the government of the United States, with roughly an additional twelve pages covering the twenty-seven Amendments ratified by the several States. The second Constitution consists of well over fifteen hundred pages, creating a constitution that has become bloated and dysfunctional due to rulings made by the Supreme Court. Rulings that have stretched the original constitution beyond the intent of the Founding Fathers. Far too many Supreme Court decisions have been based on the political whims of the justices in the majority or as a result of outside pressures. Rulings that are often detrimental to our Republic. Marxist-Communist Supreme Court Justices, when in the majority, are unconstitutionally legislating from the bench in violation of separation of power, as articulated in Article I, Section 1 of the Constitution.

Our elected officials have embarrassed and weakened America and shown themselves to be no more than weak, corrupt, power-hungry charlatans. We have elected officials who are criminally incompetent to represent the American people. We have hoped and prayed for our congressional members to come to their senses and correct the path they are leading us down but to no avail. We can no longer wait for someone special to come along and fix the Washington mess. That someone special is already here, and that someone special is you. Every American citizen has the power to change the destructive course our country is on, but only if they are willing to take risks by coming out of their comfort zone, stop standing on the sideline, and becoming united to challenge the corrupt government institution. Patriotic American citizens can only save our Constitutional Republic from Marxist-Communist elected officials if each American becomes engaged and makes it crystal clear to those sworn to represent us that we have had enough and demand that they act accordingly. Elected and unelected Washington Marxist-Communist officials know that much of what they are doing is unconstitutional and not in the best interest of our Constitutional Republic or the people. These members of Congress and the leadership in the bureaucratic Washington swamp are radical sociopaths who are promoting the idea, to an uninformed and ill-educated minority of the American population, that our Constitution is no longer relevant, has failed to keep up with the passage of time, and no longer reflects the America of today. In short, our Constitution is standing in the way of imposing a Marxist-Communist governing system upon an unsuspecting citizenry who are so short-sighted that they only see the "free" benefits that they believe will be provided under a Marxist-Communist form of government and not the loss of freedoms American citizens currently enjoy.

The Washington elitists are redefining the meaning and intent of many aspects of our Constitution to create their Marxist-Communist ideological euphoria. A nation based on equity, not equality, a nation based on division, not on inclusion, a country where all things must be shared equally by all American citizens and not retained by those who have worked hard and committed to achieving those personal gains. A place of fairy tales. Suppose these Marxist-Communist ideologists believe so strongly in this fairytale world of Marxist-Communist Globalism. In that case, they should propose changes to our governing system through Amendments to the existing Constitution. If these radical Marxist-Communist politicians and their radical constituents, who are actually in the minority, are so hell-bent on fundamentally changing America, our Founding Fathers made a constitutional provision by which they can attempt to make such changes constitutionally. This avenue is found under Article V of the Constitution. *(If you do not recall what Article V allows, please go back to the beginning of this Chapter for review.)*

These Marxist-Communist ideologists will not do so because they know that they could never get two-thirds of both chambers of Congress to pass such proposals. If they would somehow get Congress to propose their Marxist-Communist Amendments, then they would have to convince three-quarters of the existing States to ratify their radical Amendments. Such changes would result in a one-party ruling system and eliminate our God-given rights to the freedoms provided under our Constitution. This is why these Marxist-Communist members of Congress choose to pass unconstitutional legislation to circumvent the Constitution. Once such legislation is passed, the American citizenry ignorantly and passively accepts such new laws. Those anti-constitutional laws challenged in our court system can drag out through our inept and corrupt court system for years.

America's Constitution has promoted, protected, and assured equal justice under the law to every citizen in America since its adoption in 1787. Under our Constitution, America has survived the depression and prevailed over the aggressive power of Nazism, Fascism, and Communism. Over the last two centuries, it has been stated that if America's constitutional form of governance ever falls, it will come from internal forces. Those predicted internal forces are alive and well today in the Marxist-Communist radicals of the Democrat Party and their Marxist-Communist radicals within the Republican Party, all determined to destroy America's Constitutional Republic by any means possible.

Changing Electoral Process: Marxist-Communist Joe Biden made recommendations to change our electoral processes to promote diversity, but such proposed changes would skew the election results in favor of Marxist-Communist candidates. On December 1st, 2022, Biden addressed a letter to the Democratic National Committee's (DNC) Rules and Bylaws Committee to request consideration of potentially changing the Democrat Party presidential nomination process calendar and voting practices. His first point of focus was on the scheduling of Democrat presidential election campaigning and debates, stating black voters did not get a proper say in proceedings until too late in the calendar. This remark came alongside a Democrat National Conference controversy over whether Iowa should remain the first state to hold caucuses, as it has for the last five decades. The Democrat National Conference's rule-making committee voted to hand the first caucus to South Carolina due to its larger black population. Biden's letter notes that giving more African American voters the chance to select their preferred candidate early in the calendar will allow more of them to pick from the complete list of those running. Again, smoke and screens by a corrupt president to make it appear that he and his Marxist-Communist Party leadership are looking out for minorities. In reality, many candidates on the primary ticket in South Carolina will never survive Super Tuesday, making their votes in South Carolina irrelevant.

Joe Biden also took issue with caucuses in the letter. He highlighted that public voting events require voters to travel long distances at potentially inconvenient times, disadvantaging those with fixed working schedules. He then discussed the importance of diversity from a regional standpoint, suggesting that representation from suburban and rural areas was important to the party and urban voters. He concluded the letter by reiterating his emphasis on equal opportunities, stating he had "the most diverse Cabinet in history" and that he had appointed more minorities to official roles than any previous president. He also noted that he had nominated the first black woman to the Supreme Court, Brown Jackson. President Biden has never made a secret of his ambition to be the president to promote the selection of the most minorities within a president's administration. However, his focus would be more useful in other areas. Opinion polls have shown that American voters are currently most concerned about issues like immigration, abortion, and the economy. Unfortunately, his most diverse cabinet in history also turns out to be the most dysfunctional and destructive cabinet in our nation's history.

Election of Senators: One of the most significant errors made by the Congress of the United States was the repealing of Article I, Section 3, Clauses 1 and 2 of the Constitution, which articulated that individual State's legislators shall elect Senators of the United States and not by direct election by the citizens of that state. The Founding Founders included this method of electing Senators because Senators were intended to be ambassadors representing the interests of their State and not the citizens of the State. This method of selecting Senators was further intended to impede any attempt by the House of Representatives to pass legislation detrimental to the State or the citizens thereof. In this manner, the States dictated how their Senators would vote on any proposed legislation. Failure to vote accordingly subjected that Senator to recall by his or her state's legislators. Under this Article, Senators would have no need or incentive to develop relationships with donors, lobbyists, or any other entity, as none of these entities could directly influence either the decisions made by a Senator or the election of the Senator. This all changed with the addition of the Seventeenth Amendment to the Constitution by the 62nd Congress in 1912, becoming a part of the Constitution on April 8, 1913, on ratification by three-quarters (36) of the State legislatures.

The Seventeenth Amendment now conveniently allows for the election of Senators by the people and not by State legislators, thereby taking any legislative decision-making out of the control of the States and providing all decision-making to the federal government. This advanced the takeover of State sovereignty and the centralization of power in Washington.

This Amendment essentially eliminated the checks and balances of Congress as intended by our Founding Fathers. It opened the door to outside influences, such as campaign donors, lobbyists, and big business, subjecting senators to the same temptations of power, greed, bribes, and corruption as the members of the House of Representatives. If State legislatures still chose Senate members, as intended by the founding fathers, we would not have states wherein the majority of the red republican counties lose to the very few blue counties. Example: Our President is federally elected by the electoral college; if not done in this manner, California and New York would control every election outcome because there is more majority in those two states than in the United States combined. That is precisely what is happening to our country because Senate members are elected by the people rather than the State's legislators. This is why you see a state such as Georgia, which has a majority of red-Republican-dominated counties, losing to the very few blue-Democrat-dominated counties.

For example, this Amendment is why Democrat Senate Majority Leader Chuck Schumer and Republican Senate Minority Leader Mitch McConnell were able to push through President Obama's bankrupting Affordable Care Act in 2010, the $1.7 trillion Omnibus Bill of 2022, and the Respect for Marriage Act of 2022. These initiatives would probably not have been supported by states with Republican majorities, making the passage of these unconstitutional initiatives highly unlikely. Another prime example of the horrendous flaw in the Seventh Amendment is President Biden's March 21st, 2023, federal overreaching takeover of 510,000 acres of land in Nevada and Texas. Biden confiscated this land without input from or notification to the State's governors or State legislators. Biden used the Antiquities Act of 1906 to seize the land for the purpose of creating two new national monuments, Avi Kwa Ame National Monument in Nevada and Castner Range in Texas. The move federally protects these lands from development or mining for rich minerals, including lithium, a vital element in manufacturing electric car batteries. The protection blocked Nevada's plans to mine areas of the confiscated land for their rich mineral deposits and for providing economic opportunities to its state's citizens.

Opportunities were lost over the special interests of the Marxist-Communist movement to overthrow our constitutional Republic by eliminating economic and employment opportunities and ensuring our continued dependency on China for these rare earth minerals. This confiscation will stop the United States from moving towards becoming independent and free from Chinese lithium, which only serves to prove further that Biden was a Chinese-bought-off traitor to the United States. Biden justified his confiscation of this state land, stating Avi Kwa Ame National Monument is home to "one of the largest contiguous wildlife corridors in the United States," which he described as "breathtaking," and the Texas location, Castner Range, a nearly 7,000-acre patch near El Paso, which the president described as beautiful. However, it is improbable that he has ever visited either location—another historic example of federal government overreach by the Biden Marxist-Communist Administration.

The Seventh Amendment is the ultimate example of federal overreach and disregard for the Constitution as written and intended by our Founding Fathers. This Amendment eliminated any State input on any legislation purposed by the House of Representatives and sent to the Senate for debate and consideration. Individual States lost their ability to act as a check against federal overreach through instructions and preferences made to their State's legislatively elected senators. We must repeal the Seventh Amendment and return Senator elections to the State Legislators as our founding fathers originally intended. This would genuinely help restore power to the States and the people.

Federal Government's Role: Where does the federal government fit in our Constitution? First, understand that the federal government did not create the several states subservient to the federal government. The states needed a centralized entity to provide protection from foreign enemies and to perform a limited role on behalf of the several States. It was for this reason that the existing states created the federal government. A federal government intended to be subservient to the sovereign States, limited to only those authorities enumerated in the Constitution. These enumerated powers include the power to regulate international and interstate commerce, establish a uniform law of naturalization, establish federal courts (subordinate to the Supreme Court), make treaties, establish post offices, establish and maintain a military, declare war and levy taxes to fund these limited authorities. The Tenth Amendment enumerates the limited authority the federal government has over the states and the legal citizens of this Nation: "The powers not delegated to the United States by the Constitution, nor prohibited by it to the states, are reserved to the states respectively, or to the people." The Constitution and the Tenth Amendment to it have been ignored by our elected politicians for decades, as is evident by the fact that instead of eight or nine constitutionally approved federal agencies, we currently have well over four hundred and fifty departments, agencies, and commissions.

The Founding Fathers rightly insisted on preserving the prominent governing role of the State legislatures as a crucial mechanism to contain the power of the newly formed federal government. Let me emphasize that it was the existing states that established the American Republic and the Constitution and, within it, retained for themselves significant authority to ensure the republic's durability. To this end, Article V of the Constitution grants State legislators considerable authority to rebalance the constitutional structure to restore our founding principles should the federal government exceed its limitations, abandon its original purpose, and grow too powerful, as the founders had worried might happen. As evidenced by the current existence of well over four hundred and fifty federal government entities, this provision of the Constitution, which has never been exercised, should have been employed shortly after the Lyndon Johnson Administration enacted his "Great Society," which began the horrendous growth of our federal bureaucracy.

What was to be a harmless federal government, operating from a defined enumeration of specific grants of power has now become an ever-present and unaccountable opposing force governing far beyond the will of the citizens. It is the nation's most significant creditor, debtor, lender, employer, consumer, contractor, granter, property owner, tenant, insurer, healthcare provider, and pension guarantor. Moreover, what it does not control directly, it bans or mandates by regulations. To satisfy its greedy appetite for power through initiatives, entitlements, and grants, the federal government not only completely consumes the Treasury's annual revenue but continues to fund unconstitutional initiatives with ever-increasing taxes on a diminishing number of productive citizens, thus requiring the need to either print money which leads to inflation or borrow exuberant amounts of money from foreign nations, most adversaries of the United States. All of which was precisely what our Founding Fathers most feared would happen with the passage of time. Unfortunately for our Constitutional Republic, Congress has been relegating unconstitutional authority to unelected federal government bureaucrats over the past sixty to seventy years on matters that constitutionally belong to the sovereign states. The depth and breadth of the unconstitutional federal bureaucracy have grown so massive that gaining control of and reining in their overwhelming power over our lives will be extremely difficult at best. It will require unprecedented effort and cooperation between a strong-willed president and a strong, fearless conservative congress. These bureaucrat entities must be abolished, and the authority for federal agencies to pass regulations must be reclaimed and returned to the individual sovereign states or Congress as authorized by the Constitution.

The Founding Fathers never intended nor implied that the governance of the United States should be delegated to unelected officials. Therefore, no authority to do so was written into the Constitution. Our Constitution clearly states that our Republic will be managed by a federal government consisting of a legislative, judicial, and executive body. This manner of a federal government was established at the request of the several states to serve the needs of the states and not intended to be emperors over the states. Our Founding Fathers' intent when they created the federal government was that "the sole purpose of the federal government is to manage certain aspects of government," not to consume the responsibilities of the individual sovereign states, thereby increasing the federal government's power. The Founding Fathers intended that this newly authored Constitution would serve as a guide to those who would represent the citizens *"and to do so with honor and integrity."*

Let me repeat those critical words in the above paragraph, *"the sole purpose of the federal government is to manage certain aspects of government and to do so with **honor** and **integrity**."*

Where is the honor and integrity within our federal government when it sends billions of tax payer's dollars to our enemies to build their armed forces with which they then threaten our country? Where is the honor and integrity when our federal government spends billions of tax payer's money to lavish countries with foreign aid who hate America and our life of freedom and liberty? All the while, we dramatically reduce funding to our military forces, have veterans who honorably served our country sleeping on the streets, and American families living in distress.

Where is the honor and integrity in an oppressive federal government which no longer abides by our Constitution? An oppressive federal government that has evolved into a regime of revolving tyrannical elites. Where is the honor and integrity when we have less freedom with each passing year and, like a signpost to the coming reign of terror, we submit ourselves to the demands of a godless cancel culture, which, like cancerous growth, is metastasizing throughout our culture? We have traded the American Revolution for the Cultural Revolution. We cannot defend our borders, history, monuments to past greatness, or streets. Our cities have become anarchist playgrounds. We are a nation of dependents, panhandlers, and misplaced charities. Homeless veterans camp in the streets while illegal aliens are put up in lavish hotels. Where is the honor and integrity when our government allows this to happen?

Today, pro-American citizens who peacefully protest the injustices being imposed upon them are harassed, arrested, and jailed. Conservatives who are loyal Make America Great Again (MAGA) followers or who are strongly associated with former President Trump are detained for politically motivated purposes and handcuffed in full view of the general public for accusations that are either false or minor in nature—done for no other purpose than to embarrass these individuals publicly. Actions meant only to intimidate and send a message to all conservatives that the Marxist-Communist elitists will not tolerate conservative ideology.

Our Constitution once created a bond between all American citizens, which tied our fates and fortunes together. At least, this was true until the turn of this century. Now, we are a nation severely divided between constitutional conservatives and Marxist-Communist factions. If our Nation and the political elements charged with representing the wellbeing of this Nation and its people cannot or will not find a means by which to once again unite our country as "one nation under God," then the United States is doomed to fall into a third-world corrupt Marxist-Communist nation much like Venezuela. Unless the American people acknowledge what is happening to our Constitutional Republic and take steps to correct course, America will no longer be a self-governing Nation. Could this possibly happen to the United States of America? Let me share an eyewitness account of the corruption of a once free and prosperous constitutional republic, much like the United States.

In the 1970s, Venezuela was one of the most prosperous countries in Latin America. However, from 2015 to 2019, its economy shrank by thirty-five percent in just four short years. This eventual collapse can be traced back to 1999 when Marxist-Communist Hugo Chavez became president. Chavez was heralded as the purveyor of a "socialist paradise." Venezuela's socialist paradise rapidly denigrated into a Marxist-Communist hell under Hugo Chavez's dictatorship.

On September 20th, 2022, I had the privilege of meeting and hearing Omar Lugo speak. Omar grew up in Venezuela during the period that his country transitioned from a Constitutional Republic patterned after the United States into a Marxist-Communist country. Omar related his traumatic experiences during the collapse of Venezuela's Constitutional government. Omar's father, who was a Diplomat under Venezuela's Constitutional government, was shot on two separate occasions in front of his home. Shot in full view of his family and neighbors. Shot by thugs Omar described as being exactly like the members of Antifa and Black Lives Matter, who Hugo Chavez was using to intimidate and eliminate nonconformists. Fortunately, Omar's father survived those two attempts on his life and continued his vocal opposition to the dictatorial Marxist-Communist rule of Hugo Chavez.

By the time Omar was twelve, Hugo Chavez and his followers had transformed Venezuela into a Marxist-Communist country. A country with a collapsed economy, double-digit inflation, out-of-control crime, destructive riots, and full-flung anarchy. It was also at this age that Omar was kidnapped for ransom by elements of Venezuela's criminal organizations. Like his father, Omar was extremely fortunate to have come out of that situation with his life. Was anyone ever prosecuted for his kidnapping or the shooting of his father? The simple answer is no because the country no longer had a legal system that protected its citizens but protected only the elitist class of Venezuela. Having suffered through that transition, the shooting of his father, and his kidnapping, Omar made his way to the United States at the age of nineteen in 1999, where he believed he would find safety and security under a genuinely constitutional government. When Omar turned thirty-three, he learned that his father had died of poisoning, most probably by the Marxist-Communist government, because his father continued to refuse to conform to the demands of Venezuela's Marxist-Communist government and spoke out against what was happening to his country.

Omar shared with his audience the steps and processes Venezuela went through in its transition from a free Constitutional government into a Marxist-Communist country. He advised the audience that what he had lived through in Venezuela, he was now seeing occurring in the United States. This compelled Omar to begin speaking out at every opportunity possible, to try and warn anyone who would listen that the United States was rapidly traveling down the same road that Venezuela had traveled to its transformation. Omar issued a stern warning that whether you are a Republican, Democrat, or member of any other patriotic American group or organization, if "We the People" do not put our differences aside soon and begin to become active in stopping what is happening to the United States, then sooner rather than later, it will be too late for our Constitutional government. Like Venezuela, we will find ourselves struggling to survive in a Marxist-Communist environment.

On March 17th, 2023, the Department of State announced that it would provide over $170 million in aid for humanitarian and development projects to help Venezuelans facing various urgent needs within their country. According to the Department of State, some of the funds would be used for food, water, and sanitation projects in Venezuela, while other portions of the funds were designated for immediate shelter, healthcare, and other services for any Venezuelans who had migrated to other nations in South America. This funding was announced by the United States ambassador to the United Nations, Linda Thomas-Greenfield, during a conference in Brussels, which aimed to raise awareness of Venezuela's ongoing economic and political crisis that has driven millions of Venezuelans into poverty and forced over seven million others to migrate out of Venezuela to mostly South America countries. Can any sane American taxpayer believe for one moment that American taxpayer dollars being infused into a dictator-led Marxist-Communist nation would actually find its way to those intended and not into the pockets of the corrupt leadership of that country? Only a naive fool would believe such a probability.

Chapter 4
Incompetent Federal Government

Democrats and Democratic-leaning independents (78%) say the government should do more; only 21% say it is doing too many things better left to businesses and individuals. Liberal Democrats (85%) are especially likely to support an active role in government; 72% of moderate Democrats also say the government should do more. By contrast, most Republicans prefer a limited role for government: 71% of Republicans and Republican leaners say that the government is doing far too many things better left to individuals and businesses, compared with 28% who say it should play a more significant role. Eight in ten conservative Republicans say the government is doing too many things better left to others. When asked to consider other aspects of government's role and performance, most Americans say government is inefficient. Fifty-six percent of Democrats say government is almost always wasteful and inefficient, compared with 42% who say it often does a better job than people give it credit. Nearly 70% of Republicans say the government is wasteful and inefficient.

<u>Source & Additional Information</u>: ((www.pewresearch.org/politics)

Out-of-Control Government: The United States federal government has become corrupt at levels that could dwarf third-world countries. The corruption of our elected members of Congress and unelected federal bureaucrats covers multiple means of corruption and is typically used concurrently with similar aims. These corrupt methods include but are not limited to bribery, embezzlement, theft, fraud, graft, extortion, blackmail, influence peddling, networking, abuse of discretion, favoritism, nepotism, and clientelism. Far too many politicians, or in my opinion, a majority of our elected officials, are involved with one or more of these corrupt actions by utilizing their office of trust to become wealthy while disregarding the expectations of and the promises made to their constituents. This corruption and ineptness span the full spectrum of our federal government.

An army of foreign citizens is invading our country through our southern border. An army consisting of millions of illegal immigrants, which includes unknown numbers of terrorists, human traffickers, M-13 gang members, murderers, and drug smugglers. Drugs that are killing tens of thousands of young American citizens. Those in the highest leadership positions are openly violating Section 8 of Article I, which charges the federal government with the responsibility of providing for the common defense of our country and, by extension, the security of our borders. Millions of illegal immigrants are pouring into the United States. This invasion force is significantly larger than the armed forces of most countries in the world. It is bringing death and destruction not only to the communities and states along the Mexican border but has penetrated the very heart of our nation. In reaction to this invasion, our treasonous Marxist-Communist Administration openly conspires with this enemy by assisting them in their invasion of the United States. It is well known that Biden's Marxist-Communist Administration provided aid and assistance to this enemy in anticipation of giving amnesty and citizenship to these invaders, who they believe will then vote to help keep the Democrat Party in absolute power.

Trucker's Protest: How many people still remember the Spring of 2022, when social and news media were covered with stories about Canadian and American truckers who had come together in their respective countries and drove their trucks in convoys cross-country to their national seats of government in protest of the draconian mandates placed on them and their fellow countrymen during the COVID epidemic? Men and women who willingly stood up against the draconian Marxist-Communist governments of Canada and America, knowing that they were risking their professional careers and their livelihoods. Canadian truckers had their banking accounts frozen by their Marxist-

Communist Canadian regime to stop those brave Canadian patriots by eliminating their ability to provide for their families. But this did not discourage them, and they went on with their protest. American truckers, fortunately, live in a country in which our federal government cannot "yet" arbitrarily shut down or confiscate a citizen's bank accounts without legal justification and warrants to do so. But that day is fast approaching with Biden's March 9th, 2022, Executive Order #14067, directing all Federal agencies to begin developing plans for the implementation of digital currency, which will give our federal government direct access to our bank accounts, enabling them to freeze or confiscate our money at their discretion.

These individuals put everything on the line, not just for their own sake but for their families, neighbors, and country. They stepped forward against the odds, willing to at least try to rein in government overreach and unconstitutional mandates. One would have thought that their heroic effort would have energized the citizens of both countries to join these peaceful protesters. These heroic truckers intended to inspire their fellow countrymen and women to also organize and conduct protest rallies at every state Capitol in the Nation, demanding their legislators stop ignoring the fact that, as sovereign entities, they are not subject to adherence to unconstitutional mandates handed down from a tyrannical Marxist-Communist federal government. It would have been wonderful if our state legislators, who took an oath to protect their State and its citizens from the federal government's overreach, had stood up and vocally supported these truckers. Unfortunately, our state legislators did not have the courage and fortitude shown by these truckers to stand against the Marxist-Communist federal government's unconstitutional mandates imposed during the COVID pandemic. It would seem that far too many of our State-level representatives are more interested in protecting all the free grant money the federal government provides as bribes to persuade states into relinquishing their sovereignty than in protecting their state sovereignty and citizens. As things now stand, our children and grandchildren are on a path to inheriting a Marxist-Communist nation, thus losing all their God-given rights and freedoms only found under our Constitution. We are being severely weakened as a Constitutional Republic as a direct result of the unwillingness of our state legislators to act as a firewall against federal government overreach and abuses by rejecting federal monies, which require the State to relinquish control and oversite to the federal government.

Section I: Secretary of State

The United States Department of State is charged with advising the President of the United States and leading the nation in foreign policy issues. It does not state that the Secretary of State is responsible for coordinating the signatures on a falsely written document to protect a Presidential candidate and his family. The State Department's mission calls for protecting and assisting American citizens living or traveling abroad. I am sure that all those American citizens left behind in Afghanistan feel incredibly comfortable in the knowledge that the State Department would be there to protect and assist them in evacuating from Afghanistan. The Department of State's mission statement indicates that it is responsible for immigrant and nonimmigrant visas to enhance the security of the United States border. How is that working out, America? The mission statement further indicates that the Department of State is responsible for guaranteeing the diplomatic readiness of the United States Government. The inept and unqualified head of the United States Department of State, Antony Blinken, was the highest-ranking member of President Biden's Cabinet and paid an annual salary of $221,400. Much taxpayer money was spent on someone incompetent to accomplish the Department's mission and willing to conspire with high-level political officials to sign a document containing a false narrative to protect a corrupt Presidential candidate in 2020.

A former Central Intelligence agent official testified that then-Biden campaign senior adviser and future Secretary of State Antony Blinken "played a role in the inception" of the public statement signed by past intelligence officials that claimed the Hunter Biden laptop was part of a Russian disinformation campaign. Former Central Intelligent Agent Deputy Director Michael Morrell testified before the House Judiciary and Intelligence Committees that Blinken was "the impetus" of the public statement signed in October 2020 that implied the laptop belonging to Hunter Biden was disinformation. Blinken orchestrated the obtaining of fifty-one former intelligence official's signatures on a statement that falsely discredited a New York Post story regarding Hunter Biden's laptop as supposed Russian disinformation. Blinken created this scandalous letter containing known false statements just weeks before the presidential election debates, clear election interference on the part of Blinken and the fifty-one ex-national security officials who signed the letter.

Source & Additional Information: (https://judiciary.house.gov/media/press-releases/new-testimony-reveals-secretary-blinken-and-biden-campaign-behind-infamous)

The lawmakers found that based on Morell's testimony, it was "apparent" that the Biden campaign "played an active role in the origins of the public statement, which had the effect of helping to suppress the Hunter Biden story and preventing American citizens from making a fully informed decision during the 2020 presidential election." Blinken obtained fifty-one individuals who held positions of trust by the American public and used that trust and their national security credentials to lend credibility to their story that the laptop was purely Russian disinformation, implying that this conclusion was based on access to specialized information unavailable to other Americans. This conspiracy, which Blinken led, minimized and suppressed public dissemination of the serious allegations about the Biden family and was a grave disservice to all American citizens' informed participation in our democracy.

Morell testified that on or around October 17, 2020, Blinken reached out to him to discuss the Hunter Biden laptop story. Blinken, at the time, was a senior adviser to the Biden campaign. According to Morell, although Blinken implied the outreach was for gathering Morell's reaction to the Post story, it set in motion the events that led to the issuance of the public statement. Morell testified that the Biden campaign helped strategize the statement's public release. Morell further explained that one of Blinken's two goals in releasing the statement was to support Joe Biden in the debate with Trump, thereby assisting Biden in winning the election. Morell went on to testify that the second intent was to share their fabricated concern with the American people that the Russians were playing an active role in helping Donald Trump win the election. None have been held accountable for election interference, which is a federal felony.

In mid-March of 2021, Secretary Blinken held his first face-to-face meeting with his Chinese counterpart, Chinese Communist Party foreign affairs chief Yang Jiechi, in Anchorage, Alaska. This initial meeting was televised and clearly showed that Yang had taken total control as he publicly scolded Secretary Blinken, indicating that China would no longer accept direct criticism from the United States and demanded respect as a new world great power. Yang unloaded on Secretary of State Antony Blinken with a list of Chinese complaints about the United States, accusing Washington of hypocrisy for daring to criticize Beijing for human rights violations while human rights violations and domestic discontent were occurring within the United States. Secretary Blinken failed to respond adequately, reacting more like an elementary school student being scolded by his teacher for misbehaving in the classroom. Secretary Blinken's handling of that meeting shattered any illusions that he had the strength and courage to be assertive with China.

On January 28th, 2023, a Chinese spy balloon entered United States airspace over Alaska and then into Canadian airspace.

The spy balloon again reentered the continental United States on January 31st, 2023. A sighting over Montana kicked off what became a media frenzy as the balloon made its way across the United States. The general public also began reporting sightings over Wyoming, North Dakota, Kansas, Missouri, North Carolina, and South Carolina on social media. The discovery of the balloon was finally officially announced on February 2nd, 2023, by Pentagon officials who said the spy balloon was spotted over the state of Wyoming's Warren Air Force Base near Cheyenne, which maintains two hundred and twenty remote missile facilities; Montana's, Malmstrom Air Force Base which maintains one-hundred and fifty Minuteman III intercontinental ballistic missiles; and North Dakota's Minot Air Force Base which is armed with one-hundred and fifty nuclear missile silos. This balloon was found to be remotely controllable and was being controlled to fly over these critical nuclear defense locations for intelligence-gathering purposes.

Joe Biden, senior leadership at the Pentagon, and the Secretary of State decided to allow this spy balloon to travel over these critical bases, deciding not to shoot the balloon out of the sky until it had completed its spying mission and was off the coast of South Carolina. Their justification was that its size would have created a debris field large enough to put people at risk. This ridiculous excuse was presented to the American citizens, although they were aware of this spy balloon's approach to the United States before its entry over the Aleutian Islands. This Chinese spy balloon could have been safely shot down over water before its entry over the Aleutian Islands, most uninhabited, or while it was over large portions of unpopulated Alaskan territory.

So why would the balloon be allowed to fly, unhindered, over America and its defensive nuclear bases by the Biden-Harris Marxist-Communist administration? A question that leads one to believe that this balloon was intentionally allowed to continue its spying mission by a Chinese compromised and bought off

President. A President who acted and behaved as though he had little to no concern for the defensive safety of America and its citizens. According to Chinese state media, all the blame for the balloon incident was laid upon the "absurd and hysterical" reaction of the Biden-Harris administration, denounced the destruction of the balloon as an "abuse of the use of force," and told Secretary Blinken that the United States would have to repair the "damage" it has caused to United States-China relations. This blatant violation of our sovereign air space by the Chinese Communist Party and their response to the spy balloon incident further indicates their total lack of respect for or fear of America under the Biden-Harris Administration.

While serving under Vice President Biden, who opposed the reckless overthrowing of Libya's dictator, Colonel Muammar Gaddafi, Blinken went around his boss and strongly encouraged President Obama to move forward under the guise of humanitarianism. This against his boss Vice President Biden's position not to overthrow Gaddafi. In July 2020, Blinken admitted that his support for the overthrowing of Libya's dictator, Colonel Muammar Gaddafi, was wrong. This move on the part of the United States was a disastrous failure that left Libya in chaos without any form of government, allowing for the Islamic State of Iraq and al-Sham (ISIS) terrorists to take control of the country.

The rapid turn of events in Afghanistan following the United States' disastrous retreat caught Blinken by total surprise, indicative of his naivety when dealing with foreign adversaries. At the time of the fall of Kabul, the Afghan Capital, Blinken was visiting his elderly father. When Blinken chose to leave Washington to visit his father, his schedule was packed with work-related calls and meetings about the situation in Afghanistan. The surprise and following frustrations over the Afghan situation were of his own making. Critics argue that many of the challenges throughout the evacuation of our military forces in Afghanistan came down to differences between the Pentagon and the State Department over the Afghan government's expectations of survival following the withdrawal of United States troops. Military leaders warned that the country could collapse within weeks, though few, if anyone, correctly predicted the fall would come within days. The State Department believed it had more time. A senior defense official told POLITICO that there appeared to be "a clear disconnect between the military estimate and what the Department of State believed. When this is investigated, we will find that the Department of State overestimated their ability to continue a diplomatic presence and underestimated the demand that a government collapse would engender Special Immigrant Visa applicants to flee," the defense official stated.

During a town hall meeting, which Secretary Blinken held with State Department employees in mid-September 2021, attendees grew emotional, complaining about what they saw as a muddled and confusing response to the chaos in Afghanistan, where many of them had served. A platform allowing anonymous comments during the event was filled with harsh statements. "At what point will the department finally take crisis response seriously…? This was worse than the blind leading the blind," one person wrote, according to images obtained by POLITICO. Another comment questioned why there was no better planning, especially for worst-case scenarios as opposed to the most likely scenarios: "There is a lot of anger. This amount of suffering did not have to occur." Employees of the State Department demonstrated disappointment in Blinken because he was viewed as an inexperienced leader, having only been a Senate committee member and having served on the National Security Council.

Republican Representatives Ralph Norman of South Carolina and Andy Harris of Maryland co-sponsored a resolution introducing articles of impeachment on August 27th, 2021, arguing that Secretary of State Antony Blinken failed to advise the president properly and abandoned American interests in Afghanistan.

"Secretary Blinken has failed to faithfully uphold his oath and has instead presided over a reckless abandonment of our nation's interests, security, and values in his role in the withdrawal of American forces and diplomatic assets from Afghanistan," reads the articles. They add that "in direct conflict with the intelligence and advice provided by his diplomats and the intelligence community, Secretary Blinken failed to counsel and advise the President accordingly and did not inform the Congress nor American citizens at home and abroad of the dangers." The move by Representative Ralph Norman and Representative Andy Harris comes as many Republicans have called for some level of accountability for the attacks that left thirteen American service members dead. But with a Marxist-Communist lead Senate, nothing came of this or any other resolution to impeach Blinken. That resolution remains in the House Committee on Judiciary, not having the required votes to pass the resolution due to Marxist-Communist members of the Republican party obstructing its move forward.

"Under the Constitution of the United States of America, the Secretary of State is tasked with informing Congress and the American citizens on the conduct of United States foreign relations," said Norman in a statement provided to Fox News. "In Afghanistan, he failed to do so, leaving American citizens exposed in a city under the control of the Taliban. Secretary Blinken is also responsible for the safety of American citizens abroad and, in the case of danger, the safe and efficient evacuation of those Americans, which he failed to do." Republican Representative Mike Gallagher of Wisconsin, a former Marine intelligence officer and a House Armed Services Committee member, stated, "My working hypothesis was that most of the dysfunction we saw was the result of State Department leadership — or lack thereof — rather than the Pentagon. But I do not think that means the Pentagon gets a pass on investigation from Congress." Kelley Currie, who served as ambassador-at-large for global women's issues during the Trump administration and has been involved in evacuating at-risk Afghans, made the following statement regarding Secretary of State Antony Blinken, "He's not doing well; he's in over his head, should never have been in this job and should probably resign and take everyone involved in this debacle with him."

As if Secretary Blinken weren't embroiled in enough foreign debacles, he now stands accused of meddling in Albanian elections on behalf of billionaire financier George Soros and is being sued for defamation in an international court. One of Blinken's curious first actions on taking office was to sanction the former president and prime minister of Albania, Sali Berisha, the anti-Communist ally of Presidents George H.W. and George W. Bush. Sali Berisha has been a vocal opponent of Soros and his Open Society Foundations, pushing judicial and electoral "reform" in Albania. In an official statement and accompanying tweet in April of 2021, Blinken alleged that Berisha was "corrupt" and had "undermined democracy in Albania" and barred him, his wife, and two children from entering the United States. Berisha strenuously denies the allegations, is outraged that Blinken never provided any proof, claims the United States government is trying to prop up the socialist Albanian government of Soros ally Prime Minister Edi Rama, and has launched a defamation action against Secretary Blinken in a Paris court. In late 2022, the disciplinary tribunal of Paris agreed to hear his case.

Source & Additional Information: (https://www.washingtontimes.com/news/2021/oct/28/sali-berisha-gets-antony-blinken-defamation-lawsui/)

The strengthening relationship between China and Russia is more than rhetoric. Chinese President Xi Jinping and Russian President Vladimir Putin are trying to usher in a "new world order." The two rising powers have changed how they and their allies treat the United States with their increasingly disrespectful attitude towards the United States. For example, Saudi Arabia did not join the Abraham Accords but opted to enter a Chinese-organized deal with Iran. Similarly, India has boosted its "trade with Russia by

300% since the start of the Russian invasion of Ukraine." China and Russia are asking the rest of the world to "bet on them" rather than side with the United States moving forward. After President Joe Biden pulled American troops out of Afghanistan; Russia, China, and Iran saw weakness in President Biden and began to test him strenuously.

Section II: United States Attorney General

The mission of the Department of Justice is to uphold the rule of law, to keep our country safe, and to protect our civil rights. As the Attorney General of the United States, Merrick Garland has criminally failed in his sworn oath to the office to protect the legal and constitutional rights of all American citizens regardless of their political ideology. He has failed to maintain a neutral approach to implementing our laws. He has corrupted the Department of Justice to the point that the Department is now referred to as the Department of Injustice. As the chief law enforcement officer in the Federal government, United States Attorney General Merrick Garland has used his position to politicize and weaponize our federal law enforcement agencies against the people he has sworn to protect. Merrick Garland has corrupted the DOJ and the FBI to the point that the citizens of this country no longer have faith or confidence in this department and agency. He has willingly chosen to break his oath to be nonpartisan by covering up the criminal acts of the Biden family. Merrick Garland took an oath to perform his duties in the strictest manner of nonpartisanship when making legal decisions or taking legal actions. Again, in his role as the Attorney General, he has allowed the Department of Justice and the Bureau of Investigation, which he provides leadership and oversight, to evolve into a purely partisan law enforcement entity supporting the Marxist-Communist agenda of the Democrat Party.

When it comes to the day-to-day administration of the laws of the United States, Merrick Garland's misuse of the DOJ's powers for partisan, political purposes is improper. It seriously undermines this country's longstanding commitment to the rule of law. Attorney General Garland has damaged public confidence in the fairness of the DOJ's evenhanded enforcement of the law. The Department's responsibility to uphold the rule of law is appropriately proclaimed in these words inscribed on the Robert F. Kennedy Justice Department Building in Washington, D.C.: "No Free Government Can Survive That Is Not Based on The Supremacy of Law. Where Law Ends, Tyranny Begins. Law Alone Can Give Us Freedom."

Source & Additional Information: (https://journals.law.harvard.edu/lpr/wp-content/uploads/sites/89/2013/05/2.2_3_Robinson.pdf)

Inspector General Michael Horowitz's report in December of 2019 told a complex story about extraordinary events related to the investigation of officials in Donald Trump's 2016 presidential campaign. The report shows that serious reforms are vitally needed in how the FBI and the Department of Justice open and conduct investigations—especially those related to politicians and political campaigns.

Sources & Additional Information: (https://www.theatlantic.com/ideas/archive/2019/12/fisa-process-broken/603688/)

While Attorney General Garland drags former President Donald Trump through the courts via the "lawfare" charges manufactured against him, Garland conveniently ignores former President Obama's history in Chicago, Hillary Clinton's history with hard drives, and Biden's history in Ukraine and China.

Attorney General Merrick Garland has consistently failed to maintain a nonpartisan neutrality within the DOJ. Garland has blatantly ignored the Constitution of our Republic and the legislative laws of our Nation. Garland has reduced our Justice system to nothing more than a third-world, corrupt legal defense arm of a corrupt and evil Marxist-Communist bureaucracy. He allowed the Biden-Harris Administration to utilize this once revered Department to attack any opponent of Joe Biden and members of his family and Administration. In early March of 2023, Attorney General Merrick Garland testified in front of the Senate Judiciary Committee at a hearing titled "Oversight of the United States Department of Justice." In Garland's written testimony submitted to the Committee under the header "Uphold the Rule of Law," Garland writes, "The integrity of our legal system is premised on adherence to the rule of law, in order to have confidence in our department and in our democracy, the American people must be able to trust that we will adhere to the rule of law in everything that we do." Garland continues, "The Justice Department strongly values a free press, and we are committed to protecting the First Amendment and the journalists who rely on it to keep the American people apprised of the workings of their government." Garland's testimony may have articulated what the Department once represented, but he lied under oath about what he has morphed the Department into: the Department of Injustice. He has denied citizens their First Amendment rights when those rights to free speech did not meet the Marxist-Communist's agenda or citizens refused to accept the dictates and narratives of the Marxist-Communist Democrat Party.

Consider, if you will, the legal actions taken against President Trump, his associates, and MAGA patriots over the term of his Presidency. Legal actions demonstrate that the United States of America has been transformed into a third-world, corrupt, two-tier justice system. One for the anti-American Marxist-Communist elitists, politicians, and wealth, and a second for patriotic Republicans, conservatives, and MAGA patriots. This two-tier justice system rose its ugly head when Donald Trump announced that he was running for the 2024 presidency. Comparisons are abundant and include such actions as:

> ➢ Former President Trump's indictment for allegedly unlawfully moving classified documents from the White House to his home, for which he potentially faced imprisonment. The DOJ was well aware that as President

Trump, he had the legal authority to declassify those documents and was authorized under the Presidential Records Act to keep and maintain any documents he had declassified with him following the end of his presidency.

Source & Additional Information: (https://www.cbsnews.com/news/donald-trump-indictment-explained-summary-federal-charges-documents/)

On the other hand, while he was a senator and vice president, Biden illegally smuggled classified documents out of the White House, which he maintained in numerous unsecured locations. Joe Biden had no legal authority to either declassify or remove those documents from the White House. Joe Biden has yet to face any accountability by the corrupt Marxist-Communist DOJ.

Source & Additional Information: (https://time.com/6692166/biden-classified-documents-justice-department-investigation-findings-charges/)

One oppressive legal system of justice for Republican Donald Trump and another corrupt favorable legal system of justice for Marxist-Communist Democrat Joe Biden.

> ➢ Former President Donald Trump's impeachment for delaying foreign aid to Ukraine until the Ukrainian government could guarantee that the Biden cartel was no longer engaged in corrupt influence peddling in Ukraine.
>
> Yet Joe "The Big Guy," Biden, bragged while being televised that he had gotten fired a Ukrainian prosecutor who was investigating both his son's and his son's employer, Ukraine Energy Company, Burisma's, corrupt schemes. Biden threatened to cancel forthcoming American foreign aid if that prosecutor was not immediately fired. The prosecutor was fired that day. To this day, he has yet to be held accountable.

Source & Additional Information: (https://www.bbc.com/news/world-us-canada-50323605) (https://www.politifact.com/article/2019/dec/09/ask-politifact-does-video-show-joe-biden-confessin/)

One oppressive legal system of justice for Republican Donald Trump and another corrupt favorable legal system of justice for Marxist-Communist Democrat Joe Biden.

- Former President Donald Trump's indictment for supposedly conspiratorially "unlawfully discounting legitimate votes" and failing to acknowledge his presidential loss in the 2020 election.

So, will we see Hillary Clinton, who to this day declares that she won the 2016 presidential election, and Stacey Abrams, who continues to falsely claim that she is the real governor of Georgia and toured the country in hopes of "discounting" the state vote count? Will Jack Smith indict Hillary Clinton and Stacey Abrams for conspiratorially "unlawfully discounting legitimate votes?" Highly unlikely!

Source & Additional Information: (https://www.pbs.org/newshour/politics/read-full-the-indictment-against-trump-for-his-efforts-to-overturn-the-2020-election)

One oppressive legal system of justice for Republican Donald Trump and another corrupt favorable legal system of justice for Marxist-Communist Democrats Hillary Clinton and Stacy Abrams.

- Former President Donald Trump's indictment for allegedly attempting to erase video material from his personal home security cameras. He was further indicted for loosely indiscreetly talking about classified material to visitors at his home.

Yet Hillary Clinton, who illegally received and transmitted classified documents over her unsecured private server, destroyed subpoenaed communication devices, and deleted thousands of emails, has yet to be held accountable for this illegal action.

Source & Additional Information: *(https://www.washingtonpost.com/national-security/2023/07/27/trump-carlos-deoliveira-classified-indictment/) (https://www.yahoo.com/news/hillary-clinton-maintains-2016-election-160716779.html) (https://www.pbs.org/newshour/politics/election-lawsuit-backed-by-stacey-abrams-goes-to-trial-in-georgia) (https://www.factcheck.org/2016/07/clintons-handling-of-classified-information/) (https://www.politifact.com/article/2023/jun/16/making-sense-of-bleach-and-hammer-claims-what-real/)*

One oppressive legal system of justice for Republican Donald Trump and another corrupt favorable legal system of justice for Marxist-Communist Democrat Hillary Clinton.

➢ Former President Donald Trump's indictment for allegedly undermining the 2020 election by questioning the integrity of the balloting system.

In 2016, Hillary Clinton's campaign illegally hired two foreign nationals, Christopher Steele and Igor Danchenko, to compile falsehoods about her opponent Trump. Clinton hid her payments behind three paywalls. Her team, along with the FBI, helped leak the counterfeit dossier to the media and high officials to undermine her opponent, Donald Trump, and thus subvert the election itself. Hillary Clinton has yet to be held legally accountable for her actions.

Source & Additional Information: *(https://www.cbsnews.com/news/trump-indictment-full-text-read-2020-election-charges/) (https://www.gmtoday.com/daily_news/commentary/two-sets-of-laws-for-two-americas/article_b919d546-fa5a-55ca-bd66-f818cd72f30c.html)*

One oppressive legal system of justice for Republican Donald Trump and another corrupt favorable legal system of justice for Marxist-Communist Democrat Hillary Clinton.

➢ Two Trump aides and Trump's indictment for supposedly stonewalling federal investigators by claiming either amnesia or ignorance.

That tactic is precisely what James Comey used two hundred and forty-two times while under oath before Congress. Director of National Intelligence James Clapper, former Director of the CIA John Brennan, and former interim FBI Director Andrew McCabe all admitted that they shamelessly lied under oath to Congress or federal investigators. The three were never indicted for their false and perjurious testimonies.

Source & Additional Information: (https://www.realclearpolitics.com/articles/2023/08/04/two_sets_of_laws_for_two_americas_149580.html) (https://duckduckgo.com/?q=James+Comey+claims+aminisia+two+hundred+and+forty-two+times+while+under+oath+before+Congress&atb=v428-1&iax=videos&ia=videos) (https://www.judiciary.senate.gov/imo/media/doc/05-08-17 Clapper Testimony.pdf)

One oppressive legal system of justice for Republican Donald Trump and another corrupt favorable legal system of justice for Marxist-Communist Democrats James Comey, James Clapper, John Brennan, and Andrew McCabe.

➢ On March 31, 2023, the United States Attorney's Office for the Eastern District of New York issued a statement announcing that Douglass Mackey had been convicted by a federal jury in Brooklyn of the charge of Conspiracy Against Rights stemming from his alleged scheme to deprive individuals of their constitutional right to vote. Mackey had been found guilty by a jury of attempting to deprive individuals from exercising their right to vote for the candidate of their choice in the 2016 Presidential Election. What was the crime he committed which was deemed to have deprived individuals of exercising their right to vote? Douglass Mackey posted a meme on Twitter suggesting Hillary Clinton voters should skip the long poll lines and vote online. A manner of voting that did not exist. For this, he faced ten years in prison. Mackey was not the only person who did the same thing during the 2016 elections. As it turns out, a woman named Kristina

Wong posted an almost identical meme during the 2016 elections, but unlike Dough Mackey, Wong voted for Hillary Clinton. Her meme included the statement, 'Hey, Trump Supporters, skip poll lines and text in your vote.' It is the same crime but a different party affiliation; therefore, there is no punishment. The DOJ under Joe Biden has shown no interest in prosecuting Kristina Wong—only the tip of the iceberg of Garland's partisan, corrupt implementation of our nation's laws.

One oppressive legal system of justice for Republican MAGA supporters and another corrupt favorable legal system of justice for Marxist-Communist Democrats.

As offensive as it may seem to most Democrats who hold a Marxist-Communist ideology, moderate Democrats, who are in the majority, need to defend Trump against this lawfare so they can protect themselves in the future. A massive storm is brewing and coming their way. A storm of their own making.

Source & Additional Information: (https://thehill.com/opinion/campaign/4642644-democrats-should-fear-lawfare-tactics-being-turned-against-them/)

Department of Justice Malpractice: During the last week of March 2023, the DOJ announced that they had sent out letters to all state Attorney Generals reminding them that state laws prohibiting children from receiving "gender-affirming care" may infringe on federal constitutional protections under the Equal Protection Clause and Due Process Clause of the Fourteenth Amendment to the United States Constitution. Which Constitution exactly is Merrick Garland referring to? Nowhere in the Fourteenth Amendment is there authority for "gender-affirming care" to *minor* children without parental consent. The Fourteenth Amendment referred to in Garland's letter to state Attorney Generals reads as follows, "No State shall make or enforce any law which shall abridge the privileges or immunities of citizens of the United States; nor shall any State deprive any person of life, liberty, or property, without due process of law;

nor deny to any person within its jurisdiction the equal protection of the law." What constitutional privilege or immunity are these young children being deprived of? How is it that these young children are being deprived of life, liberty, or property? How are these young children being denied equal protection of the law when there are no laws granting minor children the legal right to receive gender-affirming care? Puzzling, at best, as to how Attorney General Garland managed to read into this Amendment a *minor's* right to "gender-affirming care," especially when that care involves the mutilation of a child's body, which in reality is child abuse and, as such, a criminal act calling for imprisonment. Total disregard for the true intent of this Amendment to push a Marxist-Communist agenda.

Source & Additional Information: (https://www.justice.gov/opa/pr/justice-department-reinforces-federal-nondiscrimination-obligations-letter-state-officials)

Since his tenure as the Attorney General of the United States, Merrick Garland stood by doing nothing while American citizens lingered in inhumane prison conditions, having allegedly participated in an insurrection against the federal government in January of 2021. Yet, to this day, not a single person has been charged with insurrection. The January 6th incident is now years behind us. Yet, many of these American citizens still linger in prison. These individuals are nothing more than political prisoners being used as political pons by the Marxist-Communist Democrat Party. Why, in the land of "life, liberty, and justice," were so many American citizens allowed to be subjected to the unconstitutional Stalinist actions of this criminally corrupt Attorney General? All earmarks of political prisoners being held only for propaganda purposes and as a deterrent measure to assure that American citizens never question the actions or behavior of the Marxist-Communist Democrat Party. Can anyone believe this is how our Founding Fathers intended the American justice system to work?

How does a renowned attorney nominated to be a Supreme Court Justice not know that our nation has a Bill of Rights that promises "no person shall be deprived of life, liberty, or property, without due process of law"? This right is articulated in the Fifth Amendment to the United States Constitution, which reads, "No person shall be held to answer for a capital or otherwise infamous crime, unless on a presentment or indictment of a Grand Jury, except in cases arising in the land or naval forces, or in the Militia, when in actual service in time of War or public danger; nor shall any person be subject for the same offense to be twice put in jeopardy of life or limb; nor shall be compelled in any criminal case to be a witness against himself, nor be deprived of life, liberty, or property, without due process of law; nor shall private property be taken for public use, without just compensation." Could it be possible that a former nominee to our country's highest court of justice, which was created to assure this country's adherence to the Constitution, knowingly and willingly ignored the Constitution because it did not fit his partisan political views and did not favor his belief in the Stalinist style approach to governance advocated by the Marxist-Communist Democrat Party, their unconstitutional dictates, or were his actions against conservatives in retaliation for the Republican Congress' failure to appoint him as a Supreme Court Justice?

Attorney General Merrick Garland has further ignored the Sixth Amendment, which states that "In all criminal prosecutions, the accused shall enjoy the right to a speedy and public trial, by an impartial jury of the State and district wherein the crime shall have been committed, which district shall have been previously ascertained by law, and to be informed of the nature and cause of the accusation; to be confronted with the witnesses against him; to have compulsory process for obtaining witnesses in his favor, and to have the Assistance of Counsel for his defense." Is it possible that this Amendment to the Constitution of the United States is not known to Attorney General Merrick Garland, a would-be Supreme Court Justice? But then again, the United

States Constitution only applies in a Constitutional Republic form of government and not in a Marxist-Communist country, which he advocates through his actions. These political detainees were not allowed to be confronted with the witnesses against them, to have a compulsory process for obtaining witnesses in their favor, nor were they allowed to know what charges they faced or allowed to post bail.

Hunter Biden: Where was our Department of Justice when it came to bringing legal justice to individuals closely associated with the top leader of the United States when they broke laws that others are strictly required to adhere to? The FBI, which answers directly to the United States Attorney General, had in its position a laptop belonging to Hunter Biden since at least 2018. That laptop contained enormous evidence of illegal treasonous acts on the part of Hunter Biden, his father, Joe Biden, and other members of the Biden family. There is enough evidence to put most of the Biden cartel behind bars for life.

Hunter Biden was supposedly under federal investigation for tax fraud and potentially treasonous foreign business endeavors by a federal grand jury in Delaware since 2018. Years of investigation have been carried out without any action being taken. Are those investigating the illegal actions documented on Hunter's laptop so incompetent that they cannot bring this case to a jury in a timely manner, or are they knowingly and willingly slow walking their investigation to run out the clock on the statute of Limitations on the crimes identified on his laptop?

With such abundant evidence already in their hands, how much more evidence do they need to proceed to a jury unless those investigating the laptop information are politically influenced?

Hunter's membership on the Board of Directors of a Ukrainian energy company and his involvement in financial activities with the Chinese government have long raised questions by Republican members of Congress questioning whether Hunter was trading on his father's political position, and that was before the evidence on Hunter's laptop was even known to the members of Congress. We know that Hunter has no expertise within the energy industry; we have recorded evidence that Hunter, along with his father, Joe Biden, extorted a Chinese businessman, Henry Zhao, for ten million dollars in payment for obtaining the firing of the lead prosecutor investigating the company on whose Board of Directors Hunter sat, for crimes of corruption. Evidence now clearly shows that Hunter, Joe, and the top officials within the Ukrainian government had an agreement regarding influence peddling by the Biden cartel. Evidence collected by congressional committees has further proven that the Biden cartel received millions of dollars from China, Ukraine, Romania, and Russia for no known legitimate business activity. The evidence clearly shows that Joe Biden, his son Hunter, and numerous members of the Biden cartel became extraordinarily wealthy from trading on Joe Biden's coattails while he was the vice president and then President of the United States.

Source & Additional Information: (https://www.mediaite.com/biden/whistleblowers-reveal-alleged-text-of-hunter-biden-demanding-cash-from-chinese-business-partner-warned-of-consequences-from-my-father/) (https://www.washingtonexaminer.com/news/1552174/hunter-biden-invoking-my-father-resulted-in-millions-flowing-from-ccp-linked-company/)

An Internal Revenue Service whistleblower contacted Republican Senator Grassley regarding information he had regarding Hunter's and Joe Biden's financial interaction with foreign entities. Mark Lytle, the attorney for the Internal Revenue Service whistleblower, wrote to lawmakers in early April of 2023 that his client had information about a "failure to mitigate clear conflicts of interest in the ultimate disposition" of a criminal investigation related to Hunter Biden's alleged tax fraud, lobbying crimes, money laundering, and whether he made a false statement in connection with a gun purchase. On or about May 10th, 2023, the Internal Revenue Service removed that whistleblower and his team from a criminal investigation into Hunter Biden's taxes and business dealings at the request of the Department of Justice, according to the whistleblower's attorneys. The whistleblower's two lawyers stated that the Internal Revenue Service's move contradicts what Internal Revenue Service Commissioner Daniel Werfel testified in Congress on April 27, 2023, that "there will be no retaliation for anyone making an allegation or a call to a whistleblower hotline." Under federal law, the Internal Revenue Service whistleblower "is protected from retaliatory personnel actions, including receiving a 'significant change in duties, responsibilities, or working conditions,' because of his disclosures to Congress." Of course, we are all aware that General Attorney Merrick Garland, like his handlers Joe Biden and Barack Obama, is above the law and not to the fair and equitable application of law in a non-partisan manner.

The Internal Revenue Service employee who courageously stepped forward to bring to light the criminal wrongdoing of Hunter Biden was Internal Revenue Service supervisor Gary Shapley, a fourteen-year veteran of the Internal Revenue Service. Shapley gave his testimony before the House Ways and Means Committee on May 26th, 2023. On June 1st, 2023, a second Internal Revenue Service agent, Joseph Ziegler, a thirteen-year Democrat veteran of the Internal Revenue Service, also came forward and testified under oath regarding Hunter Biden. Joseph Ziegler was the tax agency's lead case agent in the federal investigation into Hunter Biden, which spanned both the Trump and Biden-Harris administrations. On July 19th, 2023, the Republican-chaired House Oversight Committee summoned the two Internal Revenue Service whistleblowers to testify publicly for the first time about their claims that the Justice Department limited a tax investigation into Hunter Biden and about their allegations that they were not free to pursue leads that may have implicated President Biden. Ziegler testified that he had recommended prosecutors charge Hunter Biden with multiple felonies and misdemeanors in 2021. Among the allegations, Ziegler testified that he believed he had sufficient evidence that showed the president's son had improperly claimed business deductions for several personal expenses, including his children's college tuition, hotel bills, and payments to escorts.

Source & Additional Information: (https://nypost.com/2023/07/20/irs-whistleblower-unanimous-agreement-to-charge-hunter-biden-with-felonies/) (https://gop-waysandmeans.house.gov/wp-content/uploads/2023/12/Ziegler_FINAL-Full-Statement-to-House-Ways-and-Means-v12.01.2023.pdf)

Little known to most is that in April of 2023, a White House whistleblower came forward regarding corruption within the White House on FOX News. A former Obama administration staffer blew the whistle on the Biden family's business dealings, accusing President Biden of being involved in a "kickback scheme" in connection with his son Hunter's overseas business dealings while he was vice president. Mike McCormick, a stenographer for the White House for fifteen years, told "Fox & Friends First" the FBI ignored his alarms on the matter despite his willingness to testify under oath before the federal grand jury investigating Hunter. "In February, I went to the FBI and filed one of their tips on their website. If you do that, and you are lying to them, you go to jail. I am not lying. I am telling the truth, and I am not going to jail," McCormick stated. " Joe Biden is a criminal. He was conducting malfeasance in office to enrich his family. Jake Sullivan is a conspirator in that, and there is more. Obama officials were involved in it, I believe."

Source & Additional Information: (https://www.foxnews.com/media/ex-obama-staffer-blows-whistle-biden-kickback-scheme-hunter-joined-burisma-malfeasance-office)

McCormick, who worked with Biden from 2011 to 2017, detailed a key dialogue involving the vice president, aide Jake Sullivan, and the press on Air Force Two before a trip to Kyiv, Ukraine, on April 21, 2014. Sullivan, who was Joe Biden's national security adviser, outlined in a White House transcript Biden's priority for his trip to the country, which included United States investment in Ukraine's energy sector days after Hunter joined the board of Burisma, according to the New York Post. Months later, and well after the trip, Congress allocated $50 million to Ukraine‹s energy market. «I›m sitting back there with a tape recorder. Jake Sullivan comes back, and somebody asks about fracking. His answer is, well, we are bringing a lot of American assistance over for fracking. Burisma was the direct beneficiary of that fracking, and that is what I recorded, and that is in a White House transcript," McCormick said. "In the transcript, you don't know who Jake Sullivan is. He is a senior administrative official. I am the witness that says Jake Sullivan is the guy who said it, and he should be investigated because at the time, Hunter Biden was on the board of Burisma, and Joe Biden was bringing American taxpayer money to enrich that company and himself and his family," he continued.

Hunter joined the Ukrainian natural gas firm board on April 18th, 2014, just three days before Biden and his team traveled to Kyiv. However, that critical piece of the puzzle was not made public until May 12th, 2014. McCormick argued the timeline of the events suggests that Biden funneled American money overseas to "enrich" himself and his family and used his influence to aid his son's newcomer energy career. The former stenographer made it clear he wants to present the information under oath before the grand jury in Delaware probing Hunter's business dealings, led by United States Attorney David Weiss.

Hunter has been under federal investigation since 2018 for suspected tax and foreign lobbying violations. The probe into Hunter›s alleged violations began after suspicious activity reports (SARs) regarding suspicious foreign transactions were flagged. Those SARs involved money funneled from «China and other foreign nations,» according to sources familiar with the probe. And although reports suggested in months past that the investigation is approaching a critical juncture, Republican subpoena power accelerated the investigation. "If David Weiss can't have me in front of his grand jury explaining what I know as a witness, that's a fraudulent grand jury," McCormick said. "It's a fraudulent use of the American judicial system to cover for

Barack Obama and Joe Biden's repeatedly claiming he has not spoken to his son regarding his overseas business dealings."

McCormick argued the information he has incriminates Biden and likely more officials he worked with in connection with the alleged influence-peddling scandal. "If I went in there, I would tell them to have Barack Obama called in as a witness because he's part of the conspiracy. He is an ex-president. He has to answer who was in charge of this, putting Joe Biden into this role. Did Barack Obama know about it?" McCormick questioned. I have seen and put evidence in my Substack on April 16th, 2014, so two days before Hunter joins, Joe Biden is with Hunter in the West Wing. They have a meeting, and then later that day in the evening, Joe Biden spends a day in the limousine in the back of Barack Obama's limousine in western Pennsylvania," he continued.

Source & Additional Information: (https://www.foxnews.com/media/ex-obama-staffer-blows-whistle-biden-kickback-scheme-hunter-joined-burisma-malfeasance-office)

In an attempt to circumvent facing the more serious charges unearthed by the two whistleblowers, Hunter Biden's legal team negotiated a plea agreement with the corrupt Department of Justice prosecutors, allowing Hunter to plead guilty to two misdemeanor tax evasion charges and defer punishment for lying on a gun license application. The plea agreement was written so that, if accepted by the court, no future charges on any illegal issues would be filed against Hunter. A plea agreement that legal scholars indicate was unprecedented given the seriousness of the charges levied against Hunter Biden. On July 26th, 2023, Hunter Biden's deal with Department of Justice prosecutors to plead guilty to two misdemeanor tax evasion charges and defer punishment for lying on a gun license application collapsed dramatically in a Delaware federal courtroom. The presiding judge, Maryellen Noreika, questioned the assembled lawyers about details of the agreement, revealing that the federal team led by corrupt prosecutor David Weiss, the United States

District Attorney in Delaware who was in charge of the Biden investigation, and Hunter Biden's lawyers, had very different views on what that plea contained. Eventually, Hunter Biden's legal team agreed to the prosecution's view, but that was just the first stumbling block. The judge then questioned the gun deal, in which no charges would be filed if Hunter Biden stayed out of legal trouble and did not attempt to purchase firearms for two years. The agreement made Judge Noreika, rather than the justice department, the arbiter of whether Hunter Biden was keeping his end of the agreement, a provision she found to be of questionable legality.

Source & Additional Information: (https://apnews.com/article/hunter-biden-guilty-plea-5c7f7a00e2dae4311706ac9ab2699070) (https://www.bbc.com/news/world-us-canada-66332875) (https://www.nytimes.com/live/2023/07/26/us/hunter-biden-plea-tax-charges)

As if the level of corruption shown by the Department of Justice's attempt to downgrade charges against Hunter was not bad enough, it got even worse. Just before Hunter's trial date, a member of Hunter Biden's legal team falsely identifying herself as an associate of Theodore Kittila, senior legal counsel to Republican Representative Jason Smith, Chair of the House Ways and Means Committee, called court clerk Sam Grimes. The caller requested that information provided to the court regarding the congressional testimony of the two Internal Revenue Service whistleblowers needed to be removed from the court docket due to sensitive information contained in those documents. According to the Court Clerk, the caller represented herself as an associate of Theodore Kittila and asked to have the information kept under seal. In a July 25th, 2023, letter, Kittila informed Delaware Judge Maryellen Noreika of the misrepresentation, and that the clerk's office had "advised that someone contacted the court representing that they worked with my office and that they were asking the court to remove this from the docket." Theodore Kittila told the judge that shortly after this call, the filing made by his legal team was unexpectedly removed from the court's docket. When contacted, the clerk, Sam Grimes, revealed that an individual, purportedly representing Theodore Kittila's office, had requested the removal. "The woman who called was a Jessica Bengels," according to the court clerk. "She said she worked with Theodore Kittila, and it was important the document was removed immediately," Grimes stated.

Judge Noreika noted that "the caller misrepresented her identity and who she worked for in an attempt to improperly convince the clerk's office to remove the amicus materials from the docket." The deceitful tactic was an attempt to remove the Internal Revenue Service whistleblower testimony about the Department of Justice's inadequate criminal investigation into Hunter Biden's tax-related offenses from the court's official records. All actions one finds in a third-world dictatorship and would never expect in the United States.

Source & Additional Information: (https://nypost.com/2023/07/25/hunter-biden-lawyer-accused-of-deception-to-seal-damning-evidence/)

Whistleblowers Gary Shapley and Joseph Ziegler have both claimed the federal tax investigation into President Biden's son supported more serious charges. According to both whistleblowers, Internal Revenue Service officials recommended that Hunter Biden be criminally charged with attempting to evade taxes, committing fraud, making false statements, willfully failing to file returns, and failing to provide information on over $8.3 million in income. The two whistleblowers describe how the DOJ intervened in a campaign to protect the son of Joe Biden by delaying and denying an ongoing investigation into Hunter Biden's alleged tax crimes.

Source & Additional Information: (https://www.nbcnews.com/politics/congress/irs-whistleblowers-testify-house-oversight-committee-hunter-biden-prob-rcna95078)

The DOJ delayed the authentication of messages between Hunter Biden and a Chinese business partner, Internal Revenue Service supervisor Shapley testified to the House Ways and

Means Committee. Shapley also testified that at a September 2020 meeting, Assistant United States Attorney for Delaware Lesley Wolf said there was "more than enough probable cause for a physical search warrant." The Internal Revenue Service whistleblower further testified that the prosecutor in the case was very hesitant about authorizing a search warrant, stating that "optics were a driving factor in the decision on whether to execute a search warrant." The Internal Revenue Service whistleblowers further advised that investigators had ample reason to look into a Northern Virginia storage unit where Hunter Biden maintained his files. According to the Internal Revenue Service whistleblower, before the search warrant could be executed, Hunter Biden's lawyers were informed of the impending search of Hunter's storage unit, which provided Hunter ample time to remove any legally damaging records.

United States Attorney for Delaware, David Weiss, who was in charge of the Hunter Biden case, falsely advised the two Internal Revenue Service whistleblowers that he wanted to bring charges against Hunter Biden in the District of Columbia in March of 2022 but was denied permission, according to whistleblower testimony before the House Ways and Means Committee. The two whistleblowers also testified that Weiss had falsely informed them that he had sought special counsel status from the Justice Department in the spring of 2022 to conduct an independent inquiry. However, he advised them that his superiors at the DOJ also denied that request. Then, in the fall of 2022, Weiss falsely stated that he had recommended that charges be brought against Hunter Biden in the Central District of California. According to Weiss, the DOJ also denied that request in January 2023. None of Weiss' claims turned out to be true. According to the transcript of the testimony from whistleblower Joseph Ziegler, the DOJ used Biden's presidential campaign as a reason to move cautiously on the investigation of Hunter Biden, which began in 2018.

Source & Additional Information: (https://www.rev.com/blog/transcripts/irs-whistleblowers-testify-at-house-hearing-on-hunter-biden-investigation-transcript)

Following five years of investigation, the damning evidence provided by the whistleblowers, and Hunter Biden's laptop, the DOJ's response was to reach a plea agreement with Hunter Biden. Under the deal, the president's son pleaded guilty to two misdemeanor counts of willful failure to pay income taxes, and the DOJ recommended an unbelievable sentence of probation. He was also permitted to enter a pretrial diversion program for a serious gun charge, which will be dismissed if he successfully completes the program.

This plea agreement was not for simple misconduct on Hunter's part; these pleas were for failing to pay his federal income taxes for two years, during which he received over $1.5 million and owed over $100,000 in taxes. The average American citizen facing the exact charges would have been prosecuted and sentenced to a five-year prison sentence. There is no accountability whatsoever because Hunter's last name is Biden, and his father is the President of the United States. David Weiss, the State of Delaware District attorney who negotiated this injustice plea deal, was a Merrick Garland and Joe Biden "yes" man. Following the collapse of Weiss' plea agreement with Hunter Biden's legal team, then DOJ Secretary Garland decided that a special counsel was needed to investigate this case.

Unbelievably, Garland appointed Weiss, who worked under the supervision of the DOJ, and according to DOJ regulations, a Special Counsel <u>shall</u> be appointed from outside of the DOJ. Weiss' appointment was made for two purposes: first, to eliminate the House Committees' ability to subpoena Weiss regarding his investigation into the allegations against Hunter Biden, which should have been accomplished within five months, but Weiss had spent five years investigating the allegations. Second, to allow Weiss to continue dragging his feet until the statute of limitations had run out on all charges. Weiss' appointment as Special Counsel brought no justice and accountability for Hunter's crimes.

We have allegations confirmed by Hunter's former business partner, Tony Bobulinski, of Hunter's treasonous business dealings in Ukraine and China, as well as allegations of a $10 million pay-to-play bribery scheme involving both Hunter and Joe Biden, who was the vice president at the time of the alleged criminal activity. Were any of those allegations thoroughly investigated? According to House Ways and Means Committee transcripts released on June 15th, 2023, the answer is NO. Internal Revenue Service Supervisory Special Agent Gary Shapley testified under oath that, as an investigator for the Internal Revenue Service, he obtained messages Hunter Biden sent on the WhatsApp platform, including one in 2017 that he read demanding payment from a Chinese businessman named Henry Zhao. In the message, Hunter Biden wrote: "I am sitting here with my father, and we would like to understand why the commitment made has not been fulfilled. Tell the director that I would like to resolve this now before it gets out of hand, and now means tonight. And, Z, if I get a call or text from anyone involved in this other than you, Zhang, or the chairman, I will make certain that between the man sitting next to me and every person he knows and my ability to forever hold a grudge, that you will regret not following my direction. I am sitting here waiting for the call with my father."

Shapley was asked about Garland's sworn Senate testimony on March 1st, 2023. At that time, Garland stated: "I promise to leave the matter of Hunter Biden in the hands of the United States Attorney for the District of Delaware. I have pledged not to interfere with that investigation, and I have carried through on my pledge." The House Ways and Means Committee asked Shapley if Garland's statement, under oath, was true. His answer was, "It's not accurate." Garland testified during that same hearing about Weiss's ability to bring cases in other federal districts. Weiss "has full authority to make those kinds of referrals that you are talking about or bring cases in other jurisdictions if he feels that it's necessary," Garland responded. "And I will assure that if he does, he will be able to do that." Shapley testified that Garland's statement was not true. According to the testimonies of whistleblowers Shapley and Ziegler, search warrants included a search warrant of Joe Biden's guest house where Hunter was living, and the DOJ constantly blocked other investigative requests.

Source & Additional Information: https://www.nbcnews.com/politics/congress/irs-whistleblowers-testify-house-oversight-committee-hunter-biden-prob-rcna95078

Both whistleblowers stated that charges against Hunter Biden were downgraded, and critical related information was leaked to Hunter Biden's legal team, suppressing investigators' ability to obtain evidence. The whistleblowers also asserted that investigating agents were prohibited from asking any questions of witnesses about the president or probing into potential campaign finance violations or financial transactions involving Hunter's children. Whistleblower Ziegler stated that investigators recommended charging Hunter Biden with felony tax charges covering six years and over $8.3 million in income, not just the two years covered by the misdemeanor charges that Hunter pleaded guilty to. However, according to the whistleblower, that recommendation was blocked by Joe Biden's political appointees. Shapley alleged that Hunter Biden engaged in this conduct to hide payments he received from Burisma Holdings. Despite Hunter's total lack of expertise in the energy field, this Ukrainian energy company hired him as a consultant and placed him on its board of directors.

The laptop from hell contains insurmountable evidence against the Biden cartel, which Garland refuses to investigate for any potential criminal activity. Delaware computer repair shop owner John Paul Mac Isaac obtained the infamous laptop in April of 2019 when Hunter Biden dropped off the laptop for repair. Mac Isaac stated that while he was copying individual files and folders from the laptop's hard drive to another device, he "saw some content that was disturbing and also raised some red flags," including "criminality related to foreign business dealings, to potential money laundering, and more importantly, national security issues and concerns." Mac Isaac, unfortunately, brought the laptop to the attention of the corrupt and weaponized FBI, who took possession of that laptop in December of 2019 under the authority of a subpoena issued by a Wilmington grand jury. This treasonous national security news story was published by the New York Times but was ignored by all the other major Marxist-Communist news outlets and social media. Ignored as a result of senior leadership in both the FBI and the DOJ advising these news outlets that the laptop was Russian misinformation and directed them not to republish the New York Times story.

Since its seizure in December of 2019 by the highly discreditable and untrustworthy FBI, which reports directly to Attorney General Merrick Garland, both the politically weaponized DOJ and the corrupt weaponized FBI suppressed the existence of the laptop throughout the 2020 Presidential elections. Polls indicate that if the information found on Hunter Biden's laptop had been released to the general public, it is doubtful that Joe Biden would now be sitting in the White House destroying our constitutional republic. Biden's and Obama's personal legal team, the DOJ, and their personal legal representative, Attorney General Merrick Garland, have never instigated any investigation on the data contained on Hunter Biden's laptop. Instead, they have chosen to continue the suppression of the information contained on that laptop. This refusal by the Attorney General to act and investigate this issue was partisan and nothing short of corruption at the highest level and a clear warning that our legal rights under the Constitution are at serious risk of being eliminated, if not already lost.

Congressional lawmakers continue to look into Hunter Biden's business dealings to determine if any abuses of power and evidence of tax evasion by Joe Biden exists. While these processes can take time, the House Committee on Oversight and Accountability Chairman, Republican Representative James

Comer from Kentucky, subpoenaed Joe Biden-related bank records. These bank records have revealed over $10 million in payments to various Biden family cartel members, including grandchildren, from a businessman connected to a Chinese Communist Party-controlled energy company. On March 16th, 2023, Comer published a press release announcing that Rob Walker, a business associate of the Biden family, sent $1.3 million to Hunter Biden, Hallie Biden, James Biden, and another account labeled "Biden" between 2015 and 2017. The movement of funds began two years before Biden finished his term as Vice President under Barack Obama. China-based State Energy HK Limited sent $3 million to a Walker-owned company. Then, the Walker-owned business sent $1,065,000 to another company connected to James Gilliar, who in turn sent Biden cartel members a similar amount of money over the following three months through various deposits.

<u>Source & Additional Information</u>: *(https://oversight.house.gov/release/oversight-judiciary-and-ways-and-means-committees-release-report-on-impeachment-inquiry-finding-joe-biden-has-committed-impeachable-conduct/)*

Three former executives of the social media Twitter were called before the House Oversight Committee to testify regarding their handling of the information on that laptop. They testified that they had made a mistake in their handling of the New York Post story on Hunter Biden's laptop. The action by the social media platform just weeks before the 2020 election unleashed a wave of backlash from Republicans, who accused Twitter executives of suppressing the story to shield President Joe Biden and his criminal family from what they say was damaging material found on a laptop hard drive belonging to the president›s son. During a House Oversight and Accountability Committee hearing, Republicans grilled the three executives about Twitter's decision to block users from sharing the story on Hunter Biden and suggested the social media giant acted under orders from the government when it suppressed the story. America witnessed a coordinated campaign by social media companies, mainstream Marxist-Communist news outlets, and the intelligence communities to suppress the existence of Hunter Biden's laptop and its contents. The former Twitter employees called the platform's decision regarding the story a "mistake" but denied that they had acted in concert with government officials. Emails and Twitter conversations were later found, and they indicated ongoing conversations between senior Twitter managers and the FBI debunking their denial. Their false testimony to the Oversight Committee under oath is a felony, but will they be held accountable by our DOJ? Highly unlikely!

The federal government, under the direction of the Marxist-Communist Democrat National Committee and Joe Biden's campaign, had indeed pressured social media and news outlets to suppress the story much in the same manner commonly found in Marxist-Communist countries around the world. The House Judiciary Committee, led by Representative Jim Jordan, continues to hold hearings regarding Hunter Biden and his laptop from hell. So far, Jordan and fellow Ohio Republican Representative Mike Turner, the House Intelligence Committee chairman, have requested documents from former senior intelligence officials who wrote an open letter weeks before the 2020 election falsely stating that the information discovered on Hunter Biden's laptop bore the "classic earmarks of a Russian disinformation campaign." The data and emails attributed to the laptop have since been authenticated by CBS News, the Washington Post, and the New York Times.

The information found on Hunter Biden's laptop is also under investigation by the House Oversight Committee, chaired by Republican Representative James Comer. Comer stated that his committee is investigating an email from 2017 found on a laptop belonging to Hunter Biden. The email discusses setting aside a certain percentage of a deal for "the big guy." Comer asserts that the email text shows Joe Biden was aware of Hunter Biden's business dealings with a Chinese Communist Party-owned company. Comer also asserts that those business ties influence President Biden's policy choices toward China. While Biden campaigned for President in Iowa in September 2019 and numerous times since his initial denial of any knowledge of Hunter's overseas business dealings, he continued to assert that he had never spoken to Hunter about Hunter's overseas business dealings. A 2020 Senate investigation led by Republicans found that Hunter Biden, his business partners, and their firms made millions of dollars doing business in Ukraine while Joe Biden was Vice President, and those financial connections have "negatively impacted" diplomatic activity within the United States.

Hunter Biden's laptop includes a May 2017 email from one of his business partners laying out how percentages of equity from a proposed venture with a Chinese energy company could be divided. One line of that email asks, "10 held by H for the big guy?" Hunter Biden's former business partner Tony Bobulinski told Fox News that he believed "H" stood for Hunter and the big guy was Joe Biden. In true Marxist-Communist style, Hunter Biden's legal strategy in response to the laptop's contents is to attack the individual who disclosed the information contained on his laptop. His defense lawyer sent letters to the prosecutors requesting they investigate those involved in copying and sharing the laptop's contents. On February 1st, 2023, Hunter Biden's defense lawyer asked the attorney general of Delaware to investigate Mac Isaac for "unlawfully" accessing Hunter Biden's personal data and distributing that data to "the political enemies" of Joe Biden. Utilizing Stalinist tactics, the attorney general of Delaware was attempting to destroy those who discovered potential criminal actions and appropriately reported that information to law enforcement, then entangling them in endless court hearings and costly legal fees. This is in spite of the fact that an abundance of evidence clearly indicates that members of the Biden family are totally corrupt and have sold out America to the Communist Chinese Party for millions of dollars. These individuals are traitors and must face justice for their actions.

On March 17th, 2023, Hunter Biden filed a countersuit against Mac Issac in the United States District Court in Delaware. The fourth two-page suit accuses Mac Isaac of invading Hunter Biden's privacy and being part of a conspiracy to obtain and distribute data. In the suit, Hunter Biden states that the computer repair shop owner had no legal right to copy data from Biden's laptop and pass it on to others. Well, Hunter Biden willfully and knowingly left his laptop at the repair shop. He was informed that if he failed to retrieve his laptop within ninety days, the shop owner had the legal right to claim the laptop in payment for the repairs made on that laptop. That laptop contained information indicating that the Biden mob family had committed treason against America. Federal laws had been violated, and the shop owner, had a legal and moral obligation to notify law enforcement agencies.

What the laptop has told us about Hunter Biden's business dealings with Ukrainian and Chinese companies creates a clear impression that he was making a lot of money off the prestige of being Joe Biden's son. The fake news outlets conveniently leave out the fact that Hunter was being paid exorbitant amounts of money for serving on large corporation boards, on which he had no expertise or knowledge regarding those corporations' products. The board positions were nothing more than a smoke screen to justify the money Hunter was receiving from a corrupt Ukrainian and Chinese government.

What is also not being reported is that the money Hunter received was shared with his father, Joe Biden. The big lie being pushed by the Marxist-Communist news media is that there is no evidence that Hunter Biden's business transactions have influenced decisions that Joe Biden made as Vice President or as President. Given the level of evidence, it is surprising that these Marxist-Communist news outlets are attempting to push this ridiculous narrative with a straight face. Is it even possible to believe someone would give another person millions of dollars for doing nothing? The White House and their news media propaganda arm proclaim that there is no evidence that money from Hunter Biden's business dealings ever made its way to Joe Biden's accounts. Bank records indicate otherwise.

Source & Additional Information: (https://www.msn.com/en-us/news/politics/just-released-bank-records-show-joe-biden-received-monthly-payments-from-hunter-s-business-entity/ar-AA1kZLBr)

Devon Archer testimony: Devon Archer, Hunter Biden's former business partner, testified on July 31st, 2023, that President Joe Biden attended dinners with the younger Biden's business partners and spoke to them over the phone, according to House Judiciary Committee Representative Chairman Jim Jordan. Jordan, one of two Republican members present for the testimony, told the *Washington Examiner* in a phone interview that the testimony runs contrary to past claims Joe Biden has made about what he knew about his son's business dealings while he was vice president. Democrat Representative Dan Goldman, a former Trump impeachment lawyer, emerged from Archer›s interview and revealed that Archer said Hunter Biden put his father on speakerphone with his business associates and friends about twenty times over ten years but only for ideal chit-chat and to talk about the weather. In the end, Archer confirmed that Biden had been lying to the public when he claimed on multiple occasions that he knew nothing about his son's overseas business. No father gets on the phone with their son's overseas business partners that many times yet knows nothing about the nature of the call and who exactly he is chatting with. This revelation came from Democrat Representative Dan Goldman following the hearing and confirmed Biden's previously denied interactions on national Main Street news media. Just how many Democrat voters in our country are so naive as to continue to believe that Joe Biden was not involved with his son in influence peddling, bribery, and extortion schemes with enemies of the United States? At some point, with all of the revelations pouring out, even the most naive must finally accept the reality of the Biden family's level of corruption.

Pro-Life or Pro-Abortion: During a Senate hearing On March 1st, 2023, Republican Senator Mike Lee from the State of Utah, noted to Attorney General Garland that according to Catholic Vote statistics, there have been eighty-one recorded attacks on Catholic-sponsored pregnancy centers and one hundred and thirty attacks on Catholic churches since the overturning of Roe verses Wade by the Supreme Court. Only <u>two</u> individuals have been apprehended and charged for those violent attacks. During that same period, the DOJ charged <u>thirty-four</u> individuals for peacefully protesting at abortion clinics. General Attorney Garland is intellectually unable to distinguish between the lawful and peaceful protest by anti-abortion groups and the violent, destructive acts committed by pro-abortion activists or is purposely ignoring this minor detail. Just what one would expect from a politicalized and weaponized DOJ under Attorney General Merrick Garland.

<u>Source & Additional Information</u>: *(https://www.christianpost.com/news/pro-life-nonprofit-denounces-attack-against-aid-for-women.html) (https://www.msn.com/en-us/news/us/while-doj-locks-up-pro-lifers-hundreds-of-pro-abortion-violent-incidents-still-remain-unprosecuted/ar-BB1nUUcw)*

In late January of 2023, a jury acquitted Pennsylvania dad Mark Houck, a pro-life activist father of seven, who was accused of pushing a Planned Parenthood escort during an encounter outside an abortion clinic. The Biden-Harris administration alleged that Houck violated the Freedom of Access to Clinic Entrances (FACE) Act, which criminalizes using force to injure, intimidate and interfere with clinic workers. Houck explained how he was defending his son from volunteer Bruce Love. When Houck's son moved behind him, he could tell his boy was "visibly scared," and insults continued to be directed at them. Then, the Catholic dad told Love to return to where he usually stands. For this minor insignificant incident, a SWAT Team of approximately twenty-five individuals shockingly showed up at Houck's house, pounding on the family's door. "They said they were going to break in if he didn't open it," wife Ryan-Marie told Catholic News Agency, "and then they had about five guns pointed at my husband, myself, and basically at my kids."

Source & Additional Information: (https://www.catholicnewsagency.com/news/253523/ acquitted-pro-life-activist-mark-houck-reveals-details-of-fbi-raid-will-press-charges)

The DOJ also filed charges against eleven pro-life protesters who entered peacefully and sat down in a Mount Juliet, Tennessee, abortion clinic in March of 2021. They each face possible sentences of up to 11 years in prison for violating the Freedom of Access to Clinic Entrances Act and conspiracy against rights. Eight other peaceful protesters have been similarly charged and face similar sentences for violating the Freedom of Access to Clinic Entrances Act and conspiracy against rights for blockading a Sterling Heights, Michigan, abortion clinic by sitting and praying in front of the door in August 2020. For example, anyone found guilty of violating the Freedom of Access to Clinic Entrances (FACE) Act would bring a one-year prison term. However, individuals protesting on a public sidewalk in front of an abortion clinic are not only being charged with Freedom of Access to Clinic Entrances violations but are also being charged with Conspiracy to Violate Civil Rights. This charge by the DOJ is being leveled against abortion protesters because they posted information regarding where they were to meet for a protest rally on Facebook. The conspiracy charge adds a potential ten years in federal prison. In a separate incident, the government charged Reverend Fidelis Moscinski, a Catholic priest in Hempstead, New York, for violating the Freedom of Access to Clinic Entrances Act. He used chains to block a clinic entrance. Attorney General Garland's decision to have the FBI execute these early morning raids on the homes of law-abiding citizens has left children terrorized, homes damaged, and families worried about their future. Families' lives have been forever changed as the charged activists face the uncertainty of prison time and legal bills that quickly mount into the six-figure range.

Source & Additional Information: (https://www.detroitnews.com/story/news/local/michigan/2024/08/21/8-convicted-of-federal-civil-rights-offenses-for-blockading-mich-abortion-clinics/74880633007/)

While the DOJ is persecuting pro-life protesters, a memorandum issued by the DOJ was unveiled by Republican Senator Katie Britt of Alabama during a March 28th, 2023, budget hearing, which discouraged United States Marshals from arresting protestors in violation of laws against picketing the homes of judges. The memorandum revealed that United States Marshals were explicitly directed not to arrest protestors at the homes of Supreme Court justices. Section 1507 of the United States Code explicitly prohibits the picketing of Supreme Court justices or other federal judges in an attempt to change the outcome of a legal case through intimidation. But when protestors demonstrated at the homes of conservative justices protesting their leaked abortion decision in June of 2022, United States Marshals made very few arrests in connection to the statute.

Source & Additional Information: (https://www.britt.senate.gov/news/press-releases/senator-katie-britt-reveals-u-s-marshals-were-discouraged-from-arresting-leftwing-protesters-illegally-harassing-scotus-justices-outside-their-homes/)

Unequal treatment under the law seems to be Merrick Garland's mode of operation as the country's top law enforcement official. His actions against American citizens are identical to what citizens of a Stalinist-governed country continuously face. In the same manner as a Stalinist regime, Garland's DOJ has deployed predawn raids with dozens of armed agents and coordinated ambushes against protesters whose only alleged crimes neither damaged property nor harmed people. Yet violent attacks by pro-Marxist-Communist individuals or groups on centers that seek to give pregnant women options other than abortion have failed to attract nearly the same attention from federal law enforcement. This is what justice now looks like in the United States of America.

Supreme Court Leak: Before the official decision by the Supreme Court to overturn Wade versus Roe, a draft of that decision was leaked to Marxist-Communist news outlets by an anonymous individual who worked inside the Supreme Court.

In January of 2023, the Supreme Court announced it was unable to determine the identity of the leaker(s). Investigators determined that eighty-two employees had access to electronic or hard copies of the Supreme Court's draft decision. Despite a small number of employees with access to the draft, investigators could never uncover the leaker(s) who exposed the working draft of the Supreme Court's Dobbs v. Jackson Women's Health Organization abortion opinion overturning Roe v. Wade. Is it not astonishing that several hundreds of protesters out of a crowd in excess of a hundred thousand on January 6th, 2021, protesters could so easily and quickly be identified, tracked down, arrested, and jailed within weeks? Still, one leaker in an office of eighty people cannot be identified. Are those who investigated that leak really that incompetent, or is the leaker being protected, as is the case whenever the bad actor is a Marxist-Communist Democrat?

It is beyond belief that professional investigators were that incompetent investigating that one leak. In contrast, those investigating alleged crimes committed by constitutional conservatives are so extraordinarily capable and timely in bringing their cases to a conclusion. Could it perhaps be because they have already determined, beforehand, the crime and the conservative target to be charged with that predetermined crime? And precisely what has our DOJ done about the radical pro-abortion group "Ruth Sent Us," which posted the justices' addresses online and began urging protesters to assemble and protest at the homes of the "six conservative justices, three in Virginia and three in Maryland," and those who were called upon to join them from the activists groups Our Rights DC, Shut Down DC, Rise Up 4 Abortion Rights, and other leftist groups. Should they not also be charged and sentenced to more than ten years for "conspiracy against rights," because they acted as a group in a criminal act against the conservative Supreme Court Justices?

Terrorist Parents: This is the same General Attorney who, in late 2021, received a request from the National School Board Association to take legal action against the parents of school-aged children. Parents who attend School Board meetings to question and oppose inappropriate actions regarding boys who identified as girls and material being taught to their children. Of particular concern to these parents was the allowing of boys who identified as girls to utilize the girl's bathrooms which eventually led to the rape of two female students. These School Board members felt intimated by these parents because they dared to question and challenge the School Board's decisions regarding school curriculums and activities; they felt the need to bypass local law enforcement and go directly to the DOJ requesting intervention from the FBI. Could that decision be related to the possibility that local law enforcement was not politically motivated and would have immediately determined that no crime had been committed?

Rather than advise the National School Board Association that these parents were within their First Amendment rights to speak out at School Board meetings and express their grievances, General Attorney Garland chose to comply with the Marxist-Communist National School Board Association's request to intervene instead. He instructed the FBI to regard these concerned parents as domestic terrorists under the Patriot Act and to subject them to intimidation and harassment as such. This move against the concerned parents of school children has only emboldened the "mama bears" to increase their participation in school board meetings and to run against incumbent board members.

Trump Associates: And then we have Attorney General Merrick Garland's DOJ's political attacks, harassment, and persecution of President Trump's aids and associates.

- *Steve Bannon*: Trump's 2016 political manager was accused of a fundraising scam tied to raising dollars to build Trump's border wall. These allegations have never been proven. These charges were made to intimidate Bannon from supporting Trump in opposition to the Marxist-Communist Democrat regime—a Stalinist style act to control the Marxist-Communist narrative and discourage others from promoting constitutional conservatism.

- *Elliott Broidy*: Charged with conspiracy in an alleged lobbying effort aimed at stopping a criminal investigation into massive fraud at a Malaysian investment firm and advocating for the removal of a Chinese billionaire living in the United States. Elliott Broidy was convicted by a Marxist-Communist New York District Attorney and jury and was subsequently pardoned by then-President Trump. Hmm, it sounds very familiar to a live broadcast in which then Vice President Joe Biden bragged about telling the head of Ukraine's justice department to fire the individual who was investigating Hunter Biden and the energy firm for whom Hunter was working. He threatened that if the lead investigator were not immediately fired, he would withhold the multi-billion-dollar aid package to the Ukrainian government. Do we see a two-tier justice system here?

- *Michael Flynn*: A decorated military war veteran and retired general, Michael Flynn served our Nation with honor and distinction and spent a brief stint as Trump's national security adviser before being forced to resign after he allegedly failed to disclose contacts with Russian officials during the transition of the Obama-Biden Administration to the Trump Administration. These allegations were never proven to be accurate. As the incoming national security adviser, Michael Flynn had every right to meet with his counterparts in foreign countries to establish relationships. Accusations led to the financial ruin of General Flynn in his defense against the unlimited resources of the Marxist-Communist Democrat federal government. Accusations were made to intimidate General Flynn in the hopes that he would disclose possibly illegal actions made by President Trump.

- *Paul Manafort*: Trump's campaign manager for part of the 2016 presidential election campaign, Paul Manafort, was accused of conspiracy against the United States and conspiracy to obstruct justice due to alleged attempts to tamper with witnesses, which Manafort adamantly denied. Paul Manafort was found guilty by a Washington, D.C., jury composed of strong Marxist-Communist jurists. None of the charges made against Manafort had any relationship with Donald Trump or the Trump campaign;

- *George Papadopoulos*: A relatively junior adviser to Trump's campaign, George Papadopoulos was sentenced to twelve days in prison for lying to investigators about his contacts with individuals tied to Russia. Papadopoulos was defiant about his innocence; "The truth will all be out," he tweeted the night before reporting to prison, "not even a prison sentence can stop that momentum." Trump pardoned Papadopoulos in December 2020. Accusations made for the sole purpose of intimidating Papadopoulos and any other individuals from supporting President Trump;

- *Roger Stone*: Roger Stone spent years advising Trump, although he was only formally affiliated with the 2016 campaign for a brief period. He was convicted for lying to Congress regarding his efforts for Trump's campaign. President Trump's response upon hearing of the verdict tweeted, "So they now convict Roger Stone of lying and want to jail him for many years to come. Well, what about Crooked Hillary, Comey, Strzok, Page, McCabe, Brennan, Clapper, Shifty Schiff, Ohr & Nellie, Steele & all of the others, including even Mueller himself? Didn't they lie to Congress?" An accurate assessment of a two-tiered judicial system that protects elitist members of the Marxist-Communist Democrat Party while going after conservatives.

> *Allen Weisselberg*: A longtime chief financial officer for the Trump Organization, Allen Weisselberg was charged with tax crimes tied to perks he was given in place of salary. Weisselberg pleaded not guilty. The Trump Organization was also indicted and also pleaded not guilty. President Trump accurately called the Weisselberg accusations a "pawn in a scorched earth attempt to harm the former president." Again, one more act of injustice by the DOJ supports the reality that the United States is now living under a two-tier justice system: one for Marxist Communist Democrat Party comrades and one for constitutional conservatives.

The individuals who committed prosecutorial offenses are missing from Merrick Garland's political hit list:

> *Hillary Clinton*, who during her tenure as United States Secretary of State, maintained an illegal, unsecured private email server installed in a closet of her home for official government communications rather than using secure official State Department servers. After a year-long FBI inquiry into Clinton's illegal home-based server, it was determined that at least one hundred emails contained information that was deemed classified at the time they were sent, including sixty-five emails deemed "Secret" and twenty-two deemed "Top Secret." Over two thousand additional emails were designated confidential by the State Department. Most non-Marxist-Communist experts, officials, and members of Congress contend that

Clinton›s use of a private server for official government business violated federal law, specifically 18 U.S. Code § 1924, regarding the unauthorized removal and retention of classified documents or materials, as well as State Department protocols, procedures, and regulations governing record keeping. The exact actions that former President Trump is facing prosecution and prison time. When confronted with these allegations, Hillary Clinton had her server, computer, and mobile phone bleached and smashed to pieces, destroying evidence of criminal activity. What was Hillary charged with and sentenced for? Nothing!

➤ *James Comey*, the director of the FBI, personally oversaw the investigation into Hillary Clinton's illegal use of a private server. Four months before the presidential elections, Comey announced that his agency's investigation had concluded that Clinton had been "extremely careless" but recommended that no charges be filed against Hillary Clinton because he did not believe that she had acted with criminal intent. This decision was not one that Comey had the legal authority to make. The investigation findings should have been turned over to the Department of Justice for any legal action they deemed appropriate. Comey›s timing was controversial, with critics saying he had violated Department of Justice guidelines and precedent. The controversy received more media coverage than any other topic during the presidential campaign. What penalty or reprimand did Comey receive for his inappropriate actions and election interference, which was a felony? None!

➤ *Peter Strzok*, a senior FBI counterintelligence official, texted his mistress Lisa Page, an FBI lawyer and close adviser to former Deputy Director Andrew McCabe, anti-Trump text messages in which Strzok texted to Page,

"We'll stop a Trump presidency." Lisa Page responded to Strzok's text, asking Strzok, "Trump is never going to become president. Right?!" Strzok responded by stating, "No. No, he won't, we'll stop it." Approximately three-hundred and seventy-five text messages between Peter Strzok and Lisa Page, exchanged during the presidential campaign, were recovered, expressing deep distaste for Donald Trump and the need to stop him from becoming the President of the United States at any cost. Both Trump-bashing bureaucrats voluntarily resigned before any official disciplinary or legal action could be taken.

➢ *Bruce Ohr*, an attorney with the Department of Justice, had repeated contacts with FBI agents during the fall and winter of 2016–2017, where he shared information in the Steele dossier. During this time, Ohr failed to inform his supervisors in the Justice Department of his role, actions which were "shocking" to then Deputy General Attorney Rod Rosenstein when he learned of Ohr›s role. Rosenstein stated that Ohr «appeared to be serving as an ‹intermediary› with Christopher Steele" regarding Steele's dossier prepared under a contract between the Democrat National Conference, the Clinton campaign, and the firm Fusion GPS.

During the 2016 election, Bruce's wife, Nellie Ohr, a Russia specialist, worked for Fusion GPS as an independent contractor. Nellie Ohr conducted "research and analysis" of Donald Trump for Fusion GPS. On September 30, 2020, Bruce Ohr retired from his position at the Department of Justice after his counsel was informed that a negative final decision on a disciplinary review being conducted by Department senior career officials was imminent." Bruce Ohr has not been subjected to any legal actions for his role in presenting a known false dossier as evidence to obtain a FISA court warrant to wiretap Trump and members of his campaign team or for this obvious act of Election Interference, which is a federal felony.

- *Andrew McCabe*, former FBI Director, admittedly lied on four occasions to federal investigators, apparently with the expectation he would never be prosecuted. No legal actions have been taken against McCabe for knowingly and purposely lying to Congress under oath. McCabe also knowingly signed a false document asserting that the Hunter Biden laptop was Russian misinformation just two weeks before the presidential elections to assist Joe Biden's bid for the Presidency. This is election interference, a felony under federal law. McCabe's punishment for this criminal act? Nothing.

- *John Brennan*, former Central Intelligent Agency Director, admittedly lied under oath to Congress, not once but twice, with absolute impunity. Brennan has not been charged for knowingly and purposely lying to Congress under oath. Brennan also knowingly signed the false document asserting that the Hunter Biden laptop was Russian misinformation just two weeks before the presidential elections to assist Joe Biden's bid for the Presidency. This is election interference, a felony under federal law. Brennan's punishment for this criminal act? Nothing.

- *James Clapper*, the former director of national intelligence, not only lied under oath to Congress but boasted that he gave the "least untruthful" answers possible. He, too, faced zero consequences. Clapper also knowingly signed the false document asserting that the Hunter Biden laptop was Russian misinformation just two weeks before the presidential elections to assist Joe Biden's bid for the Presidency. This is election interference, a felony under federal law. Clapper's punishment for this criminal act? Nothing.

➢ As evidence from the Hunter Biden laptop continues to mount, also missing from the General Attorney's prosecution list are Joe and Hunter Biden and the numerous family members of the Biden cartel who have been accepting an estimated forty million dollars from the Chinese, Ukrainian, Romanian, and Russian governments in exchange for political influence on American policies affecting these countries. Blatant acts of treason, which the Biden cartel is not being held accountable for by the Marxist-Communist Department of Justice.

As the Marxist-Communist Democrat Party is politically targeting former President Donald Trump for allegedly paying hush money to a porn-actress years prior to the 2016 presidential election, President Obama's "illegal foreign influence operation" is flying under the radar. In early April of 2023, actor Leonardo DiCaprio testified in federal court that Malaysian financier Jho Low revealed to him that he had donated up to $30 million to help Obama's 2012 reelection campaign. Low allegedly recruited the founding member of the hip-hop group The Fugees to help funnel a large amount of money to Obama's reelection campaign; under federal election law, foreigners cannot donate to presidential campaigns.

***Mar-a-Lago*:** In May of 2021, the politically weaponized National Archives and Records Administration conveniently realized they were missing several Trump Administration documents, including correspondence sent from North Korean dictator Kim Jong-un to Trump. I say "conveniently" because, as we now know, many Presidents and Vice Presidents have been found to have "classified" documents in their possession after leaving office. It can be no coincidence that all of a sudden, when an unbeatable former President named Donald Trump is running against an incompetent and in-cognitive incumbent

Marxist-Communist President, a weaponized National Archives and Records Administration suddenly realized that documents are missing from the Trump presidential office. How is it then that they did not know that numerous boxes of classified documents were missing from previous Presidents and Vice Presidents? The classified documents in these individuals' possession were not determined to be missing, and the National Archives and Records Administration National Archives did not make official demands for their return. It was only after President Trump was targeted that these former Vice Presidents, including Joe Biden, through their attorneys, suddenly found classified documents in their possession and turned those documents over to the FBI. But of course, none of these individuals were charged with illegally possessing classified documents because they "voluntarily" turned those documents over to the FBI. That is all well and good, but they had already committed the crime, so why were they not charged? Answer: Their name was not Donald J. Trump, who was running in opposition to a corrupt and inept sitting president. The National Archives and Records Administration did not feel the need to instruct the FBI to purposefully raid and search the homes of these other individuals for any other potentially missing documents or records.

On May 6th, 2021, the National Archives and Records Administration emailed Trump's lawyers requesting their assistance in returning the Kim Jong-un letters and roughly two dozen boxes in Trump's possession at the Mar-a-Lago residence. As requested, those records were released by President Trump's lawyers to the National Archives and Records Administration. In June of 2021, the National Archives and Records Administration instructed a former Trump White House counsel lawyer to send these supposedly highly classified letters from Kim Jong-un to the National Archives and Records Administration via FedEx. The National Archives and Records Administration apparently did not deem those classified letters highly classified if they felt it appropriate to return them via FedEx. According to *The*

Washington Post, Trump's attorney, Alex Cannon, helped to facilitate the transfer of all requested presidential records to the National Archives. Trump then dictated a statement indicating that "everything" requested by the National Archives had been returned, stating that "the papers were given easily and without conflict and on a very friendly basis."

On February 9th, 2022, the National Archives referred the matter to the DOJ. On May 11th, 2022, the DOJ subpoenaed Trump for "any and all documents or writings in the custody or control of Donald J. Trump and/or the Office of Donald J. Trump bearing classification markings." On May 12, 2022, the DOJ issued a grand jury subpoena to the National Archives for the classified documents previously held in the custody of President Trump, which they had provided to the House select committee investigating the January 6th, 2021, United States Capitol protest. DOJ and FBI investigators met with Trump's attorneys at Mar-a-Lago on June 3rd, 2022, about the subpoenaed classified material. Based on an anonymous informant, the DOJ believed that more classified documents remained on the Mar-a-Lago premise. During that June 3rd, 2023, meeting, Trump's custodian of records, Christina Bobb, gave the DOJ a signed declaration drafted by Trump attorney Evan Corcoran, attesting that all classified material <u>requested</u> had been returned.

On June 8th, 2022, the DOJ requested Trump's team to add additional security for the storage area, to which Trump aides complied. Less than two weeks later, Trump notified the National Archives and Records Administration to add Kash Patel, a former Trump administration official, and journalist John Solomon as "representatives for access to Presidential records of my administration." On June 24th, 2022, the FBI served a subpoena to the Trump Organization for surveillance footage at Mar-a-Lago, including views from outside the storage room between January 10th, 2022, and June 24th, 2022. In response, on July 6th, 2022, the Trump Organization provided a hard drive of the surveillance footage.

Many newspapers and media organizations rightly filed motions to unseal the probable-cause affidavit, which had been submitted to the judge on August 5th, 2022, in support of the search warrant application. In court filings, the DOJ opposed the affidavit's release, writing that "this investigation implicates highly classified materials;" disclosure which would compromise the integrity of the criminal investigation and the cooperation of witnesses in the matter and "other high-profile investigations." The DOJ also cited "widely reported threats made against law enforcement personnel in the wake of the Mar-a-Lago search." The DOJ said that if the magistrate judge ordered the release of the affidavit, the necessary redactions would render the unsealed text "devoid of any meaningful context," saying the "redacted version would not serve any public interest." All politically motivated responses. These newspaper and media organizations were not asking for the release of any classified documents or investigative reports, only a copy of the affidavit that had been submitted to the judge justifying a search warrant.

On August 8th, 2022, FBI agents raided and searched the home of former President Trump's residence at Mar-a-Lago. President Trump and his family were not in residence during the raid. On Fox News, Trump's son, Eric Trump, said he received a call about the ongoing search and informed his father shortly after. Two of Trump's lawyers, Christina Bobb and Lindsey Halligan, were called and sent to Mar-a-Lago to be present for the FBI search but were not allowed inside by the FBI, which is unprecedented. If the FBI agents felt their search of Mar-a-Lago would be conducted professionally and legally, then why would the President's attorneys not be allowed to observe the process? Why? The FBI intended to neatly scatter documents on the floor stamped as classified and then photograph the neatly scattered documents as evidence of President Trump's failure to secure such documents properly. The pictures taken by the FBI did not depict documents carelessly scattered about as would be expected when documents are handled carelessly, but rather documents intentionally and neatly positioned in a manner that would show the classified markings on each document. These documents were clearly planted on the floor. Trump and his family watched most of the FBI search from their New York resident remotely via a live video feed transmitted from Mar-a-Lago's system of security cameras, which the FBI had requested to be turned off during the search process. Trump and his attorneys refused the FBI's requests. Again, what were the agents afraid of? Why did they feel a need to demand that the security cameras be turned off? This move by the Biden-Harris Administration marked Biden's worst political decision in his already lackluster federal career, equal only to his devastating decision to retreat from Afghanistan at a pace comparable to a defeated military force on the run from the enemy.

Source & Additional Information: *(https://www.ft.com/content/68ef537c-b388-4a9f-a621-17e63b044e72)*

On August 18th, 2022, the federal magistrate judge held a hearing to discuss requests to unseal investigators' probable cause affidavit. Jay Bratt, head of the DOJ's counterintelligence division, said the investigation was in its "early stages." He argued that releasing the affidavit could reveal investigative techniques, jeopardize the identities of "several witnesses" from their specific accounts of events, and expose federal agents to threats. Media organizations continued their pursuit to have the judge unseal the affidavit even with the necessary redactions, citing the public interest. The judge signaled that he planned to unseal portions of the affidavit and gave the DOJ a week to submit proposed redactions. On social media, Trump repeatedly called for the release of the unredacted affidavit.

In a thirteen-page order released on August 22nd, 2022, the judge rejected the DOJ's argument that partially unsealing the affidavit would set a dangerous precedent and highlight the significance of this case. The judge requested the DOJ to submit proposed redactions and provide additional evidence and arguments within a week. On August 25th, the DOJ submitted a legal brief proposing redactions to the affidavit. The brief was under seal, and multiple media companies requested the judge to unseal it and direct the DOJ to make any other sealed documents public. The judge soon agreed to the proposed redactions and ordered the DOJ to release the redacted affidavit the following day. The judge's decision to release the affidavit was surprising because probable-cause affidavits are typically kept under seal and not made public before charges are filed. The redacted search warrant affidavit was released on August 26th, 2022.

The affidavit listed four main goals of the FBI, which included to:

- Determine how the documents with classification markings and records were removed from the White House and came to be stored at Mar-a-Lago;
- Determine whether the storage location at Mar-a-Lago was an authorized location for the storage of classified information;
- Determine whether any additional classified documents or records may have been stored in an unauthorized location at Mar-a-Lago or another unknown location and whether they remain at any such location;

And to identify any person(s) who may have removed or retained classified information without authorization and/or in an unauthorized space.

Following a criminal referral by the National Archives and Records Administration, Attorney General Merrick Garland authorized a search warrant application, which Magistrate Judge Bruce Reinhart approved. The order unsealed a few days after the search, showed that the FBI obtained the search warrant as part of an investigation into Trump relating to three federal criminal statutes: "18 U.S.C. §§ 793, 2071, (and) 1519". The Sections cited are:

> § 793, enacted as part of the Espionage Act of 1917, makes the unauthorized retention or disclosure of documents related to national defense, which could be used to harm the United States or aid a foreign adversary, a crime. As the Congressional Research Service notes, the "affidavit supporting the warrant focuses on subsection (e), which applies when an individual is in unauthorized possession of certain national defense information."

> § 2071 criminalizes the theft or destruction of government records, regardless of their relevance to national security. The maximum penalty is ten years in prison.

> § 1519, enacted as part of the Sarbanes-Oxley Act, criminalizes the act of destroying or concealing documents or records, regardless of their relevance to national security, "with the intent to impede, obstruct, or influence the investigation or proper administration of any matter" within the jurisdiction of any federal department or agency. The maximum penalty is 20 years in prison.

If President Trump is convicted, as the Marxist-Communist Democrat Party and the Biden-Harris White House are hoping will happen, then President Trump would supposedly be "disqualified from holding any office under the United States." This would disqualify Donald Trump as a Presidential candidate against Joe Biden, or any other Marxist-Communist Democrat Party candidate should Joe Biden not run. The Marxist-Communist Democrat Party is well aware that they have no potential party member capable of beating President Trump in a fairly administered election. Therefore, they must somehow disqualify him as a Presidential candidate. However, a significant number of legal scholars, including Democrat scholars, questioned the constitutionality of disqualifying President Trump from holding any office within the United States government due to having been criminally charged or convicted. This entire move by the Biden-Harris Administration politically stinks, clearly demonstrating an attempt by President Biden, the DOJ, and the FBI to politically damage and thereby stop President Trump from running for President in 2024.

<u>Source & Additional Information</u>: *(https://www.forbes.com/sites/ alisondurkee/2022/08/26/doj-releases-redacted-mar-a-lago-search-affidavit---heres- what-it-says/)*

Since the 1988 Supreme Court decision in *Department of the Navy v. Egan*, there has been a consensus that a sitting president has broad Constitutional powers to classify and declassify information. President Trump has asserted that he had declassified the documents found at Mar-a-Lago. In 2003, Scooter Libby, former chief of staff to Vice President Dick Cheney, claimed to have received a direct but unrecorded order from President George W. Bush and Vice President Cheney to leak classified information to reporters in what became known as the Plame Affair. Libby was not charged for releasing this classified information. Steven Aftergood, a critic of the United States government's secrecy policy, said the case "highlights the fact that the president purports to, or does, stand outside of the classification system," unless your name is Donald Trump. The Presidential Records Act further gives clear authority for a President to remove any document from the White House at the end of their presidential term.

A detailed property list was unsealed on September 2nd, 2022, due to Trump's lawsuit against the United States. The list showed that items such as documents and photographs without classification markings, news clippings, unspecified gifts, clothing items, and a book were confiscated from Mar-A-Lago. A box found in Trump's office containing "forth-three empty folders with classified banners; twenty-eight empty folders labeled 'Return to Staff Secretary/Military Aide'; ninety-nine news articles and other printed media; sixty-nine government documents or photos that were not classified; and twenty-four government documents marked confidential, secret or top secret." The Marxist-Communist Democrat Party propaganda outlets did not deem it important enough to report on how many classified documents were found in the possession of Joe Biden nor in the possession of former Vice President Mike Pence—only silence from our esteemed Marxist-Communist Democrat propaganda news arm.

On October 1st, 2022, The Washington Post reported that, according to two unnamed sources, the National Archives and Records Administration had informed the House Oversight Committee that some presidential records had not been recovered from President Trump. On October 6th, 2022, the New York Times reported that, according to these two unnamed sources, the National Archives and Records Administration informed Trump's lawyers that Trump was still holding material. It is interesting how every time these Marxist-Communist propaganda arms of the Marxist-Communist Democrat Party have politically damaging information against President Trump or other conservative officials, it always comes from unnamed or anonymous sources. If these unnamed or anonymous sources were indeed providing factual information because they felt that it was their patriotic duty to do so, then they should have the courage and strength of their convictions to stand up and proudly put their names to the accusations. If our eighteen-, nineteen-, and twenty-year-old young adults can find the strength and courage to face an enemy in a war, not of their making, which puts them at a high risk of being severely wounded or killed, then surely these politically motivated unnamed or anonymous sources can find the courage to put their name on accusations which will, in all probability, never cause them any imminent life-threatening danger.

On November 18th, 2022, Garland appointed a special counsel, federal prosecutor Jack Smith, to oversee the federal criminal investigation of Donald Trump into his alleged violation of federal criminal statutes: "18 U.S.C. §§ 793, 2071, and 1519." The Department's press release stated that attack dog Jack Smith would oversee "the ongoing investigation involving classified documents and other presidential records, as well as the possible obstruction of that investigation." Jack Smith is no friend of President Trump, being a loyal member of the Marxist-Communist Democrat Party who donated to the Biden-Harris campaign. As a result of the biased investigation by Jack Smith, President Trump was indicted on alleged violation of the federal criminal statute "18 U.S.C. §§ 793, 2071, and 1519." On June 9th, 2023, a thirty-seven-count felony indictment was unsealed accusing Trump of willful retention and improper sharing of national defense information with no evidence that Trump shared any information in his possession with anyone, let alone an adversary of the United States, as is the case with the Joe Biden cartel; conspiracy to obstruct justice and corruptly concealing a document or record; and espionage. Charges could potentially carry a penalty of up to two hundred years if convicted.

Source & Additional Information: (https://www.nbcnews.com/politics/justice-department/jack-smith-special-counsel-investigating-donald-trump-rcna57944)

Contrary to the beliefs and hopes of the Marxist-Communist Democrat Party, soon after he was indicted, polls showed clear signs that Republican voters are still willing to trust, believe in, and support Trump in his 2024 bid for President. Trump's margin of lead in the crowded 2024 Republican primary was actually extended over his closest rival in obtaining the Republican nomination, and he widened his margin for being elected as President over Biden. The prospect that someone under politically motivated indictment, not once but four separate times, could somehow still be considered a viable presidential candidate underscores Trump's undying support by Republican voters. It also illustrates how effective he has become at inoculating himself against political fallout and reflects growing Republican hostility toward the federal government, particularly the DOJ, which Trump has now spent the better part of a decade accurately criticizing.

On June 13th, 2023, Trump was arraignment in Miami, Florida, on the thirty-seven federal charges related to his handling of classified documents. After leaving the courthouse, Trump's motorcade made an unannounced stop at the Cuban-owned and run restaurant, the Versailles Bakery. Trump was welcomed enthusiastically and warmly by diners at the restaurant. Former President Trump joined the diners in prayer, and then the diners sang "Happy Birthday" to celebrate his 77th birthday on June 14th, a day early. In response, Trump urged his supporters to fight back and stop the country's decline and announced that dinner for all those present was on him. Yet, when CNN reported on the arraignment and Trump's unscheduled stop at the restaurant, host Jake Tapper seemed to have a total meltdown. As soon as Tapper realized that the video clip of Trump's visit at the Versailles Bakery showed complete excitement and enthusiasm for Trump and that he was broadcasting this video clip nationally, he immediately stopped the video clip from continuing, stating, "the folks in the control room, I don't need to see any more of that." The video clip did not show the hostile reception the Marxist-Communist Democrat Tapper had believed would be seen. With the offending video safely stopped, he accused Trump of trying to turn his visit into "a spectacle, campaign ad" before repeating that he had seen enough. The level of double-standard and total fear of Donald Trump is profound.

As in every other politically motivated false accusation made against Trump, he remained determined to continue his 2024 presidential campaign and has the full backing of the vast majority of Republican voters. At the time, polling showed that Trump's lead grew to 61% support among likely Republican voters, while second-place candidate, Florida Governor Ron

DeSantis, trails far behind at 23% following Trump's indictment. Many supporters stated that this latest indictment only made them more likely to vote for him.

White House Reactions: The White House said that President Biden and White House officials were unaware of President Trump's Mar-a-Lago home search until it was reported on the news. In reality, any such move by the DOJ on a former President would have been fully discussed with the sitting President. President Biden had previously been quoted as stating that he wanted President Trump indicted for something, anything, indict him. In conclusion, the pathological liar and dictator-in-chief sitting in the White House not only was aware of the raid on President Trump's home but, in all probability, ordered the raid by his weaponized DOJ and the FBI to take whatever action necessary to eliminate Trump as his opposing Republican candidate in the 2024 elections.

On August 26th, 2022, Biden mocked former President Trump for saying he had declassified all of the material he took with him to Mar-a-Lago, and Biden further stated that he would let the DOJ decide on the risk to national security and what actions the Department chose to take. In another speech on August 30th, 2022, Biden condemned the calls by American Patriots and Republican members of Congress to defund the FBI as "sickening," He criticized Republicans for their hypocrisy in their calls for "riots in the streets," calls which the Republican members of Congress never made. Just more lies in a litany of lies from a pathological liar. Speaking of hypocrisy, at the end of Biden's term as Vice President in 2016, classified documents were removed from the Vice President's White House office and found at four different Biden-owned or leased locations, some classified documents dating back to when he was a member of Congress.

Political Motivation, Planted Evidence, and Obama Precedent: Trump likened the search of his home and offices to the 1970s Watergate scandal. He made the factual allegation that the raid was politically motivated to stop him from running for president in 2024 and a "politically motivated move" by the Biden-Harris administration. He criticized the FBI for searching his wife, Melania Trump's rooms and belongings in Mar-a-Lago. On August 11th, 2022, Trump made the highly likely claim that the FBI had doctored evidence to support its search warrant and may very well have planted incriminating materials and recording devices at Mar-a-Lago. Trump's allies echoed these claims. On August 12th, 2022, President Trump stated that his lawyers had fully cooperated with federal investigators before the search: "The government could have had whatever they wanted if we had it."

Trump Claims of Declassifying Documents: On August 12th, 2022, Trump posted to Truth Social that the documents he brought to Mar-a-Lago were "all declassified" before he left office. That day, his office issued a statement admitting that he had frequently taken home classified documents and further claimed that he had issued a "standing order" that anything he brought home was automatically and "instantly" declassified. On September 20th, 2022, his lawyers said they were refraining from mentioning Trump's "standing order" claim in court as it might reveal a potential defense in any future indictment. Trump allies in Congress and conservative media began to inform the general public that the FBI may have planted evidence, that the FBI's search was aimed at stopping Trump from exposing criminals within the federal government, and that the FBI had conducted a "military occupation" of his home.

Republican Party Reaction: The Republican National Committee, as well as conservative Republicans, responded to the FBI's search by denouncing the search as politically motivated by a weaponized FBI and by acknowledging that Trump was a victim of Marxist-Communist factions determined to destroy him and his MEGA followers utilizing Stalinist methods. Conservative Republicans further stated that the search made the United States no more than a "third-world country" or "banana republic." Republican members of Congress vowed to investigate the DOJ now that they are in control of the House of Representatives. In a tweet, then-House Minority Leader Kevin McCarthy stated the DOJ "has reached an intolerable state of weaponized politicization" and further said, "When Republicans take back the House, we will conduct immediate oversight of this department, follow the facts, and leave no stone unturned. Attorney General Garland, preserve your documents and clear your calendar." Republican Congresswoman Marjorie Taylor Greene of Georgia called for defunding the FBI. Senator Rand Paul called for the Espionage Act to be repealed. Anthony Sabatini, a Republican member of the Florida State House of Representatives, called for the state to "sever all ties with Department of Justice immediately" and called for FBI agents to be "arrested upon sight."

Many Republicans rightly accused the DOJ and the FBI of a double standard two-tiered justice system for their previous treatment of then-former Marxist-Communist Democratic Party nominee Hillary Clinton, who was investigated but not charged over classified material found on her private email server located in a closet at her home, stemming from her tenure as the Secretary of State—an action on the part of Hillary Clinton which was a violation of federal law. Senator Lindsey Graham of South Carolina predicted the likelihood of street violence if Trump were to be found guilty of any of these fruitless charges made against him. Some Republicans took a more restrained tone upon reports that the documents seized were highly classified but questioned the search. Multiple Republicans called on the DOJ and FBI to release or share with Congress documents surrounding the search, particularly the affidavit used as the basis of the warrant. Republican Mike Turner, the ranking member of the House Intelligence Committee, stated that he was "very concerned about the method that was used in raiding Mar-a-Lago;" Republican Brian Fitzpatrick questioned whether "the law is being enforced equally" and with "parity".

Republican congresswoman Liz Cheney, the top Marxist-Communist Republican on the House Unselect Committee supposedly investigating the January 6th, 2021, protest at the Capitol building, criticized her party's response to the federal investigation of Trump, writing, "I have been ashamed to hear members of my party attacking the integrity of the FBI agents involved with the Mar-a-Lago search. These are sickening comments that put the lives of patriotic public servants at risk." Spoken like a committed Marxist-Communist Trump hater. Trump-hater Liz Cheney was well rewarded for her treachery by losing her state primary by the largest margin in American history. Her treasonous behavior gained her a position as a professor at the University of Virginia's Marxist-Communist Center for Politics. She will teach a course on betraying your party and the art of stabbing people in the back. For comic relief, she said she is considering a run for the White House in 2024. I am surprised; I never saw her as having a sense of humor.

Democrat Party Reactions: As might be expected, House Marxist-Communist Democrats praised the unprecedented actions taken against President Trump as a step toward accountability. In an interview after the search, Nancy Pelosi, then Speaker of the House, said, "We believe in the rule of law. That is what our country is about. And no person is above the law. Not even the president of the United States. Not even a former president of the United States." The rule of law? Nancy and her fellow Marxist-Communist Democrats believe in the rule of law only when it serves their political agenda, and Queen Nancy truly believes she is somehow exempt from any law or constitutional mandates. This woman has no regard for the law or the Constitution.

Biden Classified Documents: The DOJ appointed a special counsel to probe the issue of Biden's possession of classified documents, which have probably already been shared with China and Russia. The first batch of documents were found in a closet at the Penn-Biden Center, where Biden worked before his current term at the White House as President. Biden became a professor at the University of Pennsylvania in 2017, where he headed the Penn-Biden Center. Biden had been vice president for two terms during the Obama administration between 2009 and 2017 during which period the documents found related too. On January 12th, 2023, Biden's lawyer announced that a second batch of classified documents had been found in Biden's Delaware residences in Rehoboth Beach, Delaware, dating back to when Biden was a Senator.

What we know about Biden's classified documents situation is that the information provided to the public came from people who work for or are close to President Biden. As expected, the information regarding these classified documents had been filtered selectively through a media predisposed primarily to protecting the president. According to Bob Bauer, Biden's attorney, a former White House counsel, and longtime Democratic power broker whose wife, Anita Dunn, was a senior adviser to the president, the classified documents were "unexpectedly discovered" on November 2nd, 2022, just six days before the midterm election by members of the president's team of personal lawyers. The documents were supposedly found in a closet in Biden's former office at the Penn Biden Center for Diplomacy and Global Engagement in Washington, D.C. and affiliated with the University of Pennsylvania. Just by pure coincidence, the University of Pennsylvania received more than $30 million in donations from anonymous Chinese donors shortly after the Penn-Biden Center was established in 2017. Anonymous means the Chinese Communist Party.

Source & Additional Information: (https://www.cnn.com/politics/live-news/biden-classified-documents-report-02-08-24/index.html)

Bauer claims that Biden's lawyers immediately notified the National Archives and Records Administration of the discovery. According to Biden's legal team and White House senior staff, because Biden's lawyers immediately contacted and returned the classified documents to the National Archives and Records Administration, this crime is somehow not as severe as Donald Trump's retention of classified information. This is tantamount to robbing a bank, but if the perpetrator returns the money stolen a few years later, it is no longer a crime and deserves a pass.

On November 4th, 2022, the National Archives Office of Inspector General notified the DOJ of the discovery. The FBI commenced an investigation five days later, and the day after, the Injustice Department notified Biden's lawyers that it was looking into the matter. On November 14th, 2022, Attorney General Merrick Garland tasked John Lausch, the United States attorney for the Northern District, with conducting a preliminary investigation. Then, on December 20th, 2022, Biden's lawyers informed Lausch that they had found another "small number" of additional classified documents in the garage of Biden's private home in Wilmington, Delaware, where he keeps his 1967 Corvette Stingray. According to Bauer, the Injustice Department took possession of those documents the next day.

On January 5th, 2023, Lausch briefed Garland about his preliminary conclusions and recommended the appointment of a special counsel. On January 9th, 2023, after the story broke about the discovery of classified documents at the Penn-Biden Center, the White House acknowledged the matter. Biden stated that he was *"surprised"* to learn about the discovery and claimed not to know what was in the documents. Neither Biden nor the White House mentioned the classified records found in his home until January 12th, 2023, after media outlets began reporting on that discovery. At that time, the White House acknowledged the discovery and added that an additional page with classified information was *"discovered among stored materials in an adjacent room"* to the garage at the home. In response to a reporter's question the same day, Biden stated, *"by the way, my Corvette is in a locked garage. It is not like it is sitting out in the street."* This is a brilliant response from someone who believes he will never be held accountable. On January 14th, 2023, the White House issued a statement that, yet another five pages of classified information had been discovered in a storage room adjacent to Biden's garage within hours after the statement had been issued on January 12th, 2023. Biden described this adjacent room as his *"personal library."* It is beyond belief that Joe Biden did not know of the existence of these classified documents in his possession, nor that, given the various locations they were found in, he did not personally place them there. How convenient it was for his lawyers to happen to *"find"* these documents after the Trump classified documents incident.

The biggest question in terms of potential criminal prosecution, of course, is whether Biden knew the documents were there, the same question that was asked about former Secretary of State Hillary Clinton about the information residing on the server that was installed at the home she shared with former President Bill Clinton in Chappaqua, N.Y. As one might expect, Biden denies any knowledge of the documents in his possession. How surprising!

Donald Trump was charged with the possession of classified documents, which as president, he had the legal authority to declassify and, in keeping with the "Presidential Records Act," had the legal authority to take possession of those documents. Documents are all located at his Mar-A-Lago home, which is heavily secured and guarded 24/7. Now, months later, with Trump's trial regarding his classified documents retention looming on the horizon, nothing has been done about any potential legal action against Biden, who, as a Vice President and Senator, had no legal authority to declassify those documents or to take those documents in his possession. More evidence of a two-tiered justice system in the third-world banana republic we have become.

Biden Responded? In one word: poorly. His answer about the documents was the worst answer we have heard since Hillary Clinton, who had issues with the misuse and improper disclosure of classified information. Moreover, Biden has been justly criticized for appearing like a hypocrite, given his reaction to the Mar-a-Lago raid when he expressed astonishment and stated, "How could that possibly happen; how could anyone be that irresponsible, and what data was in those documents that may have compromised sources and methods?"

So, what should Congress do about this criminal act on Biden's part? At the very least, Congress can and should conduct vigorous oversight hearings. While they may be hampered, Congress should do its level best to unearth exactly what happened, how it happened, why it happened, and if there should be any consequences. At the very least, Congress should review how classified documents were handled at the end of the Obama-Biden administration to minimize future national security risks. If Trump, Biden's past and potentially future political rival, is indicted and Biden is not, just as Hillary Clinton was not, there can be only one conclusion derived from these actions or lack of actions on the part of the DOJ, the United States has evolved into a corrupt double standard of justice at the Injustice Department. That is not good for the country, as it would further add to the growing perception that there are two standards of justice in this country: one for Republicans and another for members of the Marxist-Communist Democrat Party.

Judicial Fairness: Attorney General Garland has spent millions of taxpayer dollars chasing down individuals who were anywhere near the Capitol Building on January 6th, 2021. Most of those individuals just followed the crowd of protesters to the Capitol Building to peaceably assemble and make their voices heard and are innocent of any crime other than being Republican Trump Supporters. All the while, members of Antifa and Black Lives Matter were rioting in the streets of numerous Marxist-

Communist Democrat Party-run cities, destroying property and small businesses and murdering innocent people throughout 2020 and 2021. These thugs were and continue to follow the Marxist-Communist Democrat Party playbook by creating chaos, fear, and hatred among the city's citizens. These thugs are producing an environment ripe for Marxist-Communism to infiltrate into our lives, our religious practices, our education system, and our constitutional form of government, which all plays right into the hands of the Marxist-Communist Democrat Party's move to transform our constitutional republic into an irrational, oppressive, and authoritarian regime. These American versions of Germany's Brown Shirts are enabling the Marxist-Communist Democrat Party in their move to destroy America. The politicalized FBI is hunting down few of these real violent criminals. Those they do detain are released on minimal or no bail, including those who have murdered during the riots. Marxist-Communist comrade Garland has been consistently suppressing evidence or refusing to investigate any allegations against the Biden cartel, the Marxist-Communist Democrat rioters, or real criminals who pose an imminent danger to the community.

According to documents obtained by The Heritage Foundation's Oversight Project through the Freedom of Information Act., FBI agents worked about 16,000 more hours during the pay period of the Capitol protest of January 6th, 2021, than they did during the pay period of the 2020 riots that hit Washington, D.C. Payroll records for FBI agents in the Washington, D.C. field office show they worked a total of 86,262 hours in the January 4th, 2021, to January 17th, 2021, pay period, during which the Capitol protests occurred involving those opposing Congress' certification of the 2020 presidential election.

Source & Additional Information: (https://www.westernjournal.com/fbi-worked-16000-hours-around-jan-6-blm-riots-washington-dc/)

According to whistleblowers, FBI agents were pulled off serious felony investigations to work solely on January 6th, 2021, for protester misdemeanors. By contrast, during the May 25, 2020, to June 7, 2020, pay period, when the Black Lives Matter and Antifa riots were occurring in the District of Columbia involving violent felony-level activity, payroll records show that FBI agents worked a combined total of 70,367 hours. It was on May 29, 2020, at Lafayette Square in Washington, D.C., that rioters gathered near the White House and set fire to the historic St. John's Episcopal Church. The violence outside the White House prompted the Secret Service to move Trump and others into the White House bunker. The Antifa and Black Lives Matter rioters in the District of Columbia during the weeks of May and June of 2020 resulted in about one hundred and fifty local and federal law enforcement officers being injured by those rioters. The 2020 Antifa and Black Lives Matter riots ultimately incurred $2 billion in property damage nationally and resulted in at least nineteen deaths, according to news reports. In contrast, only two deaths occurred during the January 6th, 2021, protests, both of which were non-threatening protesters with no weapons murdered by Capitol police officers. Were Capitol police officers arrested and prosecuted? No, they were honored as heroes.

Source & Additional Information: (https://nypost.com/2020/09/16/riots-following-george-floyds-death-could-cost-up-to-2b/) (https://en.wikipedia.org/wiki/Violence_and_controversies_during_the_George_Floyd_protests)

Mike Howell, director of the Heritage Oversight Project, told The Daily Signal, "It's clear the FBI and Injustice Department have been weaponized." Howell added, "These numbers show the lengths they will go to surge resources towards nonviolent offenses that fit their political narratives. Amid a George Soros-funded crime wave, law enforcement should focus their resources where they are needed and put an end to the gangs, rapes, carjackings, and murders that have become all too common." Deterrence by knowing that justice will be imposed if one commits a crime has been eroded because of the inactions of the DOJ, which has truly earned the title of the Department of Injustice. What these Marxist-Communist enablers fail to understand is that what can happen to people of one ideology can and will eventually make a full circle and come back to haunt them. Not only is the problem the absence of sure punishment for criminal behavior, but the disproportionate penalties being imposed. Violent criminals are released from custody within days after they punch, club, or shoot innocent people, while others committing far lesser offenses are arrested and detained for long periods of time or subjected to outrageous bail dependent upon their political ideology.

The more the Marxist-Communist Biden-Harris Administration ignored the chaos and lawlessness within our borders by those who would bring harm to Americans from abroad, the more foreign adversaries interpret America's lack of action as American weakness and corruption ripe to be exploited. When our state and federal governments allow criminals and foreign nationals to injure our law-abiding citizens without consequences, then the freedoms we once knew will vanish, and the predictable dangers we presently face will only escalate.

Criminals no longer fear the consequences of criminal behavior. This has only encouraged these thugs to run rampant within our cities, resulting in out-of-control smash-and-grab, carjacking, and deadly gang shoot-outs. This lack of consequences and accountability is why the Antifa thugs in Atlanta are so bold in their violent attacks on the police. After four months of rioting, looting, arson, and assault in the summer of 2020, few Black Lives Matter or Antifa members have been indicted, fewer still have been convicted, and almost no one has faced imprisonment. What else could be expected from the corrupt, politicalized, and weaponized DOJ operating within a two-tiered justice system? It is a two-tier justice system that has been and continues to show its true colors when it prosecutes a conservative former President but takes no legal action against Marxist-Communist Democrat Party officials or followers for the same actions.

The bottom line is that Attorney General Merrick Garland and the Biden-Harris Administration have redefined criminality as being a lifestyle choice imposed upon the criminal by a systematically *(that impossible term again)* racist society or justifying the criminality as legitimate acts of grievances against the society they threaten. Garland has shown himself to be little more than a corrupt political hack doing the bidding of President Biden and his puppeteers against our Constitutional Republic and the persecution of a potential opponent for the 2024 Presidential elections. Merritt Garland has shown little to no impartiality as the United States Attorney General. We can only thank the good Lord that he never made his way to a seat on the Supreme Court.

Does anyone believe that Joe Biden, his weaponized and politicized Marxist-Communist DOJ, the politically weaponized FBI, CIA, or any other federal entity cares about the people they have sworn to serve and protect anymore? After all, if anyone in any of those federal entities showed any empathy, they would soon be canceled out by the woke fools and be fired from their positions.

Section III: Bureau of Alcohol, Tobacco, Firearms and Explosives

American citizens' Second Amendment right to bear arms is under heavy and constant assault by the Marxist-Communist Democrat Party and by Marxist-Communist Democrat-governed states and cities. Gun-control advocates have conveniently interpreted the Second Amendment to mean only "the arming of a state militia." Gun-control opponents rightly maintain that the "right to bear arms" and "shall not be infringed upon" is a Constitutional guarantee, not only to members of a State militia but also to every citizen.

Marxist-Communist Democrat Joe Biden, during his 2023 State of the Union Address, demanded that Congress ignore the Second Amendment and ban all so-called assault weapons "once and for all." The anti-gun Brady campaign launched a pressure campaign to try and force the Senate to pass Dianne Feinstein's tyrannical bill (S.25) that would have arbitrarily banned millions of these commonly owned AR-15 firearms, which are far from being assault weapons. Remember that in 2022, fifteen Marxist-Communist Republicans in the Senate and fourteen Marxist-Communist Republicans in the House stabbed constitutional conservatives in the back by voting for gun control. For Marxist-Communist Democrat Party leadership and their Marxist-Communist Republican allies, facts and logic mean nothing to these gun-grabbers. Also, remember that for any political group to gain total control of the government and the citizens therein, they must disarm the population; otherwise, their attempts to take over a government will fail.

During his State of the Union address, Biden recounted the recent shooting in Monterey Park and politicized that tragic event to attempt to justify his assault on our Second Amendment rights. But he missed the most important takeaway from that tragic event: California already has an "assault weapons" ban law in place, and it failed to prevent the Monterey Park mass shootings. In fact, Biden's "assault weapons" ban would actually enable mass shootings by taking firearms out of the hands of law-abiding gun owners who could stop future would-be mass shooters.

On March 21st, 2023, a female transgender mass shooter who self-identified as a male shot to death three adult school employees and three nine-year-old children at a Nashville, Tennessee, private Christian school. Within hours after the shooting, the Marxist-Communist politicians, entertainers, and media propaganda machine kicked in gear with their anti-gun rhetoric. At the same time, they stayed safe with their gun-carrying security agents. Few noted that the shooter illegally purchased firearms by hiding her documented record of emotional disorders.

Source & Additional Information: (https://nypost.com/2023/03/27/everything-we-know-about-the-nashville-school-shooter/)

Predictably, two separate gun control scenarios surfaced: The first was led by none other than President Joe Biden, who lectured us on how guns were the cause of the mass deaths, not the free will of psychopathic killers, and the second, the Marxist-Communist media claimed that, while such killing was regrettable, we were supposed to be understandable because of the incorrect notion of intolerance of transgender people by Christian conservative Americans. The sick, anti-Christian Marxist-Communist Democrat Party is to have us believe that the victims of mass shootings are the oppressors, and the killers are the victims. Had the school's staff members been allowed to "conceal carry" or had an armed resource officer been within the building, the number of deaths may have been much lower or none at all.

The Marxist-Communist Democrat Party is enabling disgruntled individuals to commit these heinous crimes because the offenders believe that they will be hailed as victims of society and, therefore, justified in their actions. But of course, this minor detail regarding gun violence against innocent children and citizens matters little to uninformed and uneducated Marxist-Communist anti-gun supporters. Banning "assault weapons," which are not "assault weapons" but rather semi-automatic rifles, is only their first step towards their ultimate goal of destroying the Second Amendment, leaving American citizens wholly disarmed and at the mercy of dangerous criminals intent on harming us, our loved ones, or any individual found to be in a life-threatening situation.

This push by the Marxist-Communist Democrat regime will leave law-abiding citizens with no means of self-defense against hardened criminals, who will find a way to obtain firearms, already do not comply with our laws, nor does it provide "We the People" a means to protect ourselves against a corrupt federal government intent on gaining control of the nation's population. In his 2023 State of the Union address, Biden called for the banning of all commonly owned firearms, making this a serious threat to our Second Amendment rights.

Proponents of increased gun control in the United States falsely argue that limiting access to guns will save lives and reduce crime; opponents factually insist that it would actually do the opposite by preventing law-abiding citizens from defending themselves against armed criminals. Even in times of crisis, it is illegal for any level of government to confiscate weapons from law-abiding citizens. The Constitution cannot be put on hold because of a perceived threat. However, that does not mean firearm confiscation has not happened or will not happen again if we are not vigilant and ready to stand against any governmental attempts to restrict or eliminate our Second Amendment right to own and carry firearms.

On January 12th, 2022, Amish dairy farmer Reuben King's farm in Lancaster County, Pennsylvania, was raided by the Bureau of Alcohol, Tobacco, Firearms and Explosives (ATF). King was charged with dealing in firearms without a license and had six hundred and sixteen guns confiscated by the Bureau of Alcohol, Tobacco, Firearms and Explosives. An undercover Bureau of Alcohol, Tobacco, Firearms and Explosives agent had bought five guns from King between October 2019 and March 2020, according to court papers filed by the Bureau of Alcohol, Tobacco, Firearms and Explosives. On June 11, 2020, the Bureau of Alcohol, Tobacco, Firearms and Explosives served King with a cease-and-desist letter advising him to get a Federal Firearms License (FFL) before selling any more firearms. King told the Bureau of Alcohol, Tobacco, Firearms and Explosives that he did not sell firearms as a business and only occasionally sold personal long arms for which he had no further use. After that letter, King sold four firearms to undercover state troopers in November 2020, March 2021, and December 2021, prompting the charges.

Source & Additional Information: (https://www.inquirer.com/news/pennsylvania/guns-atf-amish-firearms-lancaster-foundry-laws-20220211.html)

Based on the Constitution, King is not constitutionally required to obtain a Federal Firearms License. Therefore, such a requirement is legally unconstitutional. The Constitution does not restrict anyone from selling or buying firearms, nor does it limit the number of firearms an American citizen can own or sell. The Second Amendment clearly states, "the right of the people to keep and bear arms, shall not be infringed." Firearms sellers, those who sell occasionally from a private collection, and those who hold a Federal Firearms License, have come under more scrutiny since June 2021 when President Joe Biden declared "zero tolerance for rogue gun dealers that willfully violate the law." Since Biden took office, there has been an increase in Federal Firearms License revocations, Mark Oliva, spokesman for the National Shooting Sports Foundation, told The Epoch Times. Attorneys defending clients facing Federal Firearms License revocations or warnings to get a Federal Firearms License say they have seen more cases than any time before Biden took office.

Written in 1791, the Second Amendment protects the right to keep and bear arms. You will not find any language in the Second Amendment of the Constitution requiring an individual to obtain a license to be able to sell firearms. It was not until 1938 that the first Federal Firearms Act requiring sellers of firearms to become licensed was enacted. The United States Supreme Court has said the understanding of the Second Amendment around the time of the founding is the best measure of what the founders intended. There is no recorded evidence that the founders intended for a license to be required to sell firearms. The government must demonstrate that the regulation requiring a license to sell firearms is consistent with the nation's historical tradition of firearm sales and the Constitution.

If King did constitutionally require a license to sell guns from his barn, the Bureau of Alcohol, Tobacco, Firearms and Explosives would not have issued King a license because the Bureau of Alcohol, Tobacco, Firearms and Explosives requires photo identification to obtain a Federal Firearms License, with no exceptions. Because of his Amish religion, King cannot allow his photo to be taken. That is why his driver's license says, "no photo required," where an individual's photo would normally be on the driver's license. King does not drive a vehicle but rather drives a horse and buggy. Pennsylvania allows religious exemptions for photos on driver's licenses and concealed carry gun permits. This is another constitutional issue because requiring a photo would violate King's First Amendment right to practice his religious beliefs without government interference.

Source & Additional Information: (https://www.thelancasterpatriot.com/king/)

On June 14th, 2023, a gun shop in Great Falls, Montana, was raided by twenty heavily armed Internal Revenue Service agents who seized thousands of documents containing private customer information. Highwood Creek Outfitters owner Tom Van Hoose said agents of the Internal Revenue Service Criminal Investigation Division (IRS-CI) showed up carrying semi-automatic rifles and dressed in full tactical gear when he arrived to open the store at 7:30 a.m. During the ten-hour search, Van Hoose said the agents confiscated documents, including financial records and over twelve thousand individual firearms transactions representing thirteen years in business. He said those records filled more than twenty boxes at six-hundred records in each box and comprised "ninety percent" of the documents seized. Whenever a person purchases a firearm, they must fill out a Firearms Transaction Record, ATF Form 4473, which contains the buyer's name, address, vital information, and photo ID. So now the gun-carrying Internal Revenue Service agents have collected all the information on all the individuals who purchase firearms at Highwood Creek Outfitters in Montana. Information that can later be used to track down gun owners by the Marxist-Communist Democrat Party to confiscate those weapons should we lose our Constitutional Republic to Marxist-Communism. Are we about to see a full-scale raid on all gun stores to confiscate documented information on American firearms owners? If the Marxist-Communist Democrat Party wins the 2024 presidential elections, do not be surprised.

Our current Marxist-Communist Democrat government, under the Biden-Harris Administration, aims to disarm law-abiding citizens and loathes the idea of any lawful private firearm ownership. This right is sacred, which is why our Founding Fathers included it in the Constitution. The Second Amendment does not allow the government to restrict or deny the ownership of firearms because of the illegal use of firearms by criminal elements within our country. Firearms do not commit crimes; criminals do. But this fact is irrelevant to the Marxist-Communist Democrat Party because the elimination of a citizen's Second Amendment rights is not to stop criminal acts by evil people. It is to assure total control over the citizens of our Nation by depriving them of any ability to protect themselves, not only against criminal attacks but against the takeover of America by the Marxist-Communist Democrat Party utilizing Stalinist measures to accomplish that goal. If we start to relegate any of our rights to second-class rights, then there are no longer rights at all, and any of those rights can fall at any time. It is our right to own a firearm in America, provided you are a law-abiding citizen. These actions are nothing more than Marxist-Communist elements of our federal government attempting to chip away at those rights, undermine the Second Amendment, and ultimately eliminate this constitutional right.

I am licensed to conceal carry a firearm. I conceal carry not because I want to be cool and macho by carrying a firearm on my hip to show off to my friends; I conceal carry because my wife and I are in our seventies and are easy targets for criminals intent on doing us harm. I don't carry a firearm to kill people, I carry a firearm to keep from being killed; I don't carry a firearm because I'm evil, I carry a firearm because I have lived long enough to see the evil in the world intent on destroying our lives; I don't carry a firearm because I hate the government, I carry a firearm because I understand the threat our federal government possess against its citizens; I don't carry a firearm because I'm angry, I carry a gun so that I don't have to spend the rest of my life hating myself for failing to be prepared; I don't carry a firearm because I want to shoot someone, I carry a firearm because I want to die at a ripe old age in my bed and not on some downtown sidewalk tomorrow afternoon; I don't carry a firearm to make me feel like a man, I carry a firearm because men know how to take care of themselves and the ones they love; I don't carry a firearm because I feel inadequate, I carry a firearm because being unarmed and facing armed thugs, I know I am inadequate; I don't carry a firearm because I love it, I carry a firearm because I love life and the people who make it meaningful to me. Police protection is an oxymoron, and as such, citizens must protect themselves because the police do not protect you from crime, they investigate the crime after it happens and then call someone in to clean up the mess. Personally, I carry a firearm because I am too young to die and too old to take a beating.

Source & Additional Information: (https://www.krtv.com/news/great-falls-news/montanas-u-s-senators-want-answers-about-the-raid-on-a-great-falls-gun-shop)

History on the Right to Bear Arms: "The definition of insanity … to continually repeat the same actions expecting a different result." – Albert Einstein

The following is a brief history of why it is so critical that we maintain our right to own and bear arms. Just the facts, not politics, but history. It is a history we do not want to be repeated in the United States and do not think for a moment that this could not happen in our country because the Marxist-Communist Democrat Party is trying very hard to make it happen:

- ➢ In 1911, Turkey established national gun controls: From 1915 to 1917, one hundred and five million Armenians, unable to defend themselves, were rounded up and exterminated.

- ➢ In 1929, the Soviet Union established national gun controls: From 1929 to 1953, about twenty million dissidents, unable to defend themselves, were rounded up and exterminated.

➤ China established national gun control in 1935: From 1948 to 1952, twenty million political dissidents, unable to defend themselves, were rounded up and exterminated.

➤ Germany established national gun controls in 1938: From 1939 to 1945, a total of thirteen million Jews who were unable to defend themselves were rounded up and exterminated.

➤ Cambodia established gun control in 1956: From 1975 to 1977, one million educated people, unable to defend themselves, were rounded up and exterminated.

➤ Guatemala established national gun controls in 1964: From 1964 to 1981, one hundred thousand Mayan Indians, unable to defend themselves, were rounded up and exterminated.

➤ Uganda established national gun control in 1970: From 1971 to 1979, three hundred thousand Christians, unable to defend themselves, were rounded up and exterminated.

➤ Fifty-six million defenseless people have been rounded up and exterminated in the 20th Century because of gun control laws within their countries.

You will not see this data on the evening news or hear politicians disseminating this information. Firearms in the hands of honest citizens save lives and property. Firearm control laws adversely affect only law-abiding citizens. With firearms, we are 'citizens'; without them, we are 'subjects'. During WW II, the Japanese decided not to invade America because they knew most Americans were ARMED! Firearm owners in the United States are the largest armed forces in the World. Remember, the purpose of fighting is to win. There is no possible victory in defense.

The sword is more important than the shield, and skill is more important than either.

The Switzerland government issues a gun to every household in their country and provides firearm training to every adult in the country. Switzerland has the lowest gun-related crime rate of any civilized country in the world. This is the model America should be following. We must not ever allow the government, at any level, to waste millions of our tax dollars in an effort to make all law-abiding citizens easy targets for the criminals that they, the Marxist-Communist Democrat Party, allow to roam our streets looking for a victim nor to protect ourselves against a tyrannical government. Americans must always support and protect the Second Amendment to the Constitution for the sake of our lives and our loved ones and to defend our Constitutional Republic from those who would destroy it.

On June 25th, 2024, the Supreme Court avoided taking up a series of new cases about the scope of the right to bear arms and left in place an Illinois law that bans assault-style weapons such as the AR-15 semiautomatic rifle, which has been used in various high-profile mass shootings.

The decision not to hear the multiple cases challenging the Illinois law means it remains in effect. Litigation over the Illinois ban, and similar laws enacted by other states continues, and the issue is likely to return to the justices.

Source & Additional Information: (https://www.nbcnews.com/politics/supreme-court/supreme-court-illinois-assault-weapons-ban-right-to-bear-arms-rcna153971)

Meanwhile, the court sent several other gun cases back to lower courts for further review in light of its recent ruling that upheld a federal law that prevents people accused of domestic abuse from possessing firearms. In doing so, the court sidestepped adding a new gun case to its docket for the following term, which begins in October.

The court has strongly backed the right to bear arms under the Constitution's Second Amendment, including in a significant ruling in 2022. However, the recent ruling indicated that some long-standing laws can still survive. The 2022 decision led to new challenges to existing gun restrictions.

There should be NO legal reason why the Supreme Court ruling should have been limited "... shall not be infringed" is an obvious and powerful argument. It is a no-brainer!

Source & Additional Information: (https://www.nbcnews.com/politics/supreme-court/supreme-court-illinois-assault-weapons-ban-right-to-bear-arms-rcna153971)

Second and Fourth Amendment Violations: The federal government is already using Americans' income and firearm purchases to conduct warrantless tracking of American citizens. The Bureau of Alcohol, Tobacco, Firearms, and Explosives provides individual salaries to the FBI to justify monitoring people's firearms purchases. The monitoring of individuals who purchase firearms, who have committed no crime or made any known threats, is an action only taken in third-world Stalinist regimes.

Knowledge of these unconstitutional actions was revealed in hundreds of pages of documents obtained by The Epoch Times as a result of their Freedom of Information Act (FOIA) lawsuit. These documents verified that the Bureau of Alcohol, Tobacco, and Firearms agents were requesting warrantless surveillance requests from the FBI, justifying their request based on a firearm purchaser's low salary, past firearm purchases, or the sending of strange messages over social media.

The FBI is secretly monitoring firearm purchasers using the warrantless surveillance authority issued to the Bureau of Alcohol, Tobacco, and Firearms. Firearm purchaser's information is being obtained from the FBI's National Instant Criminal Background Check System by the Bureau of Alcohol, Tobacco, Firearms to investigate a prohibited person's attempt to purchase a firearm based on a firearm background check on that individual and the National Instant Criminal Background Check System's denial of the purchase. Studies indicate that ninety-five percent of firearm purchase denials by the National Instant Criminal Background Check were inaccurate. The National Instant Criminal Background Check System is incapable of keeping firearms out of the hands of criminals.

Examples of violations of the Second and Fourth Amendments include but is not limited to:

- An Arizona citizen was placed under the National Instant Criminal's daily monitoring because he had a reported income of only $2,839. The Bureau of Alcohol, Tobacco, and Firearms agent who requested warrantless surveillance authority justified the request by stating that, in the agent's experience, someone with this amount of income could not afford twenty firearms.

- An Asian man in Texas was put on the background check list because the Bureau of Alcohol, Tobacco, and Firearms agent said the firearm purchaser had no work history, which could indicate that he was purchasing the weapon for a third party.

- A special agent in Kansas emailed the Bureau of Alcohol, Tobacco, and Firearms liaison to utilize the National Instant Criminal Background Check System to flag two purchasers for potential trafficking. The agent justified his request by stating that his targets were purchasing an abundance of firearms without any known financial means to obtain the firearms. An FBI's National Instant Criminal Background Check System expert instructed the agent in Kansas on what to include in his request to ensure approval for tracking the alleged suspects. The so-called expert's instructions included suggesting to the agent that he address the buyer's lack of income rather than the buyer's expenditures. The Bureau of Alcohol, Tobacco, Firearms agent emailed the requesting agent the incomes for each man, which they acquired from the Kansas Department of Labor.

- A Florida man was monitored daily by the FBI in 2020 because a Bureau of Alcohol, Tobacco, Firearms agent wrote: "Based on my training and experience, I have not seen a legal firearms purchaser purchase approximately thirty firearms in a hundred- and twenty-day window for their personal collection." Licensed firearms dealers must report to the Bureau of Alcohol, Tobacco, and Firearms the sale of two or more handguns to the same purchaser within five consecutive business days. However, no federal law or constitutional language limits the number of firearms a person can purchase within any period.

- A Wisconsin man was put under surveillance in 2020 because a Bureau of Alcohol, Tobacco, and Firearms agent saw text messages related to buying and selling firearms and suspected the individual in question was dealing without a license. The agent said the man bought guns from the website Gunbroker.com, transferred them through a local gun store, and then resold the firearms using email, text messaging, and the website Armslist.com. There was unredacted information that disclosed the number of guns the suspect bought and sold.

- A Missouri man was put into the National Instant Criminal Background Check System after a Bureau of Alcohol, Tobacco, Firearms agent emailed that a U.S. Attorney's Office asked that they monitor his activity due to recent bizarre messages he had been leaving. The agent wrote that the man had recently been released from the Bureau of Prisons and had begun making bizarre comments toward the U.S. Attorney's Office, federal judge, and the Bureau of Alcohol, Tobacco, Firearms case agent. The completed form does not indicate the man had committed any felony, which means that he would have already been in the National Instant Criminal Background Check System and prevented from buying a firearm at the point of sale. Sending bizarre messages does not make anyone lose their Second Amendment rights. This action by the Bureau of Alcohol, Tobacco, and Firearms is a blatant misuse of the background check system.

> A Hispanic woman in Texas was put into the National Instant Criminal Background Check System because an agent got an anonymous tip indicating that she had purchased ten firearms in the last two weeks. The agent wrote that the investigation was incomplete because it did not have the background check forms from the dealer nor video footage from the store.

There were no instances of the FBI denying any Bureau of Alcohol, Tobacco, Firearms request to put a person under warrantless surveillance in all the documents released to the Epoch Times. The Bureau of Alcohol, Tobacco, and Firearms headquarters denied the Epoch Times' request to disclose how they acquired suspects' incomes, employment information, and past firearm purchases. The Bureau of Alcohol, Tobacco, Firearms' spokesman Erik Longnecker told The Epoch Times: "We are unable to discuss specific techniques utilized in criminal investigations," stating that the "Bureau of Alcohol, Tobacco, Firearms utilizes a multitude of legal means in our criminal investigations to protect our communities from violent gun crime."

The FBI and the Bureau of Alcohol, Tobacco, Firearms are unconstitutional agencies that are consistently violating American citizens' Fourth Amendment rights, which state, "The right of the people to be secure in their persons, houses, papers, and effects, against unreasonable searches and seizures, shall not be violated, and no Warrants shall be issue, but upon probable cause, supported by Oath or affirmation, and particularly describing the place to be searched, and persons or things to be sized." The FBI and the Bureau of Alcohol, Tobacco, and Firearms are attempting to restrict citizen's rights under the Second Amendment. Both of these agencies are unconstitutional entities of the federal government and need to be abolished as such.

Section IV: Federal Bureau of Investigation (FBI)

According to its mission statement, the FBI is a national security and law enforcement agency that serves under the auspices of the DOJ. The Agency collects, uses, and shares intelligence with other Federal Departments and Agencies. As the only member of the United States Intelligence community with broad authority over criminal and terrorist acts on United States soil, the FBI has a sworn duty to protect all Americans by staying ahead of national security threats to the homeland, such as concerned parents and anti-abortion proponents. The FBI's mission is to uphold the Constitution and protect the American people, which is a tenant lost under the Marxist-Communist regime. The Director of the FBI receives an annual salary of $201,300 for being corrupt and leading America's version of the KGB.

The current Director of the FBI, Christopher Wray, is a career member of the Washington swamp and a lapdog of the Marxist-Communist movement. Wray's activities of carrying out acts of unconstitutional intimidation and harassment on American citizens know no bounds. The FBI is now the American version of the Russian KGB. John Durham's recently released report accuses the FBI of applying a double standard in its investigation of ties between Russia and Donald Trump's 2016 presidential campaign compared to its treatment of similar claims regarding foreign influence on Hillary Clinton's campaign or Stacey Abrams, who, to this day still claims she is the ligament governor of Georgia. Exactly what one would expect of the Russian KGB: crush your opponent with unfounded accusations, thus distracting the opposition to focus on defending themselves, causing the individual and their campaign to expend excessive amounts of time and money for legal processes.

John Durham's report severely criticizes the FBI's handling of the Trump-Russia probe, highlighting significant flaws involving ignoring the FBI's policies and procedures when executing an investigation. However, despite the lengthy investigation into the origins of the probe, Durham's report resulted in minimal criminal charges against the leadership of America's KGB thugs. After a four-year investigation, Durham only recommended filing charges against three minor FBI managers. Two of those employees were acquitted by juries, and the third pleaded guilty but avoided prison time. There are no recommended charges against any FBI senior leadership who were the individuals involved in the Russian-Trump collusion accusations.

Durham's report raised concerns about inconsistent investigation treatment of the Trump and Clinton campaigns by the FBI. Durham's report further brings attention to alleged efforts by foreign entities to influence Clinton's campaign through campaign donations, noting that the Clinton campaign was informed about some of these activities. Trump and his associates were never briefed regarding the FBI's suspicions regarding his campaign. The report does not propose major changes to the existing guidelines and policies of the DOJ or the FBI. Instead, it recommends assigning an official responsible for scrutinizing politically sensitive investigations. The bottom line is that there are no fundamental changes to the management of the Bureau or accountability of those who instigated and pushed the Russian hoax; they add more bureaucrats and expense to our bloated government. The Marxist-Communist Democrat Party has been given the green light to continue the status quo. No accountability equals no change.

Source & Additional Information: (https://en.wikisource.org/wiki/File:Durham_Report.pdf)

Wiretapping: Who can forget the extent the Marxist-Communist Party was willing to go to eliminate Donald Trump from the 2016 presidential elections? The Marxist-Communist Party illegally wiretapped the campaign office of Donald J. Trump, a candidate running for the office of the President of the United States. Wiretapping continued even after Donald Trump won the election. The wiretapping was not only conducted on Donald Trump but extended to members of Trump's campaign team. The Marxist-Communist Democrat Party hoped that they might find dirty laundry on Trump, which they could then use to force Donald Trump out of the 2016 elections.

With the win of non-political outsider Donald Trump in 2016, the Marxist-Communist Democrat Party went into melt-down mode, with Hillary Clinton and the Marxist-Communist Democrat Party making accusations that Trump had won through fraud and election interference by Russia. To prove their allegations against Trump, the Clinton Campaign and the Democrat National Conference authorized and paid for the creation of the "Steele dossier" by Christopher Steele. The dossier contained allegations that the Trump 2016 presidential campaign had connections with the Kremlin, including accusations of scandalous sexual activity between Donald Trump and Moscow prostitutes at the Moscow Ritz-Carlton. Steele's dossier alleged that these alleged sexual activities occurred while Donald Trump was staying in the "Presidential Suite" of the Moscow Ritz-Carlton. The problem is that there is no recorded evidence that Trump ever stayed at the Moscow Ritz-Carlton, nor does the Ritz Carlton website indicate that there is even a 'Presidential Suite' at their hotel. The dossier also contains claims of alleged ties between Donald Trump and Russia's President Vladimir Putin and served as a part of the basis for the FBI to obtain a warrant against Carter Page under the Foreign Intelligence Surveillance Act.

Lies created, coordinated, and paid for by Hillary Clinton and the Democrat National Conference. Corrupt high-level

FBI leadership, FBI assets, and the Hillary Clinton campaign organization created the Russian collusion lie. All at the instruction of Hillary Clinton herself, and all were eventually confirmed to be false accusations in the Robert Mueller Investigation report. Illegal actions were committed by elements of Washington's corrupt Marxist-Communist Democrat bureaucracy and influential Washington elitists. To date, not a single Marxist-Communist Democrat involved has been held accountable, while Donald Trump faces criminal trial merely for questioning the results of the 2020 elections.

Information contained in the Steele dossier regarding the allegations of scandalous sexual encounters between Donald Trump and Moscow prostitution and alleged ties between Donald Trump and Russia's President Vladimir Putin was conveniently leaked by the FBI to numerous Marxist-Communist propaganda news arms of the Marxist-Communist Democrat Party. The FBI then turned around and cited the information published by these news and social media outlets, such as Yahoo, Mother Jones, the Washington Post, Huffington Post, CNN, and the New York Times, as part of their justification for wiretapping Trump and Page. Ex- FBI lawyer Kevin Clinesmith admitted falsifying a document (Email) that was used as part of the inquiry into alleged Russian interference with the 2016 presidential election. Kevin Clinesmith changed the email from another FBI official to suggest that President Trump's aide, Carter Page, had never been a Central Intelligence Agency "source." In contrast, Carter Page was, in fact, a Central Intelligence Agency informant. The document was cited to support the contention that there was "probable cause" to suspect Carter Page was "a known agent" of Russia.

Special Counsel Robert Mueller's investigation yielded no evidence of criminal conspiracy or coordination between the Trump campaign and Russian officials during the 2016 election. The now-declassified investigation report further revealed that the

FBI knowingly had no collaboration of the claims included in the dossier.

Source & Additional Information: (https://www.nytimes.com/interactive/2019/03/20/us/politics/mueller-investigation-people-events.html)

Joe "The Big Guy" Biden Scandal: In late April of 2023, it was revealed that an FBI whistleblower made a legally protected disclosure to the office of Republican Senator Charles Grassley of Iowa. That disclosure claimed that the FBI held in its possession an FD-2023 form that alleges then-Vice President Biden and a foreign national's, most probably Ukrainian, involvement in an exchange of money for policy decisions favorable to that country. This patriotic American whistleblower risked his career to bring this information to Senator Grassley. An FD-1023 is an FBI document that documents meetings or information gathered from confidential sources. On May 3rd, 2023, the House Oversight and Accountability Committee subpoenaed the unclassified FD-2023 form from the FBI. Questions that need answering before the House Oversight and Accountably Committee include: why wasn't there any action to investigate this accusation, and why did the FBI brush this serious allegation under the rug as they had done with the Hunter Biden laptop? What is unclear is what government foreign policy was allegedly changed and when.

On May 11th, 2023, the FBI formally refused to honor the subpoena from Congress regarding the FD-2023 Biden-related corruption document. They claimed that Congress, which has constitutional oversight authority over the agency and funding them, 'has no right to see these documents.' In other words, the FBI is its own law and is not accountable to the United States Constitution, laws, or the American citizens they were established to protect. The House Oversight Committee has a confirmed case with witnesses and massive bank records showing the Biden cartel took bribes for favors from foreign nationals: Quid Pro Quo and Pay for Play. If the bribery allegation in the FBI form FD-1023 is proven to be accurate, Biden's actions would certainly meet the standard for a treason charge calling for his impeachment and incarceration. The Biden cartel business schemes with foreign entities were discovered in suspicious activity reports obtained from the Treasury Department by the House Oversight Panel. It is becoming abundantly clear that the Biden cartel is using Joe Biden's position of power to personally profit from treasonous activities involving the Chinese Communist Party, Ukraine, Russia, Romania, as well as other foreign countries.

For years, Republican lawmakers have alleged that President Joe Biden and his extended family were using his political positions for personal and financial gain. While various connections have been made over the years, Republicans lacked convincing concrete evidence to prove their point. However, after a few months of investigation, House Oversight and Accountability Republican Chairman James Comer of Kentucky announced they had established "a pattern of influence peddling" within the presidential family. On May 10th, 2023, Comer spoke at a press conference about his committee's ongoing investigation, highlighting how he and his associates have seen documents that show a minimum of $10 million moving from foreign nationals to multiple shadow companies owned and controlled by the Bidens. Comer alleged that the family "took steps to hide payments they received" through the elaborate creation of multiple shell companies used to launder the money before it was deposited into the Biden accounts. These payments were made to various Biden family members, including his grandchildren, nieces, and nephews. Money linked to Ukraine, Romania, Russia, and the Chinese Communist Party. This latest development proves what many Americans already know: Joe Biden has never had the best interest of the American people in mind; in fact, he has been exploiting us for his own and his family's financial interests since his first day as an elected official. It was reported on March 13th, 2023, that the amount the Biden cartel received from Ukraine was $10 million, five million to Hunter and five million to the

"Big Guy." Bank transactions from the Department of Treasury now indicate that the Biden family racked in well over $30 million from China, Ukraine, Romania, and Russia. As evidence continues to flow in, the estimated amount of money the Bidens extorted may be around $50 million. Transfers of large amounts of money have been supported by the Department of Treasury's filing of one hundred and seventy 'suspicious activity' financial transactions passing through United States banks.

Source & Additional Information: (https://www.washingtontimes.com/news/2023/may/18/house-probe-digs-more-foreign-deals-suggest-joe-bi/)

This is "The Big One," involving "The Big Guy," and the Marxist-Communist Democrat Party, along with their propaganda arm, the mainstream media, which will do anything to suppress this fact.

On July 20th, 2023, Iowa Republican Senator Chuck Grassley released the FBI-generated FD-1023 describing an alleged criminal scheme involving then-Vice President Joe Biden and a Ukrainian business executive. Grassley acquired the FD-1023 via legally protected disclosures by Justice Department whistleblowers. "For the better part of a year, I have been pushing the Justice Department and FBI to provide details on its handling of very significant allegations from a trusted FBI informant implicating then-Vice President Biden in a criminal bribery scheme. While the FBI sought to obfuscate and redact, the American people can now read this document for themselves, without the filter of politicians or bureaucrats, thanks to brave and heroic whistleblowers. What did the Injustice Department and FBI do with the detailed information in the document, and why have they tried to conceal it from Congress and the American people for so long? The Injustice Department and FBI have failed to come clean, but Chairman Comer and I intend to find out," Grassley stated.

Source & Additional Information: (https://www.grassley.senate.gov/news/news-releases/grassley-obtains-and-releases-fbi-record-alleging-vp-biden-foreign-bribery-scheme)

The FBI's Biden Bribery Record is closely tracked by the evidence uncovered by the Oversight Committee's Biden family influence-peddling investigation. In the FBI's record, the Burisma executive claims he did not pay 'the big guy' directly but used several bank accounts to conceal the money. That sounds an awful lot like how the Bidens conduct business: using multiple bank accounts to hide the source and total amount of the money," House Committee on Oversight and Accountability Chairman James Comer stated. "At our hearing with Internal Revenue Service whistleblowers, they testified that they had never seen or heard of this record during the Biden criminal investigation, despite having potentially corroborating evidence. Given the misconduct and politicization at the Department of Justice, the American people must be able to read this record for themselves. I thank Senator Grassley for providing much-needed transparency to the American people. We must hold the Department of Justice accountable for seeking to bury this record to protect the Bidens."

Grassley first disclosed the FBI's possession of significant and voluminous evidence of potential criminality involving the Biden family in 2022. He has since worked to unearth the FBI record, eventually partnering with Comer on a subpoena to compel its public disclosure. After delays, the FBI provided a highly redacted version of the document to select members of the House of Representatives. Still, it remained shielded from the public and omitted key details, including references to recordings. Following the FBI's failure to comply with the congressional subpoena fully, Grassley received the legally protected disclosure with limited redactions to protect a trusted FBI source, handling agents, department whistleblowers, and identifiers related to other ongoing investigations.

Source & Additional Information: (https://www.bbc.co.uk/news/world-us-canada-66272217)

According to the FBI's confidential human source, executives for Burisma, a Ukrainian gas company, brought Hunter Biden on the board to "protect us through his dad, from all kinds of problems." At the time, Burisma sought to do business in the United States but was facing a corruption investigation in Ukraine led by then-Ukraine Prosecutor General Viktor Shokin. Regarding that investigation's impact on its ambitions in North America, Burisma CEO Mykola Zlochevsky reportedly said, "Don't worry, Hunter will take care of all of those issues through his dad." Zlochevsky allegedly stated that he had to pay $5 million to Hunter Biden and $5 million to Joe Biden, an arrangement he described as 'poluchili,' which is Russian crime slang for being "forced or coerced to pay," according to the document.

<u>Source & Additional Information</u>: *(https://www.realclearpolitics.com/ video/2019/09/27/flashback_2018_joe_biden_brags_at_cfr_meeting_about_ withholding_aid_to_ukraine_to_force_firing_of_prosecutor.html)*

Zlochevsky claimed to have many text messages and recordings that show that he was coerced into paying the Bidens to ensure Shokin was fired. Specifically, he claimed to have two recordings with Joe Biden and fifteen with Hunter Biden. Zlochevsky also retained two documents, presumably financial records, as evidence of the arrangement but said he did not send any funds directly to "The Big Guy," a term he understood to reference Joe Biden. References to "The Big Guy" surfaced in communications involving other Biden family business arrangements independent of the Burisma arrangement. According to the document, Zlochevsky claimed it would take investigators ten years to uncover the illicit payments to the Bidens.

Harassment and Intimidation: Christopher Wray ordered the arrest of eleven former associates of former President Trump, at the direction of Attorney General Merrick Garland, on a variety of minor charges, all intended to intimidate and harass former associates and potential associates of President Trump. It could be argued that Director Wray was merely following the orders of the

Attorney General. However, how Director Wray chose to execute those arrests was atrocious, using extreme force and tactics by his FBI agents. Tactics included early morning raids on the homes of these individuals with numerous FBI agents in full tactical gear and armed with AR-15 rifles. Tactics more appropriately used in the arrest of violent criminals who have a high likelihood of resisting law enforcement or fleeing. These arrests were politically motivated and made in populated areas in clear view of the general public, including the handcuffing of individuals with no past criminal history, whose charges were non-violent, and who posed no imminent danger to the arresting agents or the general public. All for optical and propaganda purposes on behalf of the Marxist-Communist Democrat Party.

A prime example of the FBI's use of potentially deadly force came at 7 a.m. on Friday, September 23rd, 2022 when Mark and Ryan-Marie Houck's home was raided by approximately fifteen FBI agents in full tactical gear with guns drawn and pointed at them and their children. Attorney General Garland had ordered the arrest of Mark Houck on charges of violating the Freedom of Access to Clinic Entrances Act. Mark rightfully believes that President Joe Biden's Justice Department politically targeted his arrest to intimidate, silence, and scare his family for their pro-life work and praying outside abortion clinics for the women headed inside to abort their unborn babies. Is it possible that highly trained FBI agents deemed praying with your wife and young children outside a building as violent and life-threatening to them or the general public? Mark pleaded not guilty to the federal charges. His legal team argued that the DOJ violated the Constitution by engaging in "viewpoint discrimination" and "selective prosecution," violating the Religious Freedom Restoration Act and the First Amendment's protection of the free exercise of religion and speech. This is but one example out of countless incidents of a run-away justice system acting on the orders and behalf of Joe Biden and his Marxist-Communist Democrat Party.

Source & Additional Information: (https://www.foxnews.com/media/children-pro-life-activist-arrested-fbi-raid-home-traumatized-wife-says-crying)

Catholics: The FBI received instructions from the DOJ to target Catholics as a hate group. This allegation was based on a document obtained by the DOJ from the Southern Poverty Law Center, titled "Interest of Racially or Ethnically Motivated Violent Extremists in Radical Traditionalist Catholic Ideology Almost Certainly Presents New Mitigation Opportunities." The DOJ's decision to take this unprecedented action was based on the information found in the document received from the Southern Poverty Law Center, an organization notorious for smearing mainstream conservative and Christian nonprofits and depicting Catholics as a "hate group." The Southern Poverty Law Center's document state that there was common ground between "ethnically motivated violent extremists" and "radical-traditionalist Catholics" because of Catholic's extreme opinions on "legislation or judicial decisions in areas such as abortion rights, immigration, affirmative action, and LGBTQ protections."

The DOJ's memo requested that the FBI monitor these Catholics through "the development of sources with access to Catholics," including "places of worship." It presented a list of "hate groups" published by the Southern Poverty Law Center as a place to start this work. As a result of the memo, the FBI attempted to smear conservative Catholics as white supremacists and anti-Semites. It is slander with no facts. The FBI Investigation calls Catholics who prefer the Latin mass "Radical Traditionalist Catholics" a danger to society. What exactly is radical or dangerous about a Latin catholic mass? Do these government agencies fear Latin Mass because they do not understand the language? If this is such a concern, then learn to speak Latin and attend a Latin Mass to articulate what they heard that made Latin mass so radical and dangerous. But of course, doing so would eliminate their narrative and show the FBI to be nothing more than the armed KGB and secret police of the Marxist-Communist Democrat Party. Sadly, besides being the Marxist-Communist Democrat

Party's goon squad, the FBI is a modern-day Catholic-hating arm of satin, with their satanic robes secretly stored in their closets.

Source & Additional Information: (https://www.newsweek.com/fbi-memo-catholics-radical-traditional-leaked-1780379)

Out of Control Crime: District attorneys in all of our major cities falsely claim that crime is caused by poverty, wealth inequality, and inadequate government spending on social programs. They refer to prostitution, open drug use, and drug dealing as "victimless crimes" and refuse to prosecute individuals involved in these crimes. The result has been a dramatic increase in crime so sharp that those residents who can afford to do so are now paying for private security guards, taking self-defense classes, or purchasing firearms and obtaining concealed carry permits. Retailers like Walmart, Walgreens, and Target are closing stores throughout America's crime-ridden Marxist-Communist Democrat-governed metropolitan cities, citing rampant shoplifting as their reason for leaving. Whole Foods closed its store in San Francisco after being open for only one year. Rampant crime, shoplifting, drug addiction, homelessness, and inability to ensure employee safety led to the decision. The radical Marxist-Communist Democrat Party is now attacking Whole Foods for creating a 'food desert' by their departure when it is the city's Marxist-Communist Democrat Party leadership's failure to maintain a safe environment for their customers and workers that led to the closure. Walmart just recently closed four stores in Chicago. These stores lose tens of millions of dollars yearly to out-of-control shoplifting and lack of employee safety. It is only going to get worse with Chicago's new criminal-loving mayor. Every week, shockingly organized mobs of teenage looters ransack stores. This crime pandemic is crippling tourism and the willingness of area residents to go out to shop and are instead turning to the internet to do their shopping.

Car break-ins and shoplifting are both out of control in America. Car break-ins were 75% higher in May 2021 than in May 2019.

This rise in street crime is directly related to Soros-funded District Attorneys who refuse to prosecute these criminals. In 2019, 40% of all shoplifting resulted in arrest; in 2021, only 19% were arrested and charged; however, most of these criminals were given minor or no bail requirements and were back on the street, committing the same crimes within hours. Walgreens has stated that shoplifting is five times as high, and security costs are fifty times higher in its stores in large metropolitan areas based on their chainwide average. In the meantime, the charging rate for theft has declined from 62% in 2019 to 46% in 2021; for petty theft, it has fallen from 58% to 35%. More than half of all offenders, and three-quarters of the most violent ones, who are released on bail or released from jail before trial, commit new crimes. All the result of Soros-funded Marxist-Communist Democrat Party prosecutors who openly express great hostility toward the police. These Soros-funded District Attorneys are ignoring what they are referring to as quality-of-life crimes. Police Departments throughout the United States are dramatically short of officers, and those who remain on duty are very demoralized.

Source & Additional Information: (https://patriotfetch.com/2022/05/shocking-video-shoplifters-run-wild-in-this-left-run-city/)

The solution to our criminal problems is relatively straightforward. Arrest criminals and hold them accountable to the fullest extent of the law. Shut down the drug trafficking by closing down our open southern border and begin to become serious about arresting and deporting drug dealers who are here illegally; arrest addicts who camp and use drugs in full view of the general public and offer them rehab as an alternative to jail. The situation has degenerated to the point that an opportunity exists for conservative Republicans to wrest power away from the Marxist-Communist Democrat Party and implement a sweeping, common-sense political agenda to address these critical concerns of American citizens.

Need for Overhaul: The FBI, under the leadership of Christopher Wray and the Marxist-Communist Democrat Party, is no longer the proud arm of our justice system in which American citizens once took great pride. The upper echelon of this once great law enforcement institution has reduced the agency to nothing more than goose-stepping cronies of the Marxist-Communist Democrat Party movement in the United States. American citizens no longer have any faith or trust in the FBI. A recent poll revealed that 64% of Americans believe the FBI has been totally "weaponized" by the Marxist-Communist Democrat Party. One has to wonder, after all that has transpired over the last fifteen years involving unconstitutional political attacks and persecution by the FBI of those who do not espouse the Marxist-Communist Democrat Party ideology, if the 36% of Americans who do not believe the agency has been weaponized are brain dead or advocates of Marxist-Communist rule. Senior and mid-level leadership of the FBI are so corrupt and incompetent that they must immediately be fired. However, just firing and replacing these individuals will not change the toxic Marxist-Communist Democrat Party ideology that permeates throughout the FBI. To restore the integrity and honor of this once revered agency, the agency will need to be disbanded and rebuilt from the ground up. More appropriately, the FBI must be abolished as an unconstitutional entity, as every sovereign state can conduct its own investigations.

Source & Additional Information: (https://www.newsmax.com/newsfront/rasmussen-reports-poll-fbi/2023/03/10/id/1111859/)

Section V: Secretary of Defense

Lloyd J. Austin III is the 28th secretary of defense, sworn in on Jan. 22, 2021. A graduate of the U.S. Military Academy at West Point, N.Y., Austin served 41 years in uniform, retiring as a four-star Army general after three years as commander of U.S. Central Command.

The Chairman of the Joint Chief of Staff for the military is four-star General Charles Q. Brown, Jr., who has been the chairman of the Joint Chiefs of Staff since October 1, 2023. Brown has made the Air Force very woke and wants to do the same for all the other services. Specifically, *he wants to make white male officers a minority, and he has quotas in mind to accept transgenders* and other alternate lifestyle individuals into our military forces. This is reverse racism, and our military forces, which are already unready for any significant combat encounters, will cease to be an effective fighting force altogether. But it will be woke.

Internal documents obtained by the Daily Caller News Foundation include a slideshow from 2022 in which the Air Force outlines racial and gender quotas and details how it hopes to "achieve" a reduced number of white males in its Reserve Officers' Training Corps officer applicant program.

The documents reflect the Biden-Harris Pentagon's intense focus on implementing diversity, equity, and inclusion policies in the armed forces, even as the military continues to combat dwindling morale among its rank-and-file, recruitment and retention shortfalls, and low pay.

"The American people are rightly concerned that, at a time when our country is facing dangerous and increasing threats throughout the world, the Air Force is focused on recruitment efforts based on arbitrary racial diversity goals—not merit or increasing the force's lethality," James Fitzpatrick, director of the Center to Advance Security in America, told the Daily Caller News Foundation.

The Center to Advance Security in America requested records regarding the Air Force's new officer applicant standards through a federal transparency request in 2023. At the time, the Air Force said it couldn't find any records, according to a letter obtained by the Daily Caller News Foundation. The Center to Advance Security in America sued the Air Force for the records in April

2024 and received hundreds of documents and slides in response, which the Daily Caller News Foundation subsequently obtained.

Critical Race Theory: Success in combat depends on cohesion and competence, and critical race theory would destroy military personnel's ability to maintain these two crucial aptitudes. What would our military be like if our warriors were taught to assess their fellow warriors not on trustworthiness or capability but based on the color of their skin? Critical race theory makes race the prism through which all aspects of military life are viewed. It categorizes individuals into groups of oppressors and victims, and it is a philosophy that is undoubtedly going to create divisiveness within our military forces. Suppose these are the prisms under which our military functions, then America's ability to be combat-ready and continue its position as the greatest armed forces in the world is doomed. China, Russia, Iran, and North Korea would like nothing better.

As if our military forces have not been demoralized enough by wokism, our perverse senior leaders in the Pentagon have announced that the United States Navy has introduced a program using an enlisted sailor dressed as a drag queen to recruit sailors. The fingerprints of the Marxist-Communist Democrat Party are all over this embarrassing initiative. There seems to be no end to our Marxist-Communist Democrat Party's ability to make America the laughing stock of the world at every turn. At a time when all branches of our military, except for the Marine Corps, are failing to fill their recruitment quotas, the fools in the Pentagon have made military service even less attractive to young men and women. It is time for Secretary Austin to find new employment. These military leaders are intentionally destroying our military's ability to defend our country. Former Navy Seal Team Six member Robert O'Neill, the man who killed Bin Laden, said it best, "The Navy is now using an enlisted sailor drag queen as a recruiter. I am done. China is going to destroy us. I can't believe I fought for this bullshit." Few American service members who fought in combat would disagree with O'Neill.

Source & Additional Information: (https://www.scribd.com/document/770884913/ Production-1-in-CASA-Air-Force-Racial-Quotas-Lawsuit-1) (https://dailycaller. com/2024/02/13/exclusive-a-huge-blow-decline-in-white-recruits-fueling-the-militarys-worst-ever-recruiting-crisis-data-shows/) (https://www.scribd.com/ document/770884487/Fina-Response-to-FOIA2023-05851-F-signed-1-1)

Afghanistan: On August 18th, 2021, President Joe Biden promised America that if any United States citizens left in Afghanistan on August 31st, 2021, wanted to leave, "we're gonna stay to get them all out." But that is not what happened when the last United States soldier departed the country. Biden broke his most sacred responsibilities, protecting American citizens' lives. It was just another Marxist-Communist promise made and promise broken. But how many Americans were left behind? The White House puts the figure at one hundred to two hundred. Some suggest the figure is much closer to a thousand American citizens left at the mercy of the Taliban, who, unfortunately for those left behind, have no sense of mercy. During a House Foreign Affairs Committee hearing in March of 2023, Secretary of State Antony Blinken confirmed that there were still Americans being held captive by the Taliban in Afghanistan as a result of the United States military's withdrawal in August of 2021. Henceforth, American non-military citizen volunteers or contractors can no longer feel assured that the American government will do whatever is necessary to ensure that they are safely evacuated before American forces are withdrawn from hostile environments. We have a Marxist-Communist ruling class unwilling to compromise negotiations with foreign adversaries, even at the expense of non-military American citizen lives. Then there are the thousands of Afghanistan citizens who were left behind, who willingly risked horrific torture and death at the hands of the Taliban for cooperating with American forces. Left behind to face certain death.

The United States left behind approximately $85 billion of the world's most sophisticated military hardware. Around six-hundred and fifty thousand weapons, which consisted of three-hundred and fifty-thousand M4 and M16 rifles, sixty-five-thousand machine guns, twenty-five-thousand grenade launchers and two-thousand-five-hundred mortars and howitzers; seventy-five-thousand military vehicles, including fifty-thousand light and medium tactical vehicles, twenty-two-thousand Humvees and nine-hundred and twenty-eight mine-resistant vehicles; one-hundred and ten Black Hawk helicopters, costing $21 million each; twenty A-29 Super Tucano attack aircraft, worth $21.3 million each; and seven C-208 light attack airplanes, each costing $12.1 million; six Aerostat surveillance balloons, each costing taxpayers $8.9 million; eight ScanEagle drones, each costing $1.4 million; and more than sixteen-thousand-night vision devices costing $80 million in total.

Source & Additional Information: (https://townhall.com/tipsheet/ leahbarkoukis/2021/08/25/banks-taliban-now-has-more-black-hawk-helicopters-than-85-of-the-countries-in-the-world-n2594702) (https://thefederalist.com/2021/08/27/the-taliban-now-has-85-billion-worth-of-taxpayer-funded-us-military-equipment/)(https:// www.nbcnews.com/news/world/taliban-parade-new-weapons-seized-afghan-military-u-s-withdraws-n1273081)

Most sobering, on August 26th of 2021, the Biden retreat tactics led to a suicide bombing at Hamid Karzai International Airport, killing eleven Marines, one Army paratrooper, one Navy Corpsman, upwards of seventy Afghan citizens, and hundreds of severely wounded Americans and Afghans. These military heroes died due to the dereliction of duty on the parts of our Commander-in-Chief Joe Biden, Secretary of Defense Lloyd J. Austin, and Chairman of the Joint Chiefs of Staff General Mark Milley, for their botched tactical withdrawal strategy; and senior field commanders who denied a Marine Corps sniper's request to fire upon the individual he had in his sights carrying the bomb. Those American service members killed were:

- *Marine Corps Staff Sergeant Darin T. Hoover, 31, of Salt Lake City, Utah.*
- *Army Staff Sergeant Ryan C. Knauss 23, of Corryton, Tennessee.*
- *Marine Corps Sergeant Nicole L. Gee, 23, of Sacramento, California*
- *Marine Corps Sergeant Johanny Rosario Pichardo, 25, of Lawrence, Massachusetts*
- *Marine Corps Corporal Humberto A. Sanchez, 22, of Logansport, Indiana.*
- *Marine Corps Corporal Hunter Lopez, 22, of Indio, California*
- *Marine Corps Corporal Daegan W. Page, 23, of Omaha, Nebraska*
- *Marine Corps Lance Corporal David L. Espinoza, 20, of Rio Bravo, Texas*
- *Marine Corps Lance Corporal Jared M. Schmitz, 20, of St. Charles, Missouri*
- *Marine Corps Lance Corporal Rylee J. McCollum, 20, of Jackson, Wyoming.*
- *Marine Corps Lance Corporal Dylan R. Merola, 20, of Rancho Cucamonga, Calif.*
- *Marine Corps Lance Corporal Kareem M. Nikoui, 20, of Norco, California*
- *Navy Hospital Corpsman Maxton W. Soviak, 22, of Berlin Heights, Ohio*

Marxist-Communist Joe Biden promised the American citizens that there would be a 'peace dividend' from leaving Afghanistan. However, because of how the United States retreated from Afghanistan, there has been nor will there ever be any peace dividend. The Biden-Harris Administration left the world in a much more unsafe place because of their botched withdrawal. How the greatest fighting force in the world surrendered to some of the evilest men on earth is a black mark in the history of the United States of America that will be difficult, if not impossible, to undo. This surrender has emboldened other American adversaries, such as China, Russia, North Korea, and Iran, who no longer respect or fear our ability and willingness to fight back if necessary. In November of 2021, the Taliban showed the world the actual dividend obtained in America's retreat by holding a military parade, showcasing captured United States aircraft and helicopters, armored vehicles, and soldiers marching carrying American rifles.

This happens when the top military leadership, such as the Joint Chief of Staff members, are more concerned with woke ideology than in defeating our enemies or have no shame in retreating from the enemy. During WWII, a reporter complained to Mr. Dunn, a famous war correspondent in the South Pacific during World War II who covered General Douglas MacArthur for many years, stating that the general was an egomaniac, to which Mr. Dunn replied, "If you were going into combat, would you want to be led by a general with an inferiority complex?" That is where we are with today's military brass, with no courage to stand for what is right rather than caving in to an anti-military Marxist-Communist President such as Joe Biden.

<u>Anti-American Coalition</u>: Is America ready for war? Not even close due to Secretary Austin's and President Biden's indifference and neglect of our military forces' ability to face any foreign military force of significance. The Biden-Harris Administration has allowed wokism and unconstitutional mandates to deplete our military's ranks; they failed to modernize our military equipment, depleted our country's oil reserves necessary to operate our military equipment, and showed an inability or unwillingness to stand up to foreign adversaries diplomatically. Secretary of Defense Lloyd Austin failed to meet his obligation and responsibility to confront Biden and advise him about this fact, and, lacking Biden's willingness to correct his and his administration's anti-military attitude, he should have resigned in protest. With the building of coalitions between hostile anti-American governments, we have entered a period in our history wherein our allies are joining forces with our enemies or turning their backs on us.

French President Emmanuel Macron is cozying up to China while trashing France's oldest ally, the United States of America; there are active moves to discard the dollar as the global currency for the Chinese yuan; Japan and India are shrugging off America's request to boycotting Russian oil; the president of Brazil is traveling to China to pursue relationships; Israel is facing an increasing level of attacks by its enemies from all directions; Turkey is threatening fellow NATO member Greece; China is openly conducting military drills around Taiwan, threatening Taiwan with a forced takeover of their island and government; Saudi Arabia has entered into a new pact with Iran, its former archenemy; and Russia's President Putin talks nonstop about potentially using a tactical nuclear weapon against Ukraine. China is flying spy balloons over sensitive American military bases, and China and Russia are holding joint military training off the coasts of the Aleutian Islands. All signs that we are rapidly approaching World War III, which will lead to global devastation. All the while, the Biden-Harris Administration does nothing to prepare America's military forces, which are currently ill-prepared for this possible outcome. With the Biden-Harris Administration's show of weakness, even Mexican President Obrador openly bragged that millions of Mexicans have illegally entered the United States, and he is attempting to interfere in United States elections by urging his expatriates to vote for Democrats.

Why and how were a mentally impaired, confused, and incoherent President and his incompetent Administration able to facilitate such global chaos in just three-plus years? Under Biden-Harris's leadership, America has lost all international credibility and any ability to influence and stop hostile global moves; Biden-Harris has brought America and the world to global chaos as a result of his Administration's failed actions.

> ➢ In March 2021, at the Anchorage, Alaska mini-summit, Chinese diplomats unleashed a relentless barrage at their stunned and mostly silent American counterparts. They lectured the timid Biden-Harris administration diplomats about American toxicity and hypocrisy. And they have defiantly refused to explain why and how their virology lab birthed the COVID-19 virus that has killed tens of millions worldwide.

Source & Additional Information: (https://www.nbcnews.com/politics/politics-news/top-u-s-china-diplomats-have-public-spat-alaska-summit-n1261490)

> ➢ Abruptly pulling all American troops out of Afghanistan, leaving behind hundreds of Americans and thousands of pro-American Afghans who risked their lives to assist American military efforts in Afghanistan and the deaths of thirteen American military service members. Abandoned billions of dollars in the world's most advanced military equipment, the most extensive military air base in central Asia, and a $1 billion embassy. A debacle the Biden-Harris Administration has described as a proud and successful decision. The American citizens disagreed and saw only humiliation.

> ➢ The Biden-Harris administration allowed a Chinese high-altitude spy balloon to traverse the continental United States, spying on key American military installations. The Chinese were defiant when caught and offered no apologies. In response, the Pentagon and the administration lied about the extent to which China had surveilled top-secret sites.

Source & Additional Information: (https://www.nbcnews.com/news/investigations/secret-us-effort-track-hide-surveil-chinese-spy-balloon-rcna130991)

- In June 2021, in response to Russian cyberattacks against the United States, Biden meekly asked Russian President Vladimir Putin to at least make certain critical American infrastructure was off-limits.

- When asked what he would do if Russia invaded Ukraine, Biden replied that the reaction would depend on whether the Russians conducted a "minor incursion." Biden-Harris' weakness eventually led to the full invasion of Ukraine by Russian military forces.

- Between 2021 and 2022, Biden serially insulted and bragged that he would not meet Mohammed bin Salman, the de facto ruler of Saudi Arabia and one of our oldest and most valuable allies in the Middle East. As a result, Saudi Arabia has turned its back against the United States and is now working with Iran.

- For much of 2021, the Biden-Harris administration made it known that it was eager and ready to offer concessions to reenter the dangerous Iran nuclear deal at a time when Iran has joined China and Russia in a new geostrategic partnership.

- Almost immediately upon inauguration, the administration moved the United States away from Israel, restored financial aid to the radical Palestinians, and both publicly and privately alienated the Benjamin Netanyahu government.

- Serially, Biden-Harris stopped all construction on the border wall and opened our southern border to millions of illegal immigrants. During the 2019 Democratic presidential primary, Biden-Harris made it known that illegal immigrants were welcome to enter the United States without fear of being pursued and deported.

- ➤ Biden-Harris reinstated "catch and release." They did nothing about the Mexican cartel importation of fentanyl, which is killing over 100,000 Americans per year.
- ➤ Since Biden's inauguration, the Pentagon has embarked on a woke agenda. Our military forces cannot meet their annual recruitment quota, and the defense budget has not kept up with inflation. One of the most significant intelligence leaks in United States history occurred from the Pentagon.
- ➤ The Pentagon refused to admit culpability for misleading the country about Afghanistan and the Chinese spy balloon flight.

Is Armageddon on our doorstep? Now, we are being told that Iran is just weeks away from producing a nuclear weapon. Our dysfunctional Marxist-Communist Democrat Party government told us that they would never allow this to happen, yet here we are. It was just more lies from the swamp. It is time for the Israelis to do the job we do not have the courage to do.

Oil Reserves: Just before the 2022 mid-term elections, then-President Joe Biden attempted to buy votes by depleting our strategic oil reserves, which are held in reserve in case of war, at which time the need will be extreme. He did so to slightly bring down the fuel price and garner votes from individuals concerned about the gas price at the pump. He further attempted, on bended knees, to get OPEC not to reduce oil production until after the midterm election. In response, OPEC immediately reduced their oil production, causing the price of fuel to rise to historic levels. Attempted corruption, which backfired on Joe Biden.

Munitions: Since the start of the war between Russia and Ukraine, the United States has been providing Ukraine with the military weapons needed to oppose the Russian invasion. This includes ammunition for all the weapons of war being utilized in Ukraine. The level at which the United States has been providing ammunition to Ukraine has left the United States so critically short of ammunition that it would be implausible that the United States could fight any significant war. The Joint Chiefs of Staff Chairman has stated that our nation has a long way to go to replenish its sorely depleted stockpiles. To be sure, the Pentagon has taken steps to stop the depletion of ammunition by purchasing ammunition from other countries.

The Department of Defense has authorized the increase of ammunition production by five hundred percent. But even at five hundred percent, it will take at least eight years to bring the ammunition stockpile back to a level that would allow for American forces to be prepared for any major war. Given the recent and ongoing threats by China to invade Taiwan, with whom we have a negotiated treaty to defend, if we want to avoid World War III, we must have the munitions stockpile necessary to arm Taiwan to the teeth to ensure they are capable of repressing any military move by China. Not only does the United States immediately need to replenish its stockpile to support Taiwan, but that stockpile must also be more than sufficient for the United States to fight a war, especially given that China has been dramatically increasing spending on military initiatives for several years. An increase that the United States is failing to match and will not bode well should we be drawn into a war with China.

Leaked Military Classified Documents: How was it possible for a Massachusetts Air National Guard Airman First Class (E-3) to obtain top secret material, remove those documents from their storage site, leave the facility with those documents, and then spread them around the world via the internet? How did someone this far down the security chain, assuming that this individual even had a security clearance, obtain these sensitive classified documents? There are many pieces missing from this puzzle. Who gave these secret documents to this low-level enlisted man? It appears it was done intentionally to embarrass the Pentagon brass and harm the country. This is not some computer game. In the real world, leaking sensitive documents and information can get military and CIA personnel killed. Those old enough remember the WW II poster: LOOSE LIPS SINK SHIPS. Why did it take the FBI so long to find the leaker? This idiot traitor posted his photo on the internet along with the documents. Maybe the FBI was too busy hunting down Catholics and school parents to have noticed.

We had a compromised former Commander-in-Chief, an incompetent Secretary of Defense willing to order the teaching of divisive critical race theory to military personnel whose very lives depend on unity; who would surrender and fully retreat our military forces from enemy forces leading to the unnecessary deaths of military personal; who had no problem with abandoning American citizens behind enemy lines and the abandoning of foreign citizens who had willingly put their lives at risk to assist American forces and faced certain torture and death after our departure; who had no problem with surrendering billions of dollars of the worlds most sophisticated military weapons to our enemies; who were inept and committed to destroying our military forces readiness and strength through enforced wokeness upon our troops. Then we wonder why our young adults no longer see pride in serving in our armed forces.

And what does it say about our military forces when Pentagon brass openly cheered when they heard that FOX News media had fired conservative talk show host Tucker Carlson? Probably because these woke university-educated fools, who have all taken an oath to protect the Constitution of the United States, never got it in their minds that their oath includes the most important part of our Constitution, "freedom of speech." Tucker was not afraid to expose wasteful and corrupt spending by the Department of

Defense, the most wasteful department in the federal government. These fools must have felt threatened that Tucker Carlson would expose them as incompetent guardians of taxpayers' money.

Source & Additional Information: (https://wlos.com/news/nation-world/top-pentagon-officials-cheer-tucker-carlson-exit-from-fox-news-biden-administration-lloyd-austin-defense-secretary-military-army-navy)

As a retired four-star General, Secretary of Defense Lloyd J. Austin III and any member of the Joint Chief of Staff with any honor and integrity would have, upon receiving orders by a sitting President to implement any of the above immoral, cowardly, and incompetent orders, immediately resigned from their position in protest. Secretary of Defense Austin failed to do so, shaming the position he holds. It is evident that Secretary of Defense Lloyd J. Austin III chose to remain as Secretary of Defense out of ego and his place as a Washington elitist.

Section VI: Secretary of Treasury

The Secretary of the Treasury is responsible for formulating and recommending domestic and international financial, economic, and tax policies, formulating broad fiscal policies that have general significance for the economy, and managing public debt. The Department of the Treasury manages Federal finances by collecting taxes, paying bills, and managing currency, government accounts, and public debt. It also enforces finance and tax laws. The Secretary of the Treasury was Janet Yellen.

Debt Ceiling: After months of standoff between Speaker McCarthy and President Biden, a deal was finally reached on June 3rd, 2023, just days ahead of the Treasury Department's estimated date that the government would run out of money to pay its obligations. The disastrous agreement between these two individuals suspended the debt limit ceiling until early 2025, after the presidential election. It also locked in our non-defense spending for 2024 at 2023 levels before allowing a slight increase in 2025. This negotiated deal will add at least $4 trillion to America's already devasting $35 trillion national debt over the next two years without any substantial cuts to offset this increase in spending. Speaker McCarthy could have and should have held fast with the Republican's position that they would not agree to lifting or increasing the debt ceiling, which would have required the decrease in previously approved spending authorities provided in the $1.85 Trillion Omnibus spending bill passed in December of 2022. So, when it comes to outrageous spending by our government, it is business as usual. Political leaders in Washington have failed those they represent and our country by keeping spending levels at COVID-era levels, ignoring the fact that such spending is "unsustainable."

<u>Source & Additional Information</u>: *(https://www.nbcnews.com/politics/congress/biden-mccarthy-complete-debt-ceiling-agreement-sunday-jeffries-tells-d-rcna86191)*

Digital Currency: On March 9th, 2022, President Biden issued an executive order instructing all government agencies to form committees dedicated to researching the consequences should America shift our currency from paper currency to digital currency and to work towards creating a regulatory framework for digital crypto-asset markets. Digital currency will be a trackable monetary system providing the federal government with a new tool to track, monitor, and spy on the citizens of the United States. The Executive Order outlines a whole government approach to harnessing the potential benefits to the federal government of digital money and its inherent technology. The Order lays out a national policy for digital money across six key priorities which the Marxist-Communist Democrat Party wants American citizens to believe will be in their best interest: consumer and investor protection; financial stability; illicit finance; United States leadership in the global financial system, and economic competitiveness; financial inclusion; and responsible innovation. The digital currency will give the federal government direct access to all information regarding American citizens' income and spending habits. The federal government will then have all the information necessary to determine if an individual is failing to adhere to their Marxist-Communist doctrine should the Marxist-Communist Democrat Party remain in control after the 2024 elections. They will also have the ability to freeze or confiscate any monies held in banks if that individual were to oppose their Marxist-Communist Democrat Party's dictates.

Source & Additional Information: (https://www.reuters.com/business/finance/biden-orders-government-study-digital-dollar-other-cryptocurrency-risks-2022-03-09/)

The rise of crypto tokens sets the stage for a global whirlwind of racketeering. The marketing of thousands of ridiculous tokens backed by nothing more than white sheets of paper is only the most apparent problem with crypto tokens. Crypto tokens have given birth to many new schemes to defraud those who invest in them. Very often, the difference between a real business and a scam can get very blurry. This was the case with FTX, the crypto racket run by Sam Bankman-Fried. Thousands of American citizens suffer financial losses due to Bankman-Fried's scam. His company emerged out of nowhere to become the world's third-largest crypto exchange, promising to give all profits away to charity. It just so happens that the charities of his choice were connected with Marxist-Communist Democrat Party causes. Bankman-Fried and his brother had frequent meetings with top aides to Biden. In other words, there is every indication that the whole company was established as a money-laundering operation, all directed toward helping large donors get around campaign finance law to donate large sums of money to various Marxist-Communist Party candidates.

Source & Additional Information: (https://apnews.com/article/sam-bankman-fried-ftx-fraud-timeline-be13e3fc0e074e2edd50ba59d1f8960e)

The federal government will have full access to all the financial transaction information of every American citizen, furthering the implementation of President Obama's promise to forever fundamentally change America from a Constitutional Republic to a Marxist-Communist Nation. This transition to digital cryptocurrency will allow law enforcement to obtain seizure warrants for any transaction determined by the federal government to be illicit. Sounds like a good idea on the surface. Still, the problem is that in a Marxist-Communist dictatorship, which America is rapidly transforming into, this oppressive and controlling form of government will be in a position to confiscate the financial assets of any nonconforming American citizen. Sounds like life in China, Russia, and all the other failed Marxist-Communist countries.

Source & Additional Information: (https://www.forbes.com/sites/ nicksibilla/2022/10/25/biden-administration-wants-to-make-it-easier-to-seize-crypto-without-criminal-charges/)

Also of great concern is that today's banking system is being weaponized to enforce ideological agendas. Dissenters from prevailing beliefs on matters of politics, culture, and healthcare now risk having their accounts canceled for committing wrong thoughts. Former President Donald Trump had his Florida bank accounts closed after his disputed 2020 election defeat. Deutsche Bank also blacklisted him for political reasons. Democrat Robert F. Kennedy, Jr. has been censored on social media and had his non-profit organization threatened with bank account closures, apparently at the order of the Biden-Harris administration. Kennedy is charged with the thought crime of spreading vaccine misinformation. It does not matter that much of what the public was initially told about the COVID-19 vaccine by the CDC, the mainstream media, and President Biden himself, namely that the jab would prevent the acquirement and transmission of the disease, turned out to be misinformation. All that matters is that dissent from whatever the ideology happens to be at any given moment is grounds for being canceled.

Dissenter doctor Joseph Mercola recently had his bank accounts deactivated by JP Morgan Chase. Also recently, anti-globalist British politician and gold advocate Nigel Farage was blacklisted by his bank for having the wrong political beliefs. Farage warns that banks are beginning to work with credit bureaus to review customers' political speech as part of a de facto Chinese-style social credit system. These high-profile cases are the tip of the iceberg. Countless lesser-known individuals and businesses are being canceled by their banks for ideological reasons. In 2013, the Obama administration launched Operation Chokepoint to push banks to crack down on supposedly high-risk business clients. Operation Chokepoint specifically targeted gun dealers, payday lenders, coin shops, and other businesses with a high volume of cash transactions. The stated rationale was to combat fraud and money laundering.

The result was to set the stage for bureaucrats and bankers to determine which persons and businesses are socially desirable and which are not, which can have full access to the financial systems and which cannot. Now that the banking system has been politically weaponized, will money itself become a tool for authorities to wield against dissidents? It could be if the central bank's digital currency replaces all forms of cash. As part of the imposition of a digital dollar, the government could arbitrarily declare that paper cash may no longer be accepted as legal tender by banks or businesses. And since all digital transactions can be logged and monitored in real-time, they can also be instantly denied by the central bank issuer. Holding wealth outside the banking system and out of United States dollar-denominated assets is a must for anyone who seeks to become resilient to being financially canceled. The monetary value of physical precious metals does not change based on the political beliefs of the holder. Unlike a banknote, whose value is governed by its issuer, a gold coin has intrinsic value as determined by the free market. And unlike an account at a financial institution, physical precious metals are not cancelable.

Banking collapses: Silicon Valley Bank failed spectacularly and suddenly on March 10th, 2023, becoming the second largest bank to do so in our nation's history and triggering panic in our banking system. Just weeks later, Signature Bank failed in the same spectacular and sudden fashion as Silicon Valley Bank. Although virtually everyone now knows of Silicon Valley Bank's and Signature Bank's failure, not everyone understands exactly why they failed. Many have blamed the Banks' Environmental, Social, and Governance (ESG) policies or "stakeholder capitalism" for the banks' sudden collapse. Still, these are just symptoms of the bank's ongoing financial mismanagement in the face of catastrophic rate hikes rather than the underlying cause of the bank's downfall. These two bank failures highlight the immense risks facing our banking system. The Biden-Harris administration, Congress, and the Federal Reserve all equally share the blame for the bank's failure. The banks failed primarily because they mismanaged interest rates and duration risk by seeking yield through investments in high-duration, long-maturity assets.

Silicon Valley Bank and Signature Bank's failure will have impacts that will linger for years, indicating America is in a "vicious cycle" of decline. The collapse of these two banks has triggered a crisis of confidence in the United States banking sector, prompting financial authorities to rush through a rescue package to stem a potential run-on bank deposits that threatens broader financial instability. The Federal Deposit Insurance Corporation insures depositors at failed banks for up to $250,000. The Federal Deposit Insurance Corporation is an independent unconstitutional agency that Congress created to insure up to $250,000 of individuals' deposits. The vast majority of deposits at these two banks were held on behalf of multi-millionaires whose deposits exceeded well over the $250,000 limit, leaving these multi-millionaires with tremendous losses. It was intended that millionaires would take the necessary steps to protect and insure their deposits at their own expense, but few bought insurance to protect their deposits. To add insult to injury, bonuses were paid out to the employees just hours before the collapse of these two banks.

Biden assured the American people that the federal government would not bail these banks out and reassured the general public that the banking system in America is safe. Unfortunately, for the American taxpayers, Silicon Valley Bank, Signature Bank, and their depositors are hard-core Marxist-Communist Democrat Party supporters. In late March of 2023, the Treasury Department announced that an unconstitutional rescue plan would reimburse depositors the money these millionaires lost in excess of the $250,000 limit. Another federal government bailout at the expense of taxpayers who struggle paycheck to paycheck to reimburse millionaires who chose not to insure their investments. But this is to be expected by our Marxist-Communist Democrat government; after all, these are the individuals who donate heavily to the Marxist-Communist Democrat Party, and the Party cannot afford to see these millionaires' donations dry up. Having been saved by the Marxist-Communist Democrat Party, these millionaires will be indebted to the Party.

Some observers urged the Central Bank to pause its rate hikes, at least temporarily, to assess the fallout from the collapse of Silicon Valley Bank and Signature Bank to reduce stress in the banking system. Treasury Secretary Janet Yellen stated that large withdrawals from regional banks have "stabilized, and the banking system is sound and resilient."

Source & Additional Information: (https://apnews.com/article/yellen-banking-federal-reserve-silicon-valley-bank-dfd110d0b55d3284afaafc4677616b9e) (https://www.bankrate.com/banking/signature-bank-collapse/)

Yet another Marxist-Communist Democrat Party propaganda states that until inflation and our economy are brought under control, America's banking system will not be sound and resilient. Meanwhile, consumer prices continue to climb at a pace that American worker's wages cannot keep up with. Annual inflation in July of 2023 was 5.6%.

Fed chairman Jerome Powell told reporters during a news conference that the central bank is particularly concerned about the rising cost of consumer services, such as airline tickets and streaming TV subscriptions. He stated, "My colleagues and I are acutely aware that high inflation imposes significant hardship as it erodes purchasing power, especially for those least able to meet the higher cost of essentials like food, housing, and transportation." Does this sound like our banking system is sound and resilient?

The Fed is also facing inquiries about its failed oversight over increasing bank failures. Fed supervisors reportedly identified problems with Silicon Valley Bank's risk-management practices years ago. Still, the issues were not corrected, and the California lender had to be taken over by the federal government after suffering a massive bank run. "We need to have humility and conduct a careful and thorough review of how we supervised and regulated this firm," said Michael Barr, the Fed's vice chairman for supervision. The perfect Marxist-Communist Democrat Party response, which knows nothing of humility. A response that comes a little too late to garner any reassurances. When the fox is responsible for guarding the hen house, you can expect to see a dramatic decrease in the number of eggs to be collected. Marxist-Communist Democrat Senators Elizabeth Warren of Massachusetts and Republican Rick Scott of Florida have proposed replacing the Fed's internal inspector general with an outside inspector appointed by the president. It sounds like a great solution if the appointing president is a conservative. If the appointing president is a Marxist-Communist, you can expect no change to the outcome of the security of our banking system. Adequate and effective oversight does not lead to the chaos desired by Marxist-Communist Democrat regimes.

The failure of the Silicon Valley Bank and Signature Bank was probably music to the ears of the Marxist-Communist Democrat Party. After all, they are working so hard to destroy the American economy. Remember, you cannot have Marxist-Communism with a strong economy. Investing so heavily in GREEN energy and WOKE ideology does not work out very well for the average American consumer. Still, it goes a long way toward the Marxist-Communist's agenda of destroying American's buying power and savings accounts. These banks put politics over profits, and the citizens suffer the consequences. The banking industry in California is as incompetent as the rest of the Marxist-Communists in that state. Putting your money in the mattress seems like a good option right now.

The Feds will need to weigh the impact of the collapse of these regional lenders in deciding how much to raise interest rates in the future. Since the collapse of Silicon Valley Bank and Signature Bank, it has been learned that other un-named banks have or are expected to collapse. This situation is causing banks to become more conservative about making loans, leaving hard-working American citizens unable to obtain home loans or loans needed to cover small businesses' needs. The collapse of these banks will result in tighter credit conditions for households and companies and weigh on economic activity, hiring, and inflation. Secretary of Treasure Janet Yellen indicated that tighter credit conditions, such as rising interest rates, will lead to slower than projected economic growth. "Credit is the grease that makes small businesses' wheels run and makes the overall economy run," said Kathy Bostjancic, chief economist at Nationwide. If credit gets choked off, consumers will pull back on spending. That could assist the Fed in curbing inflation but also raise the risk of tipping the economy into recession. Still, Secretary Yellen insists that all is under control. Yellen sounds a lot like Secretary of Homeland Security Mayorkas and his continual insistence that the southern border is closed and secure.

Section VII: Internal Revenue Service

Danny Werfel serves as the 50th Commissioner of the Internal Revenue Service. As Commissioner, he presides over the nation's tax system, which collects approximately $4.1 trillion in tax revenue each year, representing about 96% of the total gross receipts of the United States. Commissioner Werfel oversees an agency of about 85,000 employees and an annual budget of over $12 billion. The Internal Revenue Service advertises itself as being one of the world's most efficient tax administrators, provides America's taxpayers with quality service by helping them understand and meet their tax responsibilities, and enforces tax laws with integrity and fairness to all. I guess that is why they need an additional 80,000 gun-carrying agents to assure their reputation as being efficient at gouging the American taxpayer and to increase the government's continuation of reckless and inappropriate spending. I am sure that every taxpayer will clearly understand their tax responsibilities and testify that they were impressed by the Internal Revenue Service's level of integrity and fairness when confronted by a tactical team of armed Internal Revenue Service agents at their front door.

Source & Additional Information: (https://openpayrolls.com/rank/highest-paid-employees/internal-revenue-service)

Just how many tax-paying American citizens do you think could be found in America who believe this propaganda? The Internal Revenue Service is the most heartless and inefficient organization in the Federal government. The federal government's Internal Revenue Service has created the world's most complex and incomprehensible tax system. They unashamedly expect average working American citizens to understand, comprehend, and meet their tax obligations. America's tax codes and laws are so complex and extensive that not only is the taxpayer required to pay the taxes owed, but they must pay additional money to have a certified tax accountant prepare and complete the massive volumes of paperwork.

This federal government entity is perhaps the most feared of the federal government's agencies by the average American citizen. If they come knocking on your door or call you with a friendly invitation to visit with them, then you know you are in trouble before that meeting even starts. They will insist that their evaluation of your tax returns and the alleged problems or issues are accurate, which will result in the taxpayer being required to pay not only the additional amount due but also an additional penalty fee.

Speaking of billionaires, on March 18th, 2023, Biden felt the need to tweet how much billionaires paid in taxes on average, which he stated was 3% of their income, shelling out less annually than firefighters and school teachers. The president noted that the excessively rich should pay at least 25%, saying, "Look, I think you should be able to be a billionaire if you can earn it, but just pay your fair share. I think you ought to pay a minimum tax of 25%. It is about basic fairness." According to the Daily Mail, the president's tweet contradicted previous information from the White House in February of 2023, indicating that billionaires pay 8% in taxes annually. A Twitter fact-check citing the Tax Foundation as its source stated the average American tax rate for 2020 was 13.6%. It noted the wealthiest taxpayers paid a 25.99% rate, while the poorest only paid an average of 3.1%. The same source stated the highest-earning 8.8% of Americans paid 97.7% of the country's federal income taxes in 2020, meaning middle and low-income taxpayers only covered about 2.3% of the country's total. Elon Musk responded to Biden's lie regarding the tax rate imposed on billionaires by stating, "I paid 53% taxes on my Tesla stock options (40% Federal & 13% state), so I must be lifting the average! I also paid more income tax than anyone ever in the history of Earth for 2021 and will do that again in 2022."

Source & Additional Information: (https://www.politifact.com/factchecks/2024/jan/26/joe-biden/president-joe-biden-distorts-income-tax-rates-for/)

Gig Economy: On December 23rd, 2022, the Internal Revenue Service was set to implement a new tax category called "gig economy." The "gig economy" is an activity in which people earn income by providing on-demand goods, services, or work, often via an online platform. Due to extensive controversial feedback, the Internal Revenue Service placed a one-year moratorium on implementing the new "gig economy" reporting rule. On March 1st, 2023, Joe Biden's Internal Revenue Service issued a notice to "gig economy" service workers that they must now report income earned under this new tax category on their tax returns, "even if the income is from part-time, temporary, or side work; paid in any form, including cash, property, goods, or digital assets not reported on an information return form like a Form 1099-K, 1099-MISC, W-2, or other income statement." This new tax-reporting rule went into effect for the tax year 2023. This new tax on individuals who make no more than $30,000 to $50,000 per year was implemented under the authority of the American Rescue Plan, which was signed into law in early 2021. The American Rescue Plan Act of 2021 was a scam on the American people at a cost of $1.9 trillion under the guise of fighting the coronavirus. The American Rescue Plan package was sold as a means to facilitate the United States' recovery from the devastating economic and health effects of the COVID-19 pandemic but failed miserably to accomplish its intent. Joe Biden's American Rescue Plan Act provided no authority for the Internal Revenue Service to create a new tax category called the "gig economy." Nowhere in that Act is there any mention of the Internal Revenue Service, let alone providing them with authorization to change or introduce new tax requirements. This authority Constitutionally rests in the hands of the House of Representatives and they alone.

Source & Additional Information: (https://www.nerdwallet.com/article/finance/what-gig-workers-need-to-know-about-taxes)

Freelancers, Tips, and Contractors: If you are one of the millions of "gig economy" composed of freelancer or contractor workers, and you received payments totaling $600 or more from any one of your jobs during the tax year, the individual or company that paid you must now provide you with a Form 1099-NEC for nonemployee compensation. If you receive payments through online payment services such as PayPal, you will also receive a form 1099-K. Payers must send these forms to the

Internal Revenue Service to report their income. Individuals who work in restaurants, hotels, salons, and similar industries and regularly receive tips must now report these tips as income. Cash tips include those received directly from customers, electronically paid tips distributed to the employee by their employer, and tips received from other employees under any tip-sharing arrangement. All cash tips must be reported to the employer, who must include them on the employee's Form W-2, Wage and Tax Statement. "Noncash tips" are defined as items of value such as passes, tickets, or goods and commodities given to the employee must also be reported on tax returns. Tips not reported to an individual's employer must be reported separately on Form 4137, Social Security and Medicare Tax as Unreported Tip Income, so employees who fall into this category pay their share of the Social Security and Medicare tax owed on tips. Employees do not have to report tip amounts of less than $20 per month per employer. For more significant amounts, employees must report tips to the employer by the 10th of the month after receiving the tips.

<u>Source & Additional Information</u>: *(https://fairtax.org/articles/vp-kamala-harris-cast-tie-breaking-vote-to-let-irs-track-workers-tips-so-they-can-be-taxed) (https://www.irs.gov/pub/irs-prior/i1040sc--2021.pdf)*

Does anyone remember that one of the primary reasons the American colonies broke away from England was the exorbitant taxes they were required to pay to the English Crown, leaving them struggling to feed themselves and their families? Again, this is where we are for our lower-income earners, many of whom rely on tips to survive even under solid economic conditions, let alone during an ever-growing inflation environment.

Okay, so what happened to the Marxist-communist Democrat party's pledge not to raise taxes on anyone making less than $400,000 per year? Is this just another pathetic lie? Suppose the Marxist-communist Democrat party truly wanted to make taxes fair for everyone. In that case, the Internal Revenue Service must be dramatically reduced to a few thousand employees by eliminating the thousands upon thousands of tax codes and thousands of multiple-page tax return forms and replacing them with a one-page tax return form and one taxable tax percentage rate on every American citizen and business. Also necessary is the passage of an Amendment to the Constitution requiring that Congress manage its congressional responsibilities within a balanced budget limited to the revenue taken in.

Walmart Verses Federal Government: Today, Americans spend $36,000,000 at Walmart every hour of every day, which works out to $20,928 profit every minute; Walmart will sell more from January 1 to St. Patrick's Day (March 17th) than Target sells all year; is bigger than Home Depot, Kroger, Target, Sears, Costco, and K-Mart combined; employs 1.6 million people and is the world's largest private employer. Wal-Mart is the largest company in the history of the world. Wal-Mart sells more food than Kroger and Safeway combined and sells more food than any other store in the world, all of which they accomplished in only fifteen years. During 2022, over seven billion different purchasing experiences occurred at Wal-Mart stores. (Earth's population is approximately 6.5 billion.) Wal-Mart has approximately 3,900 stores in the United States, of which 1,906 are Super Centers; this is one thousand more than it had five years ago. Ninety percent of all Americans live within fifteen miles of a Wal-Mart.

Source & Additional Information: (https://www.snopes.com/fact-check/how-big-is-walmart/) (https://www.hbs.edu/ris/Publication Files/13-039 Nov 2012_612ce7e2-7f81-4eea-9126-3c0964f2be2f.pdf)

Maybe "We the People" should hire those who run Wal-Mart to fix our economic problems. All patriotic Americans should recognize this Wal-Mart success: Democrats, Republicans, and Independents, including every voting member of the House of Representatives and the United States Senate. Given the above information, it is time for Congress members to reconsider their performance record on behalf of the people. Consider, for instance, Congress' performance regarding the following federal departments and agencies:

- The United States Postal Service was established in 1775. Congress has had two hundred forty-six years to get it right, and it is still broken. A stamp costs $0.73, yet the postal service's reliability in getting mail and packages to you in a timely manner is poor.

- The Social Security Administration was established in 1935, giving Congress eighty-six years to get it right, but it is still broken and dysfunctional. This program is on the threshold of bankruptcy, yet Congress cannot find the courage to make critical amendments to ensure it remains solvent.

- Fannie Mae was established in 1938, giving Congress seventy-one years to get it right. However, they have yet to make Fannie Mae work in the manner it was intended. This program needs to be abolished as it is an unconstitutional failed venture.

- The War on Poverty Act was established in 1964. Congress has had fifty-seven years to correct this unconstitutional initiative but has failed miserably. Congress confiscates $1 trillion of your money each year to subsidize the War on Poverty Act, and they want more. The Act's intent has never been productive in meeting its purpose, yet Congress continues to waste money to support this unconstitutional initiative.

- Medicare and Medicaid were established in 1965. Congress has had fifty-six years to fix these two programs, yet they remain broken and overly costly to American taxpayers.

- Freddie Mac was established in 1970. Congress has had fifty-one years to fix this program, yet it remains broken.

> The Department of Energy was created in 1977 to lessen our dependence on foreign oil. It has ballooned to 16,000 employees and a budget of $24 billion annually. With Joe Biden's inauguration, we shut down all of our country's fossil fuel production capabilities, and we are now wholly dependent on the importation of energy fuel to meet our needs from hostile foreign governments. After forty-four years of trying to get it right, the Department of Energy is an abysmal failure and a hindrance.

Currently, inflation is at its highest level in forty years. Congress's ability to provide customer-friendly "government service" has failed in every aspect of serving the American citizen while overspending our tax dollars on failed programs and initiatives.

We provide aid to Haiti, Chile, Turkey, Afghanistan, Ukraine, and Pakistan. We are funding the world for climate change and keeping a failed NATO solvent. Our southern border is being invaded by illegal immigrants who are being lavished with free living expenses at high-end hotels. Meanwhile, we have the homeless without shelter, children going to bed hungry, the elderly going without 'needed' medicines, and the mentally ill going without treatment. The United States is spending billions of taxpayer dollars on foreign entities and illegal immigrants, while many of our retired senior citizens are living on sparse 'fixed incomes.' Imagine what life in the United States for all of our citizens would be like if our federal government provided "We the People" the same support they give to illegals and foreign countries.

Source & Additional Information: (https://nypost.com/2023/03/03/city-hall-spending-10m-a-day-on-housing-feeding-migrants/)

The Biden-Harris administration did send fifteen hundred troops to the border to help Border Patrol with the wave of the thousands of illegals crossing when Title 42 expired. However, by law, the military is forbidden from exercising any policing powers on American soil. This means that these additional troops were there for only one purpose: to push reams and reams of government-mandated paperwork that will be generated by the millions of illegal immigrants crossing our open borders to be released into our country.

Illegal immigrants now crossing our open border consist of young military-age Chinese who are potential saboteurs with orders to destroy our critical infrastructure in preparation for their eventual war against the United States. Republican Representative Mark Green of Tennessee, chairman of the House Homeland Security Committee, said at a June 14th, 2023, press conference that "a Border Patrol sector chief informed him that some of the Chinese migrants at the southern border have 'known ties to the Chinese People's Liberation Army.'" We have no idea who these people are, but China is likely using the same Russian template Russia used before Russia invaded Ukraine, which consisted of sending military personnel into Ukraine before Russia invaded Ukraine to sabotage key infrastructure components. Chinese illegal immigrants are highly likely on standby to do the same with the United States' critical infrastructure components just before China's move to the United States.

Once here, the military-age fighters can link up with China's agents already in place or Chinese diplomats for instructions. How many Chinese-trained military fighters have already illegally crossed our southern border and lost themselves within America's population is unknown.

Estimates are between five to ten thousand, but the actual number is probably closer to twenty or thirty thousand Chinese "shock" troops. These Chinese "shock" troops, on the opening days of war with China, will take down America's power lines, poison water reservoirs, assassinate government and military officials, start wildfires, spread pathogens, and create terror by bombing shopping malls and supermarkets.

Given all the above harsh realities, a sizable portion of America's population still believes it can trust the federal government to manage our country's federal institutions cost-effectively while doing so with honor and integrity. These uninformed Americans have been brainwashed by corrupt career politicians and "Political Correctness."

Weaponization: The Internal Revenue Service has been weaponized against American citizens since the Obama Administration to target any conservative movement or organizations that oppose the Marxist-Communist movement to take over our Constitutional Republic. Tax-exempt conservative organizations have their tax exemption withdrawn or denied, making it extremely difficult for these non-profit organizations to survive. This weaponized move is intended to stifle the voices of conservatives against the Marxist-Communist Democrat Party, which cannot win on its merits, so they must take every legal and illegal action necessary to keep conservatives from winning elections. Many conservative movements, such as the Tea Party movement, have been financially eliminated with this method.

While campaigning for election to the presidency, Biden promised the American people that no one making under $400,000 would face any raise in their tax obligations. As noted earlier, this has become a blatant in-your-face lie. As the President of the United States, this pathological liar created the highest inflation rate since the Jimmy Carter Administration. Inflation means the price of all essential products, such as food, gas, electricity, etc., is significantly increasing. Given that the amount of taxes paid on any purchased item is based on a percentage of the cost of that product, every time you buy products on which prices have risen due to inflation, the more taxes you pay on that product. So, your taxes to the federal government have significantly increased, contrary to what the Marxist-Communist Democrat Party promised.

Section VIII: Secretary of Homeland Security

The Department of Homeland Security is responsible for border security and maintaining the safety of the citizens of our country. The Secretary of Home Land Security is Alejandro Mayorkas, a man who has allowed our southern border to be open to any illegal immigrant wishing to enter America without any vetting whatsoever. The number of terrorists that have entered our country is not known but can be assumed to be vast in numbers. Unknown numbers of fighting-age Chinese men, very likely military members of the Chinese Communist Party, are illegally entering our country without any female companions, suggesting that they are not coming to America for a better life.

It is only a matter of time before we are confronted with a devastating terrorist attack that will cripple our Nation and its citizens. Illegal immigrants from South America are already reigning terror throughout our country. They have raped, tortured, and killed young girls indiscriminately. Organized gangs are vicious, heavily armed, and are taking control of apartment complexes and utilizing them as their base. Illegal immigrants are overwhelming our cities, depleting community resources such as our emergency care facilities and our school systems. They are costing billions of dollars daily to support their personal needs.

Secretary Alejandro Mayorkas was born in Communist Havana, Cuba. His family fled from Castro's authoritarian regime to Florida shortly after the Cuban Revolution and the full institutionalizing of Cuba into a Marxist-Communist country. His family lost everything to the Marxist-Communist-controlled government. Still, he is now fully willing to embrace the very form of inhumane governance from which he and his family had fled. It would appear that Mayorkas had been thoroughly indoctrinated into Marxist-Communism before he departed from Cuba. What a horrible disappointment to the courage shown by his parents by risking their lives to flee to a country that would guarantee their children a free and prosperous life. It is even more disturbing given the success afforded him by our Constitutional Republic, which he now wants to destroy and turn into another Cuba.

Border Security: Alejandro Mayorkas inherited the most secure border in United States history. Under his leadership and with the full approval and guidance from the Marxist-Communist Biden-Harris Administration, Mayorkas intentionally and maliciously terminated every border protective measure and safeguard put in place by President Trump. Mayorkas has failed to meet his constitutional obligation to protect our borders and the citizens of the United States.

Alejandro Mayorkas has consistently and knowingly made false statements under oath while testifying before Congress, assuring that our southern border is under control and secure. Mayorkas, with the help of fake news, is misleading American citizens foolish enough to believe whatever propaganda is fed to them by Marxist-Communist news outlets. The Biden-Harris Administration's open border policies have resulted in the deaths of hundreds of thousands of human beings, both foreign immigrants and American citizens. Biden, Harris, and Mayorkas are well aware of the carnage occurring as a direct result of their failure to carry out their constitutional obligations to keep our country's borders closed and secure. This failure to protect the lives of both American and foreign citizens to advance their Marxist-Communist ideologies is murder, plain and simple. Their refusal to secure our borders, allowing the illegal entry of hardened criminals, terrorists, and deadly drugs laced with fentanyl, makes all three of them complaisant cohorts in the deadly crimes being committed by cartels, illegal immigrants, and terrorists. Not only are American citizens being harmed by these three Marxist-Communist, but thousands of illegal immigrants are being raped, robbed, murdered, or die during their migration through cartel-infested areas and the near desert-like environment which many illegal immigrants must traverse once they have illegally entered the United States; they further willingly accommodated the trafficking of children and young women into the United States, many for prostitution or to sell the cartel's illegal drugs. Of most significant concern is the three hundred and fifty thousand young children who have gone missing under their watch. Many most probably murder, while others have been forced into prostitution or hard labor.

While the Biden-Harris administration and its fake news propaganda arm are gas-lighting American citizens into believing that illegal immigration has dropped considerably since the termination of the Trump restrictions, the truth of the matter is that a record number of illegal immigrants, in the millions, including suspected terrorists, have entered the United States through our open southern border since they assumed office.

According to the FBI, the total number of individuals with links to terrorist organizations who crossed our open border in April of 2023 was more significant than the total number of known terrorists caught attempting to cross the southern border in the four years Trump was in office combined. This unprecedented number should cause incredible alarm among congressional lawmakers and all American citizens. Meanwhile, Homeland Security Secretary Mayorkas insists that our southern border is safe and secure.

Source & Additional Information: (https://www.newsweek.com/record-number-suspected-terrorists-crossed-us-mexico-border-opinion-1754869)

Cartels: The cartels are a compartmentalized organization of ruthless monsters who are divided into smuggling cells, transportation cells, and resupply cells. "Coyotes" are the full-time employees of the cartels and know the routes out of Mexico across our southern border into America. These individuals lead groups of illegal immigrants into America regularly. Those traveling with the coyotes are usually those who do not want to encounter Border Patrol, those with serious criminal records in their country of origin, or those carrying drugs for the cartels across the border in payment for the coyotes' help. Heroin, fentanyl, cocaine, and methamphetamine are the most common drugs being smuggled into the United States.

Source & Additional Information: (https://www.thecipherbrief.com/column_article/the-structure-and-psychology-of-drug-cartels)

Members of Mexico Cartel organizations are repeatedly raping girls as young as eleven- and twelve-year-old, only to then sell them into a life of slavery as prostitutes or workers in unsafe working environments and circumstances. From my perspective, it is my opinion that certain aspects of the federal government are engaged with the Mexican cartels in a win-win strategy of enormous profits while decreasing the number of military-age Americans with fentanyl. So, Mr. Mayorkas, I ask you, the citizens of America ask, you: how many more innocent people are you willing to allow to be tormented, abused, and killed for your globalist Marxist-Communist ideology; how many more children are you willing to allow to be sold into sexual slavery; how many more migrants are you willing to be raped, beaten, drowned, and murdered; how many more billions of dollars are you and your Marxist-Communist Democrat party willing to allow Mexican cartels to extort because of your insane border policies; how far into the heartland of our nation are you and your Marxist-Communist Democrat party willing to let the disease, crime, and drugs spread; just how far are you and your Marxist-Communist Democrat party willing to go to dilute Republican votes making the United States a one political party nation, bringing destruction to our Constitutional Republic, our citizens, and our constitutional freedoms?

Law Enforcement Intercepts: When law enforcement intercepts a vehicle smuggling drugs, the car is confiscated, and the driver is arrested. In contrast, when police stop a vehicle smuggling people, there is little law enforcement can do other than call the Border Patrol. If Border Patrol cannot respond immediately, law enforcement officers must release the human smuggler and the illegal immigrants they are transporting, as they do not have the legal authority to detain illegal aliens. If the driver does not run from the police, and the Border Patrol is too busy to come to the scene, law enforcement officers can do nothing but wish them a safe trip.

Source & Additional Information: (https://www.dailysignal.com/2023/03/16/behind-scenes-look-mexican-cartels-smuggling-routes-methods/)

Fentanyl: The DOJ and the Department of Homeland Security are failing to implement any deterrence that would stop Mexican-manufactured fentanyl-laced drugs from entering America and killing Americans. Nothing is being done to prevent China from sending Mexican cartels the raw ingredients needed to make fentanyl. Every seven minutes, an American citizen dies from Fentanyl poisoning or overdose in the United States, smuggled into our country by Mexican cartels. Our elected leaders are failing to secure our southern border and repel this deadly invasion. Every Marxist-Communist Democrat, from Joe Biden down, is complicit in this massive humanitarian and national security crisis.

Source & Additional Information: (https://usafacts.org/articles/are-fentanyl-overdose-deaths-rising-in-the-us/)

Border Patrol Agents: The Biden-Harris administration refuses to allow Border Patrol agents to do their job. Because of the sheer number of illegal aliens crossing the border under the Biden-Harris administration, many agents have been pulled off the border and are instead processing asylum claims. In fiscal year 2022, which ended September 30th, 2022, Customs and Border Protection reported a record 2.3 million land encounters with migrants at the southern border. From the start of fiscal year 2023 on October 1st, 2022, to May 2023, agents have encountered more than one million migrants at the border. In addition to the migrants encountered or apprehended at the border, there are hundreds of thousands of "gotaways." There were well over 1.2 million confirmed illegal immigrants that evaded capture in the last two years," Chris Cabrera, vice president of the National Border Patrol Council union, stated during a congressional hearing in Texas on March 15th, 2023.

Source & Additional Information: (https://www.nbcnews.com/politics/immigration/migrant-border-crossings-fiscal-year-2022-topped-276-million-breaking-rcna53517)

Title 42: Former President Donald Trump implemented Title 42 in 2020 to ensure that immigration officials could quickly and effectively return illegal aliens to their countries of origin on the grounds of public health. As a result of Title 42, approximately three million border crossers and illegal aliens were removed from the United States and returned to their home of origin.

The Biden-Harris administration allowed the Title 42 public health order, which provided for the expulsion of migrants at the border due to the pandemic, to expire on May 11th, 2023. The Biden-Harris Administration introduced several border measures to deal with the significant surge that ensued after the May 11th expiration of Title 42, including a new rule to limit who can make asylum claims and a humanitarian parole program to allow thirty thousand migrants a month from some countries into the United States. Rules no one expects the Marxist-Communists to enforce, and which are too little too late. Meanwhile, the Republican members of Congress ineffectively continued to argue that Biden's administration was not doing enough to resolve the catch-and-release process of releasing migrants into the United States, which is at the core of the border crisis.

The Department of Homeland Security issued a memo instructing Customs and Border Protection to release illegal immigrants directly into United States communities without the ability to track their movements or with any set pre-arranged court dates. This policy of releasing illegal immigrants without monitoring their movement and location or assigning court dates was supposedly to alleviate overcrowding, but at what cost? Many of those migrants were part of a program called Alternatives to Detention, which allowed illegal immigrants to use a federal government-issued taxpayer mobile phone to access an app on that mobile phone to pre-apply for asylum without the need to be detained at the border and to advise them of their scheduled date to appear in court for their Asylum hearing. The new policy seems to trust that released illegal immigrants who have already broken American law will do the respectful thing and report to their assigned Immigration Compliance Enforcement (ICE) officer.

When globalist Marxist-Communist Secretary of Homeland Security was asked if he had any concerns about the impact all these illegals would have on the United States economy, education system, medical care system, and American citizen's standard of living, he replied that this was what the United States was all about, a "Nation of Immigrants." However, nowhere in our Constitution does it say or imply that the United States is a "Nation of Illegal Immigrants" with the constitutional right to entry without being vetted and going through our legal immigrant processing procedures. Mayorkas is a strong advocate of no borders and the acceptance of millions upon millions of illegal immigrants. He was obviously indoctrinated in Marxist-Communist ideology and anti-American reasoning at Berkley. A mind filled with disregard for the rule of law. This is from a man born in Communist Cuba, from which his family was forced to flee, and now wants to turn our Country into a tyrannical, out-of-control, massive Cuba.

Alejandro Mayorkas has coordinated the disbursement of hundreds of thousands of illegal immigrants throughout the country via buses and midnight flights to targeted cities. A majority were sent to cities in conservative red states in an attempt to dilute the number of republican voters with individuals the Marxist-Communist Democrat Party is hopeful will be given a free path to citizenship and then vote for Marxist-Communist candidates. Mayorkas claims that we are a "Nation of Immigrants," implying that the United States is now the *land of the illegals* and the *home of the uninvited*. This Marxist-

Communist agenda is intended to overwhelm the American population, create chaos, increase taxes to support these millions of unwelcome intruders, and further bankrupt America. All for people not even willing to assimilate into the American culture but rather impose their failed cultures upon America.

Meanwhile, American veterans and the poor are sleeping on the street, going hungry, and lacking appropriate health care. Not so for these uninvited and unwanted burdens on our institutions. According to the report announcing this new influx of illegals, it was noted that three illegal immigrants are entering the United States for every four American citizen births every day. America is beginning to sound more like Venezuela with each passing day. The anti-American Marxist-Communists in Washington D.C. must be overwhelmed with anticipation with this potential new block of Marxist-Communist voters to help them overthrow our Constitutional Republic. Ironically, the Mayors of New York City and Chicago, which are declared sanction cities, are now screaming foul because Texas Governor Abbott is sending a measly few thousand illegals to their illegal immigrant sanctuary cities.

Source & Additional Information: (https://www.politifact.com/article/2022/oct/11/charlie-kirks-comparison-migrant-entries-us-births/)

***Big Business*:** Do you know who else is ecstatic over the flood of illegal immigrants? Big business organizations only see more profits through cuts in blue-collar wages and white-collar salaries. Big business groups care little for their community and fellow Americans because, for them, it is all about making more money off the illegal immigrants. These big business owners care little about the rule of law as long as the profit in dividends to their stakeholders and investors is increased. Not only must the United States take all necessary actions to locate and deport these illegal immigrants, but it must also identify those businesses that are employing these illegal immigrants and impose staggering penalties upon them for the act of betrayal against their fellow citizens to deter other companies from committing these acts.

***Illegal Immigrant Community*:** Mayorkas has made it clear in numerous press statements that his interests are aligned with those of the illegal immigrant community and that border management is all about achieving equity of outcome. Mayorkas implies that the United States must ensure equity between American citizens and foreign nationals, many of whom are terrorists, murderers, rapists, drug dealers, and traffickers of young children and women. For Mayorkas, it is more about global equity than human safety.

***Congress*:** The Marxist-Communist members of our revered Congress are failing to act on our behalf. So, "We the People" must act and loudly demand that our state legislators act as a buffer between the State and federal government as our Founding Fathers intended and take the collective actions needed to secure our southern border. An excellent place to start would be to use Article V of the Constitution to save the Constitution and our Republic. If State Legislators and "We the People" do nothing, then we are complicit. Texas State Representative Matt Schaefer officially filed a bill in the Texas legislature that established a Texas Border Defense Unit to defend Texans from cartels and help end the humanitarian and national security crisis on the southern border. This move on the part of the Texas legislation will hopefully mobilize all other states to follow suit by sending law enforcement agents to the south border to join forces with Texas to end the overwhelming destructive flow of illegal immigrants into the United States.

Source & Additional Information: (https://library.fiveable.me/key-terms/constitutional-law-i/article-v)

***Sanctuary Cities*:** New York City, which declared itself a safe zone for illegal immigrants, has received busloads of illegal immigrants from Texas since the last months of 2022. New York City's taxpayers are paying $5 million per day to house and care for these illegal immigrants who were sent to the Big Apple from Texas. That is too much money to waste on people who should not be in the country in the first place. Irresponsible Marxist-Communist liberals have managed to spend the Big Apple into bankruptcy, and then they wondered how it happened. The answer is straightforward: you go nowhere when you have too many people in the wagon and not enough people pulling it.

Source & Additional Information: (https://www.politico.com/news/2023/08/09/eric-adams-new-york-migrants-cost-00110472)

The New York Post ran a great story about New York City's mayor, Eric Adams, opening a former New York Police Department Police Academy as a shelter for illegal immigrants. The building is located on East 20th Street, right amid wealthy Marxist-Communist Democrat-voting liberals. Every conservative patriot in red states across the country is going to enjoy this moment, just thinking about the anguish these hypocritical Marxist-Communist Democrats must be feeling watching the man they voted for now destroying their neighborhood. It would be beyond exciting to see these rich Marxist-Communist reactions as they watch hundreds of illegal immigrants swarming across the Gramercy Park and Flatiron districts. Imagine the pain and torment these hypocrites are feeling for supporting the declaration of New York City as a sanctuary city. Now that New York City is feeling the financial and social disaster that its sanctuary city proclamation is creating, Marxist-Communist Mayor Adams is beginning to sing a different tune, proposing to end their sanctuary city status.

Source & Additional Information: (https://nypost.com/2023/05/05/hundreds-of-migrants-to-be-housed-in-nypds-former-police-academy-building/)

America is at the point of experiencing what Olivia Murray, an American Thinker, wrote about the German government evicting the poor and elderly citizens to make room for migrants. Olivia noted that the move is Orwellian, even communistic. Murray ends with this troubling comment, "If history is an indicator, communism doesn't peak at wresting capital by despotic inroads," but instead wholly embodies Orwell's famous line, "imagine a boot stomping on the human face, forever."

<u>Source & Additional Information</u>: *(https://www.npr.org/2023/04/17/1170571626/fbi-arrests-2-on-charges-tied-to-chinese-outpost-in-new-york-city)*

<u>American Safety and Fairness Through Expedited Removal Act</u>: House Republicans reintroduced the American Safety and Fairness Through Expedited Removal Act, which would significantly expand the use of deportation authority to quickly remove illegal immigrants at the southern border following the expiration of Title 42.

The American Safety and Fairness Through Expedited Removal (SAFER) Act, introduced by Rep. Pat Fallon, R-Texas, would expand the use of expedited removal, a Clinton-era authority that allows DHS to quickly remove illegal immigrants without a hearing if they have not been in the U.S. for more than two years.

Currently, the process is limited to illegal immigrants who are apprehended within 100 miles of the border or who have entered the U.S. within two weeks. Fallon's legislation would rescind that requirement and bar DHS from making additional limitations on using the authority.

It would also require all illegal immigrants who did not obtain valid entry documents and have been in the U.S. for less than two years to be removed via the authority. Most critically, it would require proof of citizenship for election participation. States like Oregon, Virginia, Texas, and Arizona have found thousands of illegals registered and, in some cases, have already voted. There are 30+ MILLION illegals in our country right now – we cannot allow them to vote, thereby negating an American citizen's vote.

Welfare offices and other agencies in at least 46 US states are providing voter registration forms to migrants without requiring proof of citizenship. Every state but North Dakota, New

Hampshire, Wisconsin and Wyoming gives applicants for welfare benefits or driver's licenses, federal voter registration forms without demanding proof of citizenship.

Federal voting forms currently do not require proof of US citizenship, though it is illegal to falsely claim one is a citizen or for a non-citizen to cast a ballot in a federal election. However, millions of migrants with humanitarian parole, refugee, or asylum status are eligible for benefits that would bring them to the offices where voter registration occurs.

This act still lingers in the House after the Republican-controlled House caved, once again, to Marxist-Communist elitist pressure and passed a Continuing Resolution on September 24th, 2024, without attaching this critical act. The vote came after Speaker Mike Johnson tried to move forward a six-month continuing resolution paired with a noncitizen voting measure, which the House rejected. A small group of House Republicans joined with most Democrats to oppose the measure.

House Republicans who voted against Speaker Johnson's six-month continuing resolution paired with a noncitizen voting measure were Jim Banks, Indiana; Andy Biggs, Alabama; Lauren Boebert, Colorado; Tim Burchett, Tennessee; Elijah Crane, Arizona; Matt Gaetz, Florida; Wesley Hunt, Texas; Doug Lamborn, Colorado; Nancy Mace, South Carolina; Cory Mills, Florida; Mike Rogers, Alabama; Matt Rosendale, Montana; W. Gregory Steube, Florida; Beth Van Duyne, Texas.

Source & Additional Information: (https://www.foxnews.com/politics/house-republican-bill-expand-fast-removals-illegal-immigrants-title-42s-end-nears) (https://www.cbsnews.com/news/house-vote-continuing-resolution-government-shutdown/) (https://www.newsweek.com/full-list-republicans-broke-trump-government-funding-bill-1956017) (https://www.msn.com/en-us/news/politics/how-non-citizens-are-getting-voter-registration-forms-across-the-us-and-how-republicans-are-trying-to-stop-it/ar-BB1ofh9J)

Illegal Immigrant Financial Support: Unlike any of the mainstream networks, Newsmax regularly reports on the activity on our southern border, allowing its viewers to be informed about what is actually happening on our southern border and the extent to which illegal immigrants are invading America. Like most at this point, it is hard to be surprised by any news reports of illegal and unconstitutional activities being perpetuated by the Marxist-Communists on American citizens. But surprised I was when Newsmax reported on the source of funding for the day-to-day expenses of all these illegal immigrants. No, it does not come from Soros or other far-left billionaires. It comes from "We the People" via our taxes to the federal government. This has not only been reported by Newsmax but also by the New York Times. The Marxist-Communist Democrat Party Administration has been funneling billions of dollars to the Federal Emergency Management Administration and other federal departments and agencies, who then funnel that money to non-profit organizations. The non-profit organization then, in turn, provides financial assistance to non-citizen illegal immigrants for their day-to-day needs, such as food, transportation, rental assistance, and other financial needs. The Federal government, via these non-profit organizations, is also providing these illegal immigrants debit cards with an initial $800 at the time of release into the United States following apprehension. The non-profit organization replenishes This card every month with an additional $800. No set maximum amount or any time limits are specified.

This money does not come from private donations or church collections. These organizations, which include United Way, Catholic Charities, and the Central American Refugee Center, are hauling billions of taxpayer dollars under government contracts to facilitate illegal immigration. We, taxpayers, are getting scammed by these groups identifying as charity organizations who should be expending American tax dollars on needy Americans, and there are plenty of them, but are instead giving away our tax dollars to illegal immigrants while Americans suffer. There are food banks collecting donations for our homeless military veterans, while illegal aliens are given so much food they are throwing it out. Military veterans live in cardboard boxes on the sidewalk, while illegals live in five-star hotels. Billions of dollars are given to finance illegal immigrant's general welfare while our citizens go hungry. This is the Marxist-Communist Democrat Party's priority.

Even while still in Mexico, illegal immigrants are being handed debit cards loaded with $800, which is replenished every month. These cards are being distributed in Mexico by the non-profit "Organization for Migration," thanks to money provided by the Department of State. After crossing and surrendering to United States Border agents, many migrants are directed to Catholic Charities, which provides them hotel rooms, meals, and clothing and pays for their bus or plane tickets to their chosen destinations. Sister Norma Pimentel, executive director of Catholic Charities of the Rio Grande Valley explain that the mission is merely to "give a cup of water in Jesus' name." Who can argue with that? Except that the money is not coming from Sister Norma Pimentel. Sister Pimentel admits the federal government fully finances her organization, so it comes from taxpayers who do not know they are supporting this operation. This is very charitable. However, that cup of water was funded by American tax dollars and should be provided to Americans who are just as desperately in need of that cup of water.

The Marxist-Communist Democrat Party has intentionally chosen non-profit organizations as emotional weapons to facilitate the hundreds of thousands of illegal immigrants' daily needs and transportation throughout the United States. The Marxist-Communist Democrat Party has correctly assumed that Republicans would not have the courage to criticize these charity groups' let alone shut them down by ending all federal funding. So long as this remains true, the Marxist-Communist Democrat Party will continue using these organizations as weapons to achieve their goals. It is the Republican Party's fear of these organizations that is partially responsible for allowing illegal immigration numbers to grow to the levels we see today. For more than three years, the Biden-Harris administration mass-released millions of illegal immigrants into the United States, relying on non-profit organizations to feed, transport, and lodge these illegal immigrants. These non-profit organizations receive billions of taxpayer dollars annually through Federal Emergency Administration, Homeland Security, Health and Human Services, Department of State, and Department of Justice entities.

The Marxist-Communist Democrat Party is hiding behind faith-based organizations to keep federal tax dollars flowing to meet the needs of these illegal immigrants and to keep the American taxpayer from realizing the actual extent of dollars being poured into meeting the daily needs of these individuals. It is also ironic that these faith-based charity organizations are, on the one hand, providing welfare and assistance to illegal immigrants and, on the other hand, are being complicit in the horrific conditions many of these immigrants eventually end up living under. These illegal immigrants who receive care from individuals who believe they are being merciful are, in reality, sending many of these individuals to a life of sexual exploitation, child abuse by sponsors with criminal records, mule runners for drug dealers, forced child labor, American national security threats, and public safety threats. The active and willing support obtained from faith-based organizations is especially concerning as one would assume that they would be at the forefront of ending all means that would allow such harm to come to those they provide for under God's name. These faith-based organizations began their involvement with immigrants with honor and integrity by supporting the State Department to resettle genuine refugees within the United States after a legitimate application process. Like so many other charity organizations with good intentions, they have evolved into organizations that are no more than lawless accomplices of the illegal immigration process because of the enormous profits available to them for providing these needs.

These same faith-based organizations actively advocate for the acceptance of all illegal migrants into the United States against our country's illegal immigration law. They claim they are merely helping these vulnerable illegal immigrants, but these non-profit organizations are profiting financially from the illegal immigration business. Examples of non-profit organizations profiting from federal grant money include Catholic Charities USA which has been receiving on average $1.4 billion of federal government funding annually; Lutheran Immigration and Refugee Service which received more than $93.1 million from the Federal Emergency Management Administration for illegal immigration adults and families and $182.6 million from the Department of Health and Human Services for unaccompanied illegal immigrant children and refugee services; the Church World Services which has received more than $20 million in the form of grant funds and is a New York City-based 501(c)(3) organization under the Internal Revenue Code, so it pays no federal income taxes, but it spends more than $3.7 million in advocacy at taxpayer expense; and the Hebrew Immigrant Aid Society which received more than $40.9 million in grants from the departments of Health and Human Services, Department of State, and Department of Homeland Security for illegal immigration activities. Based on the Biden-Harris administration's descriptions of nongovernmental organization "movement" services, it is reasonable to allege that the administration is paying non-profit organizations to smuggle illegal immigrants the final miles of their journey.

<u>Source & Additional Information</u>: *(https://www.newsnationnow.com/us-news/immigration/border-coverage/ngos-american-tax-dollars-migrants/)*

Republican members of Congress can no longer sit silently by while the Marxist-Communist Democrat Party and faith-based organizations claim the moral high ground in their mass illegal-migrate operations as they seek to protect their billion-dollar government-funded industry. The Marxist-Communist Democratic Party, through various federal government departments and agencies, wants to maximize its financial support for the cost of living for these illegal migrants but does not want their fingerprints on any of it. Their solution: funnel money through federal departments and agencies, then funnel that money to non-profit organizations who then provide this money to illegal immigrants. It is the House of Representative's responsibility and obligation to cut off all funding to these departments and agencies until reform is made within those departments and agencies to cease all funding activity of any initiative supporting any element of the financial support of illegal immigrants within the United States.

Abortions for Illegal Immigrant Minors: Since October 2021, the Biden administration's Office of Refugee Resettlement (ORR) has been flying or driving pregnant illegal-immigrant minors from migrant shelters in Texas, which bans abortions after a fetal heartbeat is detected, to other states with greater access to legal abortion. The transporting of pregnant illegal immigrant minors has been going on under the radar.

Because of the Texas abortion law, the ORR, which is under the Department of Health and Human Services (HHS), instructed its employees not to place pregnant migrant girls in shelters within the state of Texas "to the greatest extent possible." In its field guidance, the ORR instructs its team to "identify available and appropriate bed space at a licensed care provider facility outside of the state of Texas. . . ."

The Biden-Harris administration has been taking measures to ensure that unaccompanied illegal immigrant minors can obtain abortions, at least until the end of Biden's term. This is happening on the taxpayer's dime.

Source & Additional Information: (https://amac.us/newsline/national-security/the-biden-administrations-abortion-taxi-service-for-migrant-minors/)

Illegal Immigrant Child Labor: The New York Times ran a series of articles documenting labor abuse of illegal immigrant children that should shock all Americans. For the most part, these children are the unaccompanied children who have been entering the country in unprecedented numbers since President Biden took office. In the administration's haste to release these kids from protective custody, they have handed many of them over to "sponsors," who often turn out to be operatives or clients of the criminal cartels that brought them here in the first place. All the while, the Marxist-Communist Biden-Harris administration and federally funded Marxist-Communist non-government non-profit organizations have been pretending that open border policies are humane.

The Department of Labor reports that some four thousand kids were discovered to be working in violation of federal labor laws in 2022 alone. We can be confident that many more federal labor law violations have gone unreported. Hundreds of United States companies, including well-known companies such as General Mills, Frito-Lay, and Fruit of the Loom, are employing underage illegal child immigrants. "Migrant children, who have been coming into the United States without their parents in record numbers, are ending up in some of the most punishing jobs in the country. This shadow workforce extends across industries in every state, flouting child labor laws that have been in place for nearly a century," writes Hannah Dreier of the New York Times. Even children who enter the United States illegally with their parents are often subject to exploitation, as they are pressed into dangerous and physically demanding labor to help the family pay their debts to the cartel. Countless numbers of children end up in even more horrific circumstances at the hands of sex traffickers.

Source & Additional Information: (https://journalistsresource.org/media/migrant-children-labor-abuse-goldmith/)

Destruction of Property: Farmers along the Arizona-Mexico border are being hit with an estimated loss of $1 million worth of crops every season because of illegal immigrants crossing and camping in their fields. Federal food safety laws require farmers to destroy any crop field in which illegal immigrants enter, as it is unknown whether these illegal immigrants have urinated, defecated, or left behind potentially contaminated items in the crop fields. The cost of lost crops is solely on the shoulders of the farmer growing the crop. There is no insurance to cover such losses, and then, obviously, that crop never makes it to market to feed the citizens of our country. I am surprised that these farmers have not yet joined forces and filed lawsuits against the federal government for their losses, as the federal government has openly and knowingly allowed this destruction of their crops by failing to carry out their constitutional responsibility to maintain a closed and secure border.

Source & Additional Information: (https://www.agriculturedive.com/news/farm-immigration-border-crossings-food-safety-oped/703265/)

House Committee on Homeland Security: On February 28th, 2023, the Congressional House Committee on Homeland Security held its first Full Committee hearing of the 118th Congress, entitled "Every State is a Border State: Examining Secretary Mayorkas' Border Crisis." This first committee hearing focused on the widespread and debilitating impact President Biden and Secretary Mayorkas' border crisis was having on communities across the United States of America. "Whether it's the overwhelming presence of MS-13 gang violence on Long Island in New York, the crippling impact of the fentanyl crisis across Tennessee, or the influx of illegal aliens being dropped in small towns in Mississippi and North Carolina, every American community bears the brunt of weak border security," said Chairman Marjorie Taylor-Green. "It does not matter how far you physically live from the U.S-Mexico border, this border crisis is taking a toll on every taxpayer's wallet and Americans' safety." This first hearing clearly and articulately laid out the devastation this crisis is having on American communities and how President Biden and Secretary Mayorkas abandoned Americans as this crisis surfaces in their backyards."

On March 15th, 2023, the House Committee on Homeland Security Chairman Marjorie Taylor-Green led a full committee field hearing in McAllen, Texas, to examine the direct link between President Biden and Secretary Mayorkas' reckless border policies and the unprecedented crisis at our Southwest border. Chairman Green delivered the following opening remarks at the field hearing in Pharr, Texas, outlining how the crisis at the Southwest border is a direct result of Secretary Mayorkas' failure to enforce our country's laws.

"Good morning, and welcome to the Committee on Homeland Security's field hearing in Pharr, Texas. We came to Texas for this hearing for several reasons. To get members of Congress and their staff out of the cubicles back in Washington, and down here to the border to see it for ourselves. You cannot read about being a doctor, and then do brain surgery. My life experience has taught me, whether it was as an Army infantry commander, a physician needing a CT scan before deciding a treatment plan, or the Chief Executive Officer of my company, it takes the leader getting on the ground, seeing what is going on to make well-informed decisions. We also want the people on the border to know that Congress cares. That we see the plight of your communities."

This was to be a full committee meeting, but the Marxist-Communist Democrat members of the committee were all no-shows. They decided not to attend the committee meeting in Pharr, Texas, because they said coming to the southern border to hold a committee hearing to conduct a firsthand review of the border crisis was a political stunt. It is challenging to believe that holding a hearing at the point of the crisis is a political stunt. Marxist-Communist Democrat members of this committee needed to see firsthand what was occurring at our southern border to be viable members of that committee. Boycotting that hearing and refusing to see and acknowledge the devastating situation at the border is the real political stunt. Truth be known, every single Marxist-Communist Democrat member of that committee knows full well the depth and extent of the border crises and the crises that our unsecured southern border is having on communities across the United States. They realize that if they are televised viewing the inhumane crisis at the border, their ability to continue gaslighting the naive members of their party will be shattered.

The Marxist-Communist Democrat members of Congress talk about the need for bipartisanship to solve problems, but how is this committee to be bipartisan if opposing party members of that committee do not attend? For Marxist-Communist Democrat members of Congress, bipartisanship is defined as "agreeing exactly with their Marxist-Communist viewpoints." Bipartisanship is supposed to be a willingness by both parties to sit down together, debate the issues, and try to find common ground. The Marxist-Communist Democrat's obligation as committee members was to be present at that hearing, but they failed to report for duty in Pharr, Texas. The committee was in Pharr, Texas, to see first-hand the extent of the border crisis. To see firsthand illegal immigrants streaming across the Rio Grande, across our border into the United States, leading to millions of encounters and millions of 'gottaways.' These 'gottaways' are unaccounted for, and there is no knowledge of who these people are, where they came from, or where in the United States they are located. But what is known is that the number of drug seizures is at record highs, and the number of individuals on the terrorist watch list crossing our southern border is up significantly. In just the four years of Secretary Mayorkas' dictatorship at the Department of Home Land Security, more people have come into this country illegally than all of the eight years of the Obama presidency and all four years of the Trump presidency combined. Marxist-Communist Democrat members of that committee failed to travel to Texas because doing so would deny them the ability to deny that there was a border crisis.

Why the dramatic increase in the number of illegal crossings? The Marxist-Communist members of Congress will tell you it is a lack of sufficient funding. However, there was no decrease in the budget when Mayorkas was confirmed as Secretary; the budget increased. A lack of money did not cause this massive, sudden surge. It was Joe Biden's constant inviting immigrants to come to the United States and then those who do come, contacting their families back in their country of origin and advising them that the border is open to all; what else can be expected. Some Marxist-Communist members of Congress will tell you that it is the number of Border Patrol agents that is insufficient to secure the border. Well, when Secretary Mayorkas took over as Secretary, there were the same number of agents as when the Trump Administration was in office, so obviously, the size of the Border Patrol is not the reason for the massive surge in people, crime, and drugs. Some Marxist-Communist members of Congress from both parties will tell you that it is the technology, the systems; perhaps it is the wall or the absence of a wall. But no portion of the wall has been taken down between administrations. Yet illegal immigrants keep pouring across our southern border by the millions.

This only leaves Secretary Mayorkas and Biden-Harris' border policies that were the problem. Problems that included the movement of Border Patrol agents from border security to administrative functions processing illegal immigrants. Joe rescinded Eighty-nine successful migration control policies implemented by the Trump administration, which Biden immediately rescinded upon taking office as President. Trump policies such as the Migrant Protection Protocols and the 'Remain in Mexico,' policies. Biden and his Administration blatantly subverted the immigration laws passed by Congress because those laws were intended to deter crossings, so they were offensive to the Marxist-Communist administration.

Companies that actually have Immigration and Customs Enforcement (ICE) detention center contracts, such as CoreCivic, which has a capacity for twenty-five thousand people, are only receiving approximately eight thousand illegal immigrants a month. You would think that during the middle of a massive surge of illegal immigrants, those detention beds would be at full capacity. Why are they not at total capacity? These illegal immigrants are not being detained because Mayorkas knows that detention is deterrence, and deterrence was contrary to the Biden-Harris Administration's policies. Therefore, these illegal immigrants are being processed, immediately paroled, and then sent to the four corners of the United States. There is no provisional internment until the Judiciary Branch determines the legitimacy of a migrant's claim for asylum as required by law. A law that Secretary Mayorkas is trying to change, removing the Judiciary Branch from the decision-making process on asylum requests. Why would Secretary Mayorkas want to do away with the Judiciary? Why would he want to subvert laws written by Congress? It is because the Marxist-Communist Democrat Party wants more people to come into the country, hopefully, to be given blanket citizenship, granting them the right to vote in our elections, thereby diluting Republican votes to keep their Marxist-Communist Democrat Party regime in power.

Source & Additional Information: (https://markgreen.house.gov/2023/2/chairman-green-opening-statement-in-full-committee-hearing-examining-secretary-mayorkas-border-crisis) (https://markgreen.house.gov/2023/3/chairman-green-delivers-opening-remarks-at-field-hearing-on-mayorkas-border-crisis-this-human-tragedy-is-the-result-of-decisions-and-the-incompetence-of-this-secretary) (https://www.msn.com/en-us/news/us/why-the-biden-administration-is-closing-the-largest-ice-detention-center-in-the-us/ar-BB1oOtQn) (https://www.congress.gov/118/chrg/CHRG-118hhrg52122/CHRG-118hhrg52122.pdf)

And now the Marxist-Communist Democrat regime has developed a mobile phone app that allows illegal immigrants to fill out their asylum application and automatically get parole when they show up at a crossing site. That is in total violation of what the laws passed by Congress require from immigrants seeking entry into our country. Just more profit for drug cartel coyotes who will complete the app on behalf of the illegal immigrant for an additional fee.

Border Patrol Hindrance: Secretary Mayorkas' Fiscal Year 2023 budget strictly prohibits any funds being utilized to secure the southern border. A detailed budget analysis clearly shows that the Department of Homeland Security is prohibited from spending any funds to increase Border Patrol agents on the border or utilizing any of those funds to increase surveillance technology. All the increases in funding, and we are talking billions of dollars, are specifically committed to the processing and shipping of illegal immigrants throughout the United States. This act of funding negligence and malpractice occurred because the Democrat-controlled House passed the Fiscal Year 2023 budget appropriations via The Consolidated Appropriations Act just before the Republican Party assumed control of the House. This should not have been an issue because, without Republican support in the Senate, the bill would never have been passed. This would have allowed the Republican Party to implement a more financially sane budget, illuminating this restriction when they assumed control just a few months later. What happened in the Senate? Marxist-Communist Democrat supporter Senator Mitch McConnell is what happened when he and enough of his RINO Republican Senators supported the passage of the bill containing these restrictions.

Border Patrol sector chiefs have confirmed that they have received orders from their superiors that they cannot return illegal immigrants to their countries of origin, supposedly because the State Department has not yet renegotiated any return agreements. The State Department has failed to renegotiate return agreements because it was Biden's policy to allow illegals to invade our country in massive waves. Secretary Mayorkas' Department of Homeland Security, with the full approval of Joe Biden, wanted more illegals flooding into our country in mass. This policy has only further empowered and emboldened narco-human traffickers and terrorist Mexican cartels. The drug cartels who captured and killed American citizens but graciously apologized for their murders are making billions by bringing illegals into the United

States, many of whom, once they are in the United States, must continue paying the cartels through forced criminal labor.

On May 2, 2023, House Republicans introduced H.R.2, The Secure the Border Act of 2023. Sponsored by Rep. Mario Díaz-Balart (R-Florida), the expansive proposal represents an enforcement approach to migration-related challenges at the United States-Mexico border and beyond. It combines three bills from the 118th Congress: The Border Security and Enforcement Act of 2023, the Orderly Requirements Designed to Enforce and Regulate Latin American Migration (ORDER) Act, and the Border Reinforcement Act of 2023.

Source & Additional Information: (https://www.congress.gov/bill/118th-congress/house-bill/2640?q={"search"%3A%5B"h.r.+2640"%5D}&s=2&r=4) (https://www.congress.gov/bill/118th-congress/house-bill/1690/text?s=4&r=1&q={"search"%3A%5B"H.R.1690"%5D}) (https://www.congress.gov/bill/118th-congress/house-bill/2794?s=1&r=1&q={"search"%3A%5B"HR.2794"%5D})

***The Border*:** The Biden-Harris Administration's lack of adequate border control and security has led cartels to put out advertisements around the world that the cartel will escort illegal immigrants into the United States. They are charging individuals from China $50,000 in United States currency. In contrast, those coming from Iran are being charged $30,000. This is a large amount of money, given that those migrating from Central America are only charged $15,000. How is it possible for the average Chinese citizen who wants to escape China to produce $50,000 or for Iranian citizens in the same situation to deliver $30,000 to be illegally guided into the United States? Unless the governments of these authoritarian countries are funding these individuals, it would not make any sense. Common sense would tell you that these individuals are potential terrorists sent to the United States to create fear and chaos among our citizens and to act as in-country special operations units to attack our vulnerable infrastructure to facilitate the destruction of the United States.

Source & Additional Information: (https://www.nbcsandiego.com/news/local/chinese-migrants-pay-higher-fee-to-be-smuggled-into-u-s/2229405/)

Cartel Strategy: The cartel's strategy is to flood illegal immigrants across the border at or near Ports of Entry, compelling the Border Patrol to focus its limited resources at the Ports of Entry. In this manner, the cartels are neutralizing Customs and Border Patrol by forcing them to thin out their lines of defense in the rural areas. The cartels then smuggle fentanyl, illegals with dangerous criminal backgrounds, and potential terrorists into the United States across these rural areas. In one sector of our southern border, approximately thirty miles long, typically, two hundred agents patrol that area. That number is now down to seven men and women pulling three shifts daily to cover those thirty miles. Why is this shortage of manpower occurring? Answer: border patrol agents are being moved to processing centers to babysit illegals and coordinate their transportation across America. While Border Patrol agents are being utilized to process illegals, video cameras placed by ranchers on the border show cartel members in camouflage outfits, wearing carpet shoes and backpacks full of fentanyl pouring into our country.

So why are over six million illegal immigrants flooding into the United States now? Why are over 100,000 Americans dying per year from drugs like fentanyl? Why are we seeing massive crime increases at our border cities and throughout all the major cities of this country? Why has every city in every state now become a border state? The answer is a simple one. The Biden-Harris Administration's failure to provide adequate security on our southern border and the corrupt decisions being made by the inept, corrupt Secretary of the Department of Homeland Security, Alejandro Mayorkas. A man who lacks any sense of honor or integrity.

Fentanyl: With all the problems at our southern border, instead of a President, Vice President, and Secretary of Homeland Security working to find and implement solutions, we had a president who chuckled during a response to a reporter about a mother who lost two children to fentanyl, and a secretary of the of Homeland Security who seems to be okay with Chinese Nationals being released into our country with verified direct connections to the Chinese Communist Party and the Chinese army. You would think that with so many American youths dying from fentanyl and drug cartels taking over operational control of our border, Secretary Mayorkas would produce something a little more effective at halting the flow of illegal immigrants than an app that further incentivizes people to enter illegally. But no, the failure to secure the southern border is not about money, the number of Border Patrol agents, or technology; this massive human tragedy is the direct result of decisions being made by Secretary Mayorkas at the behest of the Biden-Harris Administration to destroy America and bring in a Marxist-Communist governance.

Mayorkas repeatedly stated that the Department of Homeland Security's primary goal was to achieve operational control of a southern border that no longer exists. Mayorkas noted that his department was making every effort possible to support Border Patrol agents with the resources, technology, and policies needed to secure the border. Border Patrol Agent Raul Ortiz, who testified at the Committee's field hearing, stated that contrary to Secretary Mayorkas repeated claims, the agency did not have operational control of the southern border and did not have the resources to secure the border. After four years as the Secretary for Homeland Security, there are no indications that Mayorkas is trying to provide desperately needed help and resources to the Border Patrol agents on the southern border. Mayorkas' statements are just more smoke-and-screen responses to failed policies and the Marxist-Communist Democrat Party's fundamental goal of permanently eliminating the southern border. Republican Representative Dan Bishop asked Border Patrol Agent Ortiz whether he, Ortiz, believed that the changes in border policy made by the Biden-Harris administration to release migrants into the interior of the country rather than detain and release exasperated the border crisis. Ortiz responded by stating that the Biden border policies not only exasperated the crisis but that there needs to be congressional action taken against those whose actions or lack of action created the devasting border crises.

Child Trafficking: During the week of April 24th, 2023, testimony was heard from a Homeland Security whistleblower who viewed first-hand what she testified as a "sophisticated network" of child migrant smuggling into forced labor and other forms of slavery. The hearing, "The Biden Border Crisis: Exploitation of Unaccompanied Alien Children," was held by the House Judiciary Subcommittee on Immigration Integrity, Security and Enforcement and included Health and Human Services whistleblower Tara Lee Rodas as a witness. Rodas, who was detailed to an Emergency Intake Site in Pomona, California, testified about what she experienced while with the Emergency Intake Site. Rodas testified, "I thought I was going to help place children in loving homes. Instead, I discovered that children are being trafficked through a sophisticated network that begins with recruiting in their home country of origin, smuggled to the United States border, and ends when the Office of Refugee Resettlement delivers a child to a sponsor. Some of the sponsors are criminals, traffickers, and members of Transnational Criminal Organizations. Some sponsors view children as commodities and assets to be used for earning income. This is why we are witnessing an explosion of labor trafficking," according to Rodas.

Source & Additional Information: (https://www.foxnews.com/politics/whistleblower-tells-congress-that-govt-delivering-migrant-children-human-traffickers)

When child migrants are encountered at the border, they are transferred into the custody of Health and Human Services and then united with a sponsor, supposedly a parent or family member already in the United States. The New York Times has received several reports detailing a rise in child exploitation, where children are forced into the labor force, sometimes to pay back their smuggling costs. This situation regarding the transporting of children to sponsors makes the Biden-Harris Administration complicit in child trafficking. "Whether intentional or not, it could be argued that the United States government has become the middleman in a large scale, multibillion-dollar child trafficking operation that is run by bad actors seeking to profit off the lives of children," Rodas testified. Rodas described how she saw children becoming captive to their "sponsors" as they could not seek help in English and sponsors used multiple addresses to obtain sponsorships of children.

On January 10th, 2023, Representative Pat Fallon of Texas filed impeachment articles against Alejandro Mayorkas, accusing him of not taking any steps to secure the southern border. Representative Fallon introduced House Resolution 8, seeking to impeach Mayorkas for "high crimes and misdemeanors." Mayorkas stood accused of failing to execute the "Secure the Fence Act of 2006," which requires the Homeland Security Secretary to "maintain operational control" over America's land and maritime borders, which he has abdicated to the Mexican Cartels. Unfortunately, the Marxist-Communist Republican allies of the Marxist-Communist Democrat Party will not support Fallon's Resolution for impeachment. As a result, Homeland Security Secretary Alejandro Mayorkas will not be held accountable for his failures to carry out his sworn duties, which has brought devastation upon our Nation, its citizens, and illegal immigrant children. He will be allowed to continue to ensure our southern border remains non-existent and deadly drugs, violent criminals, traffickers of young children, and terrorists continue to be allowed free entry into the United States. Even Speaker Kevin McCarthy, who thrilled conservatives in 2022 when he opened the door to impeachment proceedings, reversed his position and did not support the Resolution. It's just business as usual in the Washington swamp.

Source & Additional Information: https://www.govtrack.us/congress/bills/109/hr6061/text

His willful and continuous failures to carry out his oath of office are crimes against humanity and acts of treason. Alejandro Mayorkas was eventually impeached but failed to be convicted by the Marxist-Communist Democrat Party-controlled Senate. He must face the consequences of his actions by being criminally charged for his intentional criminal actions.

Section IX: Secretary of Education

The Secretary of Education serves as the principal advisor to the president and the federal government on policies, programs, and activities related to all education activities in the United States.

Secretary Cardona's biography indicates that his focus throughout his career has been on raising the bar for ***equity*** and ***inclusion*** in education for all learners and teachers under his leadership, NOT equality and excellence, to assure that all students have an equal opportunity to a level of education that will give every student the best chances of being successful in their adult life.

P.T. Barnum was known for his comment that "There's a sucker born every minute." This great showman had people figured out. With this in mind, we should erect a tent over this whole country because, thanks to Woke Marxist-Communist Democrats, America has become a three-ring circus with an overabundance of clowns. We no longer live in a rational country. We have replaced reality with fantasy to the point of allowing it to enter our schools. We enable students to use pronouns that make absolutely no sense. Schools should teach proper grammar, yet teachers are addressing an individual student as "They." It makes no sense, yet far too many teachers are buying into this insanity. Those teachers who still understand and appreciate their role as educators responsible for teaching their students the basics, which will provide them the greatest opportunity to succeed and refuse to go along with woke ideologies, are reprimanded by the school administration and may even lose their jobs. They are being forced to drink the proverbial Kool-Aid.

We all know that the human brain is not fully developed until an individual is in their mid-twenties, and it is a teacher's responsibility to teach and nurture students, not buy into and play along with lunacy. How about "Furries," now that's a screwed-up bunch of people who have lost touch with reality. They make all the 'theys' almost look sane. I read recently that a girl in elementary school comes dressed as a cat and purrs. As if this is not bad enough, the teacher treats her like a cat. Does this child have mental issues, or does she just want attention? Either way, she would have lasted about thirty seconds with "no-nonsense" Sister Anastasia, my eighth-grade teacher. This child would have been grabbed by the scruff of the neck and thrown out of the classroom, as well as "they" should be. This behavior disrupts the rest of the class and makes it difficult for the other students to focus. Aren't teachers supposed to be the adults in the room? Let us not forget those cross-dressing teachers who were allowed to tutor our younger children. I am pretty sure this confuses the children to no end. What child can concentrate on math lessons when Mr. Smith wears a dress, heels, and pearls? I am sure that this behavior by their teacher does not make any sense to the children in Mr. Smith's class. This behavior harms young students and should be ridiculed and not embraced in any school setting. Then we wonder why our federally funded schools fail to provide our children with the education we expect from our education system.

Federally Funded School System: The harshest and most devasting reality in our Republic is our federally funded school system, which is a total failure. One of the major problems is the Teacher's Union, which prioritizes power, control, and money over the education of our children. The level of knowledge in essential reading, writing, and math is now comparable to third-world education in these fundamental subjects. Our failed education system compromises the next generation of American leaders and citizens. Our children no longer learn about America's true history and the Constitution, and they do not recite the Pledge of Allegiance to our flag and nation or begin the school day with a silent prayer.

We have a federally funded school system in a Nation founded upon Judeo-Christian values whose children and educators are no longer allowed to take a knee to pray at school events or on school grounds, silently or otherwise. The school system's justification: The Constitution does not allow religion into any aspect of government. They are very wrong. The Constitution states, *"Congress shall make no law respecting the establishment of religion."* Starting the day out with a silent prayer or taking a knee at a school sporting event is hardly establishing a religion, nor does it require any child to choose one religion over another. During the morning prayer, a child can say a short prayer in keeping with their religious beliefs, think about sports or plans for the day, or remain silent until the morning prayer period is over. Again, those who find it appropriate to take a knee at a game are not establishing a religion. In any of these circumstances, the child is not being indoctrinated in any particular religion but would be introduced in some small way to the Judeo-Christian values on which our Nation was founded.

Our failed education system makes little to no attempt to teach our children the facts regarding our form of government and the freedoms and liberties that come with a Constitutional Republic. We have a failed school system that ignores the teaching of our children that, unlike any other country in the world, Congress can constitutionally propose Amendments to the Constitution of the United States under Article V of the Constitution to correct any flaws in our constitution. Our failed school system has failed to teach our children that if our federal government becomes tyrannical and out-of-control, our Constitution also allows for "We the People" through our state legislators to bring about needed changes through Constitutional Amendments to rein in such a government. Again, this Constitutional authority is articulated in Article V.

Our school system has failed to teach our children that, unlike any other country, we have a governing system that governs by, for, and of the people. They have failed to teach our children patriotism and love of country. Instead, our children are taught that our Constitution is out-of-date and no longer applicable to our ever-changing world because it is not a living, evolving document able to recognize these changes and evolve accordingly. This is factually untrue because our Founding Fathers created this document in a manner that would withstand the passage of time. Therefore, in their great wisdom, they included in the Constitution Article V, which states that: "The Congress, whenever two-thirds of both houses shall deem it necessary, shall propose Amendments to this Constitution, or, on the application of the legislatures of two-thirds of the several States, shall call a Convention for proposing Amendments, which, in either Case, shall be valid to all Intents and Purposes as Part of this Constitution, when ratified by the Legislators of three-fourths of the several States, or by Conventions in three-fourths thereof, as the one or the other Mode of Ratification may be proposed by the Congress....." The ability to change our Constitution is there, but changing it was purposefully made challenging to restrain Congress or any other group, such as the Marxist-Communist movement, from arbitrarily changing the Constitution on a whim. Do our children realize that this mechanism for change is available? No, because our failed federally funded school system does not deem the teaching of our Constitution relevant.

We must live with the harsh reality that, although America is the wealthiest country in the world, spending the most money on education per student, America consistently ranks among the world's most poorly educated students. Our federally funded public school system is failing to teach our children a core curriculum that will prepare them for success, preferring to waste valuable learning time and tax dollars indoctrinating our children in Critical Race Theory, gender identification, surgical gender alteration, LGBTQ lifestyles, and other radical far-left beliefs and lifestyles. A failed school system that teaches our children that America is and has always been systematically racist and evil from its founding. All at the expense of the American taxpayer.

Source & Additional Information: (https://www.theatlantic.com/education/archive/2013/12/american-schools-vs-the-world-expensive-unequal-bad-at-math/281983/)

What is needed is the return of our Education Department to the states as required by the Constitution. Short of this action, legislation authorizing "school choice" and providing tax dollars to families with school-age children will allow them to escape our failed federally funded schools. As parents await such legislation, many states have taken it upon themselves to use state funds to provide parents with school choice. Republican-led states such as Iowa, Utah, and Arkansas have passed legislation allowing families to access thousands of state dollars annually for private K to twelve education, allowing families to send their children to private schools. Parents can choose where their children go to school regardless of income or the area they live in. An action far past due from our federal government and the Department of Education, which constitutionally belongs to the sovereign states.

Lack of Constitutional Competency: It is also evident that many American citizens were never adequately educated about our form of governance. Few students graduate from high school or college, having learned that the United States is a republic and not a democracy.

Democracies and republics are both forms of government in which supreme power resides in the citizens. The word *republic* refers specifically to a government whose citizens elect representatives who govern according to the law, which is the case for the United States. The word *democracy* can refer to this same kind of representative government, or it can refer instead to what is also called a *direct democracy*, in which the citizens themselves directly participate in the act of governing.

The definition of a Republic does not include wokism. The United States Republic governs under a constitution in which all states are sovereign, and the federal government is subservient to the states. It is evident that far too many American citizens have never taken the time or tried to read at least, if not study, our Constitution and the affixed Amendments. It is by having at least a general knowledge of the Constitution that American citizens can know their rights and begin understanding the extent to which the citizens of our Nation are now being denied those rights and freedoms as the result of an ever-increasing Marxist-Communist government. To be able to recognize the extent to which our Constitution is being denigrated, ignored, and misinterpreted to fit the Marxist-Communist Democrat Party's narrative and agenda, you have to have at least a general understanding of the Constitution.

Source & Additional Information: (https://www.diffen.com/difference/Democracy_vs_Republic)

Class Segregation: A report from the Daily Caller revealed that a high school located in Illinois faced serious accusations of civil rights violations for offering several math classes that are restricted by a student's race. Things are so serious that a civil rights complaint was filed against Evanston Township High School by Mark Perry, Senior Fellow for a medical watchdog group, Do No Harm. The high school offers classes for black or "Latinx" students in algebra, precalculus, and calculus. Still, students of other races are restricted from participating in these classes. The complaint, which was filed with the Chicago Office for Civil Rights, pointed out that several of the codes for these classes are "restricted to students who identify as Latinx, all genders," or are limited to kids who "identify as Black, all genders," according to information from the 2023 course catalog.

More and more, we are seeing a growing tendency to return to the 1960s and the segregation that the black community was subjected to. Today, we are experiencing reverse segregation in that white citizens are being targeted as systematically racist and have privileges not available to others of different races. The action on the part of Evanston Township High School can be considered as wokism in that they are promoting Marxist-Communism by restricting certain activities to only black students, creating a potential conflict between students of different races. This action on the part of this school is, in fact, racist and is straight out of the Marxist-Communist playbook.

Source & Additional Information: (https://thespectator.com/topic/illinois-high-school-offers-racially-segregated-math-classes-evanston-township/)

Gabriel Nadales, the national director of Our America, stated that there is no excuse for any math class to be open only to people belonging to a certain group of individuals based on race.

Despite the apparent language on its website, the school stated that it has never had any process to restrict its students from taking AP classes based on skin color. The school then revealed that it has changed some of the language in the course requisite guide to better reflect its "goal and practice."

The "Spectator" reported that Evanston Township High School, located in an affluent suburb of Chicago, has the largest high school under a single roof in the United States. The campus sprawls over sixty-five acres and features several gyms, swimming pools, a greenhouse, and a planetarium. Understandably, an affluent suburb school would want to provide amenities unavailable in your average high school nationwide. But at taxpayer expense? This federally provided money should be spent on direct educational learning activities such as reading, writing, and arithmetic, which our high school students have found to be deficient. Given that this school is located in an affluent neighborhood, if those residents deemed these noneducation amenities important, then the district's parents should have voted on their wishes for their school to provide them. If approved by the resident's vote, local taxes should have covered the cost of these amenities through the District Board of Education and not through federal funding. It is curious that an Administration promoting equity would allow a school in an affluent suburb to offer so many federally funded amenities. In contrast, schools in poor neighborhoods can barely afford to provide books to all their students. Where is the equity here?

Source & Additional Information: (https://en.wikipedia.org/wiki/Evanston_Township_High_School)

Indoctrination: Doctor Miguel Cardona is a career educator who deems it more appropriate to spend valuable classroom hours not teaching our children the fundamental lessons needed to survive and prosper as adults in a very competitive world but instead promoting the teaching and indoctrination of our children to "Wokism," and Critical Race Theory which reinstitutes racism in America. Cardona's policies include indoctrinating our children to accept and support gender identification which has led to the raping of young girls in girls' bathrooms where boys who identified as girls were allowed to enter. Cardons is also encouraging teachers to support and assist students through gender reassignment without parental approval, children too young to understand what impact this action will have on the rest of their lives. This individual, who promotes himself as an educator, is no more than an immoral Marxist-Communist. A Marxist-Communist who believes that it is okay for young students, who are already going through a complex and confusing period in their lives, to be subjected and exposed to transgender lifestyle, which includes drag queen reading seasons and sexually provocative performances. This to children as young as five years old. This man, who is charged with the oversight of our children's educational well-being, has been a willing accomplice and supporter of utilizing our federally funded school system to teach our children that America is systematically racist and evil and has been so since its founding. Cardona has and continues to turn a blind eye towards public schools that are allowing age-inappropriate sexually explicit books to be available in school libraries. He has allowed the indoctrination of our children into

Marxist-Communist ideology and has made no attempt to support parental involvement in their children's curriculum.

Source & Additional Information: (https://www.pewresearch.org/short-reads/2024/04/04/about-half-of-americans-say-public-k-12-education-is-going-in-the-wrong-direction/) (https://www.nytimes.com/2019/05/02/learning/lesson-plans/still-separate-still-unequal-teaching-about-school-segregation-and-educational-inequality.html)

Conservative education reform would result in a common sense and moral fact: Parents are children's primary educators. Until the beginning of the Biden-Harris reign, this was not disputed, let alone controversial. But since Biden's election, it has become clear that Marxist-Communist elites who run teachers' unions, school boards, the Marxist-Communist Democratic Party, and the corporate fake news media no longer share this view. Their contempt for parents' rights has fueled a long list of abuses, including racist curricula, war on girls' sports and bathrooms, episodes of criminal cover-ups, and student grooming.

Terrorist Parents: In late 2021, Secretary Cardona requested the National School Board Association to send a letter to the United States DOJ asking for federal assistance with what he referred to in his letter as a "growing number of threats of violence and acts of intimidation." The letter cited examples from several states and listed federal statutes under which assistance could be provided, including the Patriot Act, which addresses domestic terrorism. Parents of school-age children were being accused of committing threats of violence because they refused to end their comments after their allotted five minutes or refused to leave the premises when directed to do so for failing to comply with the five-minute limitations. Parents were accused of acts of intimidation for demanding to have a voice in their children's educational curriculum. They were accused of acts of intimidation because they insisted that boys who identified as girls not be allowed in girls' bathrooms. They were accused of acts of intimidation because they demanded that their children not be exposed to sexually explicit classroom studies or activities without their direct permission. Because these parents exercised their parental responsibilities for the educational welfare of their children, they are being classified as domestic terrorists and investigated as such by the FBI.

Despite Cardona's Doctoral degree in Education, he does not seem to understand or care that the billions of citizen tax dollars appropriated to our public school system are allocated to provide age-level appropriate education that will adequately prepare them for a successful career and life. Doctor Cardona's key priority seems to be to push the indoctrination of our children into the Marxist-Communist doctrine, turning our children into loyal Marxist-Communist slaves who are being taught that all things good come from the federal government and not from hard work and determination and that "Woke" is an ideology that should be practiced with pride.

For Doctor Cardona's information, let me point out that Darwin perfectly described Wokism, to which these Marxist-Communist educators and practitioners of Wokism religiously bow too, with the following observation: "At some stage, the human species will divide. While most will continue to evolve, a minority of those lacking the intellectual capacity of thought will develop as subspecies. Being easily led, form into packs attempting to control the majority. They will deny biology, undo centuries of human development by rewriting history, and gradually revert to their Primate origins. They will expect all to conform to their point of view without question." It sounds like our current situation with our Marxist-Communist Democrat Party government.

Teachers: Teachers are the backbone of our Republic, charged with fostering curiosity and creativity, developing skillfully educated children, and strengthening our children's intellectual ability to be productive and patriotic American citizens. Early childhood educators should be dedicated to nurturing, educating, and caring for young children. Only the most effective teachers and staff can ensure children in their care have the early experiences they need to be more likely to succeed in school, read at grade level, and graduate on time. A great traditional teacher in every classroom is one of the most important resources we can provide our children.

A conventional teacher recognizes that their mission is to prepare all students for success in college and careers and to understand that their primary role is to teach our children a core academic curriculum and not sexual, political, or religious ideologies. A traditional teacher recognizes that parents are responsible for teaching their children about their family's religious beliefs and political ideologies and why they believe in and support them. It is the parent's responsibility to tutor their children about their sexual values and behavioral expectations. It is the parent's role to address their children's concerns and questions regarding their children's sexual orientation confusion and to seek professional assistance if necessary.

Source & Additional Information: (https://www.ed.gov/teaching) (https://key.theirworld.org/resources/teachers)

These lessons are not a teacher's role without the explicit permission of the child's parents. Today's teachers fail our children to learn the intellectual skills required to compete and succeed. Just in Chicago alone, fifty-five Chicago schools reported NO proficiency in math or reading skills. This devastating level of educational proficiency is playing out in a vast majority of our Marxist-Communist Democrat-run schools nationwide. This can be expected when unions and the federal government dictate what is to be taught in the classroom without the coordinated input of the student's parents. Unfortunately, parents are being excluded and uninformed regarding a school's actual curriculum because of the Marxist-Communist Democrat Party's desire to create an army of morons, preferably violent, to wage war on civilization. How better to swell the ranks of the Marxist-Communist Democrat Party's brown shirt army? Our federally funded school system intends that this entire generation of high school and college graduates be loyal to the Marxist-Communist Democrat Party throughout their lives.

Source & Additional Information:(https://www.illinoispolicy.org/most-chicago-students-still-read-perform-math-below-grade-level/)

They will out-vote the working, productive, taxpaying citizens of America and demand that we pay to ensure equity in every citizen's life regardless of their contributions. The Marxist-Communist Democrat Party is a rot that is destroying the heart and soul of America. A telling Marxist proverb states: «Give a man a fish, and you feed him for a day. Teach a man to fish, and you feed him for a lifetime. Promise a man someone else›s fish, and you create a lifetime Marxist-Communist voter.»

Teachers Unions: The teacher's union has caused more damage to the American education system than COVID-19. Randi Weingarten, the President of the United Federation of Teachers, is probably the greatest obstacle to our education system. One of our education system's worst enemies and most significant cause of our failed school system is the United Federation of Teachers union under the leadership of Randi Weingarten. Former Secretary of State and C.I.A. director Mike Pompeo, who had dealt firsthand with autocrats like Vladimir Putin and Xi Jinping, described Randi Weingarten as "the most dangerous person in the world" in November of 2022. Teachers' unions stand in the way of education reform and fearlessly and shamelessly protect underperforming educators. Unions are good for teachers but bad for students.

Ex-police detective Jim Smith, who now works in New Jersey making a living investigating "bad" teachers and working through the union-led process of firing a teacher, described the process he was required to go through to get rid of a teacher who allegedly hit students because of the teacher's union. Jim Smith stated it took him four years and $283,000 in taxpayer money to finally obtain this teacher's dismissal. Throughout the four years, this lousy teacher sat at home eating popcorn, watching soap operas, and collecting full salary and health care benefits. Terry Moe, a professor of political science at Stanford and a senior fellow at the Hoover Institution, agrees that unions create more problems than they solve. Moe told the Daily Beast, "We're not saying unions are responsible for every problem of the public schools, but they are major obstacles to reform." Moe adds that it takes on average $200,000, fifteen percent of a principal's time, and at least two years to get a bad teacher out of the school system.

<u>Source & Additional Information</u>: *(https://www.publicschoolreview.com/blog/are-teacher-unions-a-help-or-hindrance-to-public-education)*

Teacher unions are known recipients of billions of taxpayer dollars from the Federal government whenever the Marxist-Communist Democrat Party is in power. Money cleverly hidden in thousand-page Omnibus bills. Money purportedly intended to help unions better help educators perform in the classrooms and bring about reform. The raw truth is that this is no more than a myth perpetrated by union organizations and their Marxist-Communist Democrat Party allies in Congress to hide the fact that the teacher's union is no more than a money laundering operation to put money into Marxist-Communist Democrat Party election coffers. Just your basic corrupt attitude of "You scratch my back, and I'll scratch your back."

Dropout Rates: The Department of Education has declared that they are committed to shining a light on where students are making progress and where they need additional support. According to the Department of Education, this commitment has resulted in the highest school graduation rates of all time. Dropout rates are at historic lows; however, the dropout rates remain high for people of color, in particular American Indian and Alaskan Native high school students who have the highest high school dropout rate, according to a National Center for Education Statistics 2021 study. According to Secretary Cardona, more students are graduating from high school, and more graduates are going to college than ever before, which may very well be true. Although our failed federally funded school system may be graduating the highest rate of students of all time under Secretary Cardona's tenure, students who do graduate are ill-prepared for college or careers, and their level of core academic capabilities rank at the level of third-world countries.

Source & Additional Information: (https://www.nsba.org/Perspectives/2020/black-students-condition-education) (https://www.statista.com/statistics/1120207/rate-high-school-dropouts-us/)

Colleges and Universities: The cost of a college education has gotten out of control due to the federal government's never-ending increases in financial aid and student loans. Industrial Arts and Home Industrial Arts courses have been removed from public school curriculums to add space for computer labs and classes to help push students into college. This is done even though members of the Boards of Education, school Administrators, and Academic Teachers know that college is not for every student and that Industrial Arts and Home Industrial Arts courses are precisely what most of our children need. School districts are doing nothing for non-college-bound students. No "career awareness programs" exist to identify careers that do not require a college education. Simply put, guidance teachers, members of Boards of Education, and School administrators do not care! Some of the most intelligent and talented young adults have Industrial Arts and Home Economics abilities, yet academic people look down on people who work with their hands. The problem is that there are no longer individuals within the federal school system who are willing to represent curriculums in these areas to prepare non-college-bound students for careers in these areas. Guidance Departments, Boards of Education, and School Administrator members have not touched physical education, music, or art. Physical education brings money into the school system, and music and art have "snob appeal," music also feeds into the "football game half-time program" with the High School Band. It is all about show and tell and smoke screens.

Education Subsidies: The United States Department of Education spends tens of billions of dollars a year on subsidies for higher education. Most of the spending goes to student aid, with the balance going to grants for educational institutions. Federal Pell grants are more than $30 billion a year, federal student loans are about $100 billion a year, and grants to colleges and universities are $2.5 billion yearly. Taxpayers pay for federal college subsidies and benefit the universities and colleges, but not the young adults expected to earn higher future incomes due to their advanced educations. Thus, the effect of subsidies, in part, is to tax blue-collar workers who do not attend college to pay tuition for future white-collar professionals. But why should the government subsidize future high earners at the expense of average working people? For one thing, academically qualified high school graduates will have a stronger incentive to invest in their education and to study to earn their degrees because they will realize that doing so will lead to higher earnings. The potential for higher earnings is a big incentive for students and their parents to save or, if necessary, secure loans through banking markets to pay for their college costs. In 2010, the federal government unconstitutionally nationalized student lending.

Source & Additional Information: (https://www.downsizinggovernment.org/education/higher-education-subsidies)

Supporters of student aid often say higher education is "good for the public" and would be underprovided without government tax breaks and subsidies, which is far from true. While student aid programs aim to help students, the programs also transfer wealth from taxpayers to academic institutions. That is because the rise in student subsidies over the decades has fueled inflation in education costs. Tuition and other college costs have soared as subsidies have risen. As more Americans seek a college education, prices are driven up. Ordinarily, costs would be restrained by consumers' willingness and ability to pay, but because federal subsidies have helped absorb tuition increases, such restraints have been eliminated. Colleges and universities see federal subsidies as money for the taking, so tuition is set high enough to capture those funds and whatever else can be extracted from students and their parents. Rising federal aid is causing college cost inflation. Federal assistance has helped to increase student enrollment of students not ready or suited for college. As a result of a failed federally funded school system, most first-year college students need to take remedial classes. Further, higher education institutions have reduced their standards to adapt to the growth of second-rate students. The decline in the average student quality is also suggested by research showing a falling amount of time in college spent studying and that there are only small, measured gains in critical thinking as students progress through today's colleges. Finally, as college enrollment rises, that rise has been accompanied by declining adult literacy for people with degrees.

Cutting federal aid probably would not reduce accessibility for genuinely needy and deserving students. For one thing, college cost inflation induced by federal aid hurts low-income families more than others because they face sticker prices that appear daunting. Many private philanthropists support promising low-income college kids, and they would have more interest in doing so if the federal government got out of the student aid business. Also, because college education has real value, qualified young adults and their families have strong incentives to invest in higher education, and private lenders and aid providers have a stronger motive to lend to them. Unlike the government, private lenders are more incentivized to scrutinize aid applicants to judge whether they are ready for college and studying in valuable fields. Thus, private aid would likely reduce the problem of people entering college, racking up debt, and not finishing college or getting degrees the economy does not need. Cutting federal subsidies would restrain tuition and related costs as students shopped for the best deals. In turn, that would force schools to reduce their bloated costs.

There are at least three further signs of bloat. First, as many as forty percent of people who enter a four-year program do not finish, nor do roughly seventy percent of people who enter two-year programs. Second, about a third of those who finish four-year degrees end up in jobs that do not require their degrees. Third, even those who find jobs related to their degrees may have learned little in college that applies to those jobs. Numerous job categories employers advertise for people with degrees are positions where a college education is not needed to meet the required skills for those jobs. This is called "credential inflation." Employers ask for a college degree, regardless of job needs, because degrees are so abundant that not having one is seen as a sign of a deficiency.

Source & Additional Information: (https://www.the74million.org/article/alarming-statistics-tell-the-story-behind-americas-college-completion-crisis-nearly-a-third-of-all-college-student-still-dont-have-a-degree-six-years-later/)

Rising Federal Regulatory Control: Increasing top-down control and subsidization from Washington has threatened our education system. The growth in federal subsidies has been accompanied by calls for more oversight, micromanagement, and red tape imposed by Washington. The waste and bureaucracy of top-down federal control of our public school system is exemplified by Title IX of the Education Amendments Law of 1972. Title IX has created significant disruptions in activities such as college athletics, which have long since passed its need as colleges have well-established female-only programs that would remain intact because those athletic programs generate income for the college. Today, the only ones who profit are the legal industry, which administers, enforces, and litigates the complex rules of Title IX. The law is overseen by the Office of Civil Rights in the Department of Education, which had five-hundred and sixty employees as of 2022, earning an average annual compensation of $142,000. Title IX is a regulatory octopus with tentacles reaching into education programs, athletics, cheerleading, fraternities, and other activities. Federal control expansion also includes efforts to impose "national standards" on higher education. In the George W. Bush administration, Education Secretary Margaret Spellings created a commission to formulate a "comprehensive national strategy" for higher education, indicating that it wanted to tighten federal control. The commission's report stopped short of advocating outright federal imposition of standards and tests. Still, it did call for a "national strategy for lifelong learning" and a federal database with information on every college student in the country.

Source & Additional Information: (https://www.downsizinggovernment.org/education/higher-education-subsidies)

***Waste, Fraud, and Abuse*:** Most federal subsidy programs suffer from large amounts of waste, fraud, and abuse. Medicare, Medicaid, school lunches, farm aid, and other programs all suffer from these problems. When programs hand out billions of dollars of grants or loans, they attract dishonest individuals with criminal intent. For decades, federal student aid programs have been subject to waste, fraud, and abuse. In 1991, an in-depth Senate investigation found that federal student loan programs were plagued with fraud and abuse at every level. The investigation accused the Department of Education of "gross mismanagement, ineptitude, and neglect" and found a "dismal record" of dealing with loan abuses. Thirty-two years later, fraud and abuse have only gotten significantly worse.

Source & Additional Information: (https://www.nytimes.com/1991/05/21/us/panel-finds-wide-abuse-in-student-loan-program.html)

One fraud scheme in the early 1990s involved a group of Jewish schools in New York, which received millions of dollars in Pell grant money but spent little on education. One school pocketed $3.2 million in grants and spent just $21,000 on education. Another scandal involved a business college in Puerto Rico, whose leaders used $3 million of Pell Grants to buy items such as sports cars and real estate. Yet another scandal involved a college in Florida that recruited "students" at food stamp offices and housing projects and helped them get loans. The school owners then received tens of millions of dollars in loans and pocketed it. The Department of Education loses approximately $5 billion annually to waste, fraud, and loan defaults. Fraud and abuse continue to this day, and it is the American taxpayers who suffer.

The federal government issues about $100 billion in new student loans yearly. Total student loans outstanding are nearly $2 trillion. Student loans now surpass auto loans and credit cards as the second largest type of household debt, after mortgage debt. Student loan debt has a high rate of delinquency compared to other types of debt, and delayed or non-repayment is encouraged by many federal loan tolerance or forgiveness programs. Taxpayers could be hit with billions of dollars in losses in coming years. Many federal subsidy programs are targets for widespread abuse because they are such large and poorly administered programs. With college aid, over forty million loans are outstanding, and more than seven thousand are outstanding for postsecondary institutions. The Department of Education has shown itself incapable of efficiently managing such a vast system. Private alternatives are less likely to be abused and more likely to benefit those students most in need. The federal Department of Education is a total failure and an unconstitutional entity that needs to be eliminated, with education responsibilities transferred to the sovereign states as intended by our Constitution.

Source & Additional Information: (https://www.usatoday.com/money/blueprint/student-loans/average-student-loan-debt-statistics/)

Knowledge Is Power: Miguel Cardona and the Marxist-Communist ideologues realize that knowledge is power, and this power must be removed for a Marxist-Communist regime to prosper. To this end, our children are the losers, graduating from high school and unable to do basic elementary math, reading, or writing. Instead of allowing our federally funded school system to continue failing our children by focusing on heterosexual, bisexual, homosexual, transgender, or any other alternative sex education and Marxist-Communist indoctrination, maybe Doctor Cardona should be working on assuring that our children's public schools are havens of academic education and intellectual growth. Despite Doctor Miguel Cardona's background in the field of education, this man is not morally fit to be in the position of Secretary of Education. He is, in fact, abetting the sexual abuse of our children.

School Choice Discrimination: Doctor Miguel Cardona and Marxist-Communist Democrat Party-controlled states and cities are attempting to restrict parents' direct access to education assistance funds who prefer to send their children to schools of their choice. In the State of Maine, for the first 100 years of its tuition assistance program, the state allowed families to choose any school using tuition assistance dollars, whether public, private, religious, or secular. But in 1981, the state enacted a new restriction: Any school receiving tuition assistance payments had to be "nonsectarian," having no "religious practice" involved.

For example, a school could be named after a patron saint of the Catholic Church, but teachers could not celebrate those ideas or even add value-laden concepts to the school curriculum. In separating schools that were religious in name only from schools that practiced religion, lawmakers thought they could keep "truly" religious schools from accessing publicly available funds. In early 2022, the Commissioner of Maine's Department of Education was sued over this restriction. The lawsuit alleged that the "non-sectarian" requirement violated the Free Exercise Clause, the Establishment Clause of the First Amendment, and the Equal Protection Clause of the Fourteenth Amendment. The District Court rejected the petitioner's constitutional claims and granted judgment to the commissioner. The First Circuit affirmed. The District Court's decision was appealed and made its way to the United States Supreme Court as the Carson versus Makin filing. In 2022, the United States Supreme Court ruled 6-3 that Maine could not prevent parents from using otherwise generally available state school choice funds at religious schools simply because those schools provided religious instruction. The reason for this decision rests in the actual language of the Constitution and not the perceived language. The First Amendment to the Constitution reads as follows: "Congress shall make no law respecting an establishment of religion or prohibiting the free exercise thereof ...." Receiving religious instruction or attending a religious school is not "*an establishment of religion.*" In this context, "establishment" means to create, not instructing or attending. Another federal bastardization of actual meaning and intent to align with their agenda to eliminate religion in our society.

Source & Additional Information: (https://en.wikipedia.org/wiki/Carson_v._Makin)

Cases before the 2022 Supreme Court decision include the 2017 Trinity Lutheran Church versus the State of Missouri case; the Supreme Court held that Missouri could not discriminate against otherwise eligible recipients of public benefits because of their religion. In 2020, the Espinoza versus the State of Montana, the Supreme Court held unconstitutional a provision of the Montana Constitution that barred aid to a school "controlled in whole or in part by any church, sect, or denomination." In the 2022 Carson versus Makin decision, the Supreme Court determined that when private individuals use taxpayer funding to choose a religious K-12 school for their children, those individuals are not using public money to "establish" a religion, something that would be prohibited under the First Amendment to the Constitution. They are simply making the best educational choice for their children. Maine education officials are back in federal court less than a year later. The State of Maine has ignored the Supreme Court decision and is now back in court over its failure to comply. This is but one example of many similar situations occurring across our country in the Marxist-Communist Democrat Party's attempt to eliminate religion in the United States. Those schools that have not yet been sued over their policies restricting student assistance funding will hopefully be sued before all of our courts are taken over by Marxist-Communist judges and juries.

Source & Additional Information: (https://crsreports.congress.gov/product/pdf/LSB/LSB10785)

The state of Virginia's Marxist-Communist Democrat Party rejected a bill that would require children to be educated about the evils of communism and to give honor to its victims. They claim the law would be "racist" against Asian Americans. These highly educated state legislators never learned that communism originated in Europe, not Asia. The teacher's union agreed with the Democrats, which is unsurprising. In response, immigrant Xi Van Fleet, who fled Communist China, blasted the Marxist-Communist Democrats, stating, "How could the Democrat legislators and the teacher's union come to this absurd and disturbing conclusion? The only thing I can think of is that they are profoundly ignorant of real history and the history of communism, and they themselves are communists." AMEN!

Federal student aid drives up tuition costs, encourages bloat and inefficiency, and unfairly burdens taxpayers. But most importantly, because federal aid comes with top-down regulations, it threatens the core strengths of American higher education, including institutional autonomy, competition, and innovation. All efforts to impose federal regulations on colleges and universities should be rejected. At the same time, federal subsidies to students and institutions must be eliminated.

Source & Additional Information: (https://www.downsizinggovernment.org/education/higher-education-subsidies)

Section X: Secretary of Transportation

The Secretary of Transportation oversees the United States Department of Transportation, which has over 55,000 employees and thirteen agencies, including the Federal Aviation Administration, the Federal Highway Administration, the Federal Railroad Administration, and the National Highway Traffic Safety

Administration, to name a few. The Secretary of Transportation is Pete Buttigieg, who receives an annual salary of $221,400.

Secretary Pete Buttigieg is a want-to-be President of the United States who has stated that he is committed to delivering the world's leading transportation system for America's economy and the American people. He boasts of creating organizational excellence in the department's operations, focusing on the department's five policy goals: safety, jobs, *equity*, *climate*, and innovation. Yet, three-plus years into his appointment, he has done little to correct the issues plaguing America's supply chains. But how can an individual deliver on any promises if he does not have the knowledge, expertise, or qualifications to be the Secretary of Transportation? How can he deliver on any promises to correct our transportation issues if he focuses on equity, inclusion, and climate rather than the critical problems at hand? The real problem with the Department of Transportation is Pete Buttigieg, whose priorities are all in the wrong places because his only qualifications are that he is of the LGBTQ+ community and his only priority is himself. How can he deliver on any promises if he believes that implementing equity and inclusion as the two primary criteria for hiring employees rather than on experience and capability will fix the Department of Transportation's problems?

Pete Buttigieg is the Secretary of Transportation only because of Biden-Harris's emphasis on equity and inclusion, and unfortunately for America, not the necessary skills and knowledge required to lead the department. As stated, Pete Buttigieg is the real problem for the ongoing economically disastrous and dysfunctional supply chain. However, while serving as mayor, he was nationally recognized with an award for innovative streetscape design from the United States Department of Transportation—impressive qualifications, to say the least.

Commerce Clause: Clause 3 of Article I Section 8 of the United States Constitution, generally referred to as the Commerce

Clause, is one of the enumerated powers under which Congress may legislate. The clause states that Congress shall have the power *"to regulate Commerce with foreign Nations, and among the several States, and with the Indian Tribes."* The Constitutional intent of the Commerce Clause is restricted to legislating over matters involving the export and import of goods with foreign nations and between the sovereign states through transporting such goods by ship, trains, and highways. Like many other Constitutional authorities provided to the federal government, Clause 3 of Article I Section 8 of the United States Constitution has been severely bastardized and misinterpreted by Congress and the Supreme Court to meet political agendas.

Congress continuously invokes the Commerce Clause, specifically that part that addresses commerce "among the several states" as the authority for their taking control of and regulating business within the sovereign states. The Supreme Court has often interpreted the scope of Congress's authority to regulate interstate commerce under the Commerce Clause. That interpretation continually evolves further away from the original intent of this Section of Article I. The Commerce Clause does not authorize the Federal government to regulate businesses within a state or the United States. This clause states "among" the several States, and *"among"* is defined as commerce between the sovereign States and not commerce within a sovereign state or between individual businesses and the citizens within a State. Once again, pointing out how Congress and the Supreme Court have been rewriting the Constitution when politically convenient.

Every major post-1970 environment law relied on the corrupt interpretation and intent of this Constitutional power to restrict air and water pollution and protect endangered species; to enact the Americans with Disabilities Act, the Civil Rights Act of 1964, and the Federal Food Drug & Cosmetic Act, to name a few. Congress has further utilized this section of the Constitution to unconstitutionally regulate the exchanging, buying, or selling of things having economic value between two or more entities within a state. The Supreme Court also held that Congress was within its Commerce Power to prohibit discrimination in restaurants and motels and regulate firearms manufacturing. None of the above authorities addressed are given to the federal government under Clause 3 of Article I Section 8 of the United States Constitution. In all of the above cases, and numerous other cases, the Tenth Amendment to the Constitution is applicable and states that "The powers not delegated to the United States by the Constitution, nor prohibited by it to the States, are reserved to the States respectively, or to the people." Congress's use of the Commerce Clause to justify exercising legislative power over the activities within a state and its citizens has led to significant and ongoing controversy regarding the balance of power between the federal government and the states.

Source & Additional Information: (https://www.law.cornell.edu/wex/commerce_clause)

Supply Chain: Under Pete Buttigieg's watch, we have dealt with a national supply chain disruption and catastrophe, which seems unending. The most significant shock to our supply chain was the unscientifically unfounded COVID-19 pandemic restrictions and mandates that severely reduced the availability of the necessary numbers of employees required to move products from seaports and distribution centers to the marketplaces. After three-plus years as the Secretary of Transportation, although Buttigieg did initially inherit the supply chain crisis, he has yet to work on finding solutions, resulting in the supply chain crisis looming heavily over business owners and consumers alike. We have yet to see or hear of any of Buttigieg's plans to rectify the problems and return our national supply chain to a workable system with backup plans that can be immediately triggered should such a meltdown occur.

The ongoing supply chain issue has now been followed up by the collapse of our commercial airway system's antiquated computer-controlled airway tracking and passenger manifest system. This failure of an out-of-date electronic system has resulted in innumerable cancellations of commercial flights over an unacceptable period of time. Countless flight passengers have missed critical business meetings, personal endeavors, or sobering family gatherings while stranded in airports nationwide. Missed events that can never be recaptured. It took Pete Buttigieg two weeks before he found the courage to realize that he was responsible for addressing the commercial flight crisis to the American people and explaining what had happened and what would be done to fix the problem. As can be expected from someone who knows nothing about transportation, he failed miserably.

Source & Additional Information: (https://www.npr.org/2023/01/11/1148488850/ thousands-of-flights-were-delayed-or-canceled-due-to-critical-computer-system-fa) (https://www.cnn.com/2023/01/13/business/airline-meltdowns/index.html)

Highway System: Like many, my wife and I spend a lot of time traveling the highways of the United States in our RV. Most of the roads we travel on are plagued with potholes, crumbling blacktops, and deep tracks caused by the heavy loads carried by truckers. The quality of these roads is so poor that driving an RV over them is a recipe for damage, requiring a trip to an RV repair shop after a long trip.

The Interstate system is weak due to age, heavy use, and repeatedly delayed repair funding. The Interstate system is in critical need of significant reconstruction and modernization. American travelers, truckers, and traveling business sales representatives experience highway issues every day driving on our Interstate Highway System, once the world's envy. Our Interstate Highway System is now in serious need of modernization, and many parts of our Interstate Highway System have deteriorated to that near a third-world country. The Interstate system plays a critical national role in economic success, quality of life for every American, and the movement of military personnel and equipment; thus, it must be given the priority it deserves and promised by the Obama Administration, which passed a trillion-plus dollar omnibus bill for infrastructure upgrades. To this day, no one knows where most of that money went because it was not utilized to correct our transportation systems. Our rapidly deteriorating highway infrastructure is a clear and present danger to our nation's supply chain. Breakdowns in the Interstate Highway System add an annual $75 billion to the cost of freight transportation, and sixty-seven million tons of excess carbon dioxide emissions are released into the atmosphere every year from trucks stuck in traffic congestion. Where are the radical environmentalists who should be protesting this excessive amount of carbon dioxide into the atmosphere with demands that our interstate highway system be upgraded to eliminate this threat to our environment? This severe crisis underscores the urgent need for Congress to make real infrastructure investments backed by a fair and equitable user-based revenue source.

Smoothness on most segments of the Interstate system is outrageously lacking; the crumbling foundations of most highway sections need to be reconstructed and resurfaced to increase the smoothness of our highways. Based on the findings of the Transportation Research Board's Interstate report, recommended needs for restoration of the Interstate Highway System include the foundational reconstruction of Interstate highways, bridges, and interchanges; improvement to roadway safety features; system right-sizing, including upgrading of some roadway corridors to Interstate standards; adding needed additional highway capacity on existing routes; adding additional corridors; and, modifying some urban segments to maintain connectivity while remediating economic and social disruption.

The American Recovery and Reinvestment Act of 2009, signed into law by President Obama on February 17th, 2009, allocated $46 billion for transportation projects, plus an additional $27 billion for highway and bridge construction and repair. Of the

1.7 trillion dollars appropriated for the implementation of the Act, the amount allocated for highway infrastructure is a drop in the bucket. The Act was passed to put Americans back to work, and what better way to create tens of thousands of jobs nationwide than investing in transportation repairs and upgrades? Worse yet, no one in the federal government knows where the majority of these taxpayer dollars went, as there was little to no accountability or tracking of those dollars. And what happened to all the money collected from the sur-taxes we pay at the pump meant for maintaining and repairing our highways? Borrowed (confiscated) by Congress on the promise that the money taken would be replaced by future tax revenue, which has never occurred. Congress keeps on confiscating this money source as if it were a bowl of jellybeans while our highways become increasingly dilapidated and unsafe.

<u>Source & Additional Information</u>: *(https://tripnet.org/reports/interstate-system-national-news-release-06-22-2021/) (https://en.wikipedia.org/wiki/American_Recovery_and_Reinvestment_Act_of_2009)*

Railway System: On February 3rd, 2023, a potentially deadly train derailment occurred in East Palestine, Ohio. This tragic accident involved approximately fifty cars, causing numerous chemically filled tankers, including tankers filled with the highly flammable chemical vinyl chloride, to burst open, sending clouds of deadly chemicals into the air to linger in the atmosphere or settle back down in area water sources and vegetation, sparking severe health concerns. Some of these railway tankers exploded, sending shrapnel throughout the residential area surrounding the derailment site. The dangerous toxin was released into the air from five derailed cars before fire crews could ignite the tankers to gain control of the highly toxic and flammable chemicals being released. Area residents were required to abandon their homes because of the health risks from the fumes, but was it quick enough? No one knows how long it will be before we can fully comprehend the consequences of this disastrous accident. Within days of the derailment, area residents began reporting health problems and animals dying, including fish, chickens, and livestock. Those tankers did not derail because of any faulty components on the tankers. They derailed because the railway tracks they were traversing were compromised due to a lack of upgrading and repair.

Few federal officials have made public statements regarding the derailment and the toxic fire, most notably Pete Buttigieg, who did not even deem the incident worthy of mention during his February 13th, 2023, appearance at the National Association of Counties Legislative Conference in Washington. During his on-stage discussions, Buttigieg touched on topics like racial disparity and the safety risks of "balloons," drawing laughter from the audience. However, his avoidance of the topic of derailment and toxic chemical release did not go over well on social media, where critics complained that he seemed to be callously dodging the subject. Pete Buttigieg may have had little to say about the East Palestine train derailment. Still, Joyless Behar, one of the miserable Marxist-Communist Democrats on "The View," had plenty to say when she stated that the people of East Palestine, Ohio, "got what they deserved because they voted for Trump." What a hate-filled, ignorant old wet blanket to wish such suffering on innocent people. Are her viewers really as equally stupid and hateful as the individuals who host this program?

Buttigieg finally broke his silence nearly two weeks after the incident and the criticism he received by posting on Twitter, "I continue to be concerned about the impacts of the February 3rd train derailment near East Palestine, Ohio, and the effects on families in the ten days since their lives were upended through no fault of their own." He further referred to an investigation into the accident by the National Transportation Safety Board, noting that the Department of Transportation was assisting with the probe. He tweeted, "Our Federal Rail Administration and Pipelines and Hazardous Materials teams were onsite within hours of the initial incident and continue to be actively engaged. We will look to these investigation results and, based on them, use all relevant authorities to ensure accountability and continue to support safety." As if everyone impacted had Twitter Accounts.

The question that begs asking is, why wasn't Pete Buttigieg on the scene within hours of the derailment making this statement? Another of Buttigieg's failures out of many. Pete Buttigieg was not on the scene within hours because, like most other Biden-nominated Washington elites, this was a matter involving the peasant class and was not worthy of the time and effort of a high-ranking government official such as himself. He was a no-show out of fear of being asked questions by the news media on a subject he had no clue about; after all, the only credentials qualifying him to be the Secretary of Transportation were based on equity, diversity, and inclusion. Being the first gay married man with an adopted baby does not get things resolved and back on track, literally. For example, on March 26th, 2023, another train derailment occurred in North Dakota, involving one hundred oil tankers that released thousands of gallons of oil that soaked into the ground around the derailment, making its way to area creeks and rivers.

In 2020, as the former mayor of South Bend, Indiana, Pete Buttigieg ran for president, but he pulled out of the race after failing to rally enough support for his campaign. Actually, he garnered no support at all. When President Joe Biden took office, he invited the former candidate to become his Secretary of Transportation despite Buttigieg's total lack of experience in the field. Now, Buttigieg is facing criticism over his response to the train derailment in East Palestine, Ohio, which left a community reeling from toxic chemicals released into their town. When he finally visited the town, instead of addressing the town's citizens' hardships and what he planned on doing to resolve the national railroad track deterioration, he criticized conservatives who criticized his job performance harshly. In an interview with fake news CNN on March 6th, 2023, Buttigieg called out the "East

Coast elites," of which he is one, for attacking his handling of national transportation issues. He chose not to talk about the harm and suffering of the residents of East Palestine but rather about the planet's environment and lack of funding to the Environmental Protection Agency." While he lashed out at his critics, he admitted that he should have traveled to East Palestine earlier.

Buttigieg, who made it to the train derailment location a day after former President Donald Trump visited, called the 45th president's visit "somewhat maddening." He attacked the former President's policies and decision to hand out campaign swag during his visit. Some Americans critical of Buttigieg also called him out for the shoes he wore during his visit, which appeared to be expensive dress shoes rather than work shoes that would have been more appropriate for visiting a toxic chemical spill and train disaster site. Buttigieg pointed out that criticism of his wardrobe decisions was ridiculous and completely unnecessary, as the attention should be on "an agenda that will save lives on our railroads." Everyone in politics is subjected to criticism at some point, and Buttigieg has undoubtedly gotten his fair share and has earned every bit of criticism thrown his way. Americans can learn much about a person's character and plans by how the individual responds to criticism.

It will take months, if not years, before the actual cost of this disaster is known. What is already known, and has been known for decades, is that America's railway track system is in dire need of refurbishing and upgrading against potentially deadly safety issues occurring throughout the country. This failure to demand that railway companies fund and accomplish this critical endeavor is a direct failure by our federal legislators. As for Buttigieg, he is far too preoccupied, flying across the country in a government-owned jet and polluting the air as he does so to speak at fun events than do the job of the Secretary of Transportation. If he even knew how.

The railroad industry is currently in turmoil, and customers, including farmers, energy producers, and railroad executives themselves, say that the industry needs an overhaul. The rapid deterioration of the tracks on which railroad cars navigate is of most concern, resulting in constant railroad accidents and derailments—derailment of railroad cars transporting deadly toxic materials. In 2021, the Marxist-Communist Democrat Party passed a $1.7 trillion infrastructure bill from which a billion dollars in subsidies were allotted to national railway safety to bail them out of the crises they had created by placing profits above safety. This funding to major railroad companies was justified under the misinterpretation of the "*General Welfare*" clause of the Constitution.

Along with this amount not being nearly enough to repair dilapidated railroad track lines across America, this money was unconstitutionally provided to private railroad companies who carry the financial responsibility for the upkeep and maintenance of their privately owned railroad track system, not the American taxpayers. Railroad company executives refuse to reduce their profit margin for railroad track repairs because they know that if they wait long enough and accidents continue to occur, putting American lives at risk, the federal government will come to their rescue and pay the costs. Bailout, I believe, is the appropriate term to use here.

<u>Source & Additional Information</u>: *(https://en.wikipedia.org/wiki/East_Palestine,_Ohio,_train_derailment)*

(https://apnews.com/article/north-dakota-train-derailment-canadian-pacific-750e6e60 05e5387b1a4f32ba587fadba) (https://www.npr.org/2023/02/17/1157999692/railroad-workers-have-been-worried-about-safety-concerns-for-years-reporter-says)

Section XI: Secretary of Human and Health Services

The Department of Health and Human Services (DHHS) mission is to enhance the health and well-being of all Americans by providing effective health and human services and by fostering sound, sustained advances in the sciences underlying medicine, public health, and social services. The DHHS is the largest grant-making agency in the United States. Most DHHS grants are provided directly to states, territories, tribes, and educational and community organizations. These are then offered to people and organizations deemed eligible to receive funding. The United States Secretary of Health and Human Services is Xavier Becerra.

So, here are some of the better-known unconstitutional services and forms of assistance offered to people at taxpayer expense: shelter assistance; assistance with crimes and abuse; child welfare services; food and clothing assistance; general guidance and life planning help; insurance assistance; language barrier assistance; community integration programs; community improvement programs; and general community events. According to our Constitution, none of these services are authorized to be administered by the federal government. Given that the Constitution does not give the federal government the authority over these programs, they all belong under the purview of the sovereign states.

As is the reputation of our Marxist-Communist federal government, they have assumed control of these programs and have politicalized and weaponized them to fit the Marxist-Communist agenda. The DHHS has a massive impact on the federal government, from declaring public health emergencies to managing Medicare and Medicaid to its $1.6 trillion annual budget. Under former President Biden and President Barack Obama, the Department of Human and Health Services has also used its power over health policy to promote abortion and transgender ideology.

The DHHS has replaced science and medicine with politics and ideology. This Marxist-Communist takeover of the DHHS has caused more harm and abuse than real public health issues. Reform can only happen if entrenched special interests, lawless bureaucratic leaders, and Big Pharma are reined in and eliminated from impacting this Department. The DHHS must be returned to its proper role of promoting public health.

Source & Additional Information: (https://www.hhs.gov/about/agencies/iea/ partnerships/about-the-partnership-center/hhs-grants-information/index.html)

National Institute for Health: The National Institutes of Health (NIH) is the primary federal biomedical research center in the United States. Its goals are to improve national health through discovery and innovation, foster resources that prevent disease, expand the biomedical knowledge base, and promote high-level scientific conduct. These goals, if adhered to by its leadership, would support the National Institutes of Health's mission to "enhance health, lengthen life, and reduce the burdens of illness and disability" through supporting and conducting fundamental scientific research. The number of "fake" scientific papers published through the National Institute for Health is significant and alarming. The Marxist-Communists love these fake research papers to "prove" that their wacky ideas are real. In 2020, about 24% of all "scientific papers" were bogus. The number of fake scientific papers has now climbed to 34% annually, and we taxpayers pay for their creation and publication. Unfortunately, the goals of promoting and conducting high-level scientific papers to prevent disease have fallen far short of taxpayers' expectations following the spread of COVID-19.

Source & Additional Information: (https://www.science.org/content/article/fake-scientific-papers-are-alarmingly-common)

COVID-19: In 1968, Doctor Anthony Fauci began his tenure at the National Institute for Health as a clinical associate in the National Institute of Allergy and Infectious Diseases Laboratory of Clinical Investigation. In 1980, he was appointed chief of the Laboratory of Immunoregulation, a position he held until his supposed retirement on December 31st, 2022, as there are indications that he may still be involved with the National Institute for Health without disclosing such involvement. He has also held the position of Medical Advisor to Presidents Obama, Trump, and Biden.

Source & Additional Information: (https://www.britannica.com/biography/Anthony-Fauci)

The COVID-19 virus, which causes severe acute respiratory syndrome coronavirus 2 (SARS-CoV-2), was first identified in an outbreak in the Chinese city of Wuhan in December of 2019, according to the Chinese Communist Party and Doctor Fauci. The Chinese Communist Party probably identified this outbreak much earlier but purposely withheld this information from the rest of the world, resulting in millions of unnecessary deaths and an estimated $12.5 trillion worldwide in attempts to combat the virus. At its origin, the Chinese Communist Party government reportedly only attempted to contain its spread within the city of Wuhan, quarantining residents of that area from moving about throughout China. However, the Chinese Communist Party allowed individuals in this quarantined area to travel throughout the world, allowing the virus to spread to other areas of Asia and eventually worldwide. This action, or lack of action on the part of the Chinese Communist Party, is a clear indication that the Chinese Communist Party purposely intended the virus to infect individuals throughout the world by failing to quarantine Wuhan citizens from traveling anywhere outside the quarantined area.

Doctor Anthony Fauci is probably the person who was most responsible for the constant failure of the DHHS to provide reliable and consistent guidance to the American public. When the COVID-19 virus was first identified, Doctor Fauci was confused about what he shared with the general public. He consistently communicated conflicting information about how lethal and contagious the coronavirus was throughout the progressive spread of the virus. Behind closed doors, Doctor Fauci questioned whether the virus could be spread asymptomatically, whether wearing masks could help contain it, and whether it could be re-infected, but did not share this lack of knowledge regarding the virus to the general public. Doctor Fauci seemed to be all over the map with his evaluation of the severity of the pandemic, the need for social distancing, the wearing of masks, and the closure of schools and businesses. Doctor Fauci initially advised the general public that everyone should wear masks, but he reversed himself, stating that masks were unnecessary as they provided little protection. Later into the pandemic, he again reversed himself, advising that everyone needed to wear masks, suggesting that perhaps people should wear two masks layered upon one another. At this point, he began recommending to President Trump and Congress that even more stringent measures would be needed to contain the spread of COVID-19. Based on his recommendations, socializing at entertainment centers, bars, and restaurants was prohibited unless you happened to be a wealthy Marxist-Communist Democrat Party elitist or political figure; all non-essential businesses were closed, but Doctor Fauci only dictated that small businesses were non-essential while allowing large box-store companies to remain open, which resulted in the devastation of tens of thousands of small business, the driving force of our economic systems and the unemployment of millions of Americans; churches were prohibited from holding religious services while bars and strip-joints were allowed to remain open; and any traveling was highly discouraged, again, unless you happened to be a wealth Marxist-Communist Democrat Party elitist, political figure, or supporter. The stock market collapsed, unemployment spiked, and the national atmosphere devolved into collective anxiety.

<u>Source & Additional Information</u>: *(https://publichealth.jhu.edu/2020/5-ways-the-us-botched-the-response-to-covid-19) (https://www.cdc.gov/covid/index.html)*

In public speeches and interviews, Doctor Fauci warned that the United States was facing a viral apocalypse, predicting that the United States could be potentially facing millions upon millions of United States citizen deaths. As it turns out, Doctor Fauci got it all wrong, which allowed the Marxist-Communist Administration under Biden-Harris an opportunity to begin imposing control over the people. Right out of the Marxist-Communist playbook. At the very outset of the outbreak, Fauci insisted on contact tracing. An enormous amount of valuable time and resources was wasted trying to track down every last person who might have come into contact with every person who might have had COVID. He made Zoom calls to groups of hundreds of "contact tracers" to give them pep talks. For a highly infectious airborne viral infection, this was a criminal misuse of public health resources that did nothing to stop the spread of COVID. For sexually transmitted diseases such as HIV/AIDS, syphilis, and gonorrhea, tracing and treating contacts is very effective in disease prevention because the population of infected individuals is extremely small in comparison to the COVID-19 infection. That is why we have never tried to prevent the spread of commonly circulating influenzas using contact tracing, even though they kill an average of twenty thousand Americans each year.

Fauci failed to protect the most vulnerable to the COVID-19 virus, the elderly. The vulnerability of the elderly was shockingly confirmed in the following weeks by the speed at which the virus decimated the population of long-term-care centers in New York City and New Jersey. Its spread was accelerated by then-Governor Andrew Cuomo's insane policy of confining those with COVID with those who were still unaffected. Trump appointee Scott Atlas clashed with Fauci over lockdowns, urging him to focus on protecting the vulnerable rather than forcing everyone in the country to quarantine. At the same time, evidence clearly showed that the mortality risk was dramatically lower in younger age groups and that the risk was approximately zero for the very young. The Great Barrington Declaration, signed by dozens of disease epidemiologists and public health scientists, pointed out that "for children, COVID-19 is less dangerous than many other harms, including influenza." Public health professionals tried to get Fauci to focus on protecting the vulnerable. When public health scientists tried to lay out how such a program could be successfully carried out and was being carried out in places like Taiwan and Sweden, Fauci publicly attacked their ideas as "nonsense and very dangerous."

Source & Additional Information: (https://abcnews.go.com/Health/former-new-york-gov-andrew-cuomo-set-testify/story?id=113518539)

From the onset, Fauci demanded the nationwide closing of our school system. Few dared to question the all-knowing Doctor Fauci because, as he stated during a congressional hearing, "If you question me, then you're questioning science." America's response to Fauci's fearmongering about infections among children should have been rejected as a child's risk of dying from COVID-19 was nearly zero, far lower than their risk of dying from seasonal flu. The closing of American schools did not save lives but did have a devastating effect on our children's academic performance and emotional health. Many children spent a year with virtually no schooling or social interaction, suffering dangerous learning opportunities that will have a lasting impact on them.

Testimony after testimony, before congressional committees, Fauci consistently denied that he had funded controversial "*gain of function*" coronavirus research. At those same hearings, he denied that it was even remotely possible that the virus originated at the Wuhan Institute of Virology, insisting that the virus had been transmitted from bats being sold at an open market near the Wuhan Institute. As of July of 2023, it is firmly held that the virus, in all probability, leaked from the Wuhan Lab. However, whether it was accidental or purposely released into the world by the Chinese Communist Party is still being officially debated. Given China's open aggression towards America and our allies and their constant maneuvering to gain control over world politics, it is doubtful that the release was not intentional. It is, therefore, highly probable that Doctor Fauci used American taxpayers to fund the creation of the very disease that killed multiple millions of American citizens and the citizens of other nations worldwide. It should be further noted that the Chinese Communist Party military controls the Wuhan lab.

Source & Additional Information: (https://www.cbsnews.com/news/anthony-fauci-testimony-house-select-subcommittee-on-the-coronavirus-pandemic/) (https://www.nytimes.com/interactive/2024/06/03/opinion/covid-lab-leak.html)

Doctor Fauci never ceased to claim that the virus had not originated in a lab in Wuhan. At the same time, many other leading Immunologists advised the President and Congress that this virus cannot naturally originate in bats and be transmitted to humans. Fauci seemed to believe that he could direct the government's actions through his pronouncements, which he did exceptionally well to a Marxist-Communist Democrat Party-controlled Congress, even if he could not do so with President Trump. He further falsely advised that the malaria drug hydroxychloroquine would not provide a credible treatment to stave off the infection, resulting in the Center for the Control of Diseases prohibiting the use of hydroxychloroquine. Fauci further advised that there would not be a vaccine for at least a year at a minimum. All of Doctor Fauci's advice and predictions turned out to be wrong. Every recommendation made by Doctor Fauci was the worst possible recommendation possible for the United States economy, the citizens of the United States, and our workforce.

Doctor Fauci testified numerous times before Congress and held to the claim that neither he nor his agency had ever funded gain-of-function experiments. Doctor Robert Redfield, former director of the Centers for Disease Control and Prevention (CDC), told lawmakers that United States tax dollars did fund risky gain-of-function research at the Chinese virus lab at the heart of the COVID-19 origin controversy. Representative Nicole Malliotakis of New York asked Doctor Redfield whether it was likely that "American tax dollars funded the gain-of-function research that created this virus?" referring to the theory that the pathogen behind COVID-19 leaked from a lab in Wuhan. "I think there's no doubt that the NIH was funding gain-of-function research,"

Doctor Redfield replied, adding that he believed funding came from the NIH.

Whether United States tax dollars were used to fund gain-of-function research in China has been in the spotlight for some time. It remains steeped in controversy as the definition of such research is a matter of debate. Doctor Richard Ebright, a molecular biologist at Rutgers University, stated that the research conducted at the Wuhan lab amounted to gain-of-function and that Fauci and others lied when insisting it was not. "The materials confirm the grants supported the construction, in Wuhan, of novel chimeric SARS-related coronaviruses that combined a spike gene from one coronavirus with genetic information from another coronavirus and confirmed the resulting viruses could infect human cells," Doctor Ebright wrote on Twitter. Doctor Ebright was referring to Freedom of Information Act documents obtained by "The Intercept," detailing the work of the "EcoHealth Alliance," a United States-based health organization that used federal money to fund research into bat coronaviruses at the Chinese lab in Wuhan. "The documents make it clear that assertions by the National Institute for Health director, Francis Collins, and the National Institute of Allergy and Infectious Diseases director, Anthony Fauci, that the NIH did not support gain-of-function research or potential pandemic pathogen enhancement at the Wuhan Institute of Virology are untruthful," he added.

<u>Source & Additional Information</u>: *(https://www.msn.com/en-us/health/medical/nih-official-finally-admits-taxpayers-funded-gain-of-function-research-in-wuhan-after-years-of-denials/ar-BB1mwcLr)*

The NIH and the National Institute of Allergy and Infectious Diseases have denied that the funding to the Wuhan lab amounted to the funding of gain-of-function research, which Fauci himself has repeatedly insisted that it did not. "The National Institute for Health has not ever and does not now fund gain-of-function research in the Wuhan Institute of Virology," Fauci stated at a

Senate hearing on May 11th, 2021. National Institute for Health director Francis Collins said in a statement on May 19th, 2021, that "neither National Institute for Health nor National Institute of Allergy and Infectious Diseases has ever approved any grant that would have supported 'gain-of-function' research on coronaviruses that would have increased their transmissibility or lethality for humans." All false statements were made under oath to a Senate committee.

Source & Additional Information: (https://www.usnews.com/news/national-news/articles/2024-06-03/5-key-takeaways-from-faucis-covid-19-testimony)

Center for Disease Control: The Center for Disease Control (CDC) seemed incapable of answering questions regarding COVID-19 concerns and its plans to control and possibly eliminate this pandemic. From the pandemic's earliest days, this agency had been subject to extreme politicization and troubled by what looked like pathological clumsiness at the very least and total incompetency at the worst. CDC scientists had been far too slow to detect the virus, to develop an accurate diagnostic test of COVID-19, or to grasp just how quickly it was mutating. With Doctor Anthony Fauci as the lead person, their advice on mask-wearing, quarantine, and ventilation had been confusing, inconsistent, and often dead wrong. Federal agency leaders stood by while politicians and political appointees repeatedly undermined the impact of COVID-19 and how to protect American citizens from this virus. Scientists with expertise were ignored, while scientific reports were blocked or knowingly altered. Quarantine powers were used to achieve political goals to gain control over the citizenry of the United States. Dangerous strategies for controlling the virus were not only promoted but actively employed. State and local leaders were left to fend for themselves, to decide which of the agency's recommendations should be followed, modified, or ignored.

Energy Department Backs Lab Leak Theory: The question of whether American taxpayers funded gain-of-function research in China came back into sharper focus after the United States Energy Department, which oversees a network of seventeen laboratories in the United States, concluded that the virus that causes COVID-19 likely leaked from the Wuhan lab. Some scientists still back the natural origin theory even though no host animal was identified. While some United States agencies under Marxist-Communist leadership, still to this day, lean toward the natural origin theory, the Energy Department has joined the FBI in assessing that COVID-19 likely originated in the Wuhan lab.

Doctor Redfield also addressed the question of the lab leak theory in his testimony to Congress. "Even given the information that has surfaced in the three years since the COVID-19 pandemic began, some have contended that there is no point in investigating the origins of this virus.

There is a global need to know what we are dealing with in the COVID-19 virus because it affects how we approach the problem to try to prevent the next pandemic," he wrote in his opening statement. Doctor Redfield added that, "because there's evidence to support the lab leak theory and since gain-of-function research was being carried out on coronaviruses at the Wuhan lab, there should be a halt to gain-of-function experiments. Gain-of-function research has long been controversial within the scientific community, and, in my opinion, the COVID-19 pandemic presents a case study on the potential dangers of such research. While many believe that gain-of-function research is critical to get ahead of viruses by developing vaccines, in this case, I believe it was the exact opposite; unleashing a new virus on the world without any means of stopping it resulted in the deaths of millions of people." He further stated, "Because of this, it is my opinion that we should call for a moratorium on gain-of-function research until we have a broader debate, and we come to a consensus as a community about the value of gain-of-function research. This debate should not be limited to the scientific community. If the decision is to continue gain-of-function research, then it must be determined how and where to conduct this research safely, responsibly, and effectively." In addition, eleven scientists who are virologists were asked by "The Intercept" about the documents they had obtained about "EcoHealth Alliance" funding of virus research, and they stated that the work appears to meet the National Institute for Health criteria for gain-of-function research.

Source & Additional Information: (https://www.nytimes.com/2023/02/26/us/politics/china-lab-leak-coronavirus-pandemic.html)

Statements made by Doctor Fauci under oath and in sworn dispositions have been verified as lies based on evidence that contradicts his statements. This includes his claim that he had never met with Doctor Ralph Baric, an American virologist who helped perform risky research on bat coronaviruses in China. "I know who he is. I doubt whether I have ever met him," Fauci stated during his disposition in late 2022, which was the first time he answered questions under oath since the pandemic began. Fauci acknowledged that the United States National Institute of Allergy and Infectious Diseases, which he headed until late 2021, provided funding for Doctor Baric. "But you don't remember ever meeting him in person?" he was asked, to which he responded, "I do not recall. I could have met him. I run into several thousands of scientists that we refer to, but I do not recall, certainly, having a relationship with him."

Source & Additional Information: (https://www.bbc.com/news/world-us-canada-64891745)

But a review of Fauci's official calendar lists a one-on-one meeting with Doctor Baric on February 11th, 2020, and a message from a professor who recounted Doctor Baric's account of the meeting indicating they talked about man-made virus combinations. "I talked to Ralph for a long time last night. He sounds beat," Matt Frieman, a University of Maryland professor, wrote in a February 18th, 2020, message. "He said he sat in Fauci's office talking about the outbreak and chimeras."

A chimera is a combination of viruses. Materials unearthed from Freedom of Information Act requests by the nonprofits "OpentheBooks.com, Judicial Watch, and U.S. Right to Know," and other evidence, including a 2020 email of talking points for Fauci that mentioned Doctor Baric being "on our team," showing that "Doctor Fauci's testimony on this point is not credible," the attorney generals of Missouri and Louisiana told a federal court. Fauci also claimed that he was not "100 percent certain" of the name of Doctor Shi Zhengli, who was known for her experiments on bat viruses in China. "I get sometimes confused with Asian names," Fauci testified. "Yet Doctor Shi Zhengli, the so-called 'Batwoman,' is world-renowned as the researcher who may have caused the COVID-19 pandemic and has been so since the beginning of the pandemic, and the name 'Shi' is included in the title of the article that Doctor Fauci forwarded to Doctor Hugh Auchincloss after midnight on February 1st, 2020. Doctor Fauci's testimony is not credible on this point," Andrew Bailey and Jeff Landry, the attorney generals, wrote.

Source & Additional Information: (https://www.technologyreview.com/2022/02/09/1044985/shi-zhengli-covid-lab-leak-wuhan/)

Fauci also repeatedly said in his deposition that he could not recall details about a secret phone call held after he and deputies discussed how the National Institute of Allergy and Infectious Diseases had funded coronavirus experiments in Wuhan, China, where the first COVID-19 cases were detected. Shortly after the call became public, Fauci told USA Today, "I remember it very well." USA Today also noted that when Fauci did characterize the call, he said that it involved a "good faith discussion back and forth between people who knew each other" and that "the general feeling among the participants on the call is that they wanted to get down to the truth and not wild speculation about things." After the call, several participants authored papers decrying the theory that COVID-19 started in a lab at the apparent request of Doctor Fauci. "Doctor Fauci thus seeks to have his cake and eat it too. He claims both to remember little or nothing of what was said on the call and to clearly remember that the entire discussion was done in good faith and without any bias," Andrew Bailey and Jeff Landry, the attorney generals, stated. "In any event, subsequent communications and events make clear that Doctor Fauci's testimony on this point is not credible."

While interviewing Fauci, CNN played a clip of a 2021 clash between Senator Rand Paul and Fauci. Senator Paul noted that the United States government has funded risky research in China and named Doctor Baric and Doctor Zhengli participants. Senator Paul described Fauci as a liar who should be charged with perjury, while Fauci stated that Senator Paul was wrong on all points. In an appearance on Fox News, Senator Paul said Fauci has "orchestrated a cover-up," referring in part to a newly disclosed message that indicates Fauci "prompted" the drafting of a paper that said COVID-19 could not have come from a lab.

Dr. Fauci has yet to be held accountable for his actions and lying under oath.

Section XII: Secretary of Energy

Secretary of Energy is Jennifer Granholm, who has enthusiastically embraced the "go green" ideology of the radical Marxist-Communist Democrat Party. Jennifer Granholm has supported and provided oversight over the shutdown of America's natural energy production and the decline and eventual end to America's independence for energy from foreign countries. All resulted in America's critical shortage of energy, culminating in the need for President Biden's embarrassing knee-bent pleas for increased oil supplies from foreign governments and record high fuel costs to American citizens. This is while America sits over the world's most abundant natural energy fields. Does any of this even suggest that Secretary Granholm is working towards advancing the national, economic, and energy security of the United States? Does any of this even suggest that Secretary Granholm is working towards implementing policies regarding nuclear power or fossil fuels? Absolutely not. Secretary Granholm is focused only on renewable energy.

America is in an energy crisis, and the Department of Energy, in coordination with the Department of the Interior, could open up America's abundant oil and gas reserves for extraction. Unfortunately for American citizens, the Marxist-Communist Democrat Department of the Interior has done everything possible to delay requests for drilling permits, leading to the total shutdown of existing natural energy production. Joe Biden proclaimed that he intended to have his Administration be the catalyst that moves America from fossil fuel energy to an America dependent on wind and solar energy sources. We are in an energy crisis, and the Marxist-Communist Democrat Party wants to move America to an energy source that has yet to be developed to the point of being consistently reliable and available. Are Americans really buying into this ridiculous and unproven notion? Those uninformed Americans who depend on the fake news propaganda arm of the Marxist-Communist Democrat Party believe that America is ready to transition from fossil fuels to renewable energy. This is because the fake news refuses to report the truth regarding America's unreadiness to transition.

Wind turbines across the United States have been failing more frequently than the "Go-Green" ideologist anticipated, triggering concerns about additional costs resulting from such failures and their impact on power projects. Offshore windfarms, deployed in the name of environmentalism, are now seen as disastrous for ocean life. Malfunctions in wind turbines range from minor issues, like some key components becoming faulty, to full-blown collapses. According to Wallace Manheimer, in a 2022 paper published in the Journal of Sustainable Development, the "climate industrial complex," a powerful lobby of politicians, scientists, and media, is pushing climate-related falsehoods.

Source & Additional Information: (https://www.wsj.com/articles/americas-new-energy-crisis-11659153633) (https://co2coalition.org/2022/09/09/while-the-climate-always-has-and-always-will-change-there-is-no-climate-crisis/)

How reliable is solar and wind energy? Recall the disastrous and deadly winter storm in February of 2021. The state of Texas, which is heavily dependent on renewable energy sources, suffered a major power crisis, which came about during three severe winter storms sweeping across the United States. The first storm hit Texas on February 10th through the 11th of 2021, followed by a second severe winter storm from February 13th through thzz 15th, and a third severe winter storm between February 16th and 20th of 2021. The storms triggered the worst energy infrastructure failure in Texas history, leading to water, food, and heat shortages. More than 4.5 million homes and businesses were left without power, some for several days. At least two hundred and forty-six people died, directly or indirectly, with some estimates as high as seven hundred and two died as a result of the crisis. If this level of renewable energy failure can occur in Texas, which experiences minimal numbers of severe winter storms, can one even begin to imagine how renewable energy could possibly maintain the production of energy in northern states such as North Dakota, Montana, Wyoming, Minnesota, and the list goes on?

As more United States natural gas pipelines shut down due to the Marxist-Communist Democrat Administration-directed shutdowns and crushing expensive regulations, America is becoming increasingly reliant on foreign natural gas resources, prompting the Marxist-Communist Democrat Administration to go begging on bended knees for energy products from foreign sources. You would have thought that these embarrassing moments would have caused serious reconsideration of their energy policies. Instead, they have moved to cut off further development of new pipeline projects while imposing increased burdens on existing projects. Immediately after President Joe Biden took office, his Marxist-Communist Administration stopped all new oil and gas leasing on federal lands. Additionally, the Biden-Harris Marxist-Communist Administration omitted any mention of pipelines in their proposed $1.2 trillion infrastructure plan fact sheet.

Marxist-Communist environmental activists wanted the Biden-Harris Administration to shut down all pipelines, not just natural gas pipelines. Along with the Keystone pipeline project, several key natural gas pipelines have already been shut down, including the Atlantic Coast Pipeline, the PennEast Pipeline, the STL Pipeline, and the Constitution Pipeline. In lockstep with the Biden-Harris Administration's energy policies, in May of 2021, Michigan Governor Gretchen Whitmer ordered the shutdown of Enbridge's Line 5 pipeline over spillage concerns, although that line has not had any spillage issues in its 67-year existence. Line 5 goes through the Straits of Mackinac, which separates Lakes Michigan and Huron. The nearly seven-decade-old pipeline carries petroleum from Western Canada through Wisconsin and Michigan and ends at refineries in Sarnia, Ontario. Another major pipeline, the Mountain Valley Pipeline, has been held back from completion due to costly regulations, delays, and challenges. The pipeline's estimated completion cost sat around $3 billion when proposed initially but has now increased to over $6 billion. Toby Rice, the CEO of one of the largest natural gas producers, EQT Corporation, told The Daily Wire that this increased reliance on foreign supply and "green" energy is leading the country toward an energy crisis. He emphasized that reliable energy sources are crucial to quality of life and progress, countering the emissions concerns over fossil fuels with the argument that "green" energy sources were not nearly as reliable and never will be.

Source & Additional Information: (https://www.forbes.com/sites/ daneberhart/2023/10/28/biden-energy-policies-reducing-americas-global-influence/) (https://www.michigan.gov/whitmer/news/press-releases/2020/11/13/governor-whitmer-takes-action-to-shut-down-the-line-5-dual-pipelines-through-the-straits-of-mackina)

Do not be fooled by the Marxist-Communist Democrat Party when they demonize oil companies. The Marxist-Communist

Democrat Party says thousands of oil leases have been issued, but oil companies are not drilling. Here is why oil companies are not drilling: Once an oil company gets a lease, the next step is to obtain a drilling permit. This is where the environmental fascists in the Department of Energy hold up drilling. They will either deny the application or slow-walk the process for years. An oil lease is just a piece of paper without a drilling permit.

On March 27th, 2023, the Republican-held House of Representatives passed an energy cost bill. This legislation, called "The Lower Energy Costs Act," would change the energy permitting process and boost domestic energy production. The Republican-led House Committee on Transportation and Infrastructure is behind the bill. The White House asserts that it will "raise consumer costs " and set back progress. The Office of Management and Budget claims that the proposed law would eliminate household energy rebates, roll back historic investments in clean energy technologies, and replace pro-consumer policies with low-key permission to pollute, increasing prices for American households. The Marxist-Communist Democrat Party opposes the bill because they allege it would pad the profits of oil and gas companies, which are already at record levels, and undercut public health and the environment. All Marxist-Communist Democrat Party propaganda and misinformation, as the passage of this bill, would dramatically decrease the cost of fuel and energy for the American family.

Source & Additional Information: (https://www.cbsnews.com/news/house-republican-energy-bill-hr-1-lower-energy-costs-act/)

The damage that the Marxist-Communist Democrat Party has caused the United States and the world by shutting down America's oil industry is indescribable. When Donald Trump left office, oil prices were $50 per barrel. Today, it is at $71.90 per barrel and rising. The Marxist-Communist Democrat Party has recklessly depleted our Strategic Oil Reserve for political gain, and to replace our Strategic Oil Reserves at today's prices will cost the American taxpayers approximately $3 trillion. Trump kept the price of oil low by drilling, drilling, drilling, which kept Putin in check because he did not have the massive oil revenue needed to wage war against his neighbors. America was not only energy independent, but we were also an energy exporter.

Now, we are energy beggars, groveling to Russia, Saudi Arabia, and Venezuela. Today, Russia pumps ten million barrels of oil per day. At $71p/b, it gives Putin $710 million PER DAY to fund his illegal, unprovoked war against Ukraine! If Trump were president, there would have been no war in Ukraine because Russia would not have had the revenue coming in from the sale of oil to fund the war. All of the thousands of deaths caused by Putin's invasion are the responsibility of those who put Joe Biden in office. First on this list is Representative James Clyburn, who orchestrated the Marxist-Communist Democrat Party's plan to nominate the mentally impaired Biden; next are the corrupt election officials who allowed poll workers to evict Republican poll watchers and then run hundreds of thousands of phony ballots through the vote counters; next is the Marxist-Communist Democrat Party criminals who stuffed the ballots of "ghost voters" into the Zuckerberg-funded "Drop Off" boxes. All of these Marxist-Communist Democrats have the blood of these Ukrainian victims on their hands.

Renewable Energy: Europe is currently in an energy crisis, with natural gas prices up to over six times what they were in 2022. They have transformed their power grid to prioritize green, renewable solutions, such as solar and wind power. However, about twenty percent less wind power has been produced than anticipated, leaving the continent scrambling for gas to offset the loss. Europe depends on Russia for supplemental fuel when green energy is unavailable, making Russia a significant benefactor from Europe's energy crisis. During the winter months of late 2022 and early months of 2023, Russia turned off its supply of fuel energy to Europe due to Europe's open support for Ukraine in the Ukraine-Russia war. During his presidency, President Trump strongly discouraged Europe from making this move, predicting that renewable energy sources were unpredictable and would lead to their reliance on Russia for their energy needs. President Trump was right again.

Germany's environmental policies are staggering. Germans continue complaining about the ever-increasing energy costs directly resulting from those policies. Germany has been phasing out conventional fuels and phasing in less reliable, less abundant renewable energy sources, resulting in higher prices, shortages, and a greater reliance on adversarial nations like Russia and China. Energy prices in Germany have dramatically increased over the past years. In 2022, natural gas prices rose 39%, electricity prices rose 27%, food prices increased 23%, and pork prices increased 59%. The most shocking change was the almost doubling of sugar prices. The price of flour is 100% more expensive. Many bakeries are going out of business because of the high electricity prices and costly flour. Germany has placed an additional carbon tax on car gasoline, and every year, the gas tax increases." In addition, individuals pay higher yearly car taxes depending on the carbon their car produces. The country's decisions regarding their transition to renewable energy should prove to be a vital lesson for our Marxist-Communist Democrat Party members of Congress and their Marxist-Communist Republican allies.

The problem is not only that Germany was hit by the disruption in Russia's natural gas supplies because of the Russia-Ukraine war, but most significant is Germany's efforts to phase out its domestic resources of nuclear and coal-fired power, much like the Marxist-Communist Democrat Party members of Congress and their Marxist-Communist Republican allies are doing with America's natural resources. Germany's transition to renewable energy made Germany even more reliant on foreign natural gas supplies from Russia. The war in Ukraine brought the consequences of

Germany's green energy policies to the surface, profoundly limiting the amount of natural gas Russia was willing and able to sell to Germany. As a result, Germany has transitioned from relying on Russia for its natural gas to relying on China for solar panels and wind turbines. Ninety-five percent of the solar cells in Germany are manufactured in China. In addition, more than 50% of the raw materials used to construct wind turbines are sourced from China.

Source & Additional Information: (https://www.newsweek.com/wind-turbine-failures-europe-energy-crisis-warning-america-fossil-fuels-1643011) (https://www.euronews.com/next/2022/09/06/explained-why-europe-faces-soaring-energy-bills-and-a-cost-of-living-crisis)

President Trump warned Germany not to rely on China or Russia for something as critical as its energy supply. President Trump further advised that countries need to be able to care for themselves and maintain their energy independence. And now the United States has the Marxist-Communist Democrat Party shutting down all of America's natural energy resources. America already feels the harsh impact of the Biden-Harris energy policies, which mirror Germany's. Like Germany, America has given up its abundant natural energy resources and now depends on foreign countries for energy needs. Countries that no longer respect America and some that are ideological enemies of the United States.

In March of 2023, The Department of Energy announced its new energy efficiency standards for home air conditioning units, including portable air conditioners for windows and air cleaners. They are insinuating that these new regulations will lessen carbon emissions, cut air pollution, and reduce energy costs by billions of dollars for consumers. These energy efficiency standards will affect residential appliances such as gas ranges, ovens, washing machines, clothes dryers, and refrigerators. Critics point out that these new regulations were unnecessary because the industry technology has already advanced without government interference. One of the appliances targeted is gas-burning ovens, although natural gas is a clean-burning energy source. Nowhere in the Constitution is the authority given to the federal government to impose any of the above energy restrictions and regulations nor authority to dictate what American citizens may or may not purchase, regardless of the energy impact those products may have. These issues constitutionally belong to the sovereign states and not to the Marxist-Communist Democrat Party or the Department of Energy.

Source & Additional Information: (https://www.energy.gov/articles/doe-finalizes-efficiency-rules-room-air-conditioners-and-portable-air-cleaners)

***Electric Grid*:** The most frightening aspect of America's potential doom is the level of vulnerability and susceptibility of America's electric grid, which can easily and quickly bring destruction and defeat to American society by just a small group of terrorists. Terrorists who may already be in our country with knowledge of this vulnerability, having crossed our open southern border, plotting to strike our vulnerable electrical grid system and bring America to its knees. In late July 2023, Nicole Wells, a contract journalist for Newsmax media, reported on Chinese malware potentially hidden inside our critical infrastructure networks. She reported that our Marxist Communist Democrat Party Administration had finally grown concerned that the Chinese Communist Party may have already installed malware into the networks that control our power grids, communication systems, and water supplies, which provide these utilities to our military bases around the globe. It is feared that Chinese Communist Party military hackers have already inserted malicious computer code that will allow their military forces to disrupt our military operations should we become involved in an armed conflict with China or attempt to intervene militarily should China invade Taiwan.

The malicious computer code would affect not only our military but also the lives of American citizens, as the same infrastructure is often the same systems that supply our homes and businesses. According to Marxist-Communist Democrat Party officials and industry experts who responded to inquiries from the British news outlet The Times, this Chinese malware issue had been occurring for at least a year since it was reported in May of 2023. The Biden-Harris Administration has indicated that they have been working on efforts to find the code and eliminate it since the malware was discovered. As can be expected of a broken federal government led by a Marxist-Communist Democrat Party of inept and corrupt officials, it is just another case of a dollar short and a day late. It may have already created unknown problems that will not be fully known until the systems are put under tremendous pressure, as would occur in an armed conflict.

Government officials do not know the full extent of the code's presence in networks worldwide. However, they admit that the Chinese effort to disrupt our infrastructure appears broader than they had initially thought. Officials advised The Times that searches for the code have focused first on areas with a large number of American military bases. Those same military bases that our government allowed a Chinese Spy Balloon to fly over between January 28 and February 4, 2023. According to Adam Hodge, acting spokesman for the National Security Council, "The Biden-Harris administration is working relentlessly to defend the United States from any disruptions to our critical infrastructure, including by coordinating interagency efforts to protect water systems, pipelines, rail, and aviation systems, among others. The president has mandated rigorous cybersecurity practices for the first time." For the first time? It is extraordinarily difficult to understand why our federal government would not have understood that enemies would first attack our infrastructure in an age of computerized infrastructures.

<u>Source & Additional Information</u>: *(https://www.newsmax.com/newsfront/united-states-china-malware/2023/07/29/id/1128957/) (https://www.nytimes.com/2023/07/29/us/politics/china-malware-us-military-bases-taiwan.html) (https://www.cnn.com/2022/12/05/politics/power-grid-attack-what-matters/index.html)*

During the Obama and Biden-Harris Administrations, congress passed two legislative bills signed into law to fund the updating, improvement, and provision of security measures to vulnerable infrastructure components in the country. Two bills cost the American taxpayers over two trillion dollars, yet America's infrastructure is still dilapidated and unprotected. Worse yet, no one in our federal government knows where the majority of that money went because our federal bureaucracy failed to maintain accountability for that money. We do know that it did not go to upgrading and improving necessary security measures for America's most vulnerable and potentially devastating infrastructure elements. The most critical of which is our electric grid.

However, we can be assured that a significant portion of that money went to upgrading and improving the bank accounts of corrupt politicians, political allies, and contractors. Our electric grid is so outdated and deteriorated that it cannot confidently provide electricity to all American homes and businesses during extreme weather conditions or summer heat, resulting in rolling blackouts.

But it is even worse than that. Our country has twenty-one critical electric substations that, if disabled or destroyed, would shut down the entire electricity distribution to American homes, businesses, and factories. This shutdown would result in the death of ninety percent of American citizens. The question begs to be asked, what in God's name are our elected officials doing? Certainly, they must all know about this deadly vulnerability. If they do, why are they doing nothing to correct this problem immediately? If they do not, then we have very uninformed and incompetent representatives. In either case, we face a critically deadly situation where we can do little to save ourselves. Only those ten percent of Americans skilled in survival expertise could live off the land and survive.

Source & Additional Information: (https://spectrum.ieee.org/attack-on-nine-substations-could-take-down-us-grid)

***Electric Vehicle Batteries*:** Our Marxist-Communist Democrat Party and their Marxist-Communist Republican allies are attempting to force electric vehicles on America to move their agenda towards a fossil fuel-free country. But America is nowhere near being ready for a vehicle that requires a battery for its power. If you are buying an electric vehicle to save the planet because you believe that using oil and coal to produce energy is going to pollute the world, well, let me break some bad news to you: you are an uneducated fool to believe such nonsense because the electricity required to run your all-electric vehicle comes from electricity produced by fossil fuel. That electric vehicle needs a battery to produce the energy it requires to propel it forward. So, what exactly is a battery? A battery is an electricity storage unit; they do not create electricity; they store electricity. Electricity which coal, natural gas-powered plants, or diesel-fueled generators produce. So, electric vehicles are not zero-emission at all.

That electric vehicle is nothing to get excited about if the goal is for electric vehicles to be a part of the green revolution. There is an extensive process in making a battery that is equally as polluting as coal and oil. A typical EV battery weighs one thousand pounds. It contains twenty-five pounds of lithium, sixty pounds of nickel, forty-four pounds of manganese, thirty pounds of cobalt, two hundred pounds of copper, and four hundred pounds of aluminum, steel, and plastic. Inside are over six thousand individual lithium-ion cells.

Source & Additional Information: (https://www.newgeography.com/content/007478-is-it-ethical-purchase-a-lithium-battery-powered-ev)

All toxic mineral components are coming from mining these minerals from the earth. Sixty-eight percent of the world's cobalt, a significant part of a battery, comes from the Congo. Their mines have no pollution controls, and they employ children who die from handling this toxic material. And for what, a battery that is not zero emission-free and environmentalist idiots can feel good about themselves for falsely believing they are saving the planet? Going green may sound like a great idea. Still, when you look at the bottom-line cost, not in dollars, but in the destruction to the Earth's environment and the deaths of children forced to work in those mines, electric vehicles are no more environmentally friendly than gasoline-propelled vehicles.

Source & Additional Information: (https://www.nationalgeographic.com/environment/article/cobalt-mining-congo-batteries-electric-vehicles)

Section XIII: Social Security Administration

Since we all began working, most of us around eighteen years of age, we have participated in the Social Security program by making payroll tax contributions into a Social Security Trust Fund incompetently administered by the Social Security Administration (SSA). Social Security benefits are meant to provide a supplemental income source to the participant's retirement savings. It also offers social insurance protection to workers who become disabled or to families whose breadwinner dies. Almost all older adults receive Social Security benefits. According to Social Security Administration estimates, ninety percent of older adults aged sixty to ninety receive Social Security benefits.

Social Security is probably the most sacred program administered by the federal government. It is a program in desperate need of reform. However, no politician who wants to win reelection dares to stand up and confront the problems facing the program and its impending failure. The Social Security program is probably the most controversial issue plaguing our country today and the one program that American citizens least understand regarding how it really works. Given that the vast majority of retirees depend on their monthly Social Security check to assure some quality of life, a retirement safety net elicits the most anger from people when confronted with the facts about the program. This should not come as any surprise, given that the federal government has lied to us about the nature of the Social Security System since its inception.

The confusion and misunderstanding of how Social Security works has caused many American citizens to become utterly delusional about the program. Most Americans who contribute to the program believe that the Social Security program is constructed around a trust fund administered by the SSA or is funded through congressional appropriations. Most citizens believe the money they have contributed is being "held" in an account where the federal government matches the amount through fiscal appropriation. Many have also been led to believe that Social Security is becoming bankrupt because elected congressional politicians have been robbing the trust fund for decades, promising to repay what they have taken from the trust fund but failing to do so, causing the amount of money available for retirees to decrease steadily. Both of these beliefs are inaccurate.

Social Security is not just a retirement program. It also provides for disabled people, the survivors of workers who have died, and the dependents of recipients. Social Security is not a savings plan. What you pay into the system does not go into an account for your retirement—workers in each generation finance Social Security payments for retired elders and other beneficiaries. Down the road, their benefits will be paid for, in turn, by younger workers.

Social Security is funded via payroll taxes, which are also sometimes referred to as FICA taxes.

Most workers have 7.65% of their paychecks automatically deducted for FICA taxes. Your earnings are taxed at 6.2% for the first $160,200 of earnings as of 2023. Anything you earn above that isn't taxed for Social Security — which is why $160,200 is the maximum amount considered for calculating your benefits.

The remaining 1.45% goes toward Medicare, but for that there's no salary cap. In fact, individuals who earn above $200,000 and married couples making more than $250,000 get hit with an extra 0.9% Medicare tax.

Your employer matches your 7.65% contribution toward Social Security and Medicare. That means self-employed people pay 15.3% because they have to make both the employee and employer contributions.

<u>Source & Additional Information</u>: *(https://smartasset.com/taxes/all-about-the-fica-tax)*

What is really going on is that Social Security is at a tipping point. In 2021, Social Security started taking in less money than it pays out, thanks mostly to longer life expectancies and people having fewer children — which means fewer workers paying into the system. While Social Security has a $2.9 trillion trust fund it can dip into, the funds are expected to be depleted by 2035. But that does not mean the program is doomed. Social Security is funded on a pay-as-you-go basis.

Even as it starts depleting its trust fund, it will still collect payroll taxes from workers and employers. If the trust were to run dry in 2035, payroll taxes would still generate enough to pay for about 79% of the program's obligations if Congress does nothing. However, Congress could take plenty of actions to avoid Social Security cuts. For example, it could increase the tax rate, eliminate the wage cap, or raise the full retirement age, as it did in 1983. It is not very likely that Congress would not act. A Pew Research Center poll found that 74% of Americans oppose cutting benefits. Lawmakers on both sides of the aisle know the program's popularity among voters.

To begin with, the SSA does not have any mechanism for saving the money that wage earners are contributing. The SSA has no authority or means by which bank accounts or investment accounts can be opened for the benefit of retirees, no stock market investment authority that would allow contributions made to grow, and no ability to buy bonds. The reality is that a Social Security Trust Fund does not exist. It is nothing more than an accounting fiction. This myth that there is such a thing as a Social Security Trust Fund is a lie being fed to American workers since the Social Security Administration was established. As stated above, Social Security is a program into which workers pay every payday, and money is then immediately transferred directly to existing retirees. The financial benefits paid out to retirees depend on the number of workers contributing to the program.

Source & Additional Information: (https://www.thepennyhoarder.com/retirement/how-does-social-security-work/)

When the Social Security program was established, the number of wage earners contributing to it was such that retirees received retirement benefits on average fifteen times the amount of money they paid into the program. Today, that average amount has dramatically dropped to about one point five times what a retiree paid into the system. Many current retirees will receive less than they paid into the program, and the situation is only getting worse as the number of wage earners contributing to the system steadily drops. It is estimated that by 2034, significantly more workers will be retiring than workers contributing to the program, causing the program to become unable to pay out benefits and thus become insolvent.

To sustain this growing number of eligible Social Security recipients, more workers contributing to the system must be dramatically increased to offset the growing number of benefit recipients. Short of this increase in new additional employee contributors, either Social Security taxes will need to be raised, the age of retirement eligibility will need to be raised, Social Security taxes will need to be imposed on earnings over $160,000 per year, which are currently exempt; a means test will need to be adopted given that approximately twenty-five percent of retirees already have adequate pensions or investment incomes that place them in the wealthy category. However, providing benefits at current levels will probably require implementing all of the abovementioned actions. Even millionaires and billionaires are collecting Social Security benefits while young struggling families are handing money to these wealthy recipients. This means testing to remove wealthy retirees from receiving benefits would go a long way to ensuring the system's solvency. Without significant changes, which our congressional representatives are too cowardly to address and implement, individuals retiring within the next ten to twelve years will receive far less money than they paid into the system, and the number of monthly payments received will hardly allow for a comfortable retirement and will steadily decrease over the years.

People must begin to accept that Social Security was never intended to be a means by which individuals could financially support their retirement but rather intended to supplement their retirement savings or retirement pensions. Another reality that workers must understand is that today's retirement age is sixty-five with reduced benefits and sixty-seven with full benefits, while men's life expectancy is seventy-three and women's is seventy-eight. The system was not designed to support tens of millions of people collecting benefits for a decade or more. The bottom line is that the Social Security System has never been what the vast majority of wage earners were led to believe.

Section XIV: Environmental Protection Agency (EPA)

The Environmental Protection Agency is an unconstitutional federal government agency created by the Nixon Administration supposedly to protect human health and the environment. The Environmental Protection Agency develops and enforces crushing environmental regulations that dictate ecological standards to which densely populated countries such as China and India are not subjected. It cannot deal effectively with environmental problems or set rational priorities among different programs. This agency has led to the loss of job-creating businesses and the rise in the cost of products. Its issuance of crushing regulations has made operating a business in America overly expensive and led to American companies moving their operations to more environmentally friendly countries, bringing with them good-paying job opportunities that will no longer be available to American workers. The Environmental Protection Agency is one of the reasons America has become reliant on unfriendly foreign countries for many of our critically needed products, which does not incentivize those countries to address their environmental issues.

Environmental regulations raise production costs and lower productivity by requiring firms to install pollution control equipment and change production processes. Regulatory costs can influence firms' decisions about locating new plants and shifting production among existing plants. The Environmental Protection Agency provides no incentive for going beyond the limits it sets; it offers limited flexibility on where and how to reduce pollution, and it often has politically motivated loopholes. The Environmental Protection Agency has issued poorly designed regulations that cause more harm than good, stifle innovation, growth, and job creation, waste limited resources, undermine sustainable development, inadvertently harm the people they are supposed to protect, and erode the public's confidence in our government. Environmental regulations are further unfair barriers to trade. Foreign nations may have laws that must meet a lower standard than those of the United States, restricting the import of another nation's goods into the United States, which is an unfair barrier to trade.

In late June 2022, the Supreme Court ruled that the Environmental Protection Agency did not have the authority to regulate state-level caps on carbon emissions under the 1970 Clean Air Act. Such regulatory authority would, in effect, steer states away from coal and toward other types of power sources that emit less carbon. The Court ruled that the authority to decide how power is created in the United States must come from

Congress, limiting the regulatory powers of the Environmental Protection Agency to decarbonize energy production, which is anticipated to result in economic gains for energy companies, including those invested in coal-powered plants.

The Environmental Protection Agency and climate change advocates, including John Kerry, have been falsely claiming, without any scientific evidence, that manmade climate change is occurring and impacts all people's health and wellbeing. This agency and climate change advocates demand that the United States significantly reduce its carbon emissions at a horrendous cost to American consumers and businesses. This is even though they fully know that the United States population is only 4.25% of the world population. They further fail to acknowledge, to the citizenry of America, that the world's two greatest polluters are China and India, neither of which will ever reduce their carbon output. It is evident that the radical Marxist-Communist Democrat environmentalists who keep demanding that the United States meet a zero percent carbon output are not yet aware that the world is round and not flat; did not learn in our failed federally funded school systems that the earth rotates causing the atmosphere to move around the earth constantly; nor did they learn that the polluted atmosphere over China and India, as well as other unregulated heavy polluting countries, will eventually make its way over the United States. It is self-destructive for the United States to regulate its environment while other countries ignore the problem, creating economic disadvantages for the United States. Given these truths, any reduction in carbon emissions by the United States will have little to no effect on the planet's climate.

In further response to radical environmentalists, one only needs to point to the disastrous forest fires raging throughout Canada. The smoke from those fires pollutes the air throughout North America and even extends to many European countries. Suppose smoke emanating from forest fires in Canada can spread worldwide.

How is it that these radical environmentalist fools can believe and preach to American citizens that America needs to restrict carbon emissions to save the world from climate change catastrophe? If smoke can circumvent the earth, then it is reasonable to assume that carbon emissions into the air can also circumvent the globe. Unless countries such as China and India reduce their extremely high carbon emission levels, subjecting the United States to restricted carbon emission levels is like spitting into the wind. The problem is, neither China, India, nor any other high carbon emission countries are ever likely to agree to any restrictions as their politicians understand that such restrictions will destroy their countries' economies.

On May 11th, 2023, the Environmental Protection Agency unveiled its strictest-ever rules for power production using natural gas, coal, and oil that would require carbon capture technologies. The new standards will affect new and old power infrastructure, including new natural gas turbines and the country's coal fleet. In line with the Marxist-Communist Democrat Party leadership style, the agency falsely claims that technologies to capture ninety percent of carbon dioxide have become "adequately demonstrated" and "cost reasonable" while realizing "substantial emissions reductions." In response, Democrat Senator Joe Manchin of West Virginia stated, "This new rule would all but eliminate coal mining, which many of his constituent's livelihoods are dependent upon. I fear that this administration's commitment to their extreme ideology overshadows their responsibility to ensure long-lasting energy and economic security, and I will oppose all Environmental Protection Agency nominees until they halt their government overreach."

Source & Additional Information: (https://www.adn.com/nation-world/2023/05/11/epa-proposes-strictest-ever-limits-on-greenhouse-gas-emissions-from-power-plants/)

Marxist-Communist Democrat Party plans to restrict carbon dioxide emissions from power plants, and the inevitable support from environmental organizations illustrates what is wrong with the so-called green movement. Rather than encouraging more significant emissions of CO2 to enhance life on Earth, thereby greening the planet, the Environmental Protection Agency is telling us we must reduce 'carbon pollution' to save the climate. But CO2 is anything but pollution. It is an invisible, non-toxic, trace, natural component of the atmosphere, allowing plants, and thus all life on Earth, to thrive."

Carbon capture is not even scientifically developed yet, let alone proven to directly impact the plant when only the United States and a very few other small population countries are implementing such draconian measures against its people. Some of the world's most densely populated countries that contribute vast amounts of such emissions will never sign on to such restrictions, making this new rule by the Environmental Protection Agency ineffective. This is nothing more than a lawless administration imposing a lawless rule they know is constitutionally illegal. The most inconvenient truth regarding environmental protection actions, such as this new rule, is that our uneducated, no common-sense radical environmentalists are unable to comprehend that so long as there continue to be volcanic eruptions, living mammals, and the sun continue to shine upon the earth there will be climate change.

Bill Gates has pushed for wealthy nations to adopt one-hundred percent synthetic beef made from plant proteins like beans or peas, carbs like potato starch, fats like canola or coconut oil, minerals, and flavorings. In an online interaction on Reddit in January of 2022, Gates pushed for the widespread adoption of plant-based meat products. Gates' push to move away from meat consumption and adopt plant-based alternatives comes as he is busy buying up farmland in America. Probably to raise cows for those who sell beef to China and India, which will be an incredibly significant number of the world's population, or even more probable is the enormous profits which can be made by planting crops which will then be used to produce plant-based meat products. In a July 2022 letter from Republican Representative Dusty Johnson of South Dakota, Johnson seeks Gates' testimony regarding his farm purchases. The Microsoft founder is the "largest private farmland owner" in the United States, owning over 270,000 acres of farmland in nineteen states.

Source & Additional Information: (https://www.independent.co.uk/climate-change/news/bill-gates-india-climate-change-b2292753.html)

However, if Bill Gates plans to farm to create plant-based beef, he and John Kerry will find themselves at odds. This is where climate change advocacy has gone insane. On the one hand, climate change advocate Bill Gates wants the world to give up raising cattle for meat consumption and switch to plant-based meat, and then on the other hand, climate change advocate John Kerry wants to see the end of agriculture because it harms the earth's climate. It was reported that the special Presidential Envoy for Climate Change, John Kerry, is flying his environmentally damaging private jet around the world, warning that the world cannot effectively tackle "climate change" without first eliminating, or at least vastly reducing, emissions from agriculture. Kerry cited that agricultural production accounts for approximately one-third of the world's total greenhouse gas emissions. Therefore, according to Kerry, the world must eliminate agriculture to control emissions. As Bill Gates and John Kerry demonstrated, the level of stupidity a person can achieve knows no bounds. Somewhere in their education, they must have slept through the class on the critical needs of mankind's survival.

These two passionate environmentalist extremists have completely overlooked the fact that, although cattle and agriculture may well account for a certain percentage of greenhouse gas emissions, these two food sources are, without any doubt, 100 percent responsible for mankind's existence. Advocating for eliminating mankind's food sources is a criminal, treasonous, and genocidal ambition. These two solutions to climate change would then justify the federal government's seizure of America's farmlands. "No Farmers" means "No Food."

Source & Additional Information: (https://www.euronews.com/green/2023/09/01/plant-based-meat-is-the-future-billionaire-bill-gates-claims-what-has-to-change)

During that India event, Gates spoke about energy consumption. He pointed out that if governments are willing to implement tough laws, air conditioning can be banned, which would be "good for the climate." However, he admitted that this would not happen as a warmer climate will keep raising the demand for cooling as it gets hotter and the demand more electricity, which, if it is not green, then you are in a positive feedback loop." What brilliant insight. Doomsayers, such as Bill Gates and John Kerrey, and their radical ilk followers have been predicting climate and environmental disasters since the 1960s. None of the apocalyptic predictions have come true. While such predictions have been and continue to be enthusiastically reported by a media eager for sensational headlines, the failures of those predictions to materialize are typically not reported.

The following articles are doomsday predictions made over the past fifty-plus years, attesting to the overzealous mindset of environmentalists. They range from predictions of a new ice age or overheating to the earth's overpopulation. All are predicted to occur within the next twenty to thirty years from the date of their publications. None of the predictions occurred, turning out to be scientifically false, doing no more than creating anxiety among the world's population but making those pushing these false predictions wealthy.

Following are just a few of the failed predictions made regarding climate change by individuals who have faulty crystal balls to predict the future:

The Salt Lake Tribune – 17 November 1967: 'Already Too Late'

Dire Famine Forecast by 1975: By George Getze, Los Angeles Times Writer. LOS ANGELES – It is already too late for the world to avoid a long period of famine, a Stanford University biologist said Thursday. Paul Ehrlich said the "time of famines" is upon us and will be at its worst and most disastrous by 1975. He said the population of the United States is already too big, that birth control may have to be accomplished by making it involuntary and by putting sterilizing agents into staple foods and drinking water, and that the Roman Catholic Church should be pressured into going along with routine measures of population control.

Well, here we are in 2024, and no such disastrous famine has occurred to date, certainly not by 1975.

The New York Times, August 10, 1969

Foe of Pollution sees Lack of Time; Asserts Environmental Ills outrun Public Concern: By Robert Reinhold, The New York Times.

PALO ALTO, California – "The trouble with almost all environmental problems," says Paul R. Ehrlich, the population biologist, "is that by the time we have enough evidence to convince people, you're dead." While Dr. Ehrlich is gathering that evidence in his laboratory at Stanford University, he is wasting no time trying to convince people that drastic action is needed to head off what he foresees as a catastrophic explosion fueled by runaway population growth, a limited world food supply, and contamination of the planet by man. "We must realize that unless we are extremely lucky, everybody will disappear in a cloud of blue steam in 20 years." The 37-year-old scientist said during a coffee break at his laboratory. "The situation is going to get continuously worse unless we change our behavior."

Well, forty-five years after Doctor Ehrlich's dire prediction, the world is significantly more populated, and nobody has disappeared in a cloud of blue steam.

The Boston Globe, April 16, 1970

Scientist predicts a new ice age by the 21st century: Author Unknown.

Air pollution may obliterate the sun and cause a new ice age in the first third of the next century if population continues to grow and the earth's resources are consumed at the present rate, a pollution expert predicted yesterday. James P. Lodge Jr. also warned that if the current rate of increase in electric power generation continues, the demands for cooling water will boil dry the entire flow of the rivers and streams of continental United States. Looking into his "smoggy crystal ball," Lodge also warned that by the next century "the consumption of oxygen in combustion processes, world-wide, will surpass all of the processes which return oxygen to the atmosphere." Lodge, a scientist at the national center for Atmospheric Research in Boulder, Colorado, said the nation's states, with the exception of Alaska and Hawaii "are already consuming more oxygen than their own green plants replace and that we are importing the balance from the neighboring oceans." Lodge, speaking at the Institute of Environmental Sciences, at the Sheraton Boston, said three factors could prevent these disasters: population control, a less wasteful standard of living, and a major technological breakthrough in the way man consumes the earth's resources.

We are well into the twenty-first century, and no one is concerned with a new ice age, environmentalists are instead in a frenzy over global warming.

Daily Facts, Redlands, California, October 6, 1970

Dr. Ehrlich, outspoken ecologist, to speak: Author Unknown.

"Giving aspirins to cancer victims" is what Dr. Paul R. Ehrlich thinks of current proposals for pollution control. No real action has been taken to save the environment; he maintains. And it does need saving. Ehrlich predicts that: The oceans will be as dead as

Lake Erie in less than a decade. The DDT in our fatty tissues has reached levels high enough to cause brain damage and cirrhosis of the liver. America will be subject to water rationing by 1974 and food rationing by 1980.

Now at my age my memory is not as good as it used to be, but I certainly do not remember living through water rationing by 1974 or food rationing by 1980. In fact, here we are in 2024, fifty plus years past the doomsday clock and I still have all the fresh water and food I desire. As an added note, the oceans are not anywhere near being as dead as Lake Erie.

The Washington Post, July 9, 1971

U.S. Scientist Sees' New Ice Age Coming: By Victor Cohn, Washington Post Staff Writer.

A leading atmospheric scientist predicts that the world could be as little as 50 or 60 years away from a disastrous new ice age. Dr. S. I. Rasool of the National Aeronautics and Space Administration and Columbia University says that: "In the next 50 years," the fine dust man constantly puts into the atmosphere by fossil fuel-burning could screen out so much sunlight that the average temperature could drop by six degrees; If sustained over "several years" – "five to ten" he estimated – "such a temperature decrease could be sufficient to trigger an ice age!" These conclusions – including the ominous exclamation point rare in scientific publication – are printed in this week's issue of the Journal Science out today, signed by Rasool and co-worker Dr. S. H. Schneider.

It has now been fifty-two years since Doctors Rasool and Schneider published their prediction. With only ten years left before the predicted ice age materializes, not only is there no ice age looming on the horizon, but July 4th, 2023, was reported to be a record high throughout the United States. A little ice would have *been pleasantly welcomed for those celebrating Independence Day outdoors.*

Brown University, Department of Geological Sciences, December 3, 1972

Aware of your deep concern for the future of the world, we feel obliged to inform you of the results of the scientific conference held here recently. The conference dealt with the past and future changes in climate and was attended by forty-two top American and European investigators. The main conclusion of the meeting was that a global deterioration of climate, by an order of magnitude larger than any hitherto experienced by civilized mankind, is a genuine possibility and may be due very soon. Cooling has a natural cause and falls within the ranks of processes that produced the last ice age. This is a surprising result mainly based on recent studies of deep-sea sediments.

It has now been fifty-two years since that conference was held. But in 2024, we see no new formation or extension of ice glaciers, just your typical hot summer days.

The Guardian, January 29, 1974

Space satellites show new Ice Age coming fast: By Anthony Tucker, Science Correspondent.

WORLDWIDE and rapid trends towards a mini–Ice Age are emerging from the first long term analysis of satellite weather pictures. Of potentially great importance to energy strategies and to agriculture, but barely observable yet in Britain because the Atlantic strongly buffers our weather, a preliminary analysis carried out at Columbia University, New York, by the European climatologists Doctors George and Helena Kukla indicates that snow and ice cover of the earth increased by 12 percent during 1967 – 1972. This appears to be in keeping with other long-term climatic changes, all of which suggest that after reaching a climax of warmth between 1935 and 1956, world average temperatures are now falling. But the increase of snow and ice cover is much faster than expected from other trends.

Fifty-three years have passed since this article was published, yet no mini-Ice Age has materialized, and the grass is still growing, requiring constant mowing.

New York Times Book Review, July 18, 1976

THE COOLING: So, writes Stephen Schneider, a young climatologist at the National Center for Atmospheric Research in Boulder, Colorado, reflecting the consensus of the climatological community in his new book, "The Genesis Strategy." His warning that present world food reserves are an insufficient hedge against future famines has been heard among the scientific community for years – for example, it was a conclusion of a 1975 National Academy of Sciences report. However, Schneider has decided to explain the entire problem as responsibly and accurately as possible to the general public and thus has put together a useful and important book. Schneider quotes University of Wisconsin climatologist Reid Bryson as saying that 1930 – 1960 "was the most abnormal period in a thousand years – abnormally mild." In fact, conditions of steady, warm weather in the northern hemisphere during that time favored bumper harvests in the United States, the Soviet Union, and the wheat belt of northern India and Pakistan. In 1974, Schneider and Bryson tried to explain to a White House policy-making group why conditions are likely to worsen. One of the most depressing anecdotes in the book is Schneider's description of the deaf ears their warnings received.

Forty-eight years have passed since Schneider's 1976 book, predicting the coming of a cooling period, and yet there has been no new Ice Age and no dramatic change in weather patterns other than those manufactured by environmental extremists and John Kerry, who is getting increasingly rich with his dome-and-gloom predictions.

New York Times, January 5, 1978: No End in Sight' to 30-Year Cooling Trend

International Team of Specialist Finds No End in Sight to 30-Year Cooling Trend in Northern Hemisphere: By Walter Sullivan.

An international team of specialists has concluded from eight climate indexes that there is no end in sight to the cooling trend of the last 30 years, at least in the Northern Hemisphere. In some, but not all cases, the data extended through last winter. They include sea surface temperatures in the north-central Pacific and north Atlantic, air temperatures at the surface and at various elevations, and the extent of snow and ice cover at different seasons. In almost all cases, the year-to-year variations in climate are far more marked than the long-term trend. The long-term trend often becomes evident only when data from a number of years are displayed. The report, prepared by German, Japanese and American specialists, appears in the December 15 issue of Nature, the British Journal. The findings indicate that from 1950 to 1973, the cooling per decade, by most climate indexes in the Northern Hemisphere was from 0.2 to 0.4 degrees Fahrenheit. Data from the Southern Hemisphere, mainly south of latitude thirty south, are so meager that reliable conclusions are not possible, the report says. The 30th parallel of south latitude passes through South Africa, Chile, and southern Australia. The cooling trend seems to extend at least part way into the Southern Hemisphere, but there have been indications of warming at high southern latitudes.

Average surface air temperatures recorded at 338 stations north of latitude 20 degrees south from 1951 to 1975 have been analyzed by Drs. R. Yamamaio and T. Iwashima of Kyoto University in Japan on regional and season basis. A general cooling is evident in temperatures of the lower 18,000 feet of the atmosphere as charted by Dr. Horst Drosia of the Weather Office in Hanover, Germany. For the period from 1949 to 1976, he has calculated for 220 points in the Northern Hemisphere, the average temperature of the atmosphere from the separation between the pressure levels near the surface (at 1,00 millibars) and one high up (at five hundred millibars.) As increase in separation indicated expansion and hence warming. A decrease, for example, of twenty meters (66 feet) was taken to mean atmospheric shrinking, indicating a cooling in that case of 2 degrees Fahrenheit.

Now, we have studies that seem contradictory. On one hand, the studies indicate a continuing cooling, and on the other hand, upper atmospheric temperatures seem to be rising. In any case, there has been little to no real effect on mankind.

The Miami News; June of 1988

More droughts likely, expert tells senator: By Jeff Nesmith.

"1988 is on its way to being the hottest ever as world temperatures go up sharply."

So now, in 1988, all of a sudden, we have gone from an imminent ice age to climate warming, which the illogical radical environmentalists are using as scare tactics by attempting to put the fear of God in American citizens. The reality is that climate change does not significantly threaten human life or any other earthly life. If anyone uses common sense, it would be easy to realize that the earth is constantly going through climate change and has been doing so for the past four billion years.

The Canberra Times; September 1988

Threat to Islands: Author unknown.

Maldives: A gradual rise in average sea level is threatening to completely cover this Indian Ocean nation of 1196 small islands within the next 30 years, according to authorities. The Environmental Affairs Director, Mr. Huwssein Shihab, said an estimated rise of twenty to thirty centimeters in the next 20 to 40 years could be "catastrophic" for most of the islands, which were no more than a meter above sea level. The United Nations

Environment Project was planning a study of the problem. But the end of the Maldives and its 200,00 people could come sooner if drinking water supplies dry up by 1992, as predicted.

It has now been thirty-six years since this prediction was made. As of July 2024, the Maldives and its 1196 islands are still above water and doing simply fine as a tourist destination.

Lansing State Journal: December 12, 1988

Prepare for long, hot summers: By Edward Stiles, Gannett News Service.

If you liked last summer's record temperatures, you are going to love the 1990s, says James Hansen, the NASA scientist who, during congressional hearings on the Midwestern drought, linked greenhouse warming to the heat wave. Last summer was a preview of the average summer ten years from now, and the hottest summers during the 1990s will be even hotter and drier than the one we just struggled through, he says. Although many scientists argue that the dry, hot summer of '88 was not caused by greenhouse warming, it is hard to find a climate expert who will claim that the greenhouse effect is not on its way. When Hansen, head of the Goddard Institute of Space Studies, spoke recently to researchers at the University of Arizona Lunar and Planetary Laboratory, he ticked off several unpleasant changes in weather most scientists agree probably will occur during the next fifty to sixty years: If we do nothing to cut down on pumping carbon dioxide into the atmosphere, temperatures in 2050 will be six to seven degrees higher than they are today. Washington D.C., for instance, would go from its current thirty-five days a year over ninety degrees to eighty-five days a year; The level of the ocean will rise anywhere from one to six feet; The frequency and severity of storms would increase. If the amount of carbon dioxide in the atmosphere doubles – the worst-case scenario between now and 2050 – the maximum strength of hurricanes may increase by fifty percent. Hansen says. While a few degrees warmer or cooler may not seem like much, such a change can result in huge differences in climate. Hansen notes that during the last ice age the earth was only about nine- or ten-degrees cooler on average than it is now.

We are out thirty-six years and unless this dramatic change in average days over ninety degrees occurs virtually overnight, in terms of the passage of time, this prediction is on a course to becoming just another scary story. According to Extreme Weather Watch the average number of days over ninty degrees per year has been steadily falling, not rising, since 1988.

Associated Press, June of 1989

Rising seas could obliterate nations: U.N. officials.

UNITED NATIONS (AP) – A senior U.N. environmental official says entire nations could be wiped off the face of the Earth by rising sea levels if the global warming trend is not reversed by the year 2008. Coastal flooding and crop failures would create an exodus of "eco-refugees" threatening political chaos, said Noel Brown, director of the New York office of the U.N. Environmental Program, or UNEP. He said governments have a ten-year window of opportunity to solve the greenhouse effect before it gets beyond human control. As warming melts polar icecaps, ocean levels will rise by up to three feet, enough to cover the Maldives and other flat island nations. Brown told The Associate Press in an interview Wednesday.

2008 is well behind us, and the Maldives and other flat island nations are still above water and doing quite well—another prediction by our brilliant scientists.

The Guardian: 21 February 2004

Now the Pentagon tells Bush: climate change will destroy us: Author unknown.

Secret report warns of rioting and nuclear war; Britain will be "Siberian" in less than twenty years; This threat to the world is greater than terrorism. Climate change over the next twenty years could result in a global catastrophe costing millions of lives in wars and natural disasters. A secret report, suppressed by US defense chiefs and obtained by The Observer, warns that major European cities will be sunk beneath rising seas as Britain is plunged into a "Siberian" climate by 2020. Nuclear conflict, mega-droughts, famine, and widespread rioting will erupt across the world.

The only thing correct about these predictions in that secret report is that rioting is occurring in several countries worldwide. However, Britain has yet to be plunged into another "Siberia," nor has it yet sunk beneath a rising sea. Once again, the scientists have been wrong.

The Argus-Press, Owosso, Michigan: June of 2008

Artic will be ice free by 2018: By Seth Borenstein. AP Science Writer

NASA scientist: 'We're toast.' "We see a tipping point occurring right before our eyes." Hansen told the AP before the luncheon. "The Arctic is the first tipping point and it's occurring exactly the way we said it would." Hansen echoing work by other scientists, said that in five to ten years, the Arctic will be free of sea ice in the summer: Longtime global warming skeptic Senator James Inhofe, R-Okla, citing a recent poll, said in a statement, "Hansen, (former Vice President) Gore and the media have been trumpeting man-made climate doom since the 1980's. But Americans are not buying it." But Rep. Ed Markey, D-Mass., committee chairman, said, "Dr. Hansen was right. Twenty years later we recognize him as a climate prophet.

Climate prophet? Only a Marxist-Communist Democrat Party member of the House of Representatives could, fifteen years after

the predictions were made (that's only five years away from our apocalyptic demise) be blind to the fact that there has been no melting away of the glaciers or ice cap in the Arctic. Inhofe had it absolutely correct in his statement that Americans are not buying the fake science being put out to fit the Marxist-Communist narrative.

Independent: December 2019

Ten Years ago, @algore predicted the North polar ice cap would be gone. Inconveniently, it is still there: By Anthony Watts

On December 14, 2008, former presidential candidate Al Gore predicted the North Polar Ice Cap would be completely ice free in five years. As reported on WUWT, Gore made the prediction to a German TV audience at the COP15 Climate Conference. Al warned them that "the entire North 'polarized' cap will disappear in five years."

But… It is still there as of 2024. Al Gore, who is probably the worst polluter in the country with his mega-mansion homes and his constant escapades around the world in his private fossil-fueled jet plane, has no standing or credibility anymore with anyone. He has made one false prediction after another regarding global warming and our loss of ice in the Arctic. Yet, this false prophet keeps on getting richer and richer, predicting our doom because of global warming. It's time for Mr. Gore to hang up his hat and retire from making up false horror stories to fit his Marxist-Communist Globalist narrative.

The Guardian: December 2013

US Navy predicts summer ice free Arctic by 2016: By Nafeez Ahmed

Is conventional modelling out of pace with the speed and abruptness of global warming? An ongoing US Department of Energy-backed research project led by a US Navy scientist predicts that the Artic could lose its summer sea ice cover as early as 2016 – eighty-four years ahead of conventional model projections. The project, based out of the US Naval Postgraduate School's Department of Oceanography, uses complex modeling techniques that make its projections more accurate than others.

Well, the techniques used to make these inaccurate predictions are not complex enough because the ice cover is still doing fine and not melting away. Back to the drawing board, sailors, and try getting it right for a change.

The Independent: September 2015

Snowfalls are now just a thing of the past: By Charles Onias.

Sleds, snowmen, snowballs, and the excitement of walking to find that the stuff has settled outside are all a rapidly diminishing part of Britain's culture, as warmer winters – which scientists are attributing to global climate change – produce not only fewer white Christmases but fewer white Januarys and Februarys. However, the warming is so far manifesting itself more in winters which are less cold than in much hotter summers. According to Dr. David Viner, a senior research scientist at the climatic research unit (CRU) of the University of East Anglia, within a few years winter snowfall will become "a very rare and exciting event." "Children just aren't going to know what snow is." He said.

It has been more than just a few years—actually, it has been nine years—and Dr Viner's predictions are not panning out. Since 2015, the annual snowfall in Britian has been over twenty-six inches per year—plenty of snow to go out sledging, throw those snowballs, and take those peaceful walks in the crackling snow.

Washington Examiner: May 2014 and September 2015

French Foreign Minister: 'five hundred Days to Avoid Climate Chaos': By Jeryl Bier – May 2014

Secretary of State John Kerry welcomed French foreign minister Laurent Fabius to the State |Department in |Washington on Tuesday to discuss a range of issues, from Iran to Syria to climate change. Or, in the words of the foreign minister, "climate chaos." Kerry and Fabius made a joint appearance before their meeting, and the foreign minister warned that only five hundred days remained to avoid "climate chaos."

But...

Planet Still Standing Five Hundred Days After French Foreign Minister Warned of 'Climate Chaos.' – By Jeryl Bier – September 2015.

In May 2014, French foreign minister Laurent Fabius declared during a joint appearance with Secretary of State Jon Kerry that "we have 500 days to avoid climate chaos." Late last week, time ran out, and Fabius's original remarks were never fulfilled.

In 2021, Patrick Moore, one of the founders of Greenpeace, claimed that climate change is based on false narratives. In an email obtained by The Epoch Time, Moore, who left the organization back in 1986, said that Greenpeace was "hijacked" by the political Marxist-Communists when they realized the amount of money and power involved in the environment movement. "The 'environmental' movement has become more of a political movement than an environmental movement," Moore stated. "They are primarily focused on creating narratives and stories which are designed to instill fear and guilt into the public so the public will send them money." In June of 2022, the independent foundation Climate Intelligence (CLINTEL) received signatures from over 1,100 scientists and professionals worldwide for its World Climate Declaration, stating that there is no climate emergency. In an interview with The Epoch Times, Marcel Crok, the founder of CLINTEL, said that even if it is accepted that carbon dioxide is the main driver of current climate change, there still is no "climate emergency. We state that all evidence so far indicates that the increase in CO2 and the increase in temperature are not harmful to us or to nature and, therefore, the climate hysteria surrounding the topic is unjustified and that the 'cure'—getting rid of fossil fuels ASAP and replacing them with renewables—probably will be worse than the 'disease' climate change."

The above are but a small set of examples of doomsayer predictions that have never materialized. The number of published articles regarding the world's impending doom could probably take up this whole book. Still, the above examples are sufficient to demonstrate that the planet is not on the verge of dying because of man-made climate changes. Keep this in mind whenever the radical Marxist-Communists try to tell you that they know best. What they know is that if they can get the American population to believe their far-left radical dictums, they can gain control of that population, while those leading these radical environmentalists are just getting wealth off of your fears.

Section XV: United States Export-Import Bank

The Export-Import Bank of the United States is the official export credit agency of the United States federal government. Operating as a wholly unconstitutionally *owned* federal government corporation, the bank assists in financing and facilitating United States exports of goods and services, mainly when private sector lenders are unable or unwilling to provide the funding. This ownership of a corporation by the federal government is both unconstitutional and communism in its most valid form.

Between 2017 and 2021, the United States Export-Import Bank received over $234 Billion in taxpayer dollars to provide financial assistance to small businesses seeking to increase their overseas sales. An analysis by a nonprofit government watchdog found that most of the funds were instead going to corporate giants such as Boeing Company and one-hundred and forty corrupt foreign regimes and not to our small businesses as was intended. The

United States Export-Import Bank sent billions of dollars intended for small business aid to some of the most corrupt countries and repressive regimes in the world; equally disturbing is the amount that went to wealthy countries that do not need our aid.

Source & Additional Information: (https://www.exim.gov/news/reports) (https://www.openthebooks.com/export-import-bank-2007-2021--openthebooks-oversight-report/)

The largest beneficiary of United States taxpayer-guaranteed United States Export-Import Bank loans is Nigeria, ruled by a regime that is among the world's most corrupt. The probability that those dollars reached their intended recipients is highly questionable. China, with the world's second-largest economy and an enemy of the United States, also was a significant beneficiary of United States Export-Import Bank resources. Russia and Turkey are also big beneficiaries of United States Export-Import Bank funding. It is certain that a large portion of the over $1.9 billion that went to Russia likely ended up in the pockets of Russian President Vladimir Putin's oligarchs, who control most of that nation's commerce. A Russian financial institution, Sberbank, which the United States has sanctioned for Russia's invasion of Ukraine, received $29,103,807 of assistance from the United States Export-Import Bank despite the sanctions imposed by the United States. Further, while Turkey is dismantling all human rights for its citizens, the Export-Import Bank has sent over $6.2 billion to Turkey since 2007.

Source & Additional Information: (https://www.investors.com/politics/commentary/export-import-bank-subsidies/)

The United States Export-Import Bank has been the source of earned controversy for nearly a decade, with conservative Republicans demanding that it be abolished as a corrupt example of crony capitalism and Marxist-Communist Democrat members of Congress defending it as an essential tool of United States foreign policy. A tool that the Marxist-Communist Democrat Party is utilizing to allow Americans to fund corrupt and murderous regimes and dictators with American tax dollars. In

2015, the then-Republican-led Congress allowed the United States Export-Import Bank to expire. Just more smoke and mirrors by the Republican Party to make themselves appear to be fiscally vigilant because they reversed this decision not five months later. Just what one would expect from the Grand Old Party.

The level of corruption, deception, and misdirecting of tax dollars, which only increases our national debt for the benefit of sociopaths worldwide by our federal government, seems to know no bounds. This federally owned private venture belongs in the hands of private banking companies as required by our Constitution. This ownership of a private institution is further evidence of members of Congress from both parties' failure to keep their oath of office to limit their activities to those articulated within the Constitution.

Section XVI: United States Consumer Product Safety Commission

This Commission was created in 1972 through the Consumer Product Safety Act of 1972. It reports to Congress and the President and is not part of any other department or agency within the federal government. It is another unconstitutional entity that belongs to the sovereign states in accordance with the Tenth Amendment.

In December 2022, Commissioner Richard Trumka Jr. released a statement that the Consumer Product Safety Commission was considering banning natural gas-burning stoves. In May of 2023, it was announced that the Consumer Product Safety Commission was now targeting the banning of clothes washers due to excessive use of water, electric dryers due to excessive use of electricity, and dishwashers also because of their excessive use of water. The Consumer Product Safety Commission is an unconstitutionally established commission that regulates products in the United States. This commission intends to place the United

States back to the days of washing clothes on washboards, hanging clothing on clothes lines to air dry, and returning to the days of hand washing and drying dishes after each meal. These measures are meant only to reduce electricity consumption provided by renewable sources because renewable sources cannot sufficiently handle the consumption load, and none of these products harm the environment.

Source & Additional Information: (https://www.nbcnews.com/business/consumer/gas-stove-ban-proposal-when-and-why-rcna65078) (https://www.msn.com/en-us/news/technology/biden-admin-finalizes-enviromental-regulations-targeting-clothes-washers-dryers/ar-BB1j8jeL)

Nowhere in our Constitution is there any authority for the federal government to take these actions, denying American citizens the right to purchase and utilize these appliances. Only the sovereign states have the authority to implement such restrictions based on the will of the citizens within that State. This Commission is nothing more than a means for the Marxist-Communist Democrat Party and their Marxist-Communist Republican members of Congress to strip away our rights under the Constitution in an attempt to gain control of the American population. The only green these actions create is the green that goes into the pockets of wealthy environmentalists. The answer to avoiding such draconian dictates by the Marxist-Communist federal government was clearly expressed by President Trump: "Drill, Baby Drill."

Chapter 5
Democrat Party

The John F. Kennedy Democratic Party began its accelerated transformation into a Marxist-Communist Democrat Party with the Lyndon B. Johnson Administration in 1964, losing any trace of that party's original place as a constitutional party with the Barak Obama Administration. The John F. Kennedy Democratic Party has since been absorbed by hard-left Marxist-Communist ideologues. The new Marxist-Communist Democrat Party is committed to converting existing federal institutions into politicized and weaponized entities against its citizens, American corporations, businesses, and educational institutions, forcing their radical equity-based agendas on Americans. What the American people, and this includes Democrat voters, are not accepting is that the Democrat Party has morphed into a Marxist-Communist party determined to end our Nation's energy independence forever, end access to affordable gas for their vehicles and gas-powered equipment; end families' ability to afford food for their tables; end the quality of education without the radical teaching of Critical Race Theory; end American citizen's choices in home appliances by restricting all appliances be powered by electricity; the teaching and counseling of students as young as five or six years old in gender-affirming issues; the allowing of biological males to utilize girls' bathrooms or to compete in girls' sports; and cities safe from violent out-of-control crime. The average American does not want an unaffordable Green New Deal that results in heavy taxes and a dependence on the Middle East or other foreign adversaries of the United States for our energy sources.

Just like Republicans, the everyday working unracialized Democrat wants to see the federal government show fiscal restraint, live under a balanced budget, and begin reducing our national debt. Most working Democrats, just like Republicans, do not want a permanent stagflationary economy marked by bank failures, soaring interest rates, crony capitalism, school loan forgiveness, an open border, and subsidies for those who choose not to work.

Our country's problems do not rest entirely on the shoulders of our Democrat family members, friends, or neighbor voters but rather on the shoulders of the politicians they vote into office. Politicians who, upon arrival to Washington, D.C., are immediately indoctrinated by their Party Leadership on how they will or will not vote on legislation and not as their constituents expect them to vote.

Most Democrat-initiated legislative bills are anti-American Marxist-Communist legislation intended on bringing our once proud Nation to its knees and transferring power from "We the People" to a centralized federal government controlled by the ruling elitists of Washington, D.C. Initiatives which, if adequately named or accurately reported would immediately result in Democrat voter's rejection.

However, these legislative bills are given names that imply the bill is voter-friendly, in the Nation's best interest, or will help our citizens prosper and be safe in their homes and neighborhoods. This distortion of the bill's real intent is then peddled out to Democrat voters through the Democrat Party's propaganda arms: MSNBC, CNN, ABC, NBC, CBS, FOX, The Washington Post, Marxist social media platforms, etc. Because our Democrat friends are continuously bombarded by their endless consumption of false or skewed news reporting by these sources, they believe what they hear and read through these sources.

Therefore, it is incumbent upon the members of the Republican Party to find the means to educate confused or misinformed voters about the true nature of Democrat-sponsored legislation. Republicans must set aside their discomfort or outright fear of speaking the truth with our fellow American citizens who falsely believe that the current Democratic Party is still the moderate Democratic Party of the John F. Kennedy era.

The average informed American Democrat citizen knows no country can exist without a border or a border that is wide open. Thus, allowing for the invasion of America by millions of illegal immigrants, terrorists, violent criminals, deadly drugs, traffickers of young women and children into a life of prostitution or dealing in drugs on behalf of the Mexican cartels. Democrat citizens demand realistic deterrence at our border every bit as much as Republican citizens. These patriotic Democrats must take a stand against their Representatives and Senators who fail to abide by the Constitution and represent their constituent's will and not the Marxist-Communist ideology within Washington, D.C.

The Marxist-Communist Democrat Party leadership and their fanatical followers have hijacked the party, eerily embracing discredited Neo-Confederate notions of racial bigotry, discrimination, segregation, and the old card up the sleeve: racial obsession. They are turning America into a divided nation on the verge of civil war. To implement their unpopular programs and initiatives, the new Marxist-Communist Democrat Party is radically altering all of our federal institutions. To this end, the Marxist-Communist Democrat Party is using fear and uncertainty to confuse the citizenry, threaten to pack the courts, end the filibuster, destroy the Electoral College, and override states' sovereignty to establish voting laws that will lead to one political party country. It is further hard to believe that the average Democrat voter believes that radical Marxist-Communist protesters can, with impunity, be allowed to mob the homes of Supreme Court justices, or any judge's home for that matter, to influence their decisions without any consequences from our legal system.

When in the majority, congressional Marxist-Communist Democrat Party leadership in Congress will deny Republican minority leader's chosen Republican members to be seated on critical House committees. Only Marxist-Communist Democrat congressional leadership, think Nancy Pelosi here, would be so callous and disrespectful as to tear up the State of the Union address on national television. Even if they disagree with the presentation, it is a disgraceful black mark on our Constitutional Republic. The Marxist-Communist Democrat Party leadership in Congress disrespectfully allows for the unchecked temper tampers by the likes of Alexandria Ocasio-Cortez (AOC), a young American Marxist-Communist Democratic politician and activist who has been allowed to hijack the Democrat Party along with her so-called squad.

One member of that squad is racist Congresswoman Cori Bush, who got herself shredded by a young conservative oil company executive, Alex Epstein. During a congressional hearing, Bush accused Mr. Epstein of being a "white supremacist" because he espouses the view that "Western culture is superior to all others." Alex Epstein then had to provide the ignorant federally funded school system-educated Cori Bush with an explanation as to why our Western culture is superior to all others, which includes the promotion of individualism, freedom, and opportunity. He stated that he wants everyone worldwide to enjoy the same freedom Americans enjoy. That is what makes our culture the best in the world, explained Mr. Epstein. Mr. Epstein explained that cultural differences have nothing to do with race or skin color. Where else but America would an ignorant, racist clown like Cori Bush be able to get elected to public office? If Cori Bush had an I.Q. above room temperature, she would have been humiliated by Mr. Epstein's beatdown. Oddly, she did not even realize that she had just been humiliated.

Avowed Marxist-Communist Democrat university students, with the full support of Marxist-Communist Democrat university professors and deans, are disrupting invited campus speakers merely for having opposing views. Is it not the intention of our colleges and Universities to provide opportunities to hear and debate opposing viewpoints and ideas?

Marxist-Communist Democrat Party District Attorneys release violent arrested criminals back onto our streets without bail or minimal bail while jailing conservatives awaiting prosecution or requiring extremely high bail.

Woke Marxist-Communist Democrat Party four-star military generals call their Chinese counterparts to advise them that they will contact them should their commander-in-chief's military plans or actions have an impact on these enemies of the United States. An action once considered to be an act of treason and subject to life in prison or death by execution.

The Pentagon spends valuable training time lecturing military personnel about their supposed inborn racism. The United States military no longer has the will to win wars, abandons billions of dollars of the world's most sophisticated military equipment to terrorists, and allows Communist China to fly surveillance balloons into and across America, including over our most sensitive military bases, with impunity.

Source & Additional Information: (https://www.reuters.com/world/us/us-top-general-secretly-called-china-twice-trump-term-ended-report-2021-09-14/) (https://www.nytimes.com/2023/02/04/us/china-spy-balloon-time.html) (https://www.abc.net.au/news/2021-08-20/taliban-new-us-made-war-chest-afghanistan/100393572)

Once proud and distinguished federal establishments have been weaponized by the Marxist-Communist leadership of the Democrat Party and are no longer recognizable as servants of the people. The FBI of the Elliot Ness era no longer exists. Three former FBI directors have lied under oath to federal investigators or pleaded amnesia in congressional testimonies. Former Marxist-Communist Democrat Party national intelligence directors sign off on a known fraudulent letter to sway voter opinion in an upcoming presidential election and blatantly lie under oath to the Senate. The Internal Revenue Service has been weaponized against political opponents of the Marxist-Communist Democrat Party, and the Marxist-Communist Democrat Party leadership of the DOJ deems it more appropriate to send FBI agents after parents of school students than after Marxist-Communist mobs threatening the homes of Supreme Court justices.

Under the guise of the COVID-19 pandemic, the Marxist-Communist Democrat Party turned Election Day upside down with illegal and criminal election decisions by the Marxist-Communist Democrat Secretary of State, Board of Elections, and judicial systems. As a direct result of these Marxist-Communist Democrat entities, 70% of American voters did not vote on election day but rather voted over an extended period, in some states extending as much as a month.

The Marxist-Communist Democrat Party has changed the date of the founding of our Nation from 1776 to 1619, a hundred and fifty-plus years before the true year in which our Nation was born. Statues of American heroes or of those who played a significant role in America's history are toppled as being racists. Non-conforming American citizens' careers, livelihoods, and businesses are destroyed for not accepting Marxist-Communist woke narratives or ideology. Biological males who identify as women are destroying women's sports and five decades of women's hard-won efforts to achieve equal treatment and respect in athletics.

<u>Source & Additional Information</u>: *(https://www.niskanencenter.org/how-early-voting-is-changing-american-elections/) (https://www.peoplesworld.org/article/rewriting-the-united-states-past-and-future-the-1619-project-and-its-critics/)*

What triggered the collective madness of these radical anti-American Marxist-Communist Democrats? Was it just the killing of black criminals who refused to comply with police officers' commands, or was this just the excuse used by the Marxist-Communist Democrat radicals to create chaos and turmoil throughout cities across the country to push their Marxist-Communist agenda? Was it the COVID-19 pandemic with all the closing of businesses and schools and the loss of employment? Could it have been the 2016 election of Donald Trump that sent anti-Trump fanatics into a meltdown? The answer is, in all probability, all of the above. To the radical anti-American Marxist-Communist Democrats, it does not matter why, but rather that chaos, violence, and lawlessness were achieved to begin the destruction of our Constitutional Republic's law and order society.

As the country collapses under Marxist-Communist Democrat Party rule, the Marxist-Communist revolution's last gasp is to destroy Trump at any cost to ensure that he cannot win the 2024 presidential elections. It is their strategy to continue to indict, gag, and hemorrhage him legally until Election Day 2024. Trump was the first president to be impeached twice, the first American citizen to be tried by the Senate as a private citizen, and the first former President of the United States to have his private home raided by the FBI.

Now President Trump is the first former president to be indicted and formally charged, not once, not twice, but four times on the most ridiculous and tenuous of accusations, effectively ending America's moral authority abroad.

The Democrat platform reestablishes the fact that they are now a Marxist-Communist party, as their platform is pages of federal government hand-outs and control over the citizens of the United States. Their platform includes extensive racially biased benefits and the destruction of gun manufacturing to eliminate any threat to their Marxist-Communist government by armed Americans.

Source & Additional Information: (https://www.forbes.com/sites/saradorn/2024/08/19/democrats-approve-party-platform-written-before-harris-became-nominee/)

Every American citizen must read the Democrat Party's platform addressing their agenda for America. Only then will everyone understand the reality that the Democrat Party has indeed morphed into a Marxist-Communist party. I believe that very few registered Democrats are even aware of precisely what it is they are supporting by voting Democrat. Conservative-leaning Americans must encourage their Democrat family members and friends to read and understand what it is they are supporting. This one act will take great courage because we know of the backlash you will receive for even daring to suggest they read their own party's platform. Just remember that it will take significantly less courage than it took our eighteen, nineteen, and twenty-year-old children to face death on the battlefield to defend our Constitutional Republic. So, think about them and find the courage to do this one thing.

The Democratic Platform is classic government jurisdictional overreach and excessive expenditure. As the Convention of States Action movement proposes, these disastrous agenda items can only be stopped by proposing constitutional amendments restricting such overreach and requiring a balanced budget—assuming it is not too late.

Chapter 6
Republican Party

The official written platform of the Republican Party is generally based on American conservatism, promising to ensure that every citizen's constitutional rights are protected. However, the Republican body within Congress is infected with the RINO (Republicans In Name Only) virus, which consistently restricts what conservative legislation is passed and which Marxist-Communist Democrat legislation moves forward because of the support provided by these RINOs.

Ehe Republican Party's conservative fiscal policies include support for lower taxes, limited government, free market capitalism, free trade, deregulation of corporations, and restrictions on labor unions. In terms of fiscal restraint, the Republican party is often no better at restricting spending than are their Democrat colleges. The Republican Party has never initiated any action to restrict federal government overreach by returning to the sovereign states those departments, agencies, and commissions whose mandates and functions constitutionally belong to the individual states.

The party's social conservatism platform includes support for gun rights as outlined in the Second Amendment, the death penalty for violent criminals, and traditional values based on our Judeo-Christian foundation, including restrictions on abortion. In foreign policy, Republicans favor increased military spending to support America's deterrence policy through strength and strong national defense. Other Republican positions include restrictions on immigration, more specifically, opposition to illegal immigration, opposition to drug legalization, pornography, and affirmative action, and support for school choice and school prayer.

The Republican platform is noble, but for it to make any difference to the people and the country, it must be fearlessly and faithfully followed by the implementation of conservative ideologic legislation by elected Republican members within Congress. Unfortunately for conservatives, whenever the Republican party takes control of all three branches of government, little is done to move forward the truly conservative Republican agenda as articulated in the Republican platform. Republicans, unlike the Democrats, find it difficult to stand together united to get conservative legislation passed to bring our Nation back to what our Founding Fathers intended. Far too many Republican members of Congress fear the press and social media inhibiting them from standing behind their platform and completing the necessary hard work they promised their constituents when campaigning. While Democrats are street fighters and will go to any length necessary to push their agenda forward, Republicans are more inclined to go along to get along. This is why, even when the Republican party has, on numerous occasions over the past sixty years, been in control of all three branches of the government, little movement to the conservative right is accomplished.

The Democrat party is notorious for creating false narratives and crisis traps to ensnare Republican lawmakers. Although Republican members of Congress can see that they have been set up to appear racist and phobic, they will withdraw or, at the very least, allow themselves to be limited in their pursuit of conservative legislation to achieve their stated goals of keeping the United States a Constitutional Republic. A vast majority of our Republican representatives are quick to talk the talk while campaigning but, once elected, fail to walk the walk, failing to put a halt to the Democrat Party agenda of creating a Marxist-Communist country of our Constitutional Republic.

Source & Additional Information: (https://www.presidency.ucsb.edu/documents/2024-republican-party-platform)

We are at war with a Marxist-Communist ideological Democrat party, and unless Republican members can find the courage and determination to move out of their safe zones and enter the battle prepared to fight as hard and ruthlessly as the Marxist-Communist members of Congress, conservatism in the United States will surely fall. Republicans are quick to take the so-called "high road," which is very noble on the surface but does not win battles against an opposition force who have a "take no prisoners, show no mercy" mentality. Marxist-Communists want to win and convert our Constitutional Republic into another failed Marxist-Communist country. One cannot honestly say the same is true of the Republicans elected to protect the American citizen and our Constitution as written and intended by our Founding Fathers. The Republican party must shed their fears and self-imposed restrictions and place themselves on the front line, in the thick of the action.

Grand Old Party: For far too long, not only are the Republicans not sufficiently pushing back to prevent, or at least slow the transformation of our Constitutional Republic into a Marxist-Communist Nation, but many Republican members of Congress, most notably Mitch McConnell, Adam Kinzinger, John Corny, Lisa Murkowski, Mitt Romney, Tom Cotton, Fred Upton, and the list goes on and on, are Marxist-Communist in Republican coats. All of whom far too often support Marxist-Communist programs, initiatives, and outrageous spending bills in lockstep with Marxist-Communist Democrat members of Congress.

Before the 2022 mid-term elections, we were subjected to endless hours of cable news talking heads, political strategists, and analysts predicting the undebatable "Red Wave" coming in the 2022 mid-term elections. Then, when the Republican "Red Wave" failed to materialize, we were subjected to hours of endless debating about who was at fault for the Republican Party's underperformance. And, of course, it was all President Trump's fault. The only major Republican leader who constantly crisscrossed the country, holding rallies for Republican candidates. This is just another excellent opportunity to denigrate former President Donald Trump and attempt to diminish his popularity with the Republican base, hopefully forcing him out of running for President in 2024. This is despite the authentic fact that he was the most productive President in modern history, delivered on his promises to the people, and made America great again. Unheard of in modern politics.

The Republican leadership in Congress failed to make the red wave a reality. Mitch McConnel, the Senate minority leader, took millions of dollars away from the campaigns of Trump-endorsed candidates with enormous potential to win against their Marxist-Communist Democrat opponents and redirected that money to support left-leaning Republicans who would show allegiance to McConnel. McConnel even provided funding to a Republican candidate who openly announced intentions to vote with Marxist-Communist Democrats.

If Republican voters would break their addiction to far-left news outlets, such as NBC, CBS, ABC, CNN, FOX, or, worst of all, MSNBC, as well as Marxist-Communist leaning news outlets, they would have been aware of this fact. For truly factual news, Republicans and conservates need to look to NEWSMAX, One America News Network (ONNA), The Babylon Bee, Breitbart News, New York Post, The Hill, The Blaze, or the Gateway Pundit, to name a few. Bottom line – break yourself away from far-left outlets; otherwise, you will never know what is truly happening in our country and to what extent our federal government is denying our constitutional rights. Take the time to learn how to navigate the internet for the information needed to keep up with the daily changes in our constantly evolving political landscape. Those voters who watched or read these suggested news outlets or were able to research on the internet knew that the failed "Red Wave" rested solely on the shoulders of Marxist-Communist Mitch McConnel, who single-handedly lost the Republican party's chance to regain the majority in the Senate.

Good Old Boys: While America burns, co-emperors Chuck Schumer and Mitch McConnel were just two close buddies who enjoyed hanging out together in the back rooms of our Capitol building. Just two corrupt good old boys and their entourage, smoking expensive cigars and sipping Kentucky bourbon while figuring out how to push our Nation over the tipping point, totally dividing the citizens of the United States, bankrupting us, ruining our economy; and degrading our military's ability to fight a war thus earning those bonus checks from China. Who says the Republicans and Democrats cannot get along?

Chaos and crisis loom over America, so what a wonderful time for these two buddies to fuel America's state of crises by throwing a fifty-gallon container of gasoline on this fire with Marxist-Communist legislation and spending bills. They want to be sure that every American citizen feels the heat. Only McConnel and Schumer could be this generous. The Republican members of Congress are making it possible for the Marxist-Communist Democrat party to advertise that their initiatives to exert more control and dependence on American society are bipartisan, further undermining the argument that it is the Marxist-Communist Democrat party's out-of-control spending that is fueling the country's crisis.

As the adage states, "When it rains, it pours." The Marxist-Communist Democrat party officially owns the Senate with 51 Democrats and at least 12 RINO Republicans. But let us think about this: does it make a difference? Probably not. Why? Because, in reality, we currently have three major political parties in America. The Republican Party, the Democrat Party, and the Washington Elitist Party (a.k.a. The Swamp), with the Washington Elitist Party being the significantly more dominant and controlling party. It is the Washington Elitist Party, made up of long-serving Grand Old Party Republican and Marxist-

Communist Democrat members of Congress, influential billionaires, and past Marxist-Communist leaders who control the swamp and dictate what will or will not happen in America. These Washington elites serve only themselves and control the Washington agenda. An agenda that is not good for the survival of our Constitutional Republic.

Maybe it is far past time to reform the Grand Old Party into a Grand New Party and put out to pasture Grand Old members who cannot or will not accept the fact that the Grand Old way of politicking is no longer viable in an environment threatening the overthrowing of our Constitution and Constitutional Republic by radical Marxist-Communist elements. We and the Republican Party leadership have long known that the Marxist-Communist Democrat Party is unafraid of doing whatever it takes to win and implement their radical Marxist-Communist legislation. From the local level to the Federal level, Republican leadership and voters must rid themselves of Grand Old Members of this Grand Old Party. We must begin to find, support, and elect candidates to Congress who have the passion, dedication, and willingness not only to fight against the Marxist-Communist Democrat members of Congress but also the Marxist-Communist members of the Republican party.

What patriotic American citizen could have believed, just a few short years ago, that the day would ever come when our country, the world's great beacon of hope and the last vestige of liberty and freedom of choice, would be so close to becoming a Marxist-Communist Nation led in a Stalinist manner. Was it naivety, denial, or apathy which has led us to this point? We should all be gravely concerned for our Constitutional Republic, as the only party that could have held our Republic together is both internally divided and slowly sliding down the same slippery slope as the Marxist-Communist Democrat party. The Republican Party cannot seem to stand solidly united in the same manner as the Marxist-Communist Democrat Party to successfully oppose

Marxist-Communist legislation and pass desperately needed conservative legislation to save our Nation.

During the 2023 election process for the Speaker of the House position, the Marxist-Communist Democrat members of the House stood solidly behind their one nominee through fifteen rounds of voting. However, the Grand Old members of the Grand Old Party in the House of Representatives only wished to see the traditional Grand Old status quo remain. They could not or would not bring themselves together to support the critical reforms demanded by twenty heroic, truly conservative Republican members of the Freedom Caucus. Members refused to support Kevin McCarty until their demands for stronger conservative members on key congressional committees, full accountability of the Speaker of the House, and reforms to the House rules were met. Grand Old Party Republicans and fake news pundits were screeching at every opportunity afforded them that these twenty holdout members of the House Freedom Caucus would lead to handing over the gavel back to the Marxist-Communist Democrat Party and would be a disaster for the Republican Party, just for daring to oppose the immediate election of a speaker until their demands for process changes were agreed to. The twenty courageous conservatives were called insurrectionists and terrorists and were threatened by Grand Old Party Republicans to be kicked off committees. It even got physical on the House floor. Ultimately, McCarty agreed to the changes demanded and was elected Speaker.

In keeping with Speaker McCarthy's promise to America and the Republican Freedom Caucus members of the House, in late April of 2023, the House passed the "Limit, Save, Grow Act" which delivered on Speaker McCarthy's and the Republican members of the House's promise to bring back fiscal sanity to the federal government. The "Limit, Save, Grow Act" called for total base discretionary spending to return to fiscal 2022 levels, which was already the highest federal government spending year in American history due to the COVID epidemic. It further called for the capping of our national debt at the $32 trillion our nation owes to foreign countries, most of which the United States had borrowed from our greatest adversary, China. With this new proposed budget, Speaker McCarthy began negotiating with a reluctant President Biden, promising not to yield on the House Republican-passed "Limit, Save, Grow Act."

Then, on May 31st, 2023, Congress solidified what many have known for years and justified conservative's lack of confidence that the members of the Grand Old Party in Congress would do the right thing and pass the "Limit, Save, Grow Act." Unfortunately for America, in Washington, D.C., there is no difference between a Republican and a Democrat when it comes to fiscal insanity. A new and very disappointing budget package, the "Fiscal Responsibility Act," which is anything but fiscally responsible, was agreed to by McCarthy and Biden. This new Fiscal Year 2024 budget package was presented to the House for a vote. By a vote of 314 to 117 the House rejected the fiscally responsible "Limit, Save, Grow Act" and instead chose to pass the "Fiscal Responsibility Act" deal made between McCarthy and Biden. The "Fiscal Responsibility Act" was passed by the Senate by a vote of 63-36, ensuring that the federal government will continue to expend our Nation into obliteration recklessly.

One-hundred and forty-nine Grand Old Party Republican Representatives and eighteen Grand Old Party Republican Senators voted for this Marxist-Communist legislation, adding four more trillion dollars of debt to the already mind-boggling thirty-two-trillion-dollar debt owed by the United States. Instead of capping the debt ceiling at its current level as called for by the "Limit, Save, Grow Act," the so-called "Fiscal Responsibility Act" totally suspended any cap on the debt ceiling for two years, giving the Biden-Harris administration a firm blank check to spend at will over the next two years. The United States continues to "careening towards bankruptcy" after President Joe Biden's and House Speaker Kevin McCarthy's agreement to raise the debt ceiling by $4 trillion, and Congress ignored the coming financial collapse of our Nation, which was hastened by the passage of this insane fiscal year 2024 budget.

Source & Additional Information: (https://www.heritage.org/debt/commentary/whats-wrong-and-whats-right-debt-ceiling-deal)

Republican Senator Rand Paul of Kentucky slammed the "fake conservatives" in both chambers of Congress who supported this agreement. This so-called "Deal" will increase mandatory spending by 5%, increase military spending by 3%, and maintain current non-military discretionary spending at post-COVID levels. "No real cuts to see here, conservatives have been sold out once again!" Senator Paul posted on May 28th, 2023. According to Republican Representative Matt Rosendale of Montana, the fiscal package "continues to fund the Democrats' and Biden-Harris administration's radical agenda," labeling the deal the "Fiscal Irresponsibility Act." "It is frankly an insult to the American people to support a piece of legislation that continues to put our country's financial future at risk. Montanans did not send me to Washington to support business as usual, which is why I voted AGAINST the Fiscal Irresponsibility Act," Justin Amash, a former Libertarian Congressman from Michigan, described it on Twitter as "the ultimate kick-the-can-down-the-road agreement." Republican Senator Mike Lee of Utah has taken to social media to lambast the deal, calling the "promise of future spending cuts fake." Senator Lee also stated that many of his colleagues say the Marxist-Communist Democrats "love this deal. The debt-ceiling bill is a stunning success when it comes to uniting Democrats," Lee posted on social media.

The Republican House passed the "Limit, Save, Grow Act," which called for rescinding the $50 billion in unspent COVID funds. The Biden/McCarthy, "Fiscal Responsibility Act", rescinds only $28 billion of that $50 billion and transfers the remaining $22 billion into the hands of the Department of Commerce, making that money available to our federal bureaucracy to spend on Marxist-Communist initiatives. Of major concern to American citizens and included in the Republican-passed "Limit, Save, Grow Act" was rescinding the additional $70 billion in funding provided in mid-2022 to hire 80,000 additional gun-carrying Internal Revenue Service agents. The Biden/McCarthy, "Fiscal Responsibility Act", only rescinded $1.4 billion and placed no restrictions on hiring the additional 80,000 Internal Revenue Service agents. Far short of the Republican's promise to eliminate this pending attack on American taxpayers.

Source & Additional Information: (https://www.vox.com/2022/8/16/23302798/irs-audit-inflation-reduction-act)

At a time when American families are suffering from record-high inflation, record-high interest rates, and falling real take-home wages, we were promised by Speaker McCarthy and the Republican party that the federal government's fiscal insanity would be ended. Conservatives around the country rallied together with their approval and support of the "Limit, Save, Grow Act." Those twenty conservative members of the House who opposed the immediate election of a speaker and demanded changes gave our elected representatives another chance to save our nation from fiscal destruction. All they needed to do was stand together and demand the passage of the "Limit, Save, Grow Act," thereby keeping their promise to "We the People" to end the out-of-control spending by our federal government. As should have been expected, McCarthy and the Marxist Republican members of Congress once again failed the American people by allowing the passage of the Marxist-Communist favorable "Fiscal Responsibility Act." While our nation faces an unprecedented fiscal crisis and a largely unchecked, woke, and weaponized federal bureaucracy, it is business as usual in Washington, D.C.

Once again, its promises made, promises broken by those we elected to defend America and assure our Constitutional Republic's survival. It has been repeatedly said that we cannot look to our elected federal officials to come to America's rescue. Waiting for a miracle from heaven to manifest itself and save our Republic is a foolish waste of time at best. It threatens Americans' economic and social well-being at its worst. The only absolute path is convening a Convention of States under Article V of the Constitution to pass an Amendment requiring fiscal restraint and a balanced budget. We are doomed as freedom-loving American patriots without this means to correct course. Time is running out for our Republic. It is now or never for each of us to step out of our comfort zones and begin engaging with our State Representatives and very vocally advise them of our loss of faith in our federal government's ability to act on behalf of the citizens of the United States. We must all make it very clear to our State congressional members that we want them to pass a resolution calling for convening a Convention of States under Article V to pass Amendments to our Constitution, which will once and for all rein in our out-of-control and corrupt federal government.

I realize that over time, things change, which is to be expected, but never our government's respect for the Constitution, which our Founding Fathers wrote in a manner that would endure the passage of time. It is written in a manner that makes it as relevant today as it was when written by our Founding Fathers. We now find ourselves at a point in time when these truths are being severely tested. The scale of evil temptation for power, influence, and money that confronts our elected officials once they take office turns otherwise honorable men and women, many of whom go to Washington with honorable intentions, into corrupt Washington elites drawn to the dark side of politics. Drawn into corruption at the level of a third-world country.

Chapter 7
Donald J. Trump

In 2016, to the surprise of the Washington swamp, the Marxist-Communist Democrat Party, their extreme Marxist-Communist Democrat Party constituents, the never-Trumper Republicans, and members of Congress, a non-Washington non-political businessman, won the Presidential elections. Donald J. Trump, a successful businessman and television personality, was now the President of the United States. To the horror of the Marxist-Communist Democrat Party in both the Congress and the general population, President Trump began to undo years of Marxist-Communist Democrat Party denigration of our Constitutional Republic. This, of course, earned him the wrath of the Marxist-Communist Democrat Party and their loyal republican comrades. His four years in office were marred by lawsuit after lawsuit and two attempts to impeach the first President to actually follow through on his promise to Make America Great Again. In every case, Donald Trump was found "not guilty."

In just four short years, President Trump managed to make America energy independent, make our southern border the most secure in the history of our country, dramatically reduce the flow of illegal immigrants, reduce the trafficking of children, women, and deadly drugs, increase employment for minority groups, and reduce inflation. He renegotiated terrible trade agreements and treaties with other countries, which were being given economic advantages at the expense of diligent American taxpayers. Actually, because of President Trump's remarkable success at keeping his promises to the people and his ability to make America great again, he is greatly feared by the Marxist-Communists worldwide.

Source & Additional Information: (https://www.politico.com/news/magazine/2021/01/18/trump-presidency-administration-biggest-impact-policy-analysis-451479)

Donald J. Trump, speaking at the CPAC convention to a hall filled with patriots, stated that the Marxist-Communist Democrat Party was dedicated to undermining the rule of law and the Constitution and eliminating American conservatism. In his speech, he correctly said, "They [the leftists] are not coming after me, they're coming after you. I am just standing in their way," and "The Republican Party was ruled by freaks, neocons, open borders zealots, and fools. We are never going back to the party of Paul Ryan, Karl Rove, and Jeb Bush," in other words the Grand _Old_ Party is dead.

Think about what Donald Trump has been put through by the deep state Marxist-Communist Democrat Party traitors with no support from the never-Trumpers of the Grand Old Party and many other Republican congressional members who cared more about their political careers than finding the courage to stand by and support their leader. This man has been through two attempts to impeach him while president and after he left office. He has been investigated more times by different entities than any other individual, and absolutely nothing inappropriate has been found. To this day, the Marxist-Communist Democrat Party continues to harass, persecute, and prosecute President Trump in an attempt to stop him from running for President in 2024 by filing litigation after litigation to tarnish his reputation and promoting false accusations by Marxist-Communist individuals at the encouragement of the Marxist-Communist Democrat Party operatives. Donald Trump is the most feared individual within the Marxist-Communist community. They know that Donald Trump is motivated by his love of country, the Constitution as written by the Founding Fathers, and the citizens of this great Nation and not by greed or elitist status. He is the only one standing between Constitutional Conservativism and the Marxist-Communist movement, which is determined to eliminate conservativism in the United States permanently.

Source & Additional Information: (https://www.businessinsider.com/donald-trump-key-cases-civil-criminal-investigations-lawsuits-updates-2022-7?op=1)

Before Donald Trump became President of the United States, the "deep state" remained in the background while doing its dirty work to destroy our Constitutional Republic. When Trump became president, these treasonous enemies of America were flushed out in the open and exposed for what they truly were: traitors. President Trump was a serious threat to both party's politicians. With Trump's America First agenda, these anti-Americans could no longer continue to sell out American jobs to other countries, so they began their political attacks on Donald Trump and his associates. Just look at the players involved in the sinister plot to frame President Trump with their phony Russia collusion investigation and the scheme to frame General Michael Flynn. Donald Trump has been vilified and inappropriately investigated for no-crime issues and attacks on his First Amendment rights to free speech by FBI Director James Comey, CIA Director John Brennan, United States Attorney General Merrick Garland, Department of Justice Attorney Andrew Weissmann, Special Counsel Jack Smith, and numerous other Department of Justice lawyers.

With these Marxist-Communist Deep State players, it is the *process* that is the punishment. They want to wear down conservatives with massive legal fees to defend against baseless, fabricated charges. They do not care if their victim wins the case. Their goal is to intimidate, harass, and bankrupt. The DOJ conspirators win because they cause their victims financial pain. In New York, the Deep State is using the corrupt justice system to frame Trump for non-existing crimes. District Attorney Alvin Bragg is too foolish to have plotted this legal action against Trump alone. The plot had to have been created by high-level corrupt and malicious Marxist-Communist Democrat Party leaders and their wealthy supporters. Their purpose is to tie up the former president with bogus court cases to keep him from campaigning and holding rallies.

Also making false accusations and charging Trump with fabricated accusation of racketeering charges was the Marxist-Communist District Attorney for Fulton County in the state of Georgia. They will try to indict Trump for making a phone call to try to have investigated numerous reports of election tampering and fraud during the 2020 presidential election process in Georgia. We all saw the video of Marxist-Communist Democrat poll workers running Democrat ballots through the tabulator multiple times and pulling out boxes of phony ballots that were hidden under a table after the polling site had closed down. They were able to do this because they kicked the Republican poll workers and poll watchers out of the vote counting room, using a water leak as a ruse. Marxist-Communist Democrat Party Leaders are *sheepishly* telling American citizens, "Nothing to see here, move along now. "

Hillary Clinton, the Democrat National Convention, and the leadership within the FBI created a false story about Trump-Russia collusion; then, they conveniently leaked their fake story to their friends in the media. Using the media story as a pretext, they initiated the bogus, which cost American taxpayers $35 million to investigate knowingly false accusations. Mueller had nineteen lawyers from the corrupt and weaponized DOJ and fifty agents from an equally corrupt and weaponized FBI on his staff in an attempt to find non-existing evidence of Russian collusion, which they knew did not exist. So, they turned their attention and time tormenting Trump's campaign staffers, financially destroying their lives. When their politically motivated investigation ended, it was reported that many of Mueller's staff wiped their cell phones clean to eliminate evidence of their corruption. Doing this required them to enter the wrong password ten times a row. Then, they all claimed it was a mistake. These men and women are still walking around free and have yet to be held accountable for their destruction of evidence and other crimes against American citizens. When you commit crimes to destroy Trump, you are hailed as a hero by the Deep State and get Marxist-Communist Democrat immunity instead of being charged, tried, convicted, and jailed.

Source & Additional Information: (https://www.justice.gov/storage/report_volume2.pdf)

During Donald Trump's 2024 presidential campaign, the Marxist-Communist Democrat Party and their legal arm, the corrupt anti-American DOJ, never let up on their constant harassment and persecution of Donald Trump to distract him from his reelection campaign. False allegations, charges, indictments, and arrests of Donald Trump include:

- ➤ In March of 2023, Donald Trump became the first former United States president in history to face criminal charges when he was indicted in New York on state charges stemming from alleged hush money payments made during his 2016 presidential campaign to bury allegations of extramarital sexual encounters. President Trump pleaded not guilty to thirty-four felony counts of fabricated charges that he falsified business records in relationship to those payments. Those counts are linked to a series of checks that were written to his lawyer Michael Cohen to allegedly reimburse him for his role in paying off porn actor Stormy Daniels, who alleged a sexual encounter with Trump in 2006. Those payments were recorded in various internal company documents for a legal retainer that prosecutors say did not exist.

Source & Additional Information: (https://www.pbs.org/newshour/show/trump-pleads-not-guilty-to-34-felony-counts-of-falsification-of-business-records)

- ➤ On June 8th, 2023, Trump was indicted in federal court with alleged illegal retention of top-secret documents. Documents that the President had declassified and the Presidential Records Act gives a President the right to take and maintain possession of any records he desires, even after leaving office. Trump was indicted in this federal case in Florida, alleging he mishandled classified documents. The case identified forty felony counts against him, including retaining classified information, obstructing justice, and making false statements. This indictment, the first federal case against a former president, falsely alleges that Trump repeatedly enlisted aides and lawyers to help him hide records demanded by investigators. Walt Nauta, a valet for Trump, and Carlos De Oliveira, the property manager at Trump's Florida estate, were also charged with scheming to conceal surveillance footage from federal investigators and lying about it. Both Trump and Nauta have pleaded not guilty. Carlos De Oliveira was accused of conspiring with Trump to try to delete security footage sought by investigators probing the former president's hoarding of classified documents at his Palm Beach club. De Oliveira was further added to the indictment with Trump and the ex-president's valet, Walt Nauta, and faced charges including conspiracy to obstruct justice and lying to investigators.

Source & Additional Information: (https://www.npr.org/2023/06/09/1181340894/trump-indictment-classified-documents-charges)

- ➤ On August 2nd, 2023, the Injustice Department unveiled an indictment charging President Trump with four criminal counts related to alleged attempts to overturn the results of the 2020 presidential election. President Trump was formally arrested on August 3rd, 2023. The charges include conspiracy to defraud the United States, conspiracy to obstruct an official proceeding, obstruction of an official proceeding, and conspiracy against rights. This was the third time the Marxist-Communist Democrat Party's DOJ had indicted President Trump in an attempt to keep him off the 2024 ballot for President. The Marxist-Communist Democrat Party is very well aware that they have no one that can defeat Donald Trump in November of 2024. They are also well aware of the fact that once Trump assumes office, their Washington Elitist world will implode, and a significant number of those criminally corrupt elitists and elected/unelected Marxist-Communist Democrat Party members will be held accountable to the fullest extent of the law;

Source & Additional Information: (https://www.cnn.com/politics/live-news/indictment-jan-6-trump-08-02-23/index.html)

> ➢ In Georgia, Fulton County District Attorney Fani Willis charged Trump over alleged efforts by Trump and his allies to overturn his 2020 election loss in that state. Charges imposed by a corrupt and inept Georgia Marxist-Communist Democrat Party County District Attorney in further attempts to keep Trump from reclaiming the presidency. Those charges allege President Trump illegally meddled in the 2020 presidential elections in Georgia. The Marxist-Communist Democrat district attorney's investigation began shortly after the release of a recording of a January 2nd, 2021, phone call between Trump and Georgia Secretary of State Brad Raffensperger in which President Trump suggested that Raffensperger could "find" 11,780 votes, just enough to overtake Marxist-Communist Democrat Joe Biden and overturn Trump's narrow loss in the state. As is valid in all the above cases, this is a case based on a District Attorney's runaway imagination in an attempt to gain political favor from her Marxist-Communist Democrat Party for future elevated positions within the party.

Source & Additional Information: (https://crsreports.congress.gov/product/pdf/LSB/LSB11016)

Unlike the Marxist-Communist Democrat Party, which manufactured fake ballots for Marxist-Communist Democrat Party Joe Biden in the most election-corrupt county and state in the United States, President Trump did not direct Raffensperger to create or manufacture 11,780 votes but instead advised him that in an election-corrupt state such as Georgia, close review of the election results should result in the identification of at least this number of votes as a result of election fraud on behalf of Joe Biden.

A grand jury in the District of Columbia returned President Trump's January 6th, 2021, related indictment. Because an estimated ninety-five percent of registered voters in the District of Columbia are anti-Trump Marxist-Communist Democrats, jurors will show little unbiased legal judgment but rather will render a politically motivated judgment willing to find him guilty regardless of the amount of evidence suggesting otherwise.

Source & Additional Information: (https://time.com/6298840/donald-trump-indictment-jan-6-jack-smith/)

It is very suspicious that all of these and potential indictments, which could have and should have been pursued over four years ago, are now being pursued. Instead, the Marxist-Communist Democrat DOJ and their allies made a politically motivated decision to wait until after President Trump announced his run for the Presidency. And why would they choose to investigate and charge President Trump now? Three reasons: First, the Marxist-Communist Democrat Party was desperate to eliminate the frontrunner in the Republican Party's field of candidates, whose lead was insurmountable over the other Republican candidates; second, if President Trump won the nomination, the Marxist-Communist Democrat Party knew Joe Biden nor any other Democrat candidate they put forward could beat Trump; and third, Joe Biden's corrupt and treasonous acts with our foreign enemies which are unfolding as ever-increasing amounts of evidence are being brought forward by whistleblowers and those who were involved in those acts of treason, in hopes of creating a diversion from Biden's mounting evidence of corruption, bribery, and extortion. A clear indication of using the DOJ as a diversionary tactic can be seen in the following timeline:

- November 17th, 2022: House GOP outlines Hunter Biden probe.
- November 18th, 2022: Biden's DOJ appoints Trump Special Counsel.

- March 16th, 2023: Biden bank records revealed by GOP.
- March 18th, 2023: Trump advised of an imminent indictment.

- June 8th, 2023, GOP advises FBI Document indicates probable Biden bribe scheme.
- June 9th, 2023, a Classified Document indictment was issued against Trump.

- July 31st, 2023, Devon Archer Testifies before the House.
- August 1st, 2023, Trump was indicted for alleged January 6th, 2021, criminal actions.
- August 15th, 2023, Trump was indicted for alleged election interference in Georgia.

Right at the primary time of his campaigning for election to the Presidency, President Trump will be required to attend these hearings, preventing him from being on the campaign trail. You can be sure that every legal tactic will be deployed by the Marxist-Communist Democrat Party to prolong each trial for as long as possible to prevent Trump from campaigning. These tactics by the Marxist-Communist Special Counsel, District Attorneys, and judges are earmarks of the real election interference being perpetuated against President Trump, which is a felony. What these morons fail to observe is that every time an indictment is filed against Donald Trump, his favorability polling goes up.

These bogus legal attacks on Donald Trump will all eventually backfire on the Marxist-Communist Democrat Party, making Donald Trump even more determined and popular with American voters. Trump supporters will never abandon the only patriotic American who can bring sanity back to our political world. American conservatives understand that at this point in American history, America needs Donald Trump back in the White House so he can once and for all clean out the Washington swamp, bring accountability to those who criminally weaponized and politicized the State Department, the Department of Justice, the FBI, the Internal Revenue Service, and worst of all our education system. As a side note, it was President Obama, with Vice President Joe Biden by his side, who turned the Department of Justice, FBI, and Internal Revenue Service into weaponized political persecutors of their political enemies, in the same manner, found in all Marxist-Communist nations around the world. *These agencies are now 'political police', not political servants.*

The United States justice system is no longer recognizable as envisioned by our Founders. Lady Justice is shown as being blindfolded to represent the impartiality and objectivity of the law and that it does not let outside factors, such as politics, wealth, or fame, influence its decisions. Lady Justice's sword shows authority, including the power to punish injustice. It also implies being able to cut through obstacles to get to the facts of a case. The balance (scale) represents weighing facts and evidence to decide a verdict. It also shows her duty to restore balance to society. This is no longer the case in the United States. Lady Justice has been assassinated by the Marxist-Communist Democrat Party in order to maintain their tyrannical and oppressive hold on power at any cost.

Donald J. Trump Indictment One: On the evening of March 30th, 2023, our Constitutional form of governance took a potentially deadly blow with the indictment of former President Donald J. Trump by a Manhattan grand jury on ridiculously fabricated charges of falsifying business records. On April 4th, 2023, President Trump was officially charged on thirty-four counts, stemming from the slicing up of one misdemeanor charge into thirty-four separate charges, which was somehow magically turned into a felony. These charges were manufactured by an obscure, corrupt Soros-bought-off district attorney by the name of Alvin Bragg. Alvin Bragg is nothing more than a sociopath who has been trying for over a year to find something, anything on which to indict former President Trump, regardless of the consequences of his actions. Alvin Bragg's only concern was to have his moment of fame and to please his Marxist-Communist financial supporters. Similarly, a dog would jump through a hoop to please his master and receive a treat. Robert Jackson, a former Supreme Court justice, said it best: "The greatest danger to justice is an unscrupulous prosecutor who targets a person and then scours the law books to find an offense he can pin on that person." Justice Jackson described Alvin Bragg perfectly.

Source & Additional Information: (https://www.usatoday.com/story/news/politics/2023/04/04/read-the-trump-indictment/11528624002/)

The indictments against Donald Trump violate his 6th Amendment rights because the prosecutor, Alvin Bragg, failed to inform the accused, Donald Trump, of the nature and cause of the accusations. Bragg took an obscure misdemeanor and turned it into a felony by claiming it was done to advance another crime, but Bragg refused to specify that crime, thus leaving Trump's defense counsel in the dark on how to prepare for trial. This may have been done intentionally, to spring a trap on Trump at trial dishonestly, or probably, they do not have another crime to specify. The venue is Manhattan, where the rule of law and the Constitution do not apply to conservative Republicans. There is no way President Trump will receive a fair trial in Manhattan. The constitutionally illiterate and low common-sense pool of New York City jurors are classical Marxist Communist Democrat Trump haters who are willing to deny justice over hatred. In New York State, the county court having jurisdiction over felonies is called the Supreme Court. Their judges are elected for a term of fourteen years. When their term is up, they have to run for another fourteen-year term with the approval of the county nominating committee. In Manhattan, the committee is dominated by Marxist-Communist Democrat Party political hacks. Any judge who honestly rules in favor of Trump will never get re-elected. They will be shunned and ostracized for the rest of their life. In a fair venue, Trump's case would be dismissed due to the Statute of Limitations. Bragg's misdemeanor charge relates to issues supposedly occurring back in 2016 and 2017, which have two-year Statutes of limitations. For the made-up felony, there is a five-year Statute, which has also run out. If the judge applies the law fairly, he has to dismiss the case. But he will not because it would effectively end his career. The judge would become a non-person, just like in communist Russia.

The absurdity of indicting a former President of the United States, which has never before been done in the history of our country, on charges related to Trump's supposed hush money payments to a pornographic performer, Stormy Daniels, before the 2016 presidential election is beyond imagination. Even if Bragg's accusations were correct, there is no law anywhere in the United States prohibiting the payment of hush money by anyone to anyone. The prosecutor's primary witness regarding this accusation is Michael Cohen, a convicted felon who has repeatedly lied before congressional committee hearings and in affidavits. Despite the incredible character of this convicted felon, Bragg chose to push forward with charging Trump with the payment of hush money. Bragg purposefully manipulated campaign laws to determine somehow that the payment of hush money to another person is a contribution to a campaign. When Bragg realized this would not fly, he then indicted Trump for failing to appropriately enter this payment figure into his business' accounting ledgers. Bragg had to go to the back pages of New York State's Penal Law to find the statute that Trump is accused of violating, the "Business Records Act." How ridiculous is this when Hillary Clinton and her campaign gave millions of dollars to her law firm, which, in turn, paid Christopher Steele to create his fake Trump-Russia collusion dossier? Her campaign disguised these payments as «legal fees" when they were used to frame her political opponent with false charges. Is this not creating «false business records»? Of course, Hillary was never indicted because she has Marxist-Communist Democrat Immunity, and the fact that the statute of limitations has already passed will become very important to the Marxist-Communist Democrat Party as justification not to prosecute Hillary Clinton.

This is just further evidence that the Marxist-Communist Democrat government and the citizens of New York City are complicit in these atrocities by consistently voting for Marxist-Communist Democrat candidates election after election. These Trump-fearing/hating upstanding citizens of New York City will use any excuse to indict, charge, and convict Trump or any other conservative, regardless of how ridiculous the charges. President Trump was indicted, charged, and arrested, not because he was guilty of any wrongdoing, but because the Marxist-Communist Democrat machine in Manhattan managed to fabricate phony charges, get a Trump-hating judge assigned to the case, get the typical Manhattan jury which consists of gas-lighted and clueless Marxist-Communist Democrats who unknowingly vote against their self-interests; and parasitic career welfare recipient who have been brainwashed by the Marxist-Communist Democrat Party to hate all wealth people in America.

This partisan political prosecution is a direct assault on our justice system and a further degradation of our Constitution. Americans must fight back against Bragg and these dishonest hacks, or we will lose our country. It is not so much that Marxist-Communist Democrats despise the pro-America Trump; they hate us and America, and Trump represents both! All the while, Bragg refuses to focus on real criminals who are putting the citizens of New York City at extreme risk of becoming victims. Violent criminals are being released back into the community to attack innocent citizens again. At the same time, Bragg continues to fail to uphold his oath of office and hold criminals accountable for their actions. Bragg's soft-on-crime philosophy results in his refusal to prosecute these dangerous criminal felons. He significantly reduces charges in grand larceny cases, including towards notorious gangbangers with mile-long rap sheets. Since taking office, Bragg has downgraded 52% of felony cases to misdemeanors at the expense of the city's citizen's safety. Apparently, in New York, almost everyone is *above* the law. It could not be any clearer that Bragg's case against President Trump is entirely politically motivated. Harvard Law School Professor Emeritus and constitutional attorney Alan Dershowitz, a lifelong registered Democrat, harshly criticized the indictment of former President Donald Trump, describing it as an extreme case of prosecutorial misconduct.

Source & Additional Information: (https://nypost.com/2022/11/26/convictions-plummet-downgraded-charges-surge-under-manhattan-da-bragg/)

A Breitbart article on Trump's Non-Disclosure Agreement addressed the Marxist-Communist Party's obsession with referring to Donald Trump's Non-Disclosure Agreement with Stormy Daniels as a "hush money payment." Presidential candidate Vivek Ramaswamy exposed the fact that over the past twenty-five years, American taxpayers have paid out $18.2 million to settle two-hundred-ninety-one cases of sexual harassment and other misconduct committed by United States senators and Congressmen. In these cases, complainants entered non-disclosure agreements. Where are the indictments accusing these members of Congress of "hush money payments" and showing the settlement payments as "campaign expenses."
The double standard is obvious when Trump is involved. The Marxist-Communist Democrat Party is a cancer that is destroying America!

Donald J. Trump Indictment Two: On June 6th, 2023, Donald Trump became the first former president in American history to face a judge on federal charges as he pleaded not guilty in a Miami courtroom to dozens of felony counts accusing him of hoarding classified documents and refusing government demands to give them back. Charges brought against him by Special Counsel Jack Smith centered on charges that Trump had retained and mishandled government secret documents that, as commander-in-chief, he had every legal authority under the "Presidential Records Act" to keep in his possession after leaving office.

Source & Additional Information: (https://www.nytimes.com/live/2023/06/13/us/trump-indictment-arraignment-court)

Special Counsel Jack Smith is a prosecuting attorney who has had many of his convictions reversed by Appellant Courts and the Supreme Court, including a nine to zero Supreme Court ruling against Smith in one of the many failed cases on which Smith served as the lead prosecutor. Jack Smith is a failed Marxist-Communist Democrat prosecutor who was eventually sent to the Hague, Germany, international court as a prosecutor. Smith is nothing more than a Marxist-Communist Democrat Party attack dog who has openly proclaimed his disdain for Donald Trump. Smith is an attorney who has no problems with charging an individual and then finding a crime to fit the charge.

Donald J. Trump Indictment Three: Special counsel Jack Smith has been the lead Federal prosecutor investigating allegations that Trump attempted to subvert the results of the 2020 election, including his role in the Capitol incident on January 6th, 2021. On July 25th, 2023, Trump was indicted on felony charges for allegedly attempting to overturn the results of the 2020 election. These charges will be heard in a court within the District of Columbus, which is ninety-five percent Marist-Communist Democrats and an outspoken Trump hater judge. No justice will be seen in this trial.

Source & Additional Information: (https://www.npr.org/2023/08/01/1190459957/trump-indictment-jan-6-2020-election) (https://www.businessinsider.com/trump-january-6-criminal-indictment-charges-explained-2023-7?op=1)

Donald J. Trump Indictment Four: In December 2020 and January 2021, Trump sought to confirm the results of the presidential election in Georgia. Trump and his allies had found that voter fraud did occur in the state of Georgia. Security videos within the polling station were released to the general public. Clearly, they showed criminal acts being committed by Marxist-Communist Democrat Party poll workers at a significant Atlanta, Georgia, polling station. Republican poll workers and observers were sent home under the pretense of a significant water leak in one of the bathrooms. Once all these poll workers and observers departed, Marxist-Communist Democrat Party poll workers were observed, on the security videotape, repeatedly feeding into a vote tabulator the duplicate ballots over and over again. The security video also showed a Democrat poll worker pulling out a concealed container full of ballots from under a covered table and feeding those unknown source ballots into the vote tabulator. This video and affidavits from dismissed poll workers and watchers were clear evidence of voter fraud.

On January 2nd, 2021, Trump called Georgia's secretary of state, Brad Raffensperger, a Marxist-Communist leaning Republican, and urged him to look into the evidence indicating voter fraud and suggested that given these irregularities, Raffensperger should be able to find approximately twelve hundred additional legal votes for Trump which would swing the state of George into Trump's camp.

In January of 2023, after hearing evidence for seven months submitted by Fulton County Marist-Communist Democrat District Attorney Fani Willis, a special grand jury released a report, most of which remains under seal, recommending potential indictments. President Trump's indictment was unveiled on August 14th, 2023, charging President Trump with thirteen crimes related to his alleged efforts to reverse his election loss in Georgia.

Source & Additional Information: (https://www.nytimes.com/live/2023/08/14/us/trump-indictment-georgia-election)

All of the above actions and indictments against President Donald Trump were imposed with the full approval of Attorney General Merrick Garland, which is an unprecedented attack on America's judicial and political system and the constitutional rights of President Trump as protected by the First Amendment to freely discuss, debate, and contest serious election and political issues. It clearly shows that the ultimate weaponization of the Justice Department started by President Obama's attorney general, Eric Holder, and is now completed by Merrick Garland and weaponized to take out a political opponent of President Joe Biden. Nothing more, nothing less.

Out of uncontrol hatred and fear of former President Donald Trump, the Marxist-Communist Democrat Party has crafted one set of laws for themselves, the Washington Elitists, and their donners while having crafted another set of laws for Donald Trump and other patriotic Americans. The Marxist-Communist Democrats arrogantly believe their moral superiority grants them the right to apply laws unequally or to ignore them altogether. To retain power at all costs and to destroy a political rival, Marxist-Communist Democrats are systematically dismantling the constitutional foundations of the United States as we once knew them.

Donald J. Trump Assassination Attempts: On Saturday, July 13th, 2024, a 20-year-old from Bethel Park, Pennsylvania, Thomas Crooks, attempted to assassinate President Donald Trump when Crooks opened fire on Trump during the opening moments of his campaign rally at Butler, Pennsylvania. Crooks was able to wound Trump with a shot to the right ear, killing one and injuring two rally attendees seated directly behind the podium. Trump was rushed off stage with blood dripping down his face, and the sniper, Thomas Crooks, was killed by Secret Service agents.

Source & Additional Information: (https://www.npr.org/2024/07/19/nx-s1-5041734/ trump-shooting-assassination-crooks-bulter-secret-service)

On Sunday, September 15th, not two months later, another assassination attempt on President Trump was attempted while he was playing golf on his West Palm Beach golf club. The U.S. Secret Service fired on the man, reportedly identified as Ryan Wesley Routh, who fled the scene but was later arrested. And the fake news media? For their part, they twisted themselves into pretzels trying to paint Routh as a Trump supporter or someone with "unclear" political ideology (despite the fact of his political donations to the Harris campaign) and – unbelievably – blaming Trump's rhetoric for the second attempt on his life.

Source & Additional Information: (https://www.nbcnews.com/news/us-news/live-blog/ trump-assassination-attempt-live-updates-rcna171241)

Ultimately, history will document Donald J. Trump as the most persecuted, prosecuted President and former President and the most popular and effective President in American history, standing on the same pedestal as Presidents George Washington and Abraham Lincoln. Donald J. Trump is the right man, at the right time, and in the right place to save our Constitutional Republic. No other person, past or present, has the patriotism, courage, strength, and determination to stand against the Stalinist-style Marxist-Communist movement to save our country. President Trump is a man of honor and integrity and can always be depended upon to stand by and protect "We the People." The faith and hope the American population has in this man is visible in the massive number of attendees, numbering in the tens of thousands, at his speaking engagements and rallies.

Chapter 8
First Amendment

It is a fact that all politics begin at the local level. From local political party headquarters and locally elected officials, pressure can be placed on State elected officials who can pressure those in Washington to hear the people's voice. It is also typical that those who have served at the local level run for and are elected to State and Federal positions. These locally elected officials will have accumulated a history of their political ideology and positions, allowing electorates to know better who they are electing if they take the time to look.

It Is not just the locally elected officials who can shape the political environment. Local County Party leadership and committed volunteers can also have a tremendous impact by working to promote and grow the Party membership with an emphasis on underrepresented minorities and young adults. Constant contact and interactions with elected officials in elected city, county, state, and federal level positions are critical to encourage their active participation in County Party meetings and events. The County Party leadership must constantly look for individuals with the characteristics required to represent the people with honor and integrity and encourage them to run for public office. During a general election cycle, the County Party leadership must actively promote and personally campaign for their party's candidates.

Free Press and Democracy: Information and knowledge are powerful tools. A free and independent press connects the public to the information they need to advocate for themselves, make informed decisions, and hold governmental officials accountable. The draftsmen of the United States Constitution deemed freedom of the press so essential that they enshrined it in the First Amendment as a part of the Bill of Rights in 1791, which secures fundamental individual rights against government overreach. An independent press includes diverse voices and opinions, not just those politicians want covered. In the United States, media are independent of the government and do not receive government funding. Most outlets get their revenue through subscription sales or selling advertising. This model contributes to media independence from the government. Reporters Without Borders states, "Freedom of expression and information is the first and most important of freedoms."

In the United States, investigative journalists with honor and integration who still conduct deep research on important topics to uncover facts that citizens need to know and who objectively cover protests and rallies are few and far between. Today's journalists report based on ideology, severely restricting the information American citizens desperately need to make informed decisions. The majority of today's American news outlets are owned by radical Marxist-Communist individuals who have turned their news media into the political arms of the Marxist-Communist Democrat Party. This has led these media to report information in a manner that fits the Marxist-Communist Democrat Party's narrative and agenda, or if the news does not fit this criterion, it is not reported. These Marxist-Communist news outlets frequently censor conservative information and often block dissenting conservative voices. This has led former President Trump to refer to them as the "Fake News." This loss of a genuinely free and unbiased press is the key to the radical left's ability to change America into a Marxist-Communist regime forever fundamentally.

Media Indoctrination: Have you ever watched TV news or a talk show and been concerned with how much the country has changed? A poll was conducted by a national polling firm, "YouGov," questioning typical people on the street. The questions asked, and the answers to those questions were as follows:

- What percentage of the country is black? Answer forty-one percent ... actual twelve
- percent. If you watched commercials, you would think it is ninety percent.
- What percentage of marriages are mixed-race? Answer fifty percent .. actual one percent. If you watched commercials, you would think it is eighty-five percent.
- What percentage is "Latino"? Answer 39% ... actual numbers 17%.
- How many families make over $500,000 a year? Answer 26% ... actual figure 1%. We think a quarter of the country is rich.
- What percent of Americans are vegetarians? Response? Thirty percent ... actual 5%.
- What percent of Americans live in New City? Answer? Thirty percent ... actual 3%.
- What percentage of Americans are 'transgender'? Answer 22% .. actual number 1%.
- What percentage of your fellow citizens are Gay? Answer 30% ... actual 3%.

So why do people have such inaccurate thoughts on these counts? Answer: THE MEDIA! The media consistently run race, gender, and wealth advertisements and stories, resulting in their readers becoming somewhere between brainwashed and braindead. Hitler's propaganda minister, Joseph Goebbels, would be proud if he had half the success these news outlets experienced. Disney just went full-on woke on "gender" identification. They no longer welcome guests with the traditional "Welcome ladies and gentlemen, boys and girls." Why? Because 1% of our population dictates to the other 99% and, corporate America falls for it time and time again. Regardless of your opinion, fewer than 20% of Americans use "Twitter," yet Twitter controls 80% of public opinion. Why? The media.

We have all heard the phrase, "Go Along, To Get Along." We are all probably guilty of doing so once or twice in our own lives. But does this line of thinking have any place in business ownership or professional careers? Absolutely not. It would not take long before whoever you were going along with to get along with would leave you in their rear-view mirror and leave your business or career in the dust. Well, that is precisely what happens to Republican politicians we elect to office to represent the will of the people. They stomp around on the campaign trail listening to the people they hope to represent, promising they will go to Washington and make their voices heard and bring about change. Sound familiar?

Unfortunately for us, things become quite different once they get elected and show up in their nice plush offices with staff members running out of their ears, all at taxpayers' expense. It is not long after they arrived in Washington before their party leadership sit them down and inform them of how things are done in Washington. It is made clear to all new members that if they want a seat on a committee, party endorsements, and financial assistance for reelection, then they had better "go along to get along."

Suppose our representatives and senators oppose their leadership regarding pending legislation. In that case, there is tremendous pressure placed on them by that leadership and their fellow congressional members to vote along party lines rather than in line with what they promised their constituency. Congressional Party leaders and fellow party members have forgotten or are ignoring that they are all there to represent the will of their constituents and not the will of the party. Here is a novel idea: how about our elected officials did what they promised and truly represented their constituents? You know, "go along to get along" not with their leadership or the opposing party but with those who elected them and pay for that fancy office and all their staff. We know that a tremendous amount of pressure is put upon them by those long-entranced party leaders, and except for a few very strong and brave politicians, these newly elected officials soon cave into the demands of the leadership, lobbyists, and donors. I think we can all agree that these are not the people we want our representatives going along with to have a good relationship with.

We need to change this line of thinking by our elected officials and change it soon, or we will not have a free Constitutional Republic in which we can freely choose our destiny, choose how we will raise our children, decide how we will worship our creator, choose who will represent us, or live in a free and proud Nation. We are on the verge of losing these choices and becoming a one-party Marxist-Communist nation in which we will all become subjects of anti-Christian and anti-Constitution dictators—another third-world banana republic.

Chapter 9
Harsh Political Realities

We all must face the harsh reality of a federal political system in which we have an overabundance of self-serving sociopaths who are corrupt to the core and lack the honor and integrity required to serve as representatives. It is a harsh reality that far too many of those we elect to serve in Washington are quick and willing to fall to the temptations of greed, status, and worldly gains afforded by the Washington swamp. It is a harsh reality that far too many of these individuals are in Washington, not to represent and serve the people who elected them to Congress but rather to represent and serve their own personal interests, ambitions, and greed for wealth.

We now wake up daily to the harsh reality of a new phenomenon called "Wokism." A term that rejects American exceptionalism, a belief that the United States has never been a true democracy, that people of color suffer from systemic and institutional racism, that white Americans experience white privileges, that African Americans deserve reparations for slavery; that United States law enforcement agencies are designed to discriminate against people of color and so should be defunded, disband, or heavily reformed; that women suffer from systemic sexism; that individuals should be able to identify with any gender or none; that United States capitalism is deeply flawed; and that Donald Trump's election to the presidency was not an anomaly but a reflection of the prejudices held towards people of color. This woke movement is destroying lives and businesses by "canceling them out" and by affecting the operational decisions of big corporations.

The sad part of all this is the fact that out of America's population of more than three hundred million, the number of idiots who ascribe to this wake movement is only less than one percent. For some insane reason, people are afraid of them and will not just say no and end their childish behavior. What exactly are these woke malcontents even talking about when they label people "systemic" (fill in the target) because systemic means total, complete, absolute, etc.. We are human beings incapable of being systemic about anything. White people cannot all be systemic racist unless they are racist against every other human being in the world. The same would hold true to a claim that someone or a group of people are systemic phobic, that black people are systemic victims or oppressed. How oppressed and victimized was Barak Obama, who became the President of the most powerful Nation in the world, or how oppressed and victimized was Collin Powell, who rose to the rank of a four-star general and the Secretary of State? Examples could fill an encyclopedia. Nobody is systemic about anything!

Source & Additional Information: (https://en.wikipedia.org/wiki/Woke)

We are waking up to the reality that the Antifa and Black Lives Matter movements are creating chaos, rioting in our streets, and destroying American businesses that owners have worked so hard over so many years to grow, to provide for their livelihood, and employ area residents; that they are needlessly murdering police officers and innocent area residents and business owners; destroying government buildings; and are disregarding our laws. These anti-American movements reject the value of our Constitutional Republic, which offers them freedoms and rights not afforded to the citizens of any other country. It is my opinion that the Marxist-Communist billionaires and Biden-Harris coordinated these attacks on America. Another step in facilitating the installation of a Marxist-Communist government utilizing Stalinist tactics. Right out of the Marxist-Communist's playbook.

Source & Additional Information: (https://www.pewresearch.org/internet/2023/06/29/ten-years-of-blacklivesmatter-on-twitter/)

We are now being faced with the harsh reality that our federal government is unconstitutionally overreaching into America's information systems in an attempt to censor those who disagree with their ideology and to indoctrinate citizens with weak minds or who are otherwise easily influenced into believing Marxist-Communist propaganda. The federal government is actively pressuring news and social media outlets to suppress stories that do not meet the Marxist-Communist narrative. They are dictating to social media leadership that they must establish algorithms to identify any anti-Marxist conversations that could derail the Marxist-Communist takeover of America. Individuals who are using social media platforms to discuss conservative viewpoints or point out abuses of our federal institutions are being censored and canceled from those platforms at the direction of our federal legal institutions. American citizens are being denied their constitutional right to free speech to exchange information or discuss issues critical to maintaining a free society. A fitting example is the suppression of the information from Hunter Biden's laptop regarding Hunter's foreign business dealings and his father's involvement just days before the 2020 presidential election. Dealings that would have changed the outcome of the 2020 elections. This is a clear case of election interference. Still, with a Marxist-Communist legal system in place and given that the son of Joe Biden is a member of the corrupt Washington ruling class, no appropriate legal action has been taken.

Source & Additional Information: (https://reason.com/2023/09/11/the-5th-circuit-agrees-that-federal-officials-unconstitutionally-coerced-or-encouraged-online-censorship/)

The depth and breadth of our federal government's involvement in suppressing information from its citizens is being exposed by the very few actual journalists with the courage to provide the American public with the information found on Twitter Files since Elon Musk purchased the organization. The strangest thing about the Twitter Files scandal is that the Marxist-Communist Democrats do not think it is important. Over several weeks, new Twitter CEO Elon Musk released internal documents that show the social media company conspired for years with Marxist-Communist government officials and activists to promote woke socialism and censor conservatives. Yes, they were shadow-banning conservatives under the guise of "content moderation." Marxist-Communist Twitter employees tinkered with algorithms to ensure conservative Tweets did not "trend." How did they know which stories, like Hunter Biden's laptop, to "de-amplify?" By selectively hiring staff who were known to be woke extremists and radicals and hiring the relatives of prominent Marxist-Communist figures to maintain a close link between establishment power structures and social media censors. The whole country is outraged about these revelations, except for Marxist-Communist activists! They are not denying that they helped Big Tech billionaires conspire with government officials to censor criticism, manipulate public debate, and meddle in election campaigns. *They are saying they were right to do it.*

Today's Marxist-Communist members of the Democrat Party are not patriotic, hardworking hardhats, the poor and oppressed, or working-class families just trying to get ahead. The Marxist-Communist Democrat Party are woke, radical, anti-American, anti-family elites who have as much disdain for everyday Americans as they have for the Constitution. The Woke Marxist-Communist Democrat Party wants to censor, de-platform, de-bank, and discriminate against its critics. They do not even see authoritarianism as necessarily evil but rather as a means to subject non-conformists to actions that will pull them into line. Conservatives are not just in a fight for America's future. We are in a battle for our very lives. Woke elites do not think we should be free to speak, pray, work, vote, learn, teach, or parent the way we want.

We are being confronted by the reality that the federal government, its agencies, and in particular, America's scientific guru on COVID-19, Doctor Anthony Fauci, had been lying to the American public regarding the origins of COVID. The FBI Director has confirmed that coronavirus did not originate in a market selling bats carrying the virus but stemmed from a lab leak in Wuhan. The worst lies being fed to the American public regarding COVID-19 by our corrupt government's spokesperson, Doctor Antony Fauci, and their fake news media propaganda arm included: Natural immunity offers little protection compared to vaccination; Masks prevent COVID transmission; School closures reduce COVID transmission; Myocarditis from the vaccine is less common than from COVID; Young people benefit from a vaccine booster shot; and the theory that COVID originated from the Wuhan Lab is just a conspiracy theory. Because of the efforts of the very few remaining true journalists and Elon Musk's purchase of Twitter and his releasing of Twitter discussions between government officials regarding COVID, we now know that Doctor Fauci's claim was no more than propaganda lies to protect the Marxist-Communist narrative, their control over the citizens of the United States, and untold levels of wealth.

The COVID virus was indeed released from the Chinese Communist Party-controlled Wuhan lab either accidentally or on purpose, which is still being debated. However, China had the motive and the means to release this virus on the world to cripple the world's economy in their war to take over the world without firing a shot. The Chinese Communist Party's lies were supported by Biden and his Administration, by the so-called scientist Antoine Fauci, by our Marxist-Communist federal government, and by the Marxist-Communist propaganda arm referred to as news media. They willingly and knowingly engaged in political science rather than medical science to maintain their narrative and agenda. These American deceivers' primary goal is to politically damage America's conservatives, Donald Trump, and the MEGA movement. In doing so, they destroyed the lives and businesses of tens of thousands of tax-paying Americans. Doctors and scientists who tried to expose their lies were consistently silenced, as one would expect in a Stalinist regime!

Source & Additional Information: (https://www.bbc.com/news/world-us-canada-64806903)

We are left with the harsh reality that, although Conservative American Republicans always believed that the Steele Dossier was fake, we now have learned that the Marxist-Communist Democrat Party not only knew the dossier was false but that the creation of the fake dossier was paid for by the Hillary Clinton campaign and the Democrat National Conference to obtain a FISA warrant to install listening devices in Trump's campaign office and the oval office after his election.

Whether it is the Center for Disease Control, the DOJ, the FBI, news outlets, or social media companies, these entities are limiting or outright eliminating our First Amendment right to free speech under the direction of the Marxist-Communist Biden-Harris Administration through his politically weaponized agencies to target the American citizenry they are all sworn to serve. And the Marxist-Communist Democrat Party? They are wringing their hands in anticipation of taking over our Constitutional Republic and replacing it with their anti-American, anti-Constitution ideological Marxist-Communist form of governance.

The harsh reality of American politics is that with every bit of added information, we find that the truth is always worse than we thought. **ALWAYS!**

Chapter 10
America's Shift

For two hundred-plus years, our Constitution has made America the "shining star" of the world. A place where all citizens "are endowed by their creator with certain unalienable rights, among these are Life, Liberty and the pursuit of Happiness." America was to be a place where elected officials represented the best interest of their constituents and the several states, not their selfish interests, as in most of the other one-hundred and ninety-eight countries in the world. Just how true is this statement of the United States today? Not very, as there has been an increasing shift in our country from a Constitutional Republic to a corrupt and oppressive Marxist-Communist Nation.

Today, Congress operates not as the Framers intended but in the shadow of their donors and corrupt political leadership. They squander their time conspiring with fellow members of Congress to dream up notorious, oppressive, and bankrupting laws. New unconstitutional laws only come to the public's attention when the proposed law is ready to be voted on by members of Congress who are also conveniently not provided the time necessary to read these thousand-page proposed laws before being brought to the floor for a vote. The content of these frequently unconstitutional bills is not promptly shared with the general public so constituents can make their views known to their congressional representatives. As ex-Speaker of the House, Nancy Pelosi famously said, "You can know what's in the bill after it's passed." After passing such laws, only then do members of Congress come out to spin the content of the bill in a manner that makes the general public believe that the new law is in the best interest of the citizens and the Country. They declare the genius and sincerity of their legislating on behalf of the people despite their full knowledge that the new law is not in the best interest of the people but rather a furthering of their Marxist-Communist agenda.

Once knowledge of the new law is made public, American citizens are left dumbfounded about their congressional representatives' "supposed" consideration of their constituent's desires. These bills, referred to as Omnibus bills, more often than not. have few, if any, favorable provisions for the people and the nation but are rather packed full of corrupt, bankrupting, and unconstitutional provisions that will have dire impacts on our lives and the survival of our Constitutional Republic. But, of course, that is the whole point; the public is not to be informed but indoctrinated, manipulated, and misled. The Congress then delegates their constitutional law-making power to an ever-increasing bloated administrative bureaucracy that, in turn, unleashes upon the American citizenry crushing regulations. The Washington bureaucracy does this at such a rapid rate that the people cannot possibly know of their existence. If, by chance, they are aware of such regulations, they cannot possibly comprehend what the regulations allow or do not allow. Nonetheless, the federal government will tell those in non-compliance that ignorance of a law or regulation is no justification for non-compliance, and offenders are subjected to Marxist-Communist tactics, imprisonment, or other severe punishment of a dissenter.

This shift is being propelled and funded by wealthy Marxist-Communist anti-Americans such as multi-billionaires Mark Zuckerberg, CEO of Facebook; Laurence Fink, CEO of Blackrock; Michael Bloomberg, CEO of Bloomberg L.P.; and Marxist-Communist special interest groups and organizations. Few conservative Republican billionaires are willing to step up and donate at the levels that Marxist-Communist Democrat Billionaires are eager to do. This leaves conservative Republican candidates consistently trailing behind Marxist-Communist Democrat Party candidates in available campaigning and advertising funds to get their conservative message out to the American public.

This lack of financial support has allowed President Obama's 2008 promise to "fundamentally change America forever" to move forward under the Biden-Harris Administration. Moving forward, because Marxist-Communist Democrat Party politicians are willing to ignore the Constitution intentionally, they have sworn an oath to protect to push forward their Marxist-Communist agenda.

During the first one hundred and eighty years, the Federal government largely respected the Constitution as written and intended by our Founding Fathers. This all changed in 1932 with the election of Franklin D. Roosevelt. It was Roosevelt who began the Democrat Party's slow transitioning of the United States into a socialist nation, which eventually morphed into the Marxist-Communist Democrat Party of today. Roosevelt created numerous unconstitutionally federally funded programs through his Great New Deal, including legislation intended to correct the situations that led to the stock market crash of 1929. Two prominent actions were the Glass-Steagall Act of 1933, which created the Federal Deposit Insurance Corporation (FDIC), and the creation of the Securities and Exchange Commission (SEC) in 1934 to be a watchdog over the stock market and police dishonest practices. Both of these Acts are Marxist-Communist initiatives with no constitutional authority.

Source & Additional Information: (https://www.history.com/topics/great-depression/new-deal)

Great New Deal: President Franklin D. Roosevelt's "Great New Deal" was the catalyst for mushrooming the Washington Marxist-Communist bureaucracy. A newly formed unconstitutional fourth branch of the Federal government that utilizes Stalinist measures to impose their will on the American citizenry. These Marxist-Communist entities were created to manage the ever-growing number of federally funded or subsidized programs.

They began to wield ever-increasing power and control over the people of the United States with their crushing regulations and Marxist-Communist philosophy. There now exist well over four hundred bureaucratic departments and agencies with unelected Administrators and Directors making decisions regarding their operations. These entities constitutionally should have been left to each sovereign state's legislators to decide whether they desired to create these bureaucratic departments and agencies within their states. Instead, Congress federally created them, relinquishing their congressional responsibilities, authority, and power to this unelected swamp.

The Great New Deal was a series of programs and projects instituted during the Great Depression by President Franklin D. Roosevelt to restore Americans' prosperity. Roosevelt's New Deal fundamentally and permanently changed the United States federal government by expanding its size and scope, especially its economic role. Was this a Great New Deal for the American People? Perhaps at the time, it seemed to be salvation for millions of Americans who were financially struggling. However, in a Constitutional Republic, wherein states are sovereign entities, these Great New Deal initiatives should have been considered for implementation by each sovereign State. Instead, Roosevelt's Administration chose to Federally initiate and fund these innovative programs, sending our Constitutional Republic on a downhill slide towards Marxist-Communist.

Roosevelt's Great New Deal began the transition of congressional responsibilities to newly unconstitutionally formed bureaucratic departments and agencies. Congress provided these unconstitutional departments and agencies with the authority to operate under the leadership of unelected officials, allowing them to pass regulations to govern their areas of jurisdiction. This bureaucratic swamp created a means by which our duly elected members of Congress could impose control over the citizenry of America through regulations. Regulation is just another word for law and carries the same weight and authority as any law passed by Congress. Further, this transition took away the burden and responsibility of Congress passing unconstitutional laws that may be unpopular with voters and thus jeopardize their chances for reelection. With the bureaucrats in charge of regulating America, members of Congress have more time to raise money, campaign for their reelection, and hobnob with their fellow elitists.

Source & Additional Information: (https://www.history.com/topics/great-depression/new-deal)

Our Constitution gives Congress and only Congress the authority to pass legislation governing our country. In the Constitution, Congress has no authority to relinquish its responsibility to legislate to unconstitutional departments or agencies, nor is there any constitutional authority for these departments or agencies to issue regulations. The authors of the Declaration of Independence noted that they left England because of comparable crushing regulatory offices, accusing the English king of erecting these offices to establish control over their subjects, harass English citizens, and confiscate their property and food. Very similar to what is happening to the citizens of this country today. Unfortunately, unlike English citizens who had a new world available to escape the corruption and tyranny of their king, there is nowhere in this world left for us to run. The only way to unshackle ourselves from these tyrannical regulations is by fixing what is wrong with our governing system.

Great Society: With the advent of President Lyndon B. Johnson's "Great Society" initiative in 1965, the United States transition into a Marxist-Communist society was accelerated. Following Franklin D. Roosevelt's lead to mutate our constitutional form of government into a Marxist-Constitutional form of government, Lyndon B. Johnson's "Great Society" initiative was a sweeping set of socialist domestic programs that marked the beginning of the out-of-control bloating of Roosevelt's fourth branch of government and the reckless spending which has propelled

America to our current thirty-five trillion dollars of debt and growing.

Johnson's "Great Society" initiative was passed while the United States was at war in Vietnam, and the cost of the War was staggering. Despite our country's financial burden with the Vietnam War, Congress began passing significant legislation to implement and fund President Johnson's "Great Society" initiatives, which placed America on its path from a Constitutional Republic to a total Marxist-Communist Nation and from a prosperous Nation to a Nation on the cliff edge of bankruptcy. According to the Department of Treasury, before the initiation of the "Great Society" and the Vietnam War, the United States' national debt was only $312 billion, which has since grown to $35 Trillion.

Source & Additional Information: (https://www.history.com/topics/1960s/great-society)

Just in the six years, Lyndon B. Johnson served as President, all of the below-listed unconstitutional Marxist-Communist programs were enacted. These new unconstitutional "Great Society" initiatives were passed with bipartisan support. Both the so-called anti-spending Republican Party and the now Marxist-Communist Democrat Party failed their country and the people they represented by ringing up trillions of dollars in debt and wresting away the constitutional authority of the individual sovereign states. These new programs included:

- Funding for education programs.
- Funding for medical care programs.
- Creation of the U.S. Office of Economic Opportunity/Office of Community Services.
- Creation of the Department of Transportation.
- Creation of the National Highway Traffic Safety Administration.

- Creation of Head Start, providing free preschool programs.
- Creation of Volunteers in Service to America program/ AmeriCorps VISTA program.
- Creation of Model Cities Program for urban redevelopment.
- Creation of Upward Bound.
- Creation of the Food Stamps Act.
- Establishment of community health centers.
- Significant expansion of Social Security benefits, coverage, and new programs.
- The Higher Education Act increasing federal money to universities.
- Funding for federally sponsored scholarships and low-interest loans for students.
- The introduction of socialized medicine through Medicare.
- Creation of Medicaid under Title XIX of the Social Security Act.
- Creation of the National Endowment for the Arts.
- Creation of the National Endowment for the Humanities.
- Creation of Public Broadcasting.
- Funding for the construction of the Hirshhorn Museum and Sculpture Garden.
- Creation of the Water Quality Act.
- Creation of the Clean Air Act.

- ➢ Creation of the Wilderness Act.
- ➢ Creation of Endangered Species Preservation Act.
- ➢ Creation of the National Trails System Act.
- ➢ Creation of the Wild and Scenic Rivers Act.

Every initiative noted above is unconstitutional, as the decision to enact any of the above initiatives constitutionally belonged to the sovereign states, not the federal government. Since the early 1930s, with Franklin D. Roosevelt's Great "New Deal" followed by President Johnson's "Great Society" in the mid-1960s, the federal government has continued to expand its federalizing of programs and functions that constitutionally belong to the sovereign states. Both the Democrat and Republican Parties have been complaisant in this ongoing federalizing of state responsibilities, which includes but is not limited to Agriculture, Labor, Environmental Protection, Energy, Housing and Urban Development, Transportation, Museums, and Interior, to name just a very few of the over four hundred and twenty federal government departments and agencies. All hallmarks of a Marxist-Communist form of government.

This state of mind by our elected members of Congress, Department Secretaries, and unelected Administrators within the Washington bureaucracy to continuously create new agencies and sub-agencies put our country on the path to a Marxist-Communist form of government and on the threshold of bankruptcy with default looming on the horizon. America is on the verge of becoming just another Venezuela, and China will have achieved the overthrowing of America from within through uncontrolled spending addiction.

Subsequent congressional sessions in which the self-proclaimed fiscally conservative Republicans held control of both chambers of Congress and the Presidency could have defunded and returned all of the "Great Society" initiatives back to the individual states, where the people therein could decide whether to implement such programs within their states. But, as has become customary for the Republicans, they failed to act.

A landmark Supreme Court decision made by a conservative-dominated Supreme Court was the overturning of Roe vs Wade. This landmark decision to return to the individual states the constitutional authority to make decisions regarding the aborting of a baby by the citizens of the state. Following this ruling, Supreme Court Justices hinted that there were many more past Supreme Court decisions that may have been unconstitutional and require revisiting by the Supreme Court.

However, it should not be up to the Supreme Court to act; instead, Congress should take this action by rescinding laws they know to be unconstitutional. Will Congress do so? Unfortunately, the answer is no, as they do not have the courage or strength of conviction to carry out their constitutional obligations.

Chapter 11
Who Should Decide

So, here is the million-dollar question for every American citizen: "Who should decide what is best for you and your family?" Should decisions be made by a federal government that has forgotten or conveniently dismissed the fact that the sovereign states created the federal government to provide a minimal number of functions on behalf of the states and the people therein? Should critical decisions that affect you and your loved ones be decided by "We the People", or by an out-of-touch, corrupt Marxist-Communist bureaucracy in Washington, D.C.? Should decisions for you and your family be decided by elected and unelected Washington bureaucrats who no longer view the voters who elected them as constituents to be represented but rather as subjects to be ruled?

Should decisions critical to the well-being of your family be made by congressional members who have long since stopped representing those who elected them and only represent their donners, lobbyists, and their own best interests; who believe they reside in a country where they are considered royalty and expect "We the People" to bow to their demands and mandates without question; who have lived in Washington D.C. for so long they no longer even remember which State they represent; who go to Washington, D.C. with good intentions but are all too soon sucked into the Washington swamp by newly gained power, influence, and access to wealth; who are so distracted trying to gain favor from party leaders, supporters, and lobbyist to raise money for reelection, that this Nation's Constitution and we who elected them are ignored; or maybe it should be the unelected Washington bureaucrats (swamp rats) who believe they know what is best for our Nation and its people? After all, are they not already in control of our daily lives due to their crushing regulations? The answer in a free Constitutional Republic is obvious: it should be "We the People."

That, unfortunately, is not the reality we now find ourselves in because the Washington elitists are Marxist-Communists willing to use Stalinist tactics to take control of every aspect and every decision of our lives. They have infringed upon the state's sovereignty and corrupted our constitution by misinterpreting Articles and Amendments to fit their narrative and impose unconstitutional mandates on American citizens. Our corrupt and oppressive federal government has passed legislation and executive orders funding programs and initiatives that are designed to make citizens dependent on the federal government, thereby controlling them. The saddest part of our circumstances is that these corrupt, self-serving sociopaths did not take control of our government through any violent actions or insurrection. American citizens and the individual sovereign states have become subservient to the Washington elitists because "We the People" allowed it to happen. We failed to take the time necessary to keep abreast of what our legislators are spending our hard-earned tax dollars on and when that spending is inappropriate or unconstitutional, triggering our becoming proactive and loudly speaking out against such expenditures. "We the People" have failed to thoroughly research and know who those campaigning for office genuinely are and whether or not they stand for our values. Even worse are the millions of American citizens who have become so apathetic and complacent that they will not even take an hour or two to go to the voting poll and vote, justifying their inaction by claiming, "What difference will it make?" In a Constitutional Republic it can make the difference between retaining our God-given rights to life, liberty, and the pursuit of happiness under our Constitution or losing those rights to an oppressive, authoritarian Marxist-Communist regime of terror.

Other grave concerns are that far too many voters consistently vote for candidates they have not vetted to determine if those candidates represent their values and corrupt politicians who have remained members of Congress for decades and accumulated unacceptable levels of power, influence, and wealth. Politicians who have long since realized that if they are incumbents, they are highly likely to be reelected, causing them not to be overly concerned with following through on their campaign promises, politicians whose priorities are themselves and the party. Politicians, who by the time they finally retire, have done irrevocable harm to our Constitution and the people they swore an oath to serve and protect.

Politicians campaign on promises to go to Washington and fix our country's problems, to represent our values, and to protect our sacred constitution. But it is unkept promise after another as they are too preoccupied with solidifying their elitist status within the Washington swamp to spend the time and effort needed to fulfill their promises. Politicians who cover up their failure to legislate on behalf of their constituents accuse their failures on the opposing party, creating disunity between "We the People." This immature frame of mind by our politicians must be stopped if we are to retain our Constitutional Republic and our God-given right to life, liberty, and the pursuit of happiness. The alternative is not a pretty one; it is a life of depression, repression, and slavery to tyrannical dictators in the same manner as countries like China, Russia, Venezuela, Cuba, and every other Marxist-Communist country in the world. We have so much to lose if we fail to take a stand.

America's Constitution has promoted, protected, and assured diversity and equality, America's greatest strengths. Under our Constitution, America has survived the depression and prevailed over the aggressive power of Nazism, Fascism, and Communism. Over the last two centuries, it has been stated that if America's constitutional form of governance ever falls, it will come from internal forces. Now, in 2024, America finds itself facing that internal threat. Many people believe that this anti-American, anti-capitalist move to change America is being driven by Biden, Obama, the Bush empire, Soros, or the Marxist-Communist Washington elitists. All are clearly and openly dedicated to destroying our capitalistic form of government. However, these individuals are not the greatest threat to America's form of governance or our economy. Who could have the enormous amount of financial power and influence to drive America's Constitutional Republic into obliteration? Who could have the power to "allow" a sitting President to characterize half of America's voters as existential threats to democracy and be praised by the fake news for his rhetoric? The actual puppeteers who are destroying our capitalist form of government rest in the hands of just two New York City Marxist-Communist powerbrokers whose financial assets are so significant that they can dictate American policy and direction.

Just two men from New York City have engineered a "reset," which is intended to destroy the entire United States economy, sending America into chaos and anarchy. We are already experiencing food shortages, record-high inflation, and chaos at our border and city streets. Two men have been the behind-the-scenes financiers and primary architects of the chaos being rained down upon America to destroy capitalism and replace it with their vision of an equity-based society. Just two anti-American Marxist-Communists, who all of the other above-mentioned bad actors take a backseat to, are responsible for steering our Constitutional Republic toward a third-world Marxist-Communist nation. Our political system and social norms are not being corrupted by accident, nor are they the after-effects of a pandemic. The politicization and weaponizing of our governing system is a plot to reset the entire United States economic system in a manner that will destroy the very foundation of our constitutional government. In truth, our country is not being turned upside down by coincidence but rather by a well-thought-out plan meticulously engineered by two of the world's richest and most powerful men. Two unelected multi-billionaires who function outside the checks and balances established by our Constitution. These two individuals yield far more power than any politician or political party and have been the puppeteers pulling the strings of those we have elected to represent us and protect our Constitutional Republic, both Democrats and Republicans. They are using their wealth and influence to attack and destroy America from within, as predicted. These two sociopaths are manipulating the United States economy in a manner that will result in a historic crash, leading to deadly riots, anarchy, street violence, murder, increased suicide rates, homelessness, increased drug use, and potential armed conflict. The depth of division these two men have created in America between Marxist-Communists and conservatives is already at a boiling point and ready to explode.

In my opinion, one of those two evil and treasonous individuals has nearly every Fortune 500 Chief Executive Officer wrapped around his fingers, and the other owns the most influential media empire in the financial world. These two individuals and their cronies are actively taking steps to destroy us and our country both politically and financially. These two fanatics believe that they must save the planet by destroying that which they think is the root cause of our planet's problems: "capitalism." They believe they, alone, have the intellectual and influential capabilities to cause this massive reset of America's heritage and way of life. These two individuals believe that by destroying America as it currently exists, they can then rebuild America from the ground up to be the euphoria they envision. It is my opinion that these two individuals are Laurence Douglas Fink, an American billionaire businessman who is the current chairman and CEO of BlackRock, an American multinational investment management corporation that has control over ten trillion-plus dollars of financial assets and control over the majority of America's largest corporations; and the other, in my opinion, is Michael Bloomberg who owns the largest and most influential financial media in the world with the ability to shape and manipulate America's economy which is the driving force of a health society.

Source & Additional Information: (https://nationalcenter.org/ncppr/2022/10/04/bloomberg-dimon-and-fink-draw-capitalism-as-rule-by-the-noble/)

Our Constitution allows the citizens of this country the right to assemble and protest. I believe that Fink and Bloomberg are using this constitutional right to fund Marxist-Communist misinformation to encourage rioting in our streets, incite violence against American citizens, and destroy local small businesses in an attempt to intimidate American citizens into relinquishing their constitutional rights and freedoms. Those who ascribe Fink's and Bloomberg's hatred of our capitalist form of government are using the Constitution as a weapon against America. Because of these two individual's misplaced beliefs, American citizens are about to undergo the most complex and painful period in American history. The bastardization of our government institutions, the destructive failures of our elected officials to constitutionally represent constituents, and the ever-increasing anti-American mindset all have, in my opinion, the fingerprints of these two individuals all over them.

So, how did just two men become able to control the destiny of America; a once great Nation founded on Judeo-Christian principles and the rule of law get to the point that our elected officials and federal bureaucracy celebrate the destruction of our cities in the name of social justice; mobs of college students with embedded for-hire agitators come to be allowed to protest on our streets, demanding the abolishment of our police, the destruction of Israel, and the support of Palestinian terrorists; scientific researchers come to no longer abide by proven scientific methods of research but rather accept ideological reasoning; tens of millions of Americans come to believe that free speech and capitalism are dangerous to our society? It happened because we allowed it to happen through our failure to be vigilant and stand up for our heritage and values, and not allow it to happen.

Chapter 12
American Frustration

Americans are frustrated, angry, and struggling to any longer believe in our federal institutions and legal system. Frustrated with having to deal with a dwindling economy, high inflation, an invasion of millions of illegal immigrants through our unsecured southern border, and staggering rates of crime. Frustrated with rampant political corruption and a politicalized two-tiered justice system. Frustrated with "wokism" and "cancel culture." All of which is bringing America to a boiling point.

The response to this same level of sustained injustice, lack of judicial accountability, and criminal chaos in Venezuela was the rise of mob justice by way of public lynchings. Human nature detests the lack of equal treatment and justice for all, detests the denying of citizens who refuse to adapt to a Marxist-Communist ideology the same level of justice as those who identify and actively pursue this anti-constitutional ideology. America is now a two-tiered justice system that severely punishes otherwise law-abiding citizens for the most minor of crimes while turning a blind eye to criminals and destructive Marxist-Communist political activists. This lack of judicial equality from our politically weaponized federal law enforcement agencies is now occurring in the United States as it did in Venezuela. Constitutional Conservative American citizens are being characterized as terrorists, racists, bigots, or phobic for exercising their God-given and constitutional rights. If this denigration of our heritage and culture, our safety, and the corruption of our children's minds and emotions against their parents by the Marxist-Communist educators does not stop, Americans will respond.

If those who have been elected to govern fail to ensure that citizens' God-given Constitutional rights are preserved, if our legal system refuses to provide the same level of justice to every citizen regardless of their political ideology, then American citizens will eventually revolt against this oppression by any means necessary. Using the pursuit of equal justice and self-determination as justification, the oppressed will use any means necessary to regain control. Venezuelans believe that "a good criminal is a dead criminal," which is acceptable to the Venezuelans who have watched their friends and family ripped away by crime and political persecution. Will America become another Venezuela, or will America find the means and will to rectify the wrong being imposed upon our citizens before it is too late?

Enduring and destructive problems undermining our political system are the immense influence of special interest groups in politics, the politicizing and weaponizing of our federal institutions and legal system, and partisan polarization. These problems compound, creating a vicious cycle of distrust and dysfunction. Addressing them with urgency and conviction is crucial to restoring Americans' faith in our elected political officials, government, and the criminal justice system. Deepening partisan distrust and divisions within our country is distorting political and civic debate and family unity, encouraging extremism, and leading to our dysfunctional federal government's collapse. This divisiveness is preventing our country from addressing critical and destructive problems and advancing solutions that are in our Constitutional Republic's and its citizens' best interest. Weaknesses and subsequent distrust in our electoral system due to voter fraud, manipulation of election laws, partisan corruption and fraud, and disinformation by news outlets and social media are feeding polarization by encouraging radically partisan positions and undermining a sense of shared national identity.

Source & Additional Information: (https://journalistsresource.org/politics-and-government/influence-interest-groups-public-policy-outcomes/) (https://www.princeton.edu/news/2021/12/09/political-polarization-and-its-echo-chambers-surprising-new-cross-disciplinary)

Our Constitutional Republic is sick, if not terminally ill. The symptoms are all there for all to see, but our primary disease is that we have abandoned our Judeo-Christian values and our American Constitutional system of government. We now have a Marxist-Communist mindset among our citizens and governing officials, which is dismantling our Constitutional Republic as established by our Founding Fathers and reconstructing our nation into a corrupt form of Marxist-Communist governance. Our Nation's situation is grave, the threats are real and formidable, and our hope of escape without some social upheaval is in question. We still speak of our country as a Constitutional Republic. Still, it bears only an external and superficial resemblance to the Republic formed in 1787. Escape from the unbelievable infusion of treason within our government has no remedy so long as we continue to ignore our Nation's deterioration and stand by doing nothing.

Society and Government: A civilized society is not possible without adequate government, but that government itself can be the most significant social evil, as is now being demonstrated by our federal government. The men who framed our Constitution were familiar with the history of oppressive government and tyranny. They knew liberty was impossible without government, but they also knew that government has been the greatest enemy of freedom throughout history. They were confronted with the enormous task of erecting a government with all the powers necessary to guard the peace and the liberties of the people while simultaneously being unable to use those powers to impair or destroy the people's freedom.

Source & Additional Information: (https://www.tandfonline.com/doi/full/10.1080/0190 0692.2019.1638933)

In a republic, the citizens have the ultimate authority in the governance of its Nation. However, in a republic, the people must be able to trust in the wisdom of those they elect to represent them in Congress and the individual they elect as their President and Commander-in-Chief. It is these individuals who possess powers that the people must devise some means of controlling. The greatest protection "We the People" have is through the ballot box, requiring those in power to relinquish its powers back to the people until that power is either renewed or transferred to those chosen by the people to succeed it. The greatest threat in a Constitutional Republic is that the authority given by the people to the government and exercised by an elected Administration may be so irresistible that a corrupt Administration in power may be able to control the electorate by intimidation, bribes, favors, and the ignoring of our National Constitution and State Constitutions. These criminal acts are constantly being demonstrated by Marxist-Communist governed countries throughout the world and are now rearing their ugly heads in the United States. It is during our election process that the United States is at its gravest danger. The power of an Administration in office can be so great that a divided and polarized citizenry will be no match for a highly organized Administration armed with public funds and with the overwhelming machinery of a corrupt and weaponized government as is now being experienced by Donald Trump and the MEGA movement.

The state of our Constitutional Republic has implications for freedom around the world. Movements in other countries to establish a democracy for their country look to the United States for inspiration and support. At the same time, authoritarian leaders falsely point to America's problems as proof of a Constitutional Republic's inherent inferiority and as a sort of license for their abuses of power, as China has so clearly demonstrated. Make no mistakes, our Republic is not without fault and the incomprehensible truth is that our Constitutional Republic is in serious trouble and may not long be that inspirational nation. We must not allow this to happen. We must all stand together and force Congress and the Administration to prioritize strengthening and restoring lost trust in our federal institutions, restoring civic norms among our citizens, and upholding the promise of universal liberty on which our nation was founded. We must not fail ourselves or those citizens of foreign countries who look to us for their inspiration to change the governance of their country from an authoritarian form of governing to a democracy that will govern on behalf of their people.

There are no easy answers to our problems, which is entirely dependent on whether or not there are answers to be found. Our current American justice system is playing a crucial part in the oppression and mistreatment of our citizens who have opposing views from the Administration in power, leading to these individuals becoming collateral damage of a corrupt Marxist-Communist Democrat Party. If the Marxist-Communist elites have their way, American citizens will have no political power to hold politicians responsible for their anti-American anti-Constitutional activities. What comes of this predicament is a culture of riots, crime, and no trust in the judicial system to assure due process. When that becomes a norm, no one is safe. No one.

A return to a truly Constitutional Republic, pride in our country and flag, the ability to politically disagree without anger, being renounced or canceled, and a return to political debate between various ideologies can only begin in our children's classrooms. We must fix our education system by returning this function to the States in keeping with our Constitution and halting the indoctrination of our children regarding critical race theory, gender alteration, transgender lifestyles, and Marxist-Communism ideology. We must educate ourselves and our children on the actual costs of a Marxist-Communist version of governance versus that of a truly Constitutional Republic, and not just in dollars and cents. We must remove our educational system from the federal government, which is destroying the minds of our children rather than teaching them the fundamentals necessary to survive as a productive adult. As a result of our fatally flawed indoctrinating education system, mothers of school-aged children have become "Mama Bears" and are taking up the cause to seize back control of our School Boards across the nation, but they cannot do it alone. We must all join the fight to save our children and change the classroom environment.

Would those who have joined this so-called "Woke" movement still be demanding "free" education, "free" health care, and other "free" entitlements if they were forced to reside in a country where Marxism-Communism is the form of governing? Where they would realize what their Marxist-Communist ideology would cost them in the end? Would they be so quick to cancel and destroy the lives of American citizens and businesses who refuse to cave in to their radical views if they were wise enough to realize that the day will come when the tables will be turned on them? Would they be willing to give up all their private property, vehicles, computers, tablets, and their most precious possession, their mobile phones? These are the costs of a Marxist-Communist governing system that cannot allow its citizens access to information, which these woke fools do not consider. The elimination of private property is the first maxim of Marxist-Communism.

Would the "Woke" crowd be willing to accept Marxist-Communism with its denial of freedom to assemble and freely speak out at their protest rallies, or give up having a free press that expounds their radical ideology? Are they ready to see their family, friends, or themselves imprisoned for daring to dissent against what they disagree with? Are these "Woke" fools willing to give up a two-party political system for a one-party political system, removing any ability to vote ineffective, corrupt politicians out of office? Do they not realize that their ideology, which would bring in a Marxist-Communist form of governance, would eliminate their access to an independent judiciary system that sees any person accused of a crime as innocent until proven guilty or give up the rule of law, which protects them even while they demonstrate their anti-American behavior? Are they really willing to live under the dictatorship of a Marxist-Communist regime that will dictate their every decision on all matters? These people need to take an extended vacation in communist China, Cuba, North Korea, or Venezuela, then see if they still want all their freebies under a Marxist-Communist America.

Marxist-Communist members of Congress and their "Woke" followers like to say that Marxist-Communist has failed only because it has never been tried appropriately. The facts are that Marxism has been tried under various scenarios and has failed every time in every country where it has been attempted. Countries such as Russia and China are failed Marxist countries that have turned instead to an all-controlling communist form of government. Democratic countries such as Israel, India, and the United Kingdom have all attempted Marxism but have since rejected Marxism. All three democratic countries had a Marxist form of governing, adhering to Marxist principles and practices. All three countries changed direction and adopted capitalism as the better way to economic prosperity. As a result, India today has the largest middle class in the free world.

Marxism depends upon the decision-making of a central government. Without exception, every leader from Lenin to Castro promised to initiate fundamental freedoms such as free education, free health care, free elections, a free press, free assembly, and religious freedom. None fulfilled these promises. With these two failed leaders as examples, can anyone even begin to imagine a world controlled by Marxist-Communists? Is a world without freedom, without choice, without fundamental human rights the world that these "Woke" freeloaders would choose if they had a choice? The answer to this question could have been no if only our failed federally funded school system had taken the time to instruct our children about Socialism, Marxism, Communism, and Globalism as compared to a constitutional republic with a capitalist form of government.

Nations are just like men; both of whom believe they are invincible. Young man in their late teens, twenties, or thirties think they are invisible and will live forever? They only envision an endless lifetime, but as you pass seventy, it becomes harder to hide from reality as you lose family members and friends. Nations also have visions of infinite endurance: What young Roman citizen of the second century did not expect that their empire, which stretched from Britain to the Middle East, would endure the passage of time and exist forever. It lasted for about five hundred years, give or take. It was not bad, but it was gone.

France was considered unconquerable in the seventeenth and eighteenth centuries following Charles Martel's reunification of the Frankish kingdom and prevented the Muslim invasion of Europe when he defeated the Arabs at the Battle of Tours between 688 and 741. Now, France is on its way to becoming a sanctuary for Muslims fleeing the Middle East who refuse to assimilate into the French culture. In the nineteenth and early twentieth centuries, the sun never set on the British empire; now, Britain exists in perpetual twilight. Its 96-year-old sovereignty is a fitting symbol of a nation in terminal decline. In the 1980s, Japan seemed poised to buy the world with business schools teaching Japanese management techniques to businesses throughout the world. Today, its birth rate is so low, and its population is aging so rapidly that an industry has sprung up to remove the remains of elderly Japanese who die alone.

I was born in 1945, at the midpoint of the 20th century's American century. America's prestige and influence were never greater. Thanks to the 'Greatest Generation,' we won a world war throughout most of Europe, Asia, and the Pacific. We reduced Germany to rubble and put the 'rising sun' to bed. It set the stage for almost half a century of unprecedented prosperity. We stopped the spread of communism in Europe and Asia and have fought international terrorism, rebuilt our enemies' homelands, and lavished foreign aid on much of the world. We have built skyscrapers and flown men to the moon, conquered polio and COVID-19, and explored the mysteries of the universe and the wonders of DNA, the blueprint of life. Like the citizens of France, Britain, and Japan, I also believed America would endure the passage of time. But in the last few years, our country's political, federal law enforcement, and judicial systems have been compromised by an unprecedented level of evil and corruption, placing our Constitutional Republic on the doorstep of its demise.

Greatness Lost: The United States of America is rapidly moving from a free capitalist economy to Marxist-Communism, which has worked so well ***NOWHERE*** in the world. We have gone from a republic government guided by a constitution to a regime of revolving Washington elites. We have less freedom with each passing year, and the cancel culture is everywhere. We have traded the American Revolution for the Cultural Revolution. We have an economically feeble nation as a result of a corrupt and incompetent Marxist Communist Democrat Party administration. As a result, we cannot defend our borders, our history, our monuments, or our streets. Our cities have become anarchist playgrounds. We are a nation of dependents, beggars, and misplaced charity. Homeless veterans camp in the streets while illegal immigrants are put up in luxurious hotels that most of us could never afford. Ivy League graduates routinely fail history tests that fifth graders could pass a generation ago.

How does a nation slip from greatness to obscurity? The answer is in a federal government ruled by Marxist-Communist elitists who are willingly destroying our Republic by:

- Fighting endless wars that Presidents no longer intend to allow our military forces to win;
- Accumulating massive debts far beyond our ability to repay;

- ➢ Refusing to guard our borders, allowing the nation to be inundated by an alien invasion;

- ➢ Surrendering control of our cities to mob rule and anarchy;

- ➢ Allowing the indoctrination of our young to Marxist-Communist ideology;

- ➢ Moving from a republic government to a Marxist-Communist form of government;

- ➢ Losing our national identity as a result of endless illegal immigrants entering our country;

- ➢ Indulging in indifference towards what is occurring within our government; and,

- ➢ Abandoning God, faith, and family which is the real strength of any stable society.

In the United States of America, every one of these symptoms is pronounced, indicating an advanced stage of deterioration. Even if the cause seems hopeless, do we not have an obligation to those who sacrificed so much to give us what we had? We are surrounded by the ghosts of warriors who are urging us on: the Union soldiers who held Cemetery Ridge at Gettysburg, the battered bastards of Bastogne, those who served in the cold hell of Korea, and those who served in the jungles of Vietnam, Afghanistan, and Iraq. Will we listen and carry-on their sacrifices to once again save our Republic? This was the nation that took in my immigrant grandparents, whose uniform I and many of my family members wore in the Second World War, Korea, Vietnam, Iraq, and Afghanistan. I do not want to imagine a world without America, even as it becomes increasingly likely.

During Britain's darkest hour, when its professional army was trapped at Dunkirk, and a German invasion seemed imminent, Churchill reminded his compatriots: *'Nations that go down fighting rise again, and those that surrender tamely are finished.'* If we let America slip through our fingers and we lose what we have without a fight, what will posterity say of us? While the prognosis is far from good, only God knows if America's day in the sun is over.

Conservatism Lost: When the Republican leadership's "agenda" is to cave in to Big Pharma, cave in to Chuck Schumer's endless trillion dollar Omnibus bills, cave in to Democrat gun control, allow the bankrupting of America through Green New Deal "infrastructure" initiatives, and cooperate with the Marxist-Communist Democrat members of congress in supporting unconstitutional and morally wrong legislation such as the "Respect for Marriage Act," then Constitutional Conservatism loses; when the senior Republican leader in the Senate purposely transfers millions of dollars from Constitutional conservative candidates with great potential to win to left leaning candidates who will follow the Grand Old Party's way of doing business, equating to doing nothing unless Mitch McConnel gives the okay, then Constitutional Conservatism loses; when members of the House and Senate, who are all too aware of the deterioration of this once great Nation under the current leadership, reelect the same old leadership, somehow believing that doing the same thing over and over again will bring change, then Constitutional Conservatism loses.

Constitutional conservatives are the majority in America, but unfortunately, they are the minority in Congress, even when Republicans have a majority of members. Why? Because of RINO (Republican In Name Only) Republicans. It is far past time that we Constitutional Conservatives stand together to "bury" the Grand Old Party and "build something new." The Grand Old Party has consistently failed to keep its promises and has voted with the Democrat party on unconstitutional legislation again and again, bringing us ever closer to becoming a Marxist-Communist Nation that we do not support. It is time to acknowledge that if the Republican party desires to continue to have any relevance, it must abandon the Good Old Party mentality and truly become the party of the people. This will only happen under the leadership of determined fighters like Donald J. Trump. Individuals committed to and capable of showing dedication to our Constitution and delivering on their promises regardless of the consequences. In the last two months of 2022, the Democrat's control of the House should have been a lame-duck session, but it was anything but lame. They knew that they had only two months to jam through as many Marxist-Communist bills as possible, and jam they did.

On December 22nd, 2022, Congress passed a $1.7 trillion omnibus spending package with the help of nine RINO Republican Representatives and eighteen RINO Senate Republicans. This was indeed a stab in the back of all American conservatives by Mitch McConnel and those eighteen RINO Republican Senators because, without their votes, the Senate Democrats could not have gotten that bill passed. The nature of this bill required a super majority to pass, which the Democrats did not have, a fact Mitch McConnel could have utilized to force a continuing resolution until the Republicans took over the House in just two short weeks later. This would have allowed the House Republicans to dramatically reduce the amount of spending on Marxist-Communist initiatives and eliminate the money appropriated for the hiring of the additional 80,000 Internal Revenue Service gun-carrying agents. Instead, Mitch McConnel supported funding the Democrat's Fiscal Year 2024 wish list. This left the Republican House unable to challenge the funding of Marxist-Communist initiatives until the end of Fiscal Year 2023. The Marxist-Communist Democrat Party received an unprecedented farewell gift.

Chapter 13
The Biden's

Perhaps the greatest disaster to befall the United States of America is the Biden family. The family includes members who demonstrate some of the most antisocial and dysfunctional behavior one could find in an American family. The antics of this family would make for a fascinating dissertation for someone's PhD thesis—antics that were destroying the very foundation of our society and the devastation of our Constitutional Republic. When the leader of the greatest nation on earth and his family members cannot conform to the norms of civilized societies, they are a detrimental threat to every member of that society. The list of atrocities committed by this man and members of his family knows no bounds.

Joe Biden's inappropriate and obnoxious social behaviors include being a pathological liar and inappropriate, unwanted, and uncalled-for physical contact with women and young female children. On several occasions, Biden was shown in national news clips being overly physical with young girls, consistently attempting to hug them while kissing and blowing in their hair. Even when doing a presentation or speaking at an event, Biden weirdly called out young girls in his audiences to comment on their attractiveness. His daughter Ashley wrote in her diary that she feared that her past adolescent showers with her father had been inappropriate. This shell of a human being is a "creepy," "perverse," and "sick" person.

Joe Biden has been alleged by at least eight women that, in the past, he had serially and improperly touched, kissed, or grabbed them. One woman, Tara Reade, went so far as to allege that she was sexually assaulted by Joe Biden, who denied the charge. Women as diverse as former Education Secretary Betsy DeVos and Biden's daughter-in-law Kathleen Buhle have both alleged, in their memoirs, that Joe Biden made them feel uncomfortable through his intrusive, unwanted touching and embraces. In a televised speech, Biden stopped in the middle of his speech to point out a female acquaintance, informing the crowd that, "We go back a long way. She was twelve, and I was thirty, but anyway …." As a result of these inappropriate interactions, Biden was most probably repeatedly warned by his handlers to stop his intimate references to young women. His puppeteers no doubt advised him to halt close contact with young girls. Yet, like his cocaine-addicted son Hunter, Joe seemed to be addicted to inappropriate touching and kissing of young children. Like his son Hunter, Joe could not seem to stop this addictive behavior despite the eerie image he was projecting around the world.

While on the tarmac of the Helsinki, Finland airport, Uncle Joe attempted to embrace a young female child being held by her mother. While this child was trying to avoid him, Biden kept moving his mouth near the face of the young girl. He attempted to nibble the youngster's ear, from which the young child recoiled, but regardless of this child's desire not to be physically touched, Biden continued to nibble at her shoulder. When she flinched away, Biden sought a second try to smell her hair and nestle closer. Had any other prominent politician, especially a Republican politician, committed such unnerving antics, they would have been immediately ostracized by their colleagues and mercilessly hammered by the media. Not so in Biden's case. For the Marxist-Communist Democrat Party and their propaganda news arm, this is just "Old Uncle Joe" trying to be too friendly and thus not attributable to any sinister urge.

Unfortunately for the Biden family, son Hunter has a troubling habit of leaving a public trail of evidence of his drug use to the point one would begin to wonder if Hunter was not subconsciously attempting to bring the Biden family down for past perceived childhood injustices. In past events, Hunter forgot his crack pipe in a rental car; he abandoned his laptop that contained evidence of his and his father's felonious treasonous behavior with adversaries of the United States; and abandoned and disavowed his young four-year-old child as his legitimate child as well as did Grandpa Joe. Let us not forget about Hunter's unlawfully registered handgun turning up in a dumpster near a school. In sum, both Joe and Hunter have quite disturbing and all too public habits that brought dishonor to the Presidency and the White House.

The Secret Service has refused to turn over the list of individuals who may have accessed the area of the White House where authorities discovered cocaine over the Fourth of July weekend, saying that the record of such a list does not fall under the Freedom of Information Act. This highly suspicious response suggests that the Secret Service never created a list in the first place. If the Secret Service did not make a document listing those individuals, that would indicate that the agency did not take the investigation seriously. Further, the FBI did not develop latent fingerprints and claims that insufficient DNA was present for investigative comparisons, so the Secret Service concluded that it "is not able to compare evidence against the known pool of individuals," according to a Secret Service press release and "There was no surveillance video footage found that provided investigative leads or any other means for investigators to identify who may have deposited the found substance in this area." However, numerous cameras in that area constantly scan that area from every angle possible.

Biden is a man who has had a career of corruption so extensive as to warrant being the poster child of political corruption. Joe Biden is the most corrupt and anti-American president in the history of the United States. Biden will replace Jimmie Carter as the worst President in American history without even being close in comparison. He is the most racist and antisemitic person to hold the Oval Office, bar none. Biden has accomplished nothing positive on behalf of the American people during his entire political career. Instead, Biden and his family cartel have accomplished much on their own behalf and on behalf of the Chinese Communist Party at the expense of the American people.

The Biden cartel, which mob boss Joey "The Big Guy" Biden, cultivated remarkably lucrative relationships with the Chinese Communist Party, Romania, Russia, and Ukraine. Financial deals came despite a lack of any evidence that anyone in the Biden cartel was producing anything of value for these countries. The only thing of value the Biden Cartel had to offer was Joe Biden' position which would allow these foreign adversaries access to American policy-making influence and, as far as we know, may have provided our enemies with classified and sensitive information. Lucrative deals occurred while Joe Biden was steering policy regarding these countries, especially China, first as a Senator, then as Vice President, and then in his role as the President of the United States. Deals with the Chinese Communist Party government will have dangerous consequences for our national security for years to come.

The Chinese Communist Party government financially backs the energy firm on whose Board Hunter Biden sat. That firm was invested in a company that has been actively stealing United States nuclear secrets and providing dual-use technologies to the Chinese military. While global powers have been trying for years to stop China from monopolizing the world's rare mineral resources, the firm that employed Hunter Biden bought a company that helped China in its competition with the United States and other foreign countries for those rare mineral resources—treasonous acts against the United States of America.

The Republican Chaired House Oversight Committee subpoenaed Bank of America for the financial records of three of Hunter Biden's associates, including Biden family associate John Robinson Walker. Those financial records indicate that the Biden Cartel received tens of millions of dollars from a Chinese Communist Party-controlled China-based company. Those transactions have provided evidence that Joe Biden is referred to in communications between Hunter and his associates. He was knowledgeable about Hunter's business affairs and was personally involved in Hunter's overseas business affairs. Those records provide evidence of abuse of power by Joe Biden, who utilized his public office to help his family become wealthy through influence peddling with our foreign adversaries. Those subpoenaed bank records detail how Biden family associate John Robinson Walker wired members of Biden's family money after receiving $3 million from a Shanghai-based company, State Energy HK Limited, a Chinese Communist Party-owned company. Walker and his company, Robinson Walker, LLC, received that $3 million wire in March 2017 and then transferred approximately $1,065,692 to various bank accounts associated with members of the Biden family over a three-month period. It was further revealed that Biden's family member, Hallie Biden, was also a part of the family's overseas business dealings. Hallie Biden received two separate payments from Walker in 2017. According to a Republican House committee memo, bank records indicate that Walker received a $179,836.86 wire from a company with an overseas bank account in November 2015, transferred $59,900 of that money to one of his checking accounts, and sent Hunter Biden that same amount.

Source & Additional Information: (https://oversight.house.gov/release/chairman-comer-subpoenas-hunter-james-bidens-personal-and-business-bank-records/)

In late April of 2023, we learned that Secretary of State Antony Blinken admitted to a Senate committee in December of 2022 that he had met with Joe Biden's brother, James Biden, over a dozen times since he began working for Joe Biden around 2003. When asked by the Senate investigative counsel if he had discussed James Biden's business dealings, Blinked denied any such discussions had ever occurred. Secretary of State Blinken, who finds himself deeply marred in the Biden family scandals, has consistently denied any communications with the Biden cartel regarding their business dealings with America's foes. In a

Senate interview, Blinken claimed he had never communicated with Hunter Biden by email. However, when he served as Deputy Secretary of State in the Obama administration, he electronically communicated with Hunter while Hunter held a controversial post with Ukrainian energy company Burisma. Blinken has also been accused of helping cover up the scandal over Hunter's notorious laptop by coordinating with fifty-one past Directors of the Central Intelligent Agency and the FBI, a letter signed by them alleging that Hunter's laptop had all the earmarking's of Russian disinformation.

Source & Additional Information: (https://nypost.com/2022/10/19/its-been-two-years-since-51-intelligence-agents-interfered-with-an-election-they-still-wont-apologize/)

In early May of 2023, Republican Representative James Comer of Kentucky, who chairs the House Oversight Committee, reported that his Committee's findings regarding the Biden crime family showed a constant pattern of treasonous behavior. Comer's report showed that when he was the vice president, Joe Biden had set up a family network of shell companies to conceal the fact that the Biden cartel was receiving large amounts of money from foreign entities such as Romania, China, Ukraine, and Russia. The money the Biden cartel received from these foreign American adversaries cannot be tied to legitimate business transactions customarily expected. Despite this revelation, major news outlets have been silent. The New York Times, as can be expected, has ignored the facts as presented and has instead chosen to attempt to whitewash the entire affair to cover up the crimes of Joe Biden and his family. For a revelation of this magnitude to be brushed aside is a dereliction of journalism by the New York Times and all the other major news outlets. Instead of reporting the facts, the New York Times chose to use the findings of the House Oversight Committee as a tool with which to attack Republicans and to score cheap political points.

Special Counsel John Durham's report is a prime example of why Americans lack confidence in the government, according to prominent Democrat constitutional legal scholar Alan Dershowitz who stated, "I think it reveals that Americans are right to distrust the government—even civil servants in the government," Dershowitz told The Epoch Times on May 15th, 2023, "This case demonstrates that people are prepared to distort the Constitution to get their way—get their partisan, political way." Fraud, corruption, and treason are part of the soul of Joe Biden. If "The Big Guy" is willing to sell out his country for wealth, then it is no longer far-fetched to believe that Biden's 2020 election was indeed stolen so that he could continue his influence peddling and place himself in an excellent position to continue the coverup of his treasonous activities over the years. The knowledge that information supporting these allegations of influence peddling has been in the FBI's possession for several years resulted from an FBI whistleblower coming out and testifying to this fact. According to the House Oversight Committee report, the FBI's failure to release the information it held against Joe Biden and his son Hunter is tantamount to election interference, which is a federal felony. Polling clearly shows that had the general public been aware of the existence of the criminal activity of Joe Biden and his family cartel and his financial ties to China, Romania, Ukraine, and Russia, he would never have been elected.

Joe Biden is said to have no experience running a business or managing a payroll. Not so; Joe is experienced in running his family cartel and the multiple shell businesses created to launder the money received from foreign adversaries of the United States. It could be argued that these endeavors would qualify as having run a complex multi-facet endeavor like the federal government. After all, neither requires a man of integrity and honor, which makes Biden highly qualified. Joe Biden can always be relied upon to maintain a position of weakness against America's adversaries such as China, Russia, and Iran. What we also know beyond a reasonable doubt is that Joe Biden is a pathological liar, a traitor, and a mentally deranged old man filled with diabolic evil living in a fantasy world. Even in his private life, he is a heartless, evil old man who refuses to acknowledge his young granddaughter, fathered between his son Hunter and a prostitute. That is until the polls indicated a dropping in favorability because of his heartless rejection of this child. Then miraculously, in late July of 2023, Joe Biden, for the first time, publicly acknowledged his seventh grandchild, a four-year-old girl, Navy, fathered by his son Hunter with Arkansas woman Lunden Roberts in 2018. However, the White House emphatically denied that this public acknowledgment had anything to do with politics and his drop in favorability polls. The birth of this child by a prostitute may be embarrassing and unfortunate for Hunter and Joe. Still, the child bore no responsibility for those circumstances and did not deserve to be abandoned by both her biological father and grandfather.

As more evidence of wrongdoing by Joe Biden unfolded, his popularity within his base became nearly nonexistent. During the 2020 election campaign, Joe Biden never made any real personal effort to win that election. Biden rarely left his New Jersey home during the 2020 campaign session, and when he held a rally, very few people attended. His lack of campaigning was probably because he already knew that it did not matter, as he made known to the public during a videoed campaign speech in which he stated that he could not lose because there were initiatives in place to ensure he won the election. Are there no Democrats left who have a conscience?

The Marxist-Communist Democrat Party stole the 2020 election through a massive scheme involving mail-in voting, phantom/ghost votes, fraud, and incompetence. There are Democrats out there who have firsthand knowledge of how this election was stolen from Trump but who do not have the honor and integrity to come forward with that information. Instead, they have chosen to remain silent and not disclose the information they hold. Meanwhile, our country continues to slide deeper into decline and can now only be described as a blooming tyrannical and corrupt Marxist-Communist nation. Biden's attempts to appease foreign countries, in particular China, from which he has been receiving bribes, are failing miserably and may very well lead to a nuclear World War III.

In communist China fashion, Biden's Administration and the federal bureaucracy have openly and tyrannically abused or ignored our Constitution through loopholes, scare tactics, and unconstitutional mandates. The Marxist-Communist Democrat Administration, currently in power, is indoctrinating our children into Marxist-Communist soldiers indoctrinated to turn on their parents, attack our religious institutions, and keep the American public from exercising their God-given rights under the Constitution of the United States. Are these tyrannical and treasonous actions against America and "We the People" being instituted at the direction of China? Is this what China is paying Joe Biden to do? The Marxist-Communist Democrat Administration did nothing to dissuade China from its nonchalant aggression throughout Asia and over American sovereign territory (spy balloons). The Wuhan origin of the COVID-19 pandemic has yet to be acknowledged by the Marxist-Communist Democrat Party. No proactive actions, such as the expulsion of Chinese diplomats or Chinese citizen students from American universities, are being employed to punish China for the deaths of tens of millions of people globally and the trillions of dollars it costs across the world to fight this deadly virus. China continues to export fentanyl, which is killing our young with no consequences from the corrupt Marxist-Communist Bureaucracy. No prohibition of Chinese companies, or any other national companies with ties to the Chinese Communist government, from buying American farmland is being imposed. China is well on its way to destroying our constitutional republic.

Yet, the Marxist-Communist Administration refuses to rightly label China as a deadly adversary of the United States. Still, it falsely identifies China as nothing more than an economic competitor of the United States. So how can any person with any common sense not know that Joe Biden has been bought and paid for by the Chinese Communist Party?

Joe Biden and his merry men of true insurrectionists pushed Marxist-Communist agendas through Executive Orders and Legislation proposing Marxist-Communist measures to silence the American citizenry. This strategy to silence non-conformists is a total disregard of the First Amendment to the Constitution, which reads as follows: "Congress shall make no law respecting an establishment of religion or prohibiting the free exercise thereof, or abridging the freedom of speech, or of the press; or the right of the people peaceably to assemble, and to petition the Government for a redress of grievances." Our Forefathers deemed the right to the freedom of religion, freedom of speech, freedom to assembly, and freedom to protest so crucial to the new Republic that they made these God-given rights a part of the First Amendment to the Bill of Rights. God-given rights that our Founding Fathers were denied under English rule. The total disregard of our Constitution by the Biden-Harris Marxist-Communist Administration, financial supporters, and handlers has now placed American citizens into the same unbearable totalitarian and authoritarian governance that our forefathers had to endure in England.

Since the inauguration of Joe Biden to the Presidency in January of 2021, our federal government has turned America from the land of the free to the land of the oppressed. Joe Biden's America is an openly Marxist-Communist Nation that imposes mandates through loopholes, scare tactics, censorship, and unreasonable punishment for failure to comply. All to intimidate "We the People" from exercising our constitutional rights to life, liberty, and the pursuit of happiness. Under the Biden-Harris regime, we were canceled or censored on most social media platforms from speaking freely against the pandemic, forced vaccines, wearing of masks, closure of our children's schools, and the closure of small businesses, condemning many of these businesses to financial failure. Prominent people with expert information on COVID-19, the reliability and dangers of the vaccines, and the wisdom of school and business closures were suppressed by major news outlets and media from sharing this information with the general public. Suppressed at the encouragement, request, direction, and dictate of the Biden-Harris Administration and their out-of-control, corrupt, and weaponized federal government agencies. Banned from speaking out the truth because the truth did not fit the Marxist-Communist Democrat Party's narrative.

Under the Biden-Harris Marxist-Communist Democrat Administration, parents of school children who dared to speak out at School Board meetings, questioning what their children were being exposed to and taught, were branded as domestic terrorists by the DOJ and targeted for harassment and intimidation by the FBI at the direction of the Department DOJ of Injustice's Secretary, Merrick Garland. All for exercising their God-given right to free speech, parental responsibility for their children's education, and their constitutional right to present grievances. Under Biden-Harris' DOJ, we had American citizens being unconstitutionally held as political prisoners for practicing their Constitutional right to protest and verbalize their grievances regarding the 2020 elections. Held in inhumane conditions for months and for some, years, without being charged or, if charged, accused of trumped-up infringements that these political prisoners reluctantly plead guilty to in order to end their ordeal in the inhumane conditions of the Washington D.C. prison. Held without their Constitutional right to reasonable bail and a speedy trial.

Source & Additional Information: (https://www.washingtontimes.com/news/2022/may/12/whistleblowers-fbi-probed-parents-under-counterter/) (https://www.npr.org/2022/04/14/1092580753/capitol-riot-january-6-insurrection-defendants)

Why? Because This is lthe Marxist-Communist scheme in which they believe they can intimidate the American population into bowing to their ideology, strike fear in those who may dare oppose their dictates, discourage any citizen from dissenting or opposing their one-party rule over America's agenda. In line with the Marxist-Communist playbook, the Marxist-Communist Democrat Party falsely accused American citizens of insurrection for purely political propaganda advantage. All the result of an out-of-control, overreaching, corrupt, and oppressive Federal government attempting to implement President Obama's promise to fundamentally forever change America. After having left the Presidency, Barack Obama has continued this personal mission by utilizing Joe Biden as his puppet to implement necessary legislation and Executive Orders to further move our country to that place, a Marxist-Communist Nation. With the assistance of the Chinese Communist Party and other anonymous minions of the devil working in unison, Obama's dream is fast approaching reality.

The Marxist-Communist Democrat Party, in just four years, managed to spend trillions of dollars on Marxist-Communist initiatives; provided financial aid and assistance to the enemies of the United States; provided "Pork" money to congressional supporters; funneled billions of dollars to failed Marxist-Communist Democrat-run states and cities; destroyed the most secure southern border in American history; ended America's independence from adversarial foreign countries' oil; politicalized and weaponized our DOJ and the Federal Bureaucracy of Investigation; and introduced radical education policies which have launched the indoctrination of our children to Marxist-Communist and "Woke" ideology. Joe Biden, Kamala Harris and thier Marxist-Communist Democrat Administration solidified the politicizing of news outlets and social media, making them nothing more than propaganda arms of the Marxist-Communist Democrat Party.

Joe Biden and Kamala Harris masterminded the most embarrassing and humiliating American military defeat in American history with the retreat of all military forces from

Afghanistan. This incompetent strategical withdrawal of American military forces left behind hundreds if not thousands of American citizens and thousands of Afghan citizens who voluntarily risked their lives to actively support American military forces actively, leaving them to face torture and death at the hands of the Taliban; abandoned eighty-five billion dollars of the worlds most sophisticated military weapons and equipment to the Taliban; and the abandoned a strategically located military air base near the Chinese-Afghanistan border.

Source & Additional Information: (https://www.newyorker.com/news/our-columnists/does-the-great-retreat-from-afghanistan-mark-the-end-of-the-american-era)

Biden-Harris installed the most incompetent and corrupt Marxist-Communist Democrat Party members into leadership positions in all of our vital departments and agencies. Selections based solely on equity, inclusion, and diversity, not on knowledge or experience in the responsibilities and activities of the departments or agencies they were appointed to provide leadership. Incompetence rapidly leading to the destruction of our Constitutional Republic and the God-given rights afforded to all American citizens under that Constitution.

Biden's Fantasy Land: Amid a classified document scandal and speculation about whether or not Biden would seek reelection in 2024, the White House prepared a "cheat sheet" that was sent to Marxist-Communist Democratic lawmakers just prior to his April 2023 announcement to run for a second term. This "Cheat Sheet" highlighted the Biden's first two years in office, touting that he was "delivering results for the American people." The memo focused on Congress-passed legislation that Biden signed into law. "Today marks two years since President Biden and Vice President Kamala Harris were sworn into office," White House communications director Kate Bedingfield wrote in a statement. "In the past two years, we saw significant economic growth as the President built the most significant legislative record since the Johnson Administration. Due to the overwhelming popularity of the President's economic agenda, the President had the best first midterm election results of any Democratic President in sixty years." This was a bold statement, given the Party lost the House of Representatives to the Republican Party.

Source & Additional Information: (https://www.washingtonexaminer.com/ news/1816444/white-house-sends-out-cheat-sheet-to-tout-bidens-record-on-two-year-anniversary/)

The memo claimed that Biden had lowered prices, noting that the cost of gas per gallon had decreased more than $1.60 compared to the previous year, and insulin was now capped at $35 per month for seniors on Medicare. The memo claimed that Biden had created "millions of jobs" and that 2021 and 2022 "were the two strongest years of job growth in history," with nearly eleven million jobs, including 750,000 manufacturing jobs created. The unemployment rate was near a 50-year low, and Black, Hispanic Americans, and people with disabilities were experiencing record-low unemployment; restored global alliances and rallied partners across the world to stand up to Russian aggression and support Ukraine; brought together Democrats and Republicans to pass the most sweeping gun safety law in nearly thirty years. The memo went on to state that Biden had confirmed judicial nominees that are the most diverse in history and appointed the first Black woman to serve on the United States Supreme Court, Justice Ketanji Brown Jackson; that Biden was leading a manufacturing boom, citing around $33 billion in investments from private companies such as $20 billion from Intel in Ohio, $100 billion from Micron in New York, and Hanwa Q CELLS announcing, "the largest single solar investment in U.S. history in Georgia." Impressive, but just more spinning of information, as the information was all taken out of context and was not the success story the White House proclaimed.

The memo went on to further state that "This is in contrast to MAGA Republicans in Congress who are creating chaos and proposing an extreme and divisive agenda that bans abortion nationwide without reasonable exceptions for rape, incest, or life of the mother; hiked taxes on the middle class by taxing thousands of everyday items from groceries to gas, while cutting taxes for the wealthiest Americans; raises gas prices and deprives Americans of relief at the pump in the future, all to benefit Big Oil which are already making record profits; and puts Social Security and Medicare on the chopping block." All total fabrication.

The "cheat sheet" did not mention the inflation rate, which stood at 6.5 percent and reached a four-decade high of 9.1 percent in June of 2022, or the federal deficit, which was $27.6 trillion when Biden took office but had escalated to $31.38 trillion; the border crisis was also omitted. For the twelve months ending September 30th, 2022, Customs and Border Protection officials reported stopping immigrants at the United States border around 2.4 million times for the twelve months ending Sept. 30th, 2022. The previous high was 1.66 million in 2021. The memo mentioned the United States' assistance to Ukraine. Still, it did not include that the Biden-Harris administration had committed more than $24.2 billion in security funding to Ukraine since Russia invaded the country in early 2022. With our massive aid to Kyiv, the United States is already in a proxy war with Russia. Currently, the war in Ukraine has become a war of attrition, with heavy casualties on both sides. Russia, with a larger population, has the advantage here. What happens when Ukraine runs out of soldiers? And then ....?

Source & Additional Information: (https://www.telegraph.co.uk/world-news/2023/04/27/joe-biden-yoon-suk-yeol-press-conference-cheat-sheet/)

In a speech at the White House to a bipartisan group of mayors in Washington for an annual meeting, Biden highlighted various legislation passed during his term. He spoke about the American Rescue Plan in March 2021, the Chips and Science Act in July 2022, the Inflation Reduction Act in August 2022, the nearly $13 billion gun control bill, and the $1 trillion infrastructure law. "Now, two years in, it's clearer than ever that our plan is working," Biden said, "We're building the economy from the bottom up and the middle out, not just the top down." Biden did not discuss the United States stock market's performance in his first two years. The S&P 500 Index had increased 1.2 percent since January 2021, while the Dow Jones Industrial Average had climbed 6 percent. Those numbers rank as the lowest equity market over the first two years of a president's term since George W. Bush was inaugurated in 2001. Among Democratic presidents, Biden's initial two years rates as the worst equity performance since Jimmy Carter led the nation when the S&P dropped 3.1 percent, and the Dows plummeted 12.7 percent after his inauguration on January 20th, 1977.

As for Joe Biden, his forty-plus-year history as a politician has shown to be that of a sociopath who has never done anything meaningful to support anything or anyone other than himself and his family. Joe Biden's popularity polls showed that even his Democrat base was not happy with the job he was doing and did not want to see him run for reelection. A Washington D.C. proverb states, "If a clown moves into a palace, it does not make him a king. It just makes the palace a circus."

Chapter 14
The Swamp

On March 26th, 2023, President Donald J Trump held a campaign rally in Waco, Texas, announcing his strong support of an Amendment to the Constitution for Term Limits. He recognizes that convening a Convention of State is the only path open to the United States citizenry to rein in our corrupt and incompetent government. He acknowledges that passing legislation calling for term limits on our federal officials will never happen because our elitist legislators from both parties would work together to put up a strong opposition against the passage of such a law. Neither Democrat nor Republican members of Congress will be very keen on being limited to their lucrative and elite positions. However, if such a law were enacted, it would immediately be contested in the court system. Such a law would be overthrown as unconstitutional, as Congress is not given the power to set term limits in the Constitution.

Lawsuits will immediately be filed to eliminate such a law; therefore, we can only have actual sustainable Term Limits through an amendment to our Constitution. If we can achieve the convening of a Convention of States, propose an amendment limiting the terms under which any individual can serve in federal office, and obtain the ratification by three-quarters of the states, then and only then can we have sustainable Term Limits. Yes, Congress may someday have the votes in both chambers to propose an amendment to the Constitution to repeal a Term Limiting Amendment. However, they will find it extraordinarily difficult to get three-quarters of states to ratify such an Amendment, given that Term limits are way too popular with the citizens of our country.

Term limits will significantly change how our congressional representatives govern, but there is an even more significant threat to our Constitutional Republic: the Washington bureaucracy (the swamp). The Constitution clarifies that the executive power of the government "is not vested in departments or agencies" but rather in the President of the United States. A President today assumes office to find a bloated federal bureaucracy that is carrying out the policies and agenda of the radical Marxist-Communists and the 'woke' faction of the country by entranced politically motivated employees determined to hinder any constructive reforms.

Every election cycle, politicians promise to balance the budget, pass term limits, restrict overreach, and reduce regulatory burdens. Then, after being elected, all their promises are ignored, forgotten, and broken, with both parties blaming the other party for their failures to keep those promises. We all know (Republicans, Democrats, Unaffiliated) that things are very wrong with our federal government. But we foolishly continue to believe that everything will somehow work itself out. We fool ourselves into believing that this election cycle will be different. This time, people of conscience, honor, and integrity will be elected. Individuals who will represent the people's will and ensure opportunity and prosperity for all Americans. After all these years of hoping, we must finally admit that the Washington bureaucracy will never fix itself, end its abuse of power, or overreach into State affairs. Their absurd manipulation and purposeful misinterpretation of the Constitution to satisfy their ideology must be stopped. We must stop:

- The General Welfare Clause from being misinterpreted and used to allow Congress to waste tax dollars.
- The crushing regulations on our economy due to the misuse of the Commerce Clause.
- The increasing of our national debt due to inappropriate spending on projects, bribes to foreign countries (referred to as foreign aid), and wars that have no genuine national security interest but are purely political.

- ➢ The weaponization of the Federal Judicial system and its power to attack political opponents.
- ➢ Congressional members, judicial officials, and the Supreme Court from acting on behalf of their behalf of their political well-being and not for the citizens of the United States.

It is time for the citizens of this great nation to recognize the need for significant changes within our federal government if we are to retain the rights provided to us by God and our Constitution. We must, without delay, totally disband the existing Department of Justice and FBI; determine the extent of their necessity at the federal level keeping in mind that experience over these last many years would indicate that these two agencies should not remain under federal authority, where they will always be vulnerable to being weaponized against political opponents. The real constitutional solution would be to rebuild these two elements of our justice system at the state level, which would be managed and controlled with built-in mechanisms to interact with every other state.

This has been echoed time and time again. American citizens must cease to be unwilling or afraid to take a stand against a tyrannical government that has manifested itself as a result of citizens' indifference and lack of involvement in our political processes. American citizens must stop habitually voting for the same party and the same candidates, who get nothing done for the people they represent, just because that is the way their family has consistently voted or because they recognize the candidates' names.

Voters must take the time to familiarize themselves with the Party Platform of both parties; research through multiple sources of opposing views each party's accomplishments to determine if those accomplishments meet their values and beliefs; research through various sources of opposing views each candidate running for office, whether, Democrat, Republican, or Independent, and learn about their position on issues that you are concerned about; then and only will they be truly ready to make an informed decision on who you believe will best represent you, your family and America. In this day and age, learning about each party's candidate's values and past political history can be easily researched on the internet, by watching a variety of news outlets with opposing viewpoints, and by not relying on the same news outlet religiously. Does this take time? Yes, but it is time well spent if you are genuinely concerned about keeping our Constitutional Republic as founded by the Founding Fathers, not only for yourself but for your children and grandchildren.

An entrenched bureaucracy seriously hampers the will of the people. Marxist-Communist Democrat administrations have infiltrated political appointees into high-career federal government positions, This meant that President Trump's appointees could not effect constitutional conservative reform policies due to strong push-back or slow-walking of such policies from entrenched Marxist-Communist political appointees of previous administrations. Appointees who were redesignated as career federal employees, placed in senior positions, and worked at undermining President Trump's reform initiatives. My experience as a federal senior manager affirms that many critical policy-making positions were handed out to these converted political appointees who usually had no expertise in the mission of their particular Department or Agency.

My experiences as a senior federal government manager, regarding discipling or removing federal employees for poor job performance, attitude, or misconduct, was that it was always a time-consuming uphill battle due to excessively friendly employee laws, regulations, and federal government employee unions. As a result, many government supervisors and managers have given up on addressing negative employee issues, and these low-performing employees remain in their positions, damaging that Department's or Agencies' public opinion and overall satisfaction ratings. This aspect of employee management must be reformed, or, with a few exceptions, the federal Departments' and agencies' overall client performance approval will always be substandard to similar private sector corporations. Federal employees are often awarded bonuses regardless of performance and receive annual pay increases automatically rather than based on performance. To make matters worse, federal managers cannot screen applicants for basic qualifications such as intelligence. President Jimmy Carter eliminated the requirement of civil service IQ examinations based on the claim that IQ tests were racist. The only thing racist about this claim is Jimmy Carter's assumption that people of color's IQs were substandard to other citizens. Further, significant changes are needed to restrict the power of public-sector unions, which, much like teachers' unions, wield far too much power; the salaries of federal employees must also be reformed to bring them more in line with private-sector workers performing identical functions; reassign senior federal employees whose assignment to key policy-making positions were the result of a political appointment to non-policy making positions or positions which cannot influence policies being implemented under a new administration.

Federal employees receive wages twenty-two percent higher than workers in similar private sector positions, according to a 2016 Heritage Foundation study. With the value of employee benefits factored in, that ratio rises between thirty percent and forty percent. An American Enterprise Institute study found a fourteen percent pay premium and a sixty-one percent total compensation premium. They receive more vacation and paid sick leave, retire earlier (generally at age 55 after 30 years), enjoy richer pension annuities, and receive automatic cost-of-living adjustments based on where they retire. Congressional members in the House of Representatives have supported the legislation in the past years to increase the weight of performance over time of service in the federal bureaucracy. But as can be expected of the 'go along, to get along' Republicans, they caved into fierce opposition from unions rather than doing the right thing. They fear union retaliation in the form of union members getting out the vote in opposition to any congressional member who voted in favor of such a bill. This is a prime example of why 'term limits' are so essential, as 'term limits' would eliminate the union's leverage over elected officials and, for that matter, any other entity lobbying Congress for inappropriate support.

Source & Additional Information: (https://www.heritage.org/jobs-and-labor/report/why-it-time-reform-compensation-federal-employees) (https://fee.org/articles/a-look-at-pay-for-federal-employees-compared-to-their-private-sector-counterparts/)

Trump signed an executive order in 2018 requiring agencies to speed up correcting, disciplining, or firing employees who underperform. Still, Marxist-Communist Democrat President Joe Biden overturned that order. If a private-sector employee faces termination, they have a simple two-step process to appeal their termination, while federal employees facing termination have a wealth of options by which to appeal that termination, which can drag out for months while that employee continues to underperform or create chaos among the staff. They can appeal to the Equal Employment Opportunity Commission, the Merit Systems Protection Board, the Federal Labor Relations Authority, or the Office of Special Counsel. Public sector unions are why and how the federal bureaucracy has become entrenched with poor-performing, disruptive, unreliable employees. Democratic President Franklin D. Roosevelt considered federal government union representation incompatible with democracy, partly because strikes would amount to acts against the people. Yet Democrat President Jimmy Carter set public-sector bargaining in law as part of an agreement with Congress to pass the Civil Service Reform Act of 1978. Over time, federal managers' ability to take disciplinary action, when warranted, has been increasingly limited. Action must be taken to reinstitute and strengthen supervisors' and managers' authority to act against poor employee performance or disruptive behavior if America is to have a reliable, functional governing system.

Source & Additional Information: (https://www.congress.gov/bill/95th-congress/senate-bill/2640)

A strong-willed conservative president, such as Donald Trump, is desperately needed to counter the influence of Marxist-Communist bureaucrats who have entrenched themselves as career civil servants. The president, not career civil servants, is responsible for enforcing laws. Therefore, career civil servants do not have the Constitutional authority to make significant policy changes and reforms within the federal government. In October 2020, Trump created a new category of federal employees, Schedule F Employees. His executive order directed agency heads to prepare a list of federal employees in "positions of a confidential, policy-determining, policymaking, or policy-advocating character that are not normally subject to change as a result of a Presidential transition." The order created exceptions from civil service rules for careerists who hold such positions, allowing agency heads to identify and transfer these limited position employees, making them functionally serving at the will of the sitting president and thus much easier to fire.

Source & Additional Information: (https://trumpwhitehouse.archives.gov/presidential-actions/executive-order-creating-schedule-f-excepted-service/) (https://www.govexec.com/workforce/2024/04/opm-issues-final-rule-schedule-f-protections/395463/)

Chapter 15
Soros And Globalism

A Hungarian-born naturalized United States citizen, George Soros survived the holocaust and has personally stated in interviews that when the Germans invaded, his father explained to him that this was a "lawless occupation" where normal rules no longer applied. "You have to forget how you behave in normal society," his father said. Soros added that he was "adopted by an official of the Ministry of Agriculture, whose job was to take over Jewish properties, so I went with him, and we took possession of these large estates. That was my identity." Soros is now a ninety-plus-year-old multi-billionaire who founded and chaired the Open Society Foundations, which provides financial support to Marxist-Communist society groups worldwide. Over the years, Soros has donated more than $32 billion of his fortune to support and advocate for Marxist-Communism worldwide financially.

George Soros has now turned his full attention to the United States. He is providing political funding to candidates at all levels of government, in particular District Attorneys, who are highly far-left Marxist-Communists. He supports candidates who are willing to undermine the United States Constitution and the laws of the United States. For example, Soros funds the campaigns of District Attorneys who are soft on crime, who are willing to release violent rioters and criminals back into society to cause turmoil and chaos throughout the United States, and who are willing to show total loyalty to his Marxist-Communist agenda. Alvin Bragg is a product of Soros funding, which propelled him to the Manhattan District Attorney's office.

Soros puts a lot of money into political causes, pretending to be 'charities', to avoid paying taxes. Here are Soros' Top Nine causes and their portion of the $21 billion he has 'invested' since 2000. That is almost a billion dollars per year, not to help the poor or build anything constructive to help the needy, *but to destroy our Constitutional Republic and all it stands for.*

- Democracy Pac II - $175 million, owned by Soros;
- Democracy Pac - $184,000, also owned by Soros;
- Democrat National Conference Services Corporation - $1.54 million;
- Color of Change - $1 million;
- Justice and Public Safety (the funding source for woke prosecutors) - $569,000;
- Democratic Senatorial Campaign Commission - $505,000;
- Forward Majority Action - $200,000;
- State Level Democrats campaigns;
- Build Our Movement (funding source for federal level Democrat candidates) $200,000.

Soros also funds hundreds of media groups to promote Marxist-Communist causes, all of whom quote the same Marxist-Communist talking points. Why is this man allowed to pervert the system like this? Why is his naturalized United States citizenship not being revoked, and he be deported as a threat to the nation? Why is our government not considering this fanatical Marxist-Communist a 'clear and present danger' to the United States? Why does he not pay federal taxes like any other American citizen when he promotes taxpayer-funded Marxist-Communist programs? The answer is clear enough: he is the financial arm of the Marxist-Communist movement and is protected by the Marxist-Communist Democrat Party and Washington elites.

George Soros' time on earth is quickly drawing to an end, and it has been hoped by conservatism around the world that with his passing, his ideological influence and financial support of those ideologies would come to an end. Unfortunately, George Soros' son, Alexander Soros, is an ideological image of his billionaire father. Thirty-seven-year-old Alexander Soros has repeatedly stated that he fully intends to carry on his father's legacy and continue financially supporting the transformation of the United States from a Constitutional Republic into a Marxist-Communist nation. To this end, Alexander Soros has quietly become a Soros' White House "ambassador," making at least fourteen visits on behalf of his Marxist-Communist father during the Biden-Harris Administration, as verified by reviews of White House records by The Post.

Alexander Soros is a prolific Marxist-Communist Democrat fundraiser in his own right, who continuously boasts about his relationship with the Biden-Harris White House and Administration. According to White House visitor logs, Alexander Soros has participated in numerous meetings with White House staff and has attended lavish state dinners hosted by the Biden's. Alexander Soros now chairs the powerful Open Society Foundations network. According to White House visitor records, he has been meeting with the Advisor Counselor of the President, Mariana Adame, and the Deputy National Security Advisor, Jonathan Finer. Alexander Soros also met with Kimberly Lang, a National Security Advisor executive assistant, and former advisor Madeline Strasser. White House records show an expansive list of Alexander Soros' meetings with top White House officials.

Source & Additional Information: (https://www.washingtonexaminer.com/news/white-house/3155403/alex-soros-white-house-biden-two-dozen-visits/)

Ike Howell, director of the Oversight Project at the Conservative Heritage Foundation, said the younger Soros' easy White House access is troubling considering the Soros family has already "done tremendous damage to our country. The Soros agenda is one of death and destruction in the name of open borders and the ending of Western Civilization as we know it. The Biden-Harris administration and rogue prosecutors may be Alexander Soros' most damaging purchases in America to date." According to Matt Palumbo, author of "The Man Behind the Curtain: Inside the Secret Network of George Soros, the Soros family's influence over White House policy has never been more substantial. There is a Soros hold somewhere throughout the White House, and Alexander is his father's new ambassador," Palumbo told The Post.

Source & Additional Information: (https://www.amazon.com/Man-Behind-Curtain-Inside-Network/dp/163758332X)

George Soros donated over a million dollars in 2021 to the Marxist-Communist Color of Change political action committee that backed Alvin Bragg, the Manhattan district attorney who convened the grand jury that indicted Trump in late March of 2023, which then led to Trump being charged and arrested. Those charges concerned alleged hush-money payment and business records inaccuracies. Soros, whose contributions to Color of Change are part of a larger effort to finance a criminal justice revolution aimed at abolishing bail and the defunding of police, supported Bragg's campaign directly without even personally knowing the soft-on-crime District Attorney candidate. Alexander Soros is more open about his political involvement in the radical Marxist-Communist movement. Alexander Soros has donated more than $11 million to Marxist-Communist political action committees since 2010, including $2 million in 2018 to the United States Senate Majority PAC that Democrat Majority Leader Chuck Schumer has a significant amount of influence over. A review of Alexander's Instagram page shows that he has met with Schumer at least nine times since 2018 and former Marxist-Communist Democrat House Speaker Nancy Pelosi eight times. Alexander Soros' publicly released photos show him with former President Barack Obama, Vice President Kamala Harris, and other prominent Democrats at his hosted fundraisers. Scoring fourteen White House meetings in a little over a year suggests that Alexander Soros had "an outsize policy influence in the Biden-Harris administration," equaling the easy access given to American Federation of Teachers President Randi Weingarten, said Tom Fitton, president of the conservative legal watchdog group Judicial Watch. Fitton added that George Soros is pursuing an "aggressive environmental agenda," open-border initiatives, and other far-left causes. Alexander's visits to the White House are made as a representation of his father, who is still calling the shots. Until George Soros's death, it was his money and foundations that funded the Biden-Harris Administration's movement toward the transformation of the United States' governing system from a capitalist system to a Marxist-Communist form of governing. "Like his father, Alexander cozies up to White House and congressional leaders willing to do the family's bidding on such issues as crime, immigration, and election policy, as the Soros' exploit every type of donation avenues to help fund Marxist-Communist events, groups, and so-called charities," according to the Washington Examiner, which first documented the White House trips.

Globalism: Which do you prefer, a Sovereign Nation or a Globalist Nation? The term 'global citizen' seems so "with it," so "cosmopolitan," and more "evolved." Why be a simple American in a simple nation? Globalism is much more appealing to the highly educated and indoctrinated. These people envision a utopian-one-world happy place where we can all sing kumbaya together, pass the vape pipe, and contemplate the possibilities of multiple universes. The likes of the Bush family, billionaires such as Fink, Bloomberg, Zuckerberg, and Soros, and environmentalist tyrants such as John Kerry, seem to assume that it is their God-given mission to save the planet by reducing mankind's carbon footprint and reversing the rising number of pesky invasive species such as human beings. They despise God's design for a family consisting of one male father and one female mother.

In the thirties and forties, it was the third Reich eliminating the Jewish population, and now it is Marxist-Communist high-tech ideologists, Marxist-Communist elitists, and environmentalists, along with radical Marxist-Communist corporates that seek to socially and judicially eliminate anyone who disagrees with them.

We are in a culture war. Freedom is at stake. Social domination is the goal of the opposition. They are set on creating a global "consciousness" where no voice rises in protest to their dark agenda. They seek to cancel those who disagree with their planet-first ideology and anti-family, anti-religious values. They falsely accuse the innocent to incite violence against whole groups of people. They tactfully and maliciously label their targets as "deplorables," "domestic terrorists," and, yes, "insurrectionists." They particularly despise the crowd that believes God created genders and marriage. The only thing standing in the way of their "progressive" agenda is the United States Constitution and those who stand behind the Constitution regardless of political affiliation. Suppose you believe this mindset is just an anomaly in mainstream America. In that case, you are ignoring the staff infection, making a beeline straight for the heart of our national heritage. They want you to forget about being a plain old American, stating that such mind-sets are so outdated. Think of all the supposed prominence you could gain from such a global-residential status.

<u>Source & Additional Information</u>: *(https://www.thenation.com/article/culture/tara-zahra-against-world-globalism/)*

The Marxist-Communist Globalist's war with the United States Constitution is that the Constitution identifies each of us as a Sovereign citizen within Sovereign States within a Sovereign Country with God-given rights to life, liberty, and the freedom to pursue happiness. Marxist-Communist Globalists want us to question the Constitution's worth in today's lonely, virtual world. Marxist-Communist Globalists say it is a hindrance to America's growth as a contributing member of 'modern' world society. There is a constant drumbeat calling for its destruction in malicious comments like, "Can't we just do away with the Constitution already!" It shows up in the actions of those who willfully and traitorously turn their back on the Pledge of Allegiance, who kneel for the national anthem and tread on the blood-bought sacrifice of freedom. These traitorous actions are most notable on nationally televised sports programs. Dictators around the world wholeheartedly encourage this public display of American national defiance and self-destruction. Why wouldn't they? It makes the most powerful country on earth weak from within, and that's key to conquering America. Dictators do not fear our military as much as they do armed citizens unified in their devotion to national allegiance. This brings to mind Brittany Griner, a national basketball star who was arrested in Mother Russia for drug possession and was immediately imprisoned in a Russian prison under inhumane conditions.

This self-proclaimed anti-American Marxist-Communist was released back to the United States in late June of 2023, and who, as someone who consistently kneeled or raised a fist during the singing of our National Anthem, is now a confirmed American who cannot praise America's Constitutional way of life enough.

FOX News recently reported on a video taken inside a California restaurant that went viral on the internet and caused a meltdown within the Marxist-Communist Globalist woke crowd. The video depicted a crowd of patriotic customers inside a California restaurant, all proudly standing for the National Anthem being played by the restaurant's owner. This was in California, of all places, and it drew a slew of responses from anti-American Marxist-Communists. Comments ranged from such statements as being inside that restaurant. At the same time, The Star-Spangled Banner was being played would be their worst nightmare; being forced to listen to that song would be terrifying, and some responders compared it to being in a horror film. So many comments were made, filled with hate and disgust. Childish federally spoiled Marxist-Communist Globalists who would disrespect our National Anthem, forgetting the sacrifices made by so many of our service men and women over the years to ensure we never lost our rights under our Constitution and their right to comment on that internet video feed regarding their feeling without fear of reprisal. Those uneducated fools who disparage the National Anthem, which pays homage to our heritage, are no more than the products of our failed federally funded school system, which failed to teach them of America's uniqueness and greatness among the countries around the world.

Source & Additional Information: (https://www.foxnews.com/media/people-standing-national-anthem-horrifies-progressives-viral-video-dangerous-situation)

We are living with a whole army of Marxist-Communist Globalist fools who suffer from intellectual stupidity, spiritual wickedness, and dark hearts. Spiritually evil people bloodthirsty for power who need fools, mockers, and simpletons to carry out their malicious agenda. America is struggling from within to save its Christian, one-nation-under-God heritage. If America loses this fight against the Marxist-Communist Globalist agenda, our rights will then come from men who are prone to self-service rather than to self-sacrifice. Our relationships form the center of our identity and protection. Our national and state identities protect our rights as members of those social concepts. If we become global citizens, our strength of identity will be diluted to one in five billion.

In a Marxist-Communist Globalist world, we become a number that needs to be managed rather than a unique and sovereign soul with certain inalienable rights. So, should another pandemic arrive, if the disease does not kill you, non-compliance could. Global domination is the goal of the spiritual evil. God, Christian conservatives, and the United States Constitution are the buffers preventing their advancement. China is the perfect example of this dark enterprise. Xi Jinping thinks nothing of killing those who will not worship him. The United States Constitution is a life raft in an ocean of godless globalism, and I strongly recommend you learn it, live by it, and defend it with your life. The Convention of States Action organization is working tirelessly to pass Resolutions in thirty-four states to convene a Convention of States under Article V of the Constitution to reign in these Marxist-Communist globalists' unconstitutional actions to push us ever closer to globalism. The Convention of States Action organization needs our help to motivate state legislators to pass this Resolution to stop anti-American Marxist-Communist attempts to globalize America by your willingness to take a moment to make phone calls and send letters to your State Representatives and Senators demanding that they pass a Resolution to convene a Convention of States. Thomas Jefferson wisely articulated that we must educate the whole mass of people to keep our freedoms and liberties safe. State congressional leaders collectively have the power to reform the federal government and save our sovereign Constitutional Republic through an Article V convention. They need to act now and legislate with the forethought necessary to restrain heavy-handed Marxist-Communist federal administrative power. The closer constitutional power is to the people, the safer it will be because freedom is much harder to gain than maintain. Unaccountable, self-regulating, back-door bureaucracies are taking away power from the sovereign States and the people therein for themselves. They are dangerous. Tell your state leaders to pass resolutions calling for an Article V convention to use the Constitution to protect the sovereignty of the individual States and the citizens therein.

Source & Additional Information: (https://www.jstor.org/stable/26575598)

Chapter 16
Marxist-Communist

You do not need a political science degree from Cornell to know that forces within the United States are attempting to change American tradition, heritage, and culture. Non-elected woke entities use strategies to alter our lives, such as Diversity, Equity, and Inclusion (DEI), critical race theory (CRT), environmental, social, and governance (ESG) peddling, and woke mandates. State governments, particularly state legislatures, are going into overdrive to introduce a raft of bills to defeat DEI, CRT, and ESG. Florida and Texas are leading the way in this initiative, hopefully spreading nationwide. Missouri and Arizona have introduced similar bills that defend the constitutional rights and authorities under the Constitution. Even Congress is getting in on the act: Two anti-Critical Race Theory bills have been introduced in the Senate and the House of Representatives.

<u>Source & Additional Information</u>: *(https://www.whitehouse.gov/briefing-room/presidential-actions/2021/06/25/executive-order-on-diversity-equity-inclusion-and-accessibility-in-the-federal-workforce/) (https://www.britannica.com/topic/critical-race-theory/Basic-tenets-of-critical-race-theory) (https://www.financestrategists.com/wealth-management/esg/)*

State efforts, however, have a much better chance of passing such legislation than those introduced by the federal Senate and sponsored by Republican Senator Tom Cotton of Arkansas and Republican member of the House Dan Bishop of North Carolina. State legislators are also closer to their constituents, better able to represent their views, and less burdened by the type of permanent bureaucratic "swamp rats" that have so distorted the legislative power of Congress. The effects of their legislative efforts are also more immediate to the public. That is why it is so important to celebrate the United States' fifty laboratories of democracy, each of which is constantly living and growing, allowing for the formulation of different ideas and policies to work out issues and problems of governing at the state level.

Source & Additional Information: (https://ballotpedia.org/Laboratories_of_democracy)

To understand the significance of these legislative efforts, it is essential to understand the threat to our national unity and the preservation of American civic order that the Marxist-Communist Democrat Party agenda poses with what they refer to as DEI. Diversity, defined in the traditional sense, is a plus if obtained naturally due to colorblind equality of opportunity. But in today's jargon, it means coercive racial quotas, which are against federal law. When a public institution pursues diversity, it will never again accomplish anything worthwhile. In the federal government employee force, 'diversity' means 'we are putting in unqualified people and pretending they add value.' Diversity is a means by which to subsidize incompetence. Equity, meanwhile, has perversely come to mean government taking account of race, not need, when handing out benefits, the opposite of the American ideal of equality. Inclusion now means exclusion, as it pushes out anyone whose ideas and ideologies do not fit the Marxist-Communist Democrat Party's narrative. Critical race theory is a body of thought that seeks to revolutionize society by deconstructing the American system, which it sees as the platform of "systemic racism," and replacing it with something that looks a lot like central planning and other Marxist-Communist Democrat Party catchwords. Environmental, Social, and Governance (ESG) principles might be the least understood. It is a way for the woke Chief Executive Officers (CEOs) of large fund managers to force corporations into markets aligning with Marxist-Communist liberal agendas, be it the boycott of investment in fossil fuel industries in support of Climatism or the financial disclosure of racial quotas. Climatism is a form of anti-capitalism.

Vanguard, State Street, and BlackRock are fund managers pushing ESG ventures. They are mammoth institutions, managing almost as much money as the entire United States' gross domestic product. West Virginia and Tennessee, among others, have taken the fight to ESG by announcing that fund managers boycotting fossil fuels will not be allowed to manage their state pension funds. Highly trained groups, meanwhile, are pushing DEI at our major universities, companies, sports leagues, etc. Most of the administrators of our cultural institutions, as well as entertainers, teachers, college professors, and journalists, now push the CRT revolution. It becomes more evident with each passing day that federally funded institutions we all grew up believing in have become woke and bogus. They are either incompetent or out and out corrupt. From federal-level law enforcement agencies to our education and social service agencies, none of them any longer deserve our trust and respect. Instead, American citizens must be vigilant and look out for themselves and their families. All these federal agencies we have been putting our trust in have been compromised on some level and are not doing the jobs they were created to do. The well-being of the American people is no longer their concern.

Affordable Care Act: America's trip down the road to Marxism began in the 1930s with Franklin D. Roosevelt's "New Deal," was expanded upon in 1964 with the introduction of President Lyndon B. Johnson's "Great Society," then in 2008, Barack Obama promised to forever fundamentally transform America if elected as the President of the United States. Barack Obama won the election and began to implement his promise. What the majority of Americans failed to realize and understand is that Barack Obama's promise meant changing America from a Constitutional Republic into a Marxist-Communist Nation.

Source & Additional Information: (https://pubmed.ncbi.nlm.nih.gov/25731135/)

A clear and dramatic move towards further solidifying America as a Marxist-Communist Nation came with the signing into law of President Obama's Affordable Care Act, officially known as the Patient Protection and Affordable Care Act and informally known as Obamacare. This unconstitutional act of federalizing America's health care system was signed into law on March 23, 2010, causing a radical overhaul of America's health care services and insurance markets. It was pieced together in backroom negotiation deals through bribes as inducements to both Marxist-Communist Democrat and Republican party members of Congress to support this massive takeover of our health care system. This approximately one-thousand-page law was passed with absolutely no transparency. It included billions of dollars in earmarked (pork barrel) money to reluctant members of Congress for their support. Lawmakers were only provided twenty-four hours to read this bill before voting on its passage. When questioned about what was in the bill, then-Speaker Nancy Pelosi famously advised the members of Congress and "We the People" that the measure would need to be passed into law before we could know what was in the bill—a statement one would expect from a ruling member of a Marxist-Communist country.

Insurers were now mandated to accept all applicants without charging based on preexisting conditions or demographic status. Insurers were further mandated to cover a list of ambiguous "essential health benefits." The Marxist-Communist Democrat Party's Affordable Care Act mandates that all new medical health insurance policies sold to individuals and families include:

- The prohibiting of insurers from denying coverage to individuals due to preexisting conditions.

- The requirement that states ensure the availability of insurance for individual children who do not have coverage via their families.

- The allowing of premiums to vary only by age and location, regardless of preexisting conditions.

- That premiums for older applicants can be no more than three times those for the youngest.

- That essential health care benefits must be provided. (*The National Academy of Medicine defines the law's "essential health benefits" as "ambulatory patient services; emergency services; hospitalization; maternity and newborn care; mental health and substance use disorder services, including behavioral health treatment; prescription drugs; rehabilitative and habilitative services and devices; laboratory services; preventive and wellness services and chronic disease management; pediatric services, and includes oral and vision care.)*

➢ Preventive care and screenings for women.

➢ All Food and Drug Administration-approved contraceptive methods, sterilization procedures, and patient education and counseling for all women with reproductive capacity.

➢ Annual and lifetime coverage caps on essential benefits.

➢ The forbidden of insurers from dropping policyholders when they become ill.

➢ Imposing a yearly maximum out-of-pocket payment cap for an individual's or family's medical expenses. (*After the maximum out-of-pocket payment is reached, the insurer must pay all remaining costs.*)

➢ Preventive care, vaccinations, and medical screenings cannot be subject to co-payments or deductibles. (*Specific examples of covered services include mammograms and colonoscopies, wellness visits, gestational diabetes screening, HPV testing, sexually transmitted infection counseling, HIV screening and counseling, contraceptive methods, breastfeeding support/supplies, and domestic violence screening and counseling.*)

➢ The establishment of four tiers of coverage: bronze, silver, gold, and platinum. (*All categories offer essential health benefits. The categories vary in their division of premiums and out-of-pocket costs: bronze plans have the lowest monthly premiums and highest out-of-pocket costs, while platinum plans are the reverse.)*

- Insurers requirement to implement an appeals process for coverage determination and claims on all new plans.
- That insurers must spend at least 80–85% of premium dollars on health costs; rebates must be issued if this is violated.

This act further sponsored federally provided health care insurance and mandated that individuals buy insurance or pay a fine/tax (*originally, the bill referred to failure to buy insurance as a fine. When this terminology was challenged in the courts as unconstitutional, Congress redefined this charge as a tax.) This mandate was intended to increase the size and diversity of the insured population, including more young and healthy participants, to broaden the risk pool and spread the costs. All are unconstitutional and, if provided, belong to the sovereign states to decide on enacting.*

<u>Congressional Republican MIA</u>: And where were the Republican members of Congress? The party whose platform commits to protecting the Constitution as written and intended by the Founding Fathers and protecting our Constitutional Republic. The party whose platform commits to restricting government spending and governing within a balanced budget. The party whose platform commits to ending federal government overreach. Where were they when our Republic most needed them? They were standing alongside of their Marxist-Communist Democrat Party members in getting this bill passed. These morally weak and spineless Republican members of Congress feared being called racist by the far-left propaganda arm of the Marxist-Communist Democrat Party's news outlets, should they dare oppose the first black American President's agenda. These spineless Republican members of Congress voted with the

Marxist-Communist Democrat Party, knowing it was the wrong thing to do and that this legislation was clearly unconstitutional.

Not surprisingly, once the bill was passed and the election session rolled around, the Republican Party had a "Jesus" moment and campaigned on the promise that if they managed to take control of all three branches of the government, they would make it a priority to repeal the Affordable Care Act. Well, the Republicans took control of Congress and the White House in 2016, providing them the opportunity to defang this Marxist-Communist Democrat Party takeover of America's health care system. As experience has taught us over the years, Republican Party members of Congress once again broke their promise. They made no attempts to repeal the Affordable Care Act out of fear of the Marxist-Communist Democrat Party news media and backlash from woke corporations, big tech, and woke social media. Be damn the Constitution and be damn their constituents.

Far too many Republican members of Congress are unwilling to put their reelection on the line to make the sacrifices necessary to rein in the Marxist-Communist Democrat Party and save our Constitutional Republic. America has watched and endured years of Republican congressional members breaking their promises and commitments to their constituents, being more concerned with not upsetting the Washington Marxist-Communist elitists and their elitist status within the Washington establishment of evil and corruption. Republican congressional members so quickly ignored the fact that they were elected to Congress to work for the good of the people and the country, not the good of the party or their personal status and greed.

So, the question remains: when will Republican leadership at all levels of government finally find the courage and backbone to start fighting back against the lawless America-hating Marxist-Communist Democrat Party? When will Republican lawmakers stop believing that appeasing those who are out to destroy our Republic will somehow change their evil intentions and gain their cooperation? Why do they continue to believe in something that years of experience dictates otherwise? You cannot be civil and accommodating to a radical Marxist-Communist Democrat Party whose agenda it is to eliminate the Republican party to achieve a one-party governing system. Republicans and conservatives must learn to fight these arbitrators of hate and evil like street fighters. We must be willing to strike back in the same manner that the Marxist-Communist Democrat Party strikes out against conservatives. Be damn with the "high road" when the "high road" will only lead to the demise of our Constitutional Republic.

Because the Marxist-Communist Democrat Party feels assured that the Republican Party will always take the "high road," they believe that they are beginning to silence and end the political career of Donald Trump. They believe that through false accusations and constant phony charges being levied against Trump by Soros-backed District Attorneys, Republican voters will choose the "high road" and abandon Trump. They just do not get it. American Republican conservative voters, unlike their Grand Old Party Republican Representatives and Senators, will never abandon Trump, and they know that Trump will never abandon his love for America and its citizens. Trump has no problems ignoring the "high road" philosophy when appropriate. If you are stupid enough to attack Trump, he will embrace that attack as a challenge and attack back twice as hard.

But he must not be made to stand alone; now is the time for all Republicans to stand by his side and fight back with brutal counterattacks. Republicans in the House must begin by impeaching Anthony Blinken and Merritt Garland for gross misconduct, derelict of their constitutional obligation, criminal corrupt activities, and, in some cases, outright treason. The Democrat judges in Washington, D.C., who grossly violated the civil rights of January 6th defendants, must be removed from the bench for knowingly and willingly ignoring the rights of these

American citizens under the 5th, 6th, and 8th Amendments to the Constitution.

Marxist-Communist Destruction: Wal-Mart is closing both of its Portland, Oregon stores. This is where looting and rioting are considered a local pastime, and shoplifters do not get prosecuted. In Marxist-Communist Democrat-controlled Portland, city leadership does not seem to be able to grasp the concept that businesses are there to make a profit and not there to watch their merchandise being stolen by local tugs. Portland is just one of many cities being devastated and destroyed by Marxist-Communist ideology. These Marxist-Communist Democrat city officials did not just waltz in; ignorant and government-dependent greedy voters elected them. The people of Portland have no one to blame but themselves.

A girls' basketball team in Vermont forfeited a game against a team that had a transgender player. As athletes, these girls love the sport but took a heroic and courageous stand rather than submit to the travesty that is being perpetrated against women's sports by the absurd Marxist-Communist Woke mentality. Well, the full power of the Vermont Marxist-Communist Woke Machine kicked in, and these girls have been indefinitely suspended from participating in any further competition. All these young ladies were asking for was a 'level playing field.' This should not be allowed to stand, but of course, it will because these girls come from a very small Christian high school and these young Christian girls had to be taught a lesson.

House Minority Leader Hakeem Jeffries, an idiot among idiots, said that men in women's sports is an issue that does not exist. This individual is just another hack from Brooklyn, but is he that stupid? Jeffries made this ludicrous comment on the heels of a sad story of a female volleyball player who was playing against a transgender male. The transgender player spiked a ball at seventy miles per hour and struck the female player in the head, causing a concussion and other injuries. The injured girl could not play sports for months. Transgender people must understand that their decisions must come with limitations.

The Dodgers announced on May 4th,2023, that the team would bestow a "Community Hero Award" on the Los Angeles chapter of the Sisters of Perpetual Indulgence for "their countless hours of community service, ministry, and outreach to those on the edges, in addition to promoting human rights and respect for diversity and spiritual enlightenment." The Los Angeles Dodgers celebrated a group of drag queen performers who mock Christianity, Roman Catholicism in particular, by dressing up as sexualized nuns and even sexualizing Jesus himself. Marxist-Communist is not coming to America, folks – it is already here!

Chapter 17
Bankrupting America

Republicans campaigned against irresponsible and uncontrollable government spending and emphatically promised to end this reckless spending if elected. During campaigning for the 2022 mid-term elections, Republican Minority Leader Kevin McCarthy announced his "Commitment to America." This "Commitment to America" promised that if the Republicans won back the House, fiscal discipline would be its top priority. Well, Republicans won the House, so you would think they would remember their "Commitment to America" and begin curtailing wasteful spending.

<u>Source & Additional Information</u>: *(https://nypost.com/2022/09/27/the-gops-commitment-to-america-can-work-if-republicans-actually-run-on-the-issues/)*

***Earmarks*:** The most incredible federal waste of taxpayer dollars is 'Earmarks' referred to as 'pork barrel money.' 'Pork barrel' is a term used in politics referring to vast amounts of money allocated to congressional members for their use within their districts to impress their constituents and gain reelection. It is money used to entice Representatives or Senators to vote in favor of legislation they have indicated that they would not support; to provide funding to state governors for their pet projects to gain their support for federal government overreach initiatives that degrade State sovereignty; to payoff donors and supporters; and to fund pet projects within their districts to win reelections. The idea behind the practice is that the money allocated to the representative's district will benefit the lives of the local constituents, which, in most cases, is a false assumption. Support in this context typically means money provided through contracts with big business donors, family members, and personal friends, with a percentage returned to the lawmaker as a kick-back.

Precisely what 'Earmarks' means, and the impact "Earmarks" have on our national debt is not well understood or known to most voters. 'Earmarks' provide the illusion that their congressional Representator or Senator is looking out for them by supposedly securing money on their behalf. However, "Earmark' money is usually obtained for projects and initiatives that will benefit very few constituents but are instead intended as a form of payoff to donors, lobbyists, friends, and family members, but not the constituents within the District. Far too much of these tax dollars somehow seem to find its way into the pockets of congressional members increasing their wealth. Ever wonder how a member of Congress goes to Washington with a financial wealth comparable to that of the average middle-class American citizen and is paid an annual salary of $174,000 annually? After a few short years, their financial wealth is in the millions of dollars. "Earmarks" is one of the many questionable sources of that newfound wealth.

An infamous example of pork barrel politics is the tunnel project nicknamed the "Big Dig" in Boston, where a 3.5-mile highway was planned to be relocated underground. The Speaker of the House at the time, Thomas "Tip" O'Neill Jr., initiated the project in 1982 by directing federal funds "pork barrel money" to the tunnel project. The original budget of $3 billion was significantly exceeded, and the project was finally completed in 2007 at nearly $15 billion. All for a tunnel that was merely convenient for the residents of Boston and not a necessity and completed by construction firms who donated money to O'Neill's reelection campaign.

Source & Additional Information: (https://en.wikipedia.org/wiki/Big_Dig)

In less than a month after winning the House, Speaker McCarthy and the Republican party broke their promise and unreservedly embraced earmarks. On November 30th, 2022, House Republicans voted overwhelmingly against a proposal to ban earmarks by a vote of 158-2. This disproportionate vote favoring pork-barrel spending is symptomatic of Washington's out-of-touch approach to governing by Democrats and Republicans. It is not suitable for a Republican party that committed to restricting federal spending but has consistently done the opposite. How much longer will it take before American voters realize that politicians of either party will never keep their promises to balance the budget and end 'Earmarks,' both of which are bringing America ever closer to bankruptcy and the total erosion of State sovereignty? The only way to stop the addicted spending by Congress is through a new amendment to the Constitution via the convening of a Convention of States, which is being championed by the Convention of States Action movement addressed in Chapter 24.

Merry Christmas: On December 22nd, 2022, our corrupt government (AKA Santa Claus) gave the citizens of America a wonderful Christmas gift and Republicans a going-away kick-in-the-butt gift. Before heading home for the holidays, Congress passed a $1.7 trillion omnibus package. It was so important that we receive this gift before the holidays ended that the bill was flown by private jet to the Virgin Islands so Joe Biden could sign it into law. Merry Christmas and Happy New Year's from your corrupt government to one and all. Just like President Obama's "Affordable Care Act," this bankrupting package, mostly "pork," was pushed through Congress at lightning speed. Given this omnibus package was more than 4,000 pages, and members of Congress were only allowed twenty-four hours to read this 4,000-page bill, you can rest assured that Congressional members voted "yes" without having read the bill. Remember in 2010 when "Ex" Speaker of the House, Nancy Pelosi, said we must pass the proposed health care reform bill to find out what was in it? Well, here we go again. That statement by Pelosi was mocked back then; now, it is how Washington does business.

This $1.7 trillion omnibus bill passed the House with the help of nine anti-conservative and anti-American Marxist-Communist Republicans who joined the Marxist-Communist Democrats in helping get this bill passed. Those nine members were Fred Upton of Michigan, Liz Cheney of Wyoming, Adam Kinzinger and Rodney Davis of Illinois, Chris Jacobs and John Katko of New York, Brian Fitzpatrick of Pennsylvania, Jaime Herrera Butler of Washington State, and Steve Womack of Arkansas. A number of these individuals, well-known Marxist-Communist Republicans, voted for this bill not because they felt it was in the best interest of the country and its citizens but rather out of revenge and hatred for President Trump and to "go along to get along" with their Marxist-Communist Democrat Party comrades.

Senate Minority Leader Mitch McConnell and eighteen of his fellow Marxist-Communist Republican Senators: Roy Blunt, Missouri; John Boozman, Arkansas; Shelley Moore Capito, West Virginia; Susan Collins, Maine; John Cornyn, Texas; Tom Cotton, Arkansas; Lindsey Graham, South Carolina; Jim Inhofe, Oklahoma; Mitch McConnell, Kentucky; Jerry Moran, Kansas; Lisa Murkowski, Alaska; Rob Portman, Ohio; Mitt Romney, Utah; Mike Rounds, South Dakota; Richard Shelby, Alabama; John Thune, South Dakota; Roger Wicker, Mississippi; and Todd Young, Indiana, who along with the afore-mentioned Republican Marxist-Communist representatives, also voted in favor of this bankrupting bill allowing it to advance to the White House for signature and enactment. This support of the $1.7 trillion Omnibus Bill by these rouge Marxist-Communist Republicans betrayed all American conservatives.

Republican Senate Minority Leader Mitch McConnell defended this spending bill by stating to a press reporter that "Providing assistance for Ukrainians to defeat the Russians is the number one priority for the United States right now, according to most Republicans, that's how we see the challenges confronting the country at the moment." Republican Senator Jerry Moran also defended the bill, stating it would help Afghan refugees. You have to wonder if these guys are snorting some of Hunter's cocaine to insinuate that assisting the Ukrainians to defeat Russia and helping Afghan refugees justifies their voting for the passage of an unconstitutional $1.7 trillion Omnibus bill.

What about all the Americans who need help putting food on the table or gas in their vehicles? How about considering making Americans the top priority, Mitch McConnell? Surely he knew that this massive omnibus bill would eventually cost taxpayers $1.9 trillion at a time when American families are hurting from high inflation and a government already thirty-two trillion dollars in debt and will only serve to advance the Marxist-Communist big-government policy agenda significantly. Well, we now know that Republican Senate leader Mitch McConnell is an ebbed Marxist-Communist member of the Democrat Party charged with assuring that Senate Republicans always go along with the Marxist-Communist Democrats. We do need to give him credit for doing an outstanding job in swaying fellow Republican Senators into betraying their constituents.

This $1.7 trillion bill included $575 million for "family planning/reproductive health in areas where population growth threatens biodiversity or endangered species" *throughout the globe*. This literally puts foreign nation's plants and animals before American citizens. This provision sees humanity as a parasite, as a threat to the plants and animals that congressional members see as vastly more important than the American families who members of Congress have taken an oath to protect. The bill included $12 million to a non-profit organization partially funded by Marxist-Communist billionaire George Soro's Open Society Foundation to expand labor union rights in *three Latin American Countries*.

This bill also includes at least 4,000 'earmarks' to pay for the pet projects of Marxist-Communist senators and representatives for their bought-off positive vote. 'Earmarks' had been banned for ten years, but lawmakers from both parties brought them back in 2021 for their own corrupt intentions. A small sampling of the pork barrel spending included:

- $1.5 million to encourage people to eat outdoors in sunny Pasadena, California.
- $1.1 million for a solar array in cloudy Kirkland, Washington.
- $2 million for B360, a group that promotes dirt-bike culture in Baltimore.
- $3 million for the tiny and remote island of St. George, Alaska, for water infrastructure and $2.5. million for harbor improvements, for a total cost of over $82,000 per resident.
- $500,000 for a skate park in Rhode Island.
- $4.8 million for an environmental impact report on the possible expansion of Chicago's rail transit system. Bureaucracy at work.
- $13 million to expand the airport in the tiny city of Abbeville, Alabama.
- $4 million for "Soy-Enabled Rural Road Reconstruction" in Iowa.
- $1.6 million for the Leahy Center in Vermont, named after Senator Patrick Leahy, a Democrat from Vermont. The member who requested this earmark is Sen. Patrick Leahy.
- Funding for a wide array of woke organizations and left-wing activists. More corruption.

How many of the above pork barrel 'earmarks' are constitutionally the State's responsibilities and not the federal government's? Every single one! While hardworking families struggle under the weight of inflation caused by Washington's reckless spending sprees, Congress is going full steam ahead with even more wasteful and inappropriate spending on 'Earmarks.'

Source & Additional Information: (https://www.thoughtco.com/the-definition-of-an-earmark-3368076)

This massive spending package further allows Congress to divert incoming revenue from Social Security taxes. Why this diversion of Social Security funds? ***To cover union expenses and to pay Social Security Administration employees to work for their union instead of performing the jobs they were hired to do for America's disabled and retirees.*** This is a clear indicator that our Marxist-Communist congressional members have no moral or integrity problems with putting unions and the federal government before "American Families." This is just more evidence of totally corrupt spending by our elected members of Congress. Border patrol was allotted several billions of dollars, which sounds encouraging for the securing of our non-existing southern border, right? Unfortunately for America, the answer is no. The bill prohibits the spending of any of that money on border security. However, it provides millions of dollars in financial assistance to foreign countries to secure their borders.

The Marxist-Communist's proposed Fiscal Year 2024 budget fleeced working Americans and rewarded their parasitic Marxist-Communist voters. Do not believe the Marxist-Communists when they says they are only going to "tax the rich", and make the wealthy pay their "fair share." The top 1% of taxpayers pay 42.3% of the income taxes the Internal Revenue Service receives, so they are paying more than their fair share already! Marxist-Communist Democrats' definition of "the rich" means a person with a job, a working-class taxpayer who they can bully into submission. Joe Biden liked to crow about how he cut federal expenditures and how his policies were helping bring our national debt down. His Fiscal Year 2024 budget proposal did nothing to bring our debt down but rather did the exact opposite and dramatically increased our national debt. This means only one thing: tax hikes cannot and will not be restricted to those making over $400,000 per year.

Source & Additional Information: (https://www.wsj.com/articles/internal-revenue-service-income-taxes-2020-data-84aa19b3)

> Biden's fiscal year 2024 budget allowed America's debt to grow faster than the growth of our economy and the estimated $4.7 trillion in net tax increases.

> President Trump's average budget annual deficit rose by approximately 2.9%, while Joe Biden's Fiscal Year 2024 budget caused the yearly deficit to rise to an annual average of roughly 5.7%.

While Joe Biden and his administration claimed to be fiscally sensible, the reality is that their policies added another $6 trillion in America's debt in just three years through a combination of wasteful legislation and executive actions. Biden's fiscal year 2024 budget included dozens of hidden and indirect tax increases that will cost Americans $4.7 trillion. That is more than $35,000 per household. Tax rate increases will go from top-to-bottom, and the standard deduction is expected to be decreased by nearly $7,000 for single filers and $14,000 for married filers.

New tax hikes include but are not limited to:

> More funding and power to the Internal Revenue Service for more audits of small businesses and middle-class incomes in order to generate more revenue.

> Corporate income-tax rate increases by one-third.

> A 5% surtax increase on net investment income and extending this increased surtax to small-businesses income.

> Increased taxes on oil, natural gas, and mining development and exploration.

These are taxes that American small businesses, corporations, investors, and consumers cannot absorb in the current economic crisis. Taxes *will* also include those making less than $400,000 a year.

Biden's fiscal year 2024 budget with associated tax hikes created a flood of investors pulling out of America's markets, dramatically affecting American retirement accounts, small businesses folding, decreased real American wages, fewer jobs available, and consumers paying higher prices for the products they purchase.

Medicare trustees have been consistently calling upon Congress and the White House to adopt measures that will slow down the growth of Medicare spending. Still, Biden's budget increased Medicare spending from three percent to four-point-five percent of gross domestic product. Medicare's Hospital Insurance trust fund is already projected to be insolvent by 2028 under current policies, meaning that Medicare payments for hospital benefits would be automatically cut by ten percent with increasing cuts subsequently.

The Biden-Harris budget stated, "The budget builds upon the Inflation Reduction Act to continue lowering the cost of prescription drugs. For Medicare, this includes further strengthening its newly established negotiation power by negotiating more drugs and bringing drugs into negotiation sooner after they launch." Nice words to the gullible, but the hard reality is that Medicare "negotiates" nothing. This budget would reduce Medicare payments for prescription drugs, further reducing drug research and development investment. Controlling prices means controlling supply and central government control. More Marxist-Communist aggressive moves against America.

Under this scenario, the availability of new medical therapies and breakthrough drugs will be dramatically reduced, leading to unforeseen consequences on public health. Medicare will spend less, and seniors will pay more for the benefits earned through years of hard work and contribution to the system. Without reforms, this dramatic increase in spending on the Supplementary Medical Insurance program will cause our grandchildren and great-grandchildren to face exorbitantly high taxes, kill jobs, and deteriorate an already struggling economy.

The Biden-Harris defense budget indicated their lack of support and commitment to national defense. Their funding for the Department of Defense in fiscal year 2023 was $772 billion. That amount is about 1.5% less (after removing the effects of inflation) than the amount appropriated for 2022. The Biden-Harris Administration Fiscal Year 2024 Budget provides $842 billion for the Department of Defense, an increase of only $26 billion (3%) over Fiscal Year 2023. Since the Biden-Harris Administration assumed power, military equipment has deteriorated and failed to keep up with new technologies; military strength has declined as a result of draconian policies put in place due to COVID, causing the discharge of highly experienced military personnel; and readiness and recruitment have reached record lows. While America's military capability and budget needs are dramatically decreasing, China has increased its defense budget by an estimated 7.2% and is continually holding military training with its allies.

The Chinese Communist Party has adopted a doctrine of unrestricted warfare with nothing off limits: from conventional attacks on their opponent's military assets, DNA-based weapons focused on certain ethnic groups, flooding their opponent's country with deadly drugs, releasing of deadly viruses, social engineering; misinformation; and cyberattacks. Under the current Marxist-Communist regime, America stands grossly unprepared, and worse yet, nothing is being done to prepare America. Instead, the Chinese bought off Joe "The Big Guy" Biden, and his Marxist-Communist Administration are trying to convince American citizens that China is not a military threat but rather an economic competitor. While Biden plays his fiddle, China has already begun its undeclared war on America by flooding American streets with deadly drugs, social engineering Americans to accept Marxist-Communist doctrine, flooding America with military-age male illegal immigrants entering the United States through the open southern border, flooding America with misinformation, and with cyberattacks.

Source & Additional Information: (https://nypost.com/2023/03/10/bidens-budget-hes-cutting-military-spending/) (https://apnews.com/article/china-defense-budget-aircraft-carriers-cdac45c8d36a47cffda68be99b7c9ee7) (https://www.msn.com/en-us/money/markets/how-china-is-flooding-america-with-fentanyl-on-purpose-to-undermine-our-society/ar-BB1iRXMo)

In a world in turmoil, there is great potential for hostile actions against a NATO member(s). If this occurs, American forces will be required to join NATO members in defending against those hostilities. At this point, there is an excellent potential for hostile actions or a direct attack on America itself, which is probably not a matter of if but when. Under these genuine threats, President Biden only proposed a 3% increase for a depleted Department of Defense while other federal departments and agencies are receiving budget increases of approximately 10%. Biden's proposed budget for our military sends the wrong message to our enemies, inviting the Chinese Communist Party and Russian President Vladimir Putin's regime to challenge our military.

The Biden-Harris administration has allocated $4.7 billion for fiscal year 2024 to the Department of Homeland Security. This budget will incentivize more illegal immigration by explicitly stating that none of this money can be spent on border security. This budget includes $7 billion in taxpayer money to support refugees and unaccompanied children and $865 million to process the ever-increasing number of asylum seekers. The Department of Homeland Security claims the budget will fund securing our southern border and support a fair, orderly, and humane immigration system. Just more smoke and screens, as it does nothing of the sort, as no money can be directed at activities that would impede illegals from crossing our southern border. More opportunities for cartel violence, human trafficking, and deadly drugs flowing across our open border.

Source & Additional Information: (https://appropriations.house.gov/news/statements/joyce-remarks-fy24-budget-hearing-department-homeland-security-prepared)

The budget includes $145 million for Cybersecurity and Infrastructure Security, which will put the Department of Homeland Security in the business of censorship and control of the flow of information to the American public. $123 million to support America's transition from gas-fuel vehicles to emission-free vehicles, all misallocation of taxpayer resources to fund climate and censorship initiatives while neglecting to secure our southern border and our nation. None of these initiatives falls under the Department of Homeland Security preview. Still, then Alejandro Mayorkas is a faithful pawn of the Marxist-Communist Administration and will accept these non-Homeland Security initiatives without question.

Source & Additional Information: (https://www.csoonline.com/article/574761/cisa-funding-to-top-3-billion-under-bidens-fy-2024-budget.html) (https://about.bnef.com/blog/the-2024-sustainable-energy-in-america-factbook/)

The Marxist-Communist Administration budget included a massive federal education spending spree with a fiscal year 2024 budget of $90 billion in discretionary spending, a $10.8 billion (13.6%) increase over the fiscal year 2023 budget. Increased spending included:

- ➢ $20.5 billion for Title I, a $2.2 billion increase designed to change Title 1 funding for lower-income students to now including students whose families are not poor and can readily afford the cost of their children's education.

- ➢ $578 million to increase the number of non-teaching administrative staff, social workers, and psychologists in schools. Non-teaching staff has increased at a rate seven times that of increases in the number of public-school students since 1950, becoming a bloated bureaucracy of its own.

- ➢ $16.8 billion for the Individuals with Disabilities Education Act program, a significant increase of $2.1 billion over 2023.
- ➢ $100 million on initiatives to promote racial and socioeconomic diversity in schools, better known as Critical Race Theory. The budget will grow Washington's intrusion in education in two unique ways: "free" taxpayer-funded preschool and "free" community college. Neither of which are constitutional.
- ➢ $600 billion over ten years to finance failed federal school programs such as Head Start, which will see a $1.1 billion annual increase.

According to randomized, controlled trial evaluations conducted by the Department of Health and Human Services, the federal Head Start program has failed for a half-century to improve children's academic outcomes, their access to health care, or their parents' parenting practices.

The Biden-Harris $500 million budget for "free" community college is seriously flawed and only results in further increases in college costs because colleges know that the federal government will be paying these education expenses. This, in addition to the Marxist-Communist Democrat Administration's constitutionally illegal efforts to provide student loan debt amnesty, put taxpayers on the hook. This is an enormous 13.6% increase to the Department of Education's budget. Student loan forgiveness will be given to many students who do not believe in free speech and who violently attack, both verbally and physically, anyone who presents a conservative point of view at their colleges and universities. Conservative guest speakers are being disrupted from being able to complete their presentations. They want taxpayers to pay for their bad behavior and inability to find gainful employment because of the ridiculous and worthless degrees in majors that have no value in society.

The shock of the Marxist-Communist Democrat Administration's budget will severely impact the economy, resulting in more than $615,000 in federal spending per household over the next ten years. This level of spending would mean that the federal government would siphon off at least one-quarter of America's economy to run its unconstitutional Marxist-Communist programs. This budget level further represents the Marxist-Communist Democrat Administration's attempts to shrink the private sector and place the federal government in charge of our economy. It is important to remember that every dollar spent by the government is a dollar taken out of the hands of the hardworking Americans who earned it. When the government spends, it produces nothing; it merely reallocates scarce resources.

Source& Additional Information: (https://www.heritage.org/budget-and-spending/commentary/8-things-know-about-bidens-fiscal-2024-budget-bad-worse)

Further, the $1.7 trillion in new deficits will intensify stagflationary pressures, driving up unemployment and driving down wages and economic growth. The Marxist-Communist Administration seems to be banking on the Federal Reserve to print some of the $1.7 trillion required to cover his deficit, prolonging the already inflation crisis America has endured for the past three plus years as Federal money-printing has turned into an inflation tax of more than $7,000 per family. America cannot allow itself to be fooled by the Marxist-Communist Democrat Administration's hollow rhetoric: the Marxist-Communist Democrat Administration's tax hikes may look like they are only on the wealthy and large companies, but in truth, they are aimed squarely at the American middle class; will encourage investment capital to flee our nation; make new domestic investment prohibitive; drive our constitutional capitalist Nation further down the path toward Marxist-Communism; make private sector investment in productive pursuits more expensive or impractical; drive up unemployment and inflation; and, create stagflation leaving the federal government in a prime position to taking over America's economy which equates to America's conversion into a Marxist-Communist regime.

Source & Additional Information: (https://www.marketwatch.com/story/u-s-budget-deficit-swells-to-1-7-trillion-in-fiscal-2023-as-revenue-tumbles-99b978fc)

With a national debt of $35 trillion, inflation around seven percent, and no sign of spending restraint, Americans need leaders with the courage and integrity to say enough. Will that level of courage and integrity come from the House of Representatives? Maybe, if Speaker Mike Johnson stands by his promises to inject constitutional restrictions, which he has already backed off on; it will be from the failed leadership of Republican Senate Minority Leader Mitch McConnell, who signed onto the passage of the bloated Marxist-Communist omnibus spending bill allowing the Marxist-Communist Democrat Administration to cement their Marxist-Communist agenda through the end of fiscal year 2024? That would be a *NO*; or will it be the Democrat Party turned Marxist-Communist party? That would be an absolute *NO*!

How long before America goes bankrupt and can no longer pay the interest on America's loans to the foreign countries from whom we borrowed that money? How long before China, to whom America owes the most significant amount of debt, recalls that debt? Then what? We know that we will not be able to pay off that debt under our current economic situation. Will China confiscate all federally owned properties to satisfy this debt, thereby defeating America without firing a shoot? After all, isn't that what happens to us when we can no longer make payments on our homes or vehicles? So, what happened to the party of fiscal constraint? Is fiscal conservatism dead in the Republican Party?

Let us hope Speaker Johnson begins to stand by his promises, making the answer to this question a probable no. Are the Marxist-Communist leaning Republican congressional members attempting to destroy their party, which is already struggling? That would be a possible yes, as evidenced by their voting yes on retaining "Earmarks" and yes on the $1.7 trillion Omnibus Bill. These Marxist-Communist leaning Republicans seem to be doing all the right things to assure that those constitutionally conservative Republican constituents already on the fence decide that enough is enough and form a third "Conservative" party.

But wait, you say, creating a third party will only give the Marxist-Communist Democrat Party a considerable advantage in all future elections. Really? When so many Republicans can be dependent on to vote with the Marxist-Communist Democrats consistently, what is the difference? So, the question remains, if not a new Conservative Party, how much longer before American citizens wake up and realize that the "Only" other path to resolving our problems is through the convening of a "Convention of States" *(See Chapter 24)* and purposing an Amendment restricting federal spending and federal government overreach. An Amendment that would significantly curtail, if not nearly stop, the Washington swamp from financially destroying America.

Chapter 18
Retirement Woes

Fidelity's Retirement Savings Assessment Executive Summary regarding America's retirement plans indicates that retirement plans have been hit hard by the high inflation rate, which our country is struggling with due to the federal government's no-ending spending. This will require individuals to depend on their own resources and savings to fund their retirement. They can expect that social security supplement will be dramatically reduced with the passage of endless multi-trillion-dollar Omnibus bills by a Marxist-Communist Congress and Administration, which funnels money to foreign countries, pays off corrupt big tech and corporations for their support and donations, funds Marxist-Communist programs and initiatives which then kicks back money to corrupt politicians; and money which falls into a black hole and cannot be account for because of lack of accountability.

A report released by Fidelity addressed the financial readiness of American citizens for their retirement. Fidelity's Retirement Savings Assessment was built upon comprehensive data obtained from more than 3,500 individuals who responded to a survey ran through the extensive retirement planning platform Fidelity uses daily with their customers. This summary revealed that Americans are not financially prepared because inflation has denied them the ability to set aside the necessary funds each payday to grow a retirement fund account sufficient to meet the cost of their desired retirement lifestyle. Between inflation and amid continued volatility in the stock market, Americans' preparedness for retirement has declined significantly, indicating that over half (52%) of those surveyed are not on target for their retirement needs and face modest to significant adjustments to their planned retirement lifestyle if they do not take action to make up the shortfall. However, with inflation skyrocketing, workers can't set aside additional money to make up the difference for inflation. Based on Fidelity's survey, America's Retirement Score for the typical American household falls into the "Fair" zone, meaning the typical saver is on target to have 78 percent of the income Fidelity estimates they will need to cover retirement costs. The overall savings rate has declined since 2020, especially among Millennials, with Gen X alone showing an increase. Still, all generations are saving well below Fidelity's recommended rate of at least 15%.

<u>Source & Additional Information</u>: *(https://newsroom.fidelity.com/pressreleases/ fidelity-research--america-s-retirement-preparedness-level-declines-amid-continued- volatility/s/c57ac0e9-9c5c-4f5c-938c-cdf82a3aa7b1)*

The Marxist-Communist Democrat Administration's Labor Department announced a new rule that will permit money managers to play politics with trillions of dollars of people's retirement savings. The Marxist-Communist Democrat Administration is pushing environmental, social, and governance (ESG) investing, which allows retirement fund managers to select stocks of companies based on their positions on social and environmental issues. Retirement savings will be used as leverage to force companies to reduce their carbon emissions and establish racial and gender quotas and other social justice fads entirely unrelated to securing a high return on workers' lifetime savings. For example, money managers have divested from traditional oil and gas companies, such as Exxon or Chevron, to reduce greenhouse gases. Socially conscious investing has been around for decades. There is no problem with individual shareholders choosing stocks that link with their values. For example, some refuse to invest in Starbucks because the coffee company is fighting unionization by employees.

But it is entirely different when trillion-dollar investment and retirement funds such as BlackRock inject their own biases into how they invest people's savings without their knowledge or consent. It is even worse when these biases rob investors of a high rate of return on their nest eggs.

Terrence Keeley, a former executive at BlackRock, blew the whistle on this scam in The Wall Street Journal by noting that since 2017, when the ESG fad took hold, these funds have had an annual rate of return of 6.3%—versus 8.9% for the stock market as a whole. Investors lost 2.6% per year on their retirement funds. There goes the down payment on that retirement home in Arizona or Florida.

What is insidious about the new Marxist-Communist Democrat Administration's ESG rules is that they permit and even quietly encourage portfolio managers at firms such as BlackRock to violate their fiduciary duty to their clients by allowing ESG factors to trump sound investment decisions. Federal regulators should ensure the soundness of retirement funds, not shrinking them. To make matters worse, researchers at Columbia University and the London School of Economics found that ESG funds may not even achieve their goals. The study compared the ESG records of American companies in 147 ESG fund portfolios to those in over 2,000 non-ESG portfolios and found that the ESG companies were often worse regarding labor and environmental law compliance.

Source & Additional Information: (https://www.wsj.com/articles/esg-cant-square-with-fiduciary-duty-blackrock-vanguard-state-stree-the-big-three-violations-china-conflict-of-interest-investors-11662496552)

The good news is that a backlash is emerging against ESG. Late last year, one of the largest money managers, Vanguard, wisely announced withdrawing from the Net Zero Asset Managers Initiative, a major climate change alliance. Going forward, ESG investment policies should be illegal unless individual investors check the box to have their money invested in such politically motivated investments. By the way, victims of the policies are often unionized workers, America's truckers, factory workers, and teachers whose lifetime savings are put at risk.

Chapter 19
Insurrection That Wasn't

My wife and I attended the January 6th, 2021, rally in Washington, D.C., to joined hundreds-of-thousands of other like-minded citizens to protest the highly questionable results of the 2020 Presidential elections. We attended a rally whose primary goal was to draw attention to our concerns over the election results and to encourage then Vice President Mike Pence and members of Congress to return the Electoral results back to several key states that had demonstrated total disregard for their State Constitution and election laws, questionable ballots with irregularities, or illegal acts caught on polling facility security videos. As were the other attendees, we sought only to protest our grievances and seek redress of those grievances over the election process and results in those critical states and to do so peacefully and orderly.

Although it was a bitterly cold day, all the participants at the rally were in an incredibly positive mood. We listened to several individuals and President Trump speak about the attacks on our Constitution and election laws. During President Trump's speech, he never once encouraged nor insinuated that rally attendees should in any way disrupt the proceedings of Congress. He made it noticeably clear that we should all march to the Capitol building and make our voices heard peacefully and orderly. The rally attendees began to march towards the Capitol building, where they intended to encircle it and raise their voices to protest election results submitted from highly questionable states. It was hoped that Vice President Mike Pence and the Republican legislators inside the Capitol building would hear our pleas to reject the results of this election until those states with questionable results could be investigated and their vote counts were confirmed as being accurate.

My wife and I began the march to the Capitol building with all the other rally attendees, unaware of what was already taking place at the Capitol building by a ridiculously small group of fools. Fortunately, we never reached the Capitol building because my wife stated she was too cold to remain outdoors. We decided not to participate in the rally at the Capitol Building but instead return to the warmth of our RV. Upon returning to our RV, I turned on the Television to follow the news regarding the activity at the Capitol building. I became aware of individuals entering the Capitol Building. This surprised me as President Trump had clearly emphasized that he wanted us to go to the Capitol building and peacefully communicate our grievances. No speaker at that rally or anyone in the crowd at the rally site called for any violence or for entering the Capitol building to disrupt congressional proceedings. It was not until much later that videos were released showing a few individuals at the Capitol building encouraging rally attendees to enter the Capitol building. Many of the more aggressive agitators were likely embedded FBI agents or assets.

As the result of a small group of rally participants' entry into the Capitol building, hundreds if not thousands of people were tracked down by the FBI, even many who never entered the building but were merely present at the Capitol building. Those who were arrested were held as political prisoners in the neglected and humanly unhealthy environment of the Washington, D.C. jail. These individuals were jailed under the pretense that they had entered or were near the entrance of the Capitol Building as insurrectionists. Although the Constitution states, under the Speedy Trial Clause of the Sixth Amendment, that "In all criminal prosecutions, the accused shall enjoy the right to a speedy and public trial...". The Clause protects the defendant from the delay between presenting the indictment or similar charging instrument and the beginning of the trial. It should be pointed out that although the Marxist-Communist Democrat members of Congress continuously proclaimed to the general public that these individuals were insurrections, three-plus years after that incident, not a single person has been charged with insurrection. According to the DOJ, as of March 6th, 2023, approximately one thousand people have been subjected to the Stalinist actions of the Marxist-Communist Democrat Party and have been arrested on charges related to the January 6th, 2021, rally. Of those, three-hundred-fifty-one have had their cases adjudicated. Of those, one hundred and ninety-two have been sentenced and incarcerated as political prisoners of the Marxist-Communist Democrat regime in keeping with their Stalinist philosophy towards those who would dare challenge their authority.

These political prisoners attended a rally in support of investigating and recounting the votes of seven contested vital states: Arizona, Georgia, Michigan, Nevada, Pennsylvania, Texas, and Wisconsin. States in which results were highly suspected of fraud, cheating, and criminal activity. The Americans in attendance were there to make their voices heard regarding their strong suspicion that those seven critical states' election processes did not follow their state's constitution or election laws.

A minimal number of attendees of the January 6th, 2021, rally entered the Capitol building, primarily encouraged by FBI embedded agents and assets within the rally crowd with instructions to incite protesters to enter the Capitol building to disrupt the certification of state-submitted electro-college results. Most of those who did enter the Capitol building were just innocent individuals who got caught up in the moment under the encouragement of FBI agents and assets, but none had any criminal intent. None of those who entered that building hurt anyone or damaged any government property except some broken windows. Capitol police officers committed the only violence that occurred during that protest.

Congressional Marxist-Communist Democrats used the Josef Goebbels "Big Lie" technique to slander the January 6th protestors. The Nazi Minister of Propaganda believed that if you keep repeating a lie often enough, the people will begin to believe it. Congressional Marxist-Communist Democrats keep repeating the big lie that five police officers were killed on January 6th, 2021. This is not true, and they know it is not valid. One officer died of natural causes the day after the protests from a stroke. Months after the event, four officers committed suicide, but there is no evidence that their suicide was in any way related to the January 6th protest. But Marxist-Communist Democrats will not report this fact in keeping with the "Big Lie" to smear Trump supporters. Do not fall for their "Big Lie."

The thousands of hours of video security cameras' tapes, which captured the actual events during the protest, were not released to the general public because then-Speaker Nancy Pelosi refused to allow for the release of those video tapes, citing National security concerns. Nancy Pelosi was the individual who ultimately carried the responsibility for the security of the Capitol building and the members of Congress. She and the mayor of the District of Columbia jointly failed to take necessary precautions to protect the Capitol and the congressional members within that building. They both refused President Trump's offer of 10,000 Nation Guard soldiers to help protect the Capitol during the rally. In April of 2023, following the disposal of Nancy Pelosi as the Speaker of the House, the newly elected Republican Speaker of the House, Kevin McCarthy, released the security videos from within the Capitol building to Fox News host Tucker Carlson. Those videos tell an entirely different story than the "Big Lie" being pushed by Nancy Pelosi and the Marxist-Communist Democrat Party.

In an interview with then-Fox News host Tucker Carlson, Former Capitol Hill Police Chief Steven Sund called the events of January 6th, 2021, a cover-up. Unfortunately for American citizens, that interview was never aired; Fox News buried it. In that interview, Capitol Hill Police Chief Sund tells Carlson he believes that the Chair of the Joint Chiefs of Staff, Mark Milley, and then-House Speaker Nancy Pelosi had intelligence of what was to come on January 6th, 2021, but failed to communicate that information to him and subsequently covered it up in the aftermath. "Everything appears to be a cover-up," Sund told Carlson. "I'm not a conspiracy theorist ... but when you look at the information and intelligence they had, the military had, it's all watered down. I am not getting intelligence; I am denied any support from the National Guard in advance. I am denied National Guard while we are under attack, for seventy-one minutes ..." At one point, Carlson stated to Sund, "It sounds like they were hiding the intelligence." Sund responded: "Could there possibly be actually ... they kind of wanted something to happen? It is not a far stretch to believe so. It is sad when you start putting everything together and thinking about the way this played out ... what was their end goal? If I was allowed to do my job as the chief we wouldn't be here; this didn't have to happen."

I know that people throughout this country, both Democrats and Republicans, have no problem seeing those who participated in the January 6th, 2021, protest (a.k.a. Insurrection) rot in a Washington, D.C. jail under inhumane conditions or forced to plead to ridiculous charges to be transferred to more tolerable prisons. The problem with these emotional feelings is that American citizens spent years in jail, many without being charged with any crime or allowed to appear in court to be formally charged and allowed to post bail in keeping with the Constitution. This is not what justice is under the Constitution of the United States; these are the actions of a Marxist-Communist country to severely punish those who dare challenge the Marxist-Communist regime in power and intimidate those who may consider opposing that regime.

Then, as if the unconstitutional treatment of these individuals were not enough, we had to endure the one-sided political witch hunt proceedings of a Select Committee, which was supposedly formed to investigate the January 6th, 2021, incident.

A Committee that only heard testimony from those individuals who held Marxist-Communist ideological viewpoints and were willing to falsely testify as to what happened on that day; did not allow for witnesses with opposing testimony to appear before the committee; and refused to allow witnesses to be cross-examined regarding their testimony by representatives of the Republican Party. Trump haters Liz Chaney and crying Adam Kinzinger have never been Republicans but rather Republicans in name only (RINOs). All perpetuated by elected members of Congress who took a sworn oath to defend our Constitution and the God given rights afforded to every citizen of this Nation under that Constitution. Did these members of Congress forget what they learned about our Constitution? Did they attend failed federally funded public schools where learning about our Constitution had not been afforded them, or are they all just outright corrupt bureaucrats who care little about the rights of American citizens under our Constitution?

It is not hard to understand or know that our Constitution speaks directly to the above situation. The 6th Amendment to the Constitution reads: "In all criminal prosecutions, the accused shall enjoy the right to a speedy and public trial, by an impartial jury of the state and district wherein the crime shall have committed, which district shall have been previously ascertained by law, and to be informed of the nature and cause of the accusation; <u>to be confronted with the witnesses against him; to have compulsory process for obtaining witnesses in his favor, and to have the Assistance of Counsel for his defense.</u>" All the individuals who were or are still incarcerated, all the individuals who have been accused of participating in or of inciting the January 6th, 2021, incident, have been failed by the very elected officials who took a sworn oath of office to protect their Constitutional rights.

You may believe that these people deserved what they have been put through or that, in time, we will get past all this political

noise and move on. If so, you had better think this through and realize that one day, this could happen to you, a member of your family, or a friend. No matter the crime, no matter the politics, no matter how you or any individual in this country feels about the severity of the crime of those who participated in the January 6th protest, no American must ever be denied their Constitutional rights. To allow this to happen spells the end of our Constitutional Republic. Any individual or institution, including Congress, who denies any American citizen their Constitutional rights must be held accountable to the fullest extent of our laws, no matter their station or position. Remember, for our Republic and God-given freedoms to survive, our Constitutional rights must survive.
If we are to ensure a free Republic for our grandchildren and great-grandchildren, then everyone must become engaged. We cannot sit back while our Republic disintegrates. As Benjamin Franklyn famously stated, "We have a Republic if we can keep it." More than ever since the Civil War, our resolve to keep our Constitutional Republic is being gravely tested. We must not falter because there will be no turning back if we do. Every patriotic American citizen can be effective through involvement, determination, and complete support of our Constitution.

Rosanne Boyland: In July of 2022, Philip Anderson confirmed to The Gateway Pundit that he witnessed Capitol Police officer Lila Morris beat to death Trump supporter Rosanne Boyland on January 6th, 2021. Rosanne was neither armed nor in any manner a threat or threatening anyone, including Police Officer Lila Morris, who fatally beat Rosanne to death with a police baton. Philip stated that he was next to her, holding her hand when she died. Philip Anderson was gassed with clouds of pepper spray, pushed down, and then nearly trampled to death as police officers continued to press Trump supporters on top of himself and Rosanne Boyland's body as she lay on the steps into the Capitol building. Jake Lang, a second eyewitness, also contacted The Gateway Pundit and confirmed Philip Anderson's account of Rosanne Boyland's murder.

Roseanne's murder was further confirmed by surveillance cameras obtained by Gateway Pundit, which showed Capitol Police Officer Lila Morris beating an unconscious Roseanne Boyland. The footage of this video revealed the unconscious body of Rosanne Boyland lying on the steps of the Capitol building as protesters tried in vain to save her life. When their attempts failed, the protesters carried her body up to the West Capitol Entrance and turned her body over to the Metro Police, begging them for help. Rosanne's body was last seen as Metro police officers dragged her body down the tunnel by her feet. This act of violence in the beating death of Roseanne Boyland by Capitol Police officer Lila Morris was the first of two murders committed by Nancy Pelosi's Capitol Building Police officers.

Source & Additional Information: (https://www.washingtonexaminer.com/news/1857999/video-shows-officer-striking-motionless-woman-on-ground-during-capitol-riot/)

Interestingly, the January 6th, 2021, Congressional Select-Committee investigating what happened during the January 6th protest rally never took the time to call on Philip Anderson or Jake Lang to testify. Philip Anderson's amazing eyewitness account of what happened was ignored, as was Jake Lang's. Roseanne Boyland's murder and eyewitness accounts of that day were not only ignored by the January 6th Congressional Select Committee but were totally ignored by the fake news media because it did not fit their Marxist-Communist Democrat Party narrative.

Ashli Babbitt: The most publicized murder was videotaped, capturing the shooting to death of Ashli Babbitt by Capitol police officer Lt. Mike Byrd. Babbitt was shot at the entry of the Speaker of the House's lobby by Lt. Byrd. She died a half-hour later. Lt. Mike Byrd shot Ashli Babbitt even though she was not armed and posed no threat of any kind to any police officer or anyone else. Videos show Ashli standing back as others attempted to enter the Speaker's lobby by smashing out the windows to the door leading into the Speaker's lobby. If Lt. Byrd were so concerned for his life, why did he not shoot one of the individuals smashing out the window who would have seemed to be the greater threat than someone standing by passively? Ashli Babbitt's cold-blooded murder on that day by Lt. Byrd was not proclaimed as a heinous crime. Instead, it resulted in his being declared a hero by the then Marxist-Communist Speaker of the House, Nancy Pelosi, and given an award for her murder rather than charged with murder and incarcerated as would have been expected in a law-and-order nation. Ashli Babbitt was the second murder committed by the Capitol police that day. Just before her murder, released videotapes show Capitol police officers who were guarding the entry at which Ashli Babbitt was shot mysteriously and simultaneously walking away from their posts—an action which has yet to be explained by the leadership of the Capitol police department.

As can be expected in a Marxist-Communist regime, Roseanne Boyland's murder by Capitol Police officer Lila Morris, as well as Ashli Babbitt's murder by Capitol Police officer Lt. Mike Byrd, were ruled to be "objectively reasonable" by Capitol Police investigators. Investigators into the deaths of the two rally protesters never viewed or purposefully ignored the surveillance videotapes nor ever interviewed Philip Anderson or Jake Lang before the two Capitol police officers were exonerated. It is now clear that if you are a Capitol Police Officer under Marxist-Communist leadership in the House of Representatives, you can kill Trump supporters at will. You will not be held accountable but instead revered and honored for your murderous actions. As many conservatives already know, it is always open season for Trump MAGA supporters. God protect us from the criminally evil Marxist-Communist Democrat Party.

Source & Additional Information: (https://www.nytimes.com/2021/01/23/us/capitol-police-shooting-ashli-babbitt.html)

***Capitol Building Security Videos*:** William Pope of Topeka, Kansas, sought to lift the court seal on videos taken by undercover government agents to obtain full access to video evidence held by the government. Pope was representing himself in the criminal case being prosecuted against him. At a March 3rd, 2023, hearing, Judge Contreras seemed sympathetic to Pope's motion to unmask the videos. A federal prosecutor had admitted in court papers that three D.C. Metropolitan Police Department undercover officers functioned as provocateurs at the northwest steps of the Capitol building on January 6th, 2021. The admission came in a March 24th, 2023, filing before United States District Judge Rudolph Contreras that sought to keep video footage taken by the officers under court seal. Videos long hidden under court seal had become a major defense topic but withheld by Nancy Pelosi and the prosecutors against the January 6th rally defendants.

Source & Additional Information: (https://www.pbs.org/newshour/show/fox-news-uses-selective-capitol-security-footage-to-spread-misinformation-on-jan-6)

Protesters who entered the Capitol building, and many who did not enter, have been hunted down by the politically weaponized FBI. Those unfortunate individuals were held as political prisoners for prolonged periods to prolong their value as propaganda tools for the Marxist-Communist Democrat Party. Those who have been charged, as a plea agreement to end their ordeal under such inhumane prison conditions, were charged with trumped-up infringements. Why? Because they exercised their right to assemble and protest their grievances. Can the same be said of those members of Antifa and Black Lives Matter when their protests were clearly violent, destructive, and organized? Unfortunately, the answer is no, mocking our law-and-order society. But unlike the Antifa and Black Lives Matter riot participants, the January 6th, 2021, protesters were falsely accused of insurrection for the political propaganda benefit of the Marxist-Communist Democrat Party. An insurrection committed with no organized leadership, coordinated effort, and no weapons other than sticks with protest signs attached to them.

Dominic Pezzola is one of the Proud Boys members charged with obstruction and conspiracy related to the January 6th, 2021, Capitol breach. He was arrested on January 15th, 2021, and indicted the same month. Pezzola's trial began in January of 2023 but was paused due to classified FBI messages revealed in court, which the defense attorneys say show FBI agents discussing the altering of evidence. Not at all a far-fetched probability from our politicalized and weaponized FBI. Emails between FBI agents revealed their casual discussion of altering a document and destroying hundreds of pieces of evidence. Washington District Court Judge Timothy J. Kelly paused the trial due to the leaked messages. This information came to light during the testimony of FBI special agent Nicole Miller, who participated in the agency's investigations of the January 6th, 2021, defendants. When cross-examining Miller, Nick Smith, an attorney representing Proud Boys member Ethan Nordean, revealed classified FBI emails that were hidden in a tab in an Excel spreadsheet. This evidence supported a motion to dismiss the charges against Pezzola. In the motion, Pezzola's team said the emails showed that the FBI monitored communications between Nordean and his lawyer, violating the Sixth Amendment, which prohibits invasions of the right to counsel.

Source & Additional Information: (https://www.westernjournal.com/report-fbi-caught-doctoring-destroying-388-items-evidence-jan-6-proud-boys-case/)

According to a separate filing by Nordean's lawyers, Miller said in one correspondence that "her boss assigned her three-hundred and thirty-eight items of evidence she had to destroy." Nordean's lawyers allege that another email shows an agent requesting Miller to "go into an informant report she had just put together and edit out that the agent was present." The emails show Miller "admitted fabricating evidence and following orders to destroy hundreds of items of evidence," Pezzola's lawyers wrote in its motion to dismiss, and that the government obtained information that benefitted itself in the trial but failed to disclose this information to the defendant's counsel causing substantial prejudice to each of the defendants, including Pezzola.

Source & Additional Information: (https://www.ntd.com/defendant-moves-to-dismiss-jan-6-case-based-on-newly-disclosed-footage-fbi-testimony_906263.html)

In addition to their argument about the Sixth Amendment, Pezzola's lawyers also argued in their motion to dismiss, that the newly surfaced video footage of events of the January 6th, 2021, Capitol breach constitutes exculpatory evidence. The defendants' lawyers stated that by withholding that evidence, the government violated their client's constitutional rights as defined in Brady v. Maryland, a 1963 case in which the Supreme Court held that prosecutors must make exculpatory evidence available to defense counsel. The motion came two days after then-House Speaker Kevin McCarthy released more than 40,000 hours of January 6th, 2021, video footage to Tucker Carlson, previously of the Fox News lineup, which then aired some footage on his show. One tape aired by Tucker Carlson showed Capitol Police officers walking alongside Jacob Chansley, a January 6th, 2021, defendant serving a fourth-one-month sentence after pleading guilty to an obstruction charge. Chansley was unarmed and was being escorted by Capitol police officers around the Capitol building. The aired footage "is plainly exculpatory," Pezzola's lawyers said in the motion. As can be expected, the Marxist-Communist FBI declined to comment on the revelations noted in the emails or the video footage but instead chose to defer any questions regarding what appears to be misconduct on the part of the FBI to the Attorney General's Office for comment.

Tucker Carlson: Tucker Carlson did a great service to the American people by having the courage to stand against those who would silence him. Tucker was a FOX News superstar who was fired because he dared to expose wrongdoing within our Marxist-Communist government. Newly elected Republican

Speaker of the House, Kevin McCarthy, released thousands of hours of videos taken within the Capitol building on January 6th, 2021, to Tucker Carlson, who began to release footage of the January 6th, 2021, protest. Most videos exhibited peaceful demonstrators peacefully entering the Capitol, escorted or aided by Capitol police officers. These videos destroy the Marxist-Communist Democrats' phony narrative of an insurrection or riot. Marxist-Communist Senate Majority Leader Chuck Schumer was so upset about the truth being told about January 6th that he became apoplectic on the Senate floor. He demanded that FOX silence Carlson and prevent him from showing any additional video footage depicting what happened inside the Capitol building on January 6th, 2021. Maybe Schumer missed the First Amendment lecture in his Constitutional Law class at Harvard Law. Or perhaps he is an America-hating, left-wing Marxist-Communist Democrat ideologue.

Source & Additional Information: (https://www.newsweek.com/tucker-carlson-jan6-videos-capitol-riot-1785944)

Sadly, Schumer's threats to FOX were successful. After FOX host Tucker Carlson did a great service to America by showing what truly happened on January 6th, 2021, the Marxist-Communist Democrat Party leadership unleashed their attack dogs. The next day, Tucker Carlson stopped showing clips of tapes depicting peaceful Americans protesting at the Capitol. Tucker's boss, the Trump-hater and Marxist-Communist Democrat Murdoch did not want any videos released that were helpful to Trump. Sadly, the silencing of Tucker Carlson by Schumer and the Murdochs led to the firing of Tucker Carlson. If Speaker McCarthy had a spine, he would have released those tapes to Newsmax, The Gateway Pundit, Breitbart, and the defense lawyers for the January 6th, 2021, defendants. Why let Schumer and the Murdoch family keep the truth from Americans?

Following the January 6th rally, then Speaker of the House, Nancy Pelosi, convened a special House Committed to investigate the

January 6th incident at the Capitol building. Pelosi purposeful only selected members who were loyal to her and were Trump haters. Then, Minority Leader McCarthy selected two Republican House members to sit on that Committee, which is appropriate as Committees are to be represented by both parties. Pelosi unprecedentedly rejected the individuals selected by McCarty, and Pelosi instead selected two Marxist-Communist Trump haters as Republican representatives on that Committee. Pamela Geller, who is a reporter for The Geller Report, wrote that Bennie Thompson, Chairman of the corrupt January 6th, 2021, Committee, admitted that he and the other Committee members never looked at the full range of surveillance tapes that Tucker Carlson was airing on his cable news show. Yet, their final report insisted there was a "violent insurrection." Thompson is either lying or profoundly stupid, or maybe both. This unselect Committee was nothing more than a dishonest Marxist-Communist Democrat hit job! What Thompson and his Committee members did was to deceptively edit the tapes to show the few violent demonstrators while ignoring the videos that showed ordinary Americans peacefully walking through the Capitol building.

Marxist-Communist Republican Senate Minority Leader Mitch McConnell stabbed Speaker Kevin McCarthy in the back, stating that it was a mistake for Speaker McCarthy to release the actual videos of what happened on January 6th, 2021. McConnell has good reason to prevent the release of these video tapes to cover up his joining Nancy Pelosi in refusing to order the National Guard to protect the Capitol building during the protest rally. McConnell is one of the reasons that loyal Republicans despise weak, back-stabbing Marxist-Communist RINOS.

Post Capitol Attacks: Since the January 6th, 2021, protest occurred, the corrupt Marxist-Communist Majority Leader of the Senate, Chuck Schumer, along with the propaganda arm of the Marxist-Communist Democrat Party would have you believe that this incursion on the Capitol building was the first and only such act at or within the Capitol Building. This incursion was not the blood bath, killing field, or destructive acts that they would have the general public believe. The January 6th, 2021, protest resulted in only two deaths, both at the hands of the Capitol police against unarmed and non-life-threatening individuals. History paints a vastly different picture of assaults within the chambers of the Capitol than what the Marxist-Communist elements of our government and the fake news outlets would have the American people believe.

Source & Additional Information: (https://www.justice.gov/usao-dc/36-months-jan-6-attack-capitol-0?os=i&ref=app)

On July 2nd, 1915, Eric Muenter, a German spy who worked as an academic at American universities in the early 20th century, went to the Capitol building with a bomb consisting of three sticks of dynamite and a timing mechanism. He had planned to place his bomb in the Senate chamber but found it locked. Instead, he put the bomb underneath a telephone switchboard in a Senate reception room, where it exploded late at night, causing considerable damage but no casualties.

On December 13th, 1931, Marlin Kemmerer, a 25-year-old clerk at a Sears, Roebuck & Company department store in Allentown, Pennsylvania, and an excellent sharpshooter took a train to Washington with a pistol, ammunition, and two sticks of dynamite. On that same day, Kemmerer went to the gallery of the House of Representatives and stood at the railing of the House gallery, waving his pistol over his head. A page shouted a warning, and most members exited the House floor. Member Edith Rogers, who had experience counseling shell-shocked veterans of World War I, worked to calm him down. Melvin Maas, a Marine combat veteran, stood directly below on the House floor, encouraging Kemmerer to drop the gun, which Kemmerer eventually did, and Maas caught the pistol.

On March 1, 1954, Puerto Rican nationalists went to the public gallery of the House of Representatives, unfurled a Puerto Rican flag, and then began shooting at members of Congress. Five members were wounded, but all recovered.

On March 1, 1971, Weather Underground members planted a bomb in a men's restroom one floor below the chamber of the Senate. They used a stopwatch connected to a fuse to control the time of the explosion and issued a warning by telephone half an hour before the bomb detonated. The blast devastated the bathroom, smashing the plumbing fixtures. The doors to the Senate barbershop were torn off their hinges and crashed through a window ending up in a courtyard. Lighting fixtures, plaster, and tile were damaged in the corridor. A stained-glass window in the Senate dining room was severely damaged. No one was ever arrested or convicted for this bombing. Of course not; members of the Weather Underground were Marxist-Communist supporters who fit the Marxist-Communist narrative of the Democrat Party leadership.

On October 18th, 1983, Israel Rubinowits, an Israeli visiting the United States, entered the Capitol and went to the visitor's gallery of the House of Representatives. He was observed manipulating what appeared to be a bomb. When approached by four plainclothes officers, he threatened to detonate the bomb before being subdued. The device, which had been concealed under his clothes, consisted of two plastic bottles filled with a flammable liquid, gunpowder, and improvised shrapnel and was rigged to a detonator with copper wire.

The "May 19th Communist Organization" was a women-led successor to the Weather Underground. On November 6, 1983, two members of the group assembled a bomb in a restroom at the Capitol that failed to go off. The following day, they returned and constructed a second bomb, which detonated, causing extensive damage but no casualties.

On July 24, 1998, Russell Eugene Weston Jr. went to the Capitol and triggered the metal detector at the entrance. When questioned by Capitol Police, he killed the officer with a shot to his head; he then wounded a second Capitol Police officer. A tourist was also wounded. Weston then ran into an office used by Congressman Tom DeLay and fatally shot a Capitol Police detective assigned to protect DeLay.

The above-noted invasions of our federal Capitol Building are not the only attacks on a government Capitol building, as the Marxist-Communist Democrat Party would lead everyone to believe. It has happened numerous times and always by far-left Marxist-Communist Democrat Party protesters. Call to mind the take-over of the Wisconsin State Capitol building during Scott Walker's term as governor. Were those insurrectionists imprisoned as political prisoners of the State of Wisconsin? Hardly! During the week of April 11th, 2023, a group of activists stormed the Florida state Capitol building, intent on disrupting the passage of a bill banning abortion after six weeks. The White House's take on this occupation blames the lawmakers for passing a bill restricting abortions and not the criminals for this illegal action.

It is this double standard that is not only outraging Americans but is tearing the country apart. Marxist-Communist Democrat Party leaders want to win by any means necessary. Things like democratic process, free speech, the rule of law, and liberty and justice for all, are merely obstacles in their pursuit of a Marxist-Communist Country.

On December 22nd, 2022, the United States House "select" committee investigating the January 6th, 2022, unfounded accusations of an insurrection attack on the Capitol building published its final report. A report they expect Americans to accept as legitimate even though the Committee did not allow for the cross-examination of any of the witnesses testifying before the Committee and every member chosen to serve on that committee suffered from Trump syndrome. Further, the Committee's two

Republican members, Liz Chaney and Adam Kinzinger broke with their party by accepting the appointment from Pelosi, who had earlier rejected the two Republican members appointed by then-House Minority Leader Keven McCarthy. Republican Minority Leader McCarthy refused to certify the selection of Chaney and Kinzinger based on their known biased hatred of President Trump.

The Committee completely failed to investigate the cause of the lack of security at the Capitol building on that day, which, if it had been adequately secured, would have prevented the incident from occurring in the first place. President Trump had offered to bring in several thousand National Guard troops to provide security. Although he strongly recommended that these troops be allowed to provide security, Nancy Pelosi and the Mayor of Washington, D.C. declined the offer, making their refusal very suspicious, implying that they intended to allow this Capitol building incident to occur for political propaganda.

Instead of investigating the lack of security, which was the root cause of the protester's ability to enter the congressional building, the Committee chose to focus its entire time attempting to implicate President Trump in the incident. So, why would a Committee charged with investigating the January 6th, 2022, incident not make it a priority to determine why the Capitol building was not appropriately secured, knowing that hundreds of thousands of protesters would descend upon Washington? Answer: because then-Speaker Nancy Pelosi, who alone bore the responsibility for the Capitol Building's security, handpicked members loyal to her or who were Republican Trump haters, knowing the committee would never call on her and question her lack of action to ensure that the appropriate level of security had been put in place.

Source & Additional Information: (https://americanmilitarynews.com/2022/08/gen-kellogg-trump-did-request-natl-guard-troops-on-jan-6th-asks-congress-to-release-his-testimony/)

Given the makeup of the committee members, due process for the accused January 6th, 2021, protesters was never considered nor was equal application of the law applied. Comparisons have been made between the treatment of the January 6th protesters and the 2021 and 2020 Black Lives Matter and Antifa rioters. Black Lives Matter and Antifa riots were violent, destructive, and deadly. Police Stations and businesses that people worked their entire lives to build were burned to the ground or otherwise destroyed. Interestingly enough, the politicalized and weaponized Marxist-Communist FBI did not track down every individual who participated in those riots. In fact, none of the individuals who participated in those riots and the destruction of property were ever hunted down by the FBI. Those arrested were arrested on the scene and were subsequently allowed to immediately post bond and be released to go out and continue their mayhem. Some of those arrested had their bonds paid for by none other than cackling Kamala Harris, Vice President of the United States or President, according to Joe Biden. This is more evidence of a Nation with a double standard: one for radical Marxist-Communist Democrats and one for Republican conservatives. Critics of that comparison believe that the Capitol protesters, who harmed no one and destroyed no property, were more violent than the Black Lives Matter and Antifa rioters, who committed murder, burned down city government buildings, and destroyed small businesses. This blatant disparity has been demonstrated every time these two movements bring destruction to our streets with little to no accountability. A prime example of our two-tiered justice system was shown in the Colinford Mattis and Urooj Rahman, case. These were two New York attorneys who brought Molotov cocktails to an anti-police protest and used them on police vehicles, placing the officers and citizens around that area in jeopardy. These two individuals pleaded guilty to "possessing and making an explosive device," which carries a maximum sentence of 10 years in prison. However, these terrorist criminals were Marxist-Communist ideologists whose criminal actions fit the Marxist-Communist narrative, and so the DOJ revised their plea to "conspiracy," recommending no more than 18 to 24 months of imprisonment.

Meanwhile, Jacob Chansley, the now infamous "QAnon Shaman," who wore a buffalo headdress and prayed at the podium in the Senate chamber, is serving a 41-month sentence for "corruptly impeding an official proceeding." Jacob Chansley did not manufacture any Molotov cocktails, burn any police vehicles, or place anyone's life in jeopardy. In fact, the released security videotapes from the Capitol building show Chansley peaceably touring the building with two Capitol police officers serving as tour guides. The two officers were making no attempt to hinder Chansley's movements but instead were just tagging along and opening doors for him.

We have reached the point in America at which we have to accept the harsh reality that most politicians and members of the media are hypocrites who will throw principles aside and alter their treatment of people to serve their political agenda. As for federal prosecutors, the disparity and inconsistent treatment we have been seeing goes beyond mere hypocrisy. It constitutes a breach of duty that undermines due process and the rule of law. If allowed to continue, the politicization of the criminal justice system will undermine our entire system of government. We are a Nation of laws, and whether those laws are ignored or not equally applied, makes America no better than Venezuela.

Chapter 20
Social Insanity

Biological Stupidity: Our Marxist-Communist government has allowed mentally ill males and females to self-identify as being of the opposite sex that they were born. We have males who identify as females demanding access to female sports, resulting in the inability of our daughters and sisters to compete in sports fairly. Our Marxist-Communist government has allowed males to self-identify as females and allowed them access to girls' bathrooms leading to the raping of two young girls in those bathrooms. We have young children who identify as cats and other animals or self-identify as God only knows what on any given day. We have drag queens holding reading hour sessions with first and second-graders or performing age-inappropriate erotic dances for young kids. Young children are being surgically mutilated by transforming them into a different sex than they were born. All done with the approval and encouragement of our Marxist-Communist Democrat teachers, members of Congress, and the radically "sick-minded" parents of these young children or worse yet without the permission of the child's parents. All done in the Marxist-Communist Democrat Party's attempt to indoctrinate our children into a world of Marxist-Communism, ignoring that such radical decisions are creating instability and severe mental and emotional issues as these children mature and begin to understand just what they have done to their bodies.

We have become a Nation where Critical Race Theory is being injected into every aspect of our culture; most alarming is the teaching of this philosophy in our failed federally funded public schools. Critical Race Theory reestablishes racism by teaching that one race is inherently evil racist and the other inherently victim. Critical Race Theory is only the latest front in our decades-long war against those who would destroy our American values. Marxist-Communist-inspired indoctrination by our educators in American universities is hard-edged identity politics, which portrays the United States as a country so steeped in white supremacy and racism that it must be destroyed to be saved. It sounds crazy on the surface but be assured that these extreme radical supporters of Critical Race Theory are deadly serious about using its teachings to poison the minds of our children, turn them into young revolutionaries, and in the process, destroy the America that we love and cherish.

Nothing has energized parents and grandparents quite like the events surrounding the ongoing exposure of this shocking abuse of taxpayer dollars used to spread this diabolical inspired ideology in classrooms across America. An ideology that would never have come to the attention of the parents of school-age children if not for the lockdown of our failed federally funded Marxist-Communist Democrat Party school system as a result of COVID-19. How ironic that a deadly pandemic that was used to assert control over the citizenry was also the catalyst that brought to the attention of parents the teaching of Critical Race Theory, the exposure of our children to age-inappropriate activities, and Marxist-Communism indoctrination of our children.

Despite the overwhelming evidence and first-hand exposure to the teaching of Critical Race Theory in our schools, Marxist-Communist politicians continue to deny its teaching emphatically. Critical Race Theory is being promoted by the Marxist-Communist Democrat Party, the Secretary of Education, school superintendents, school boards, teachers, and organizations such as the NAACP. In other words, its radical political message is spreading throughout the federal educational system and infecting society. Our Marxist-Communist Democrat Party government is utilizing our tax dollars to abuse and attack our children and our civil rights. Social and news media utilize this politically motivated ideology to criticize or blame Americans for experiences of racism. The Marxist-Communist Democrat elements of our society argue that race advances the interests of white people at the expense of people of color and that the notion that American laws are color-blind is false and, in reality, a continuation of racial discrimination. Conservatives maintain that critical race theory is based on political motivation instead of evidence and reason, rejects truth and merit, and opposes racial tolerance.

Since 2020, conservative lawmakers at both the State and Federal levels have sought to ban the education of critical race theory in primary and secondary schools, as well as the training of this ideology inside our federal agencies and military forces. Advocates of such bans argue that critical race theory is a false anti-American villainization of white people, promotes division and indoctrinates children to hate. These advocates are accused of misrepresenting the principles of Critical Race Theory to silence discussions of racism, equity, social injustice, and the history of racism in America. In reality, critical race theory is a reinstitution of racism in America, creating renewed hatred based on skin color and ideology, all for destabilizing American institutions. Under these conditions, it will be an uphill battle for America to endure.

Transgender and drag queens are being allowed to interact with our young children in the school environment, holding reading sessions often dressed in age-inappropriate sexually erotic garments. Drag Queens are being allowed to perform age-inappropriate erotic dance routines at venues in which young children are in attendance—brought to these sexually explicit performances by morally ill parents who lack the moral decency to realize that exposing their young children to such performances is both emotionally and mentally unhealthy and is child abuse. Performances held in establishments where city codes and statutes explicitly prohibit minors from entering.

Source & Additional Information: (https://www.heritage.org/gender/commentary/the-lefts-goal-creating-new-generation-drag-kids) (https://www.westernjournal.com/public-schools-bring-in-drag-queens-to-teach-kindergartners-about-gender-ideology/) (https://eagleforum.org/publications/insights/nothing-harmless-and-fun-about-drag-queens-and-children.html)

Our young children are being exposed to and encouraged by their school teachers to take gender-altering medication, assume a name befitting their preferred gender, as well as the changing of pronouns when fellow students or their teachers address them. Gender self-identification ideology is being encouraged and supported by the Marxist-Communist Democrat Party and the Department of Education. It is an ideology that elementary school educators are imposing upon our young children without input or permission from the parents of these children. Our school teachers are destroying our trust in them to do what they were intended to do: teach our children how to read, write, and do arithmetic; teach our children the history of our great country, our Constitution, and what it means to be in a country which guarantees their God-given rights to life, liberty, and the pursuit of happiness; to teach our children social skills for them to interact with others effectively.

Our school system was never intended to be a place where young girls and boys were to be convinced that they were "born in the wrong body" and encouraged to take experimental drugs, hormones, and surgeries that would leave them stunted, scarred, and infertile. Yet that is precisely what is being pushed on our children by the Marxist-Communist Democrat Party, which not only supports this horror but dares to condemn those who would protect children from this "sinful" and "cruel" ideology. The Marxist-Communist Democrat Party has repeatedly criticized Governor Ron DeSantis' Florida Health Department's efforts that prioritize counseling over the medical transitioning of young children, going as far as calling these efforts "close to sinful" and "cruel." The Marxist-Communist Democrat Party emphasizes the humanity of children who struggle with an identity at odds with their biological sex, stating, "They love, they have feelings, they have inclinations," as if to suggest that the Florida Health Department considers these kids as subhuman. The Marxist-Communist Democrat Party knowingly and purposefully fails to address the horrific outcomes of transgender medical intervention. the Marxist-Communist Democrat Party has also failed to address Pope Francis' statement that "the ideology of gender is one of the most dangerous ideological colonization, denying the richness of men and women, and of all humanity in the tension of the differences." Instead, the Marxist-Communist Democrat Party has chosen to advance an ideology in direct opposition to the teaching of the Catholic Church, Scripture, and Christian tradition spanning over the past 2,000 years. The Marxist-Communist Democrat Party has embraced the moral authority to declare sinful, which Catholicism does not consider sinful, while promoting that which Catholicism does consider sinful.

Christians must be compassionate and remember that each one of us is often a sinner. Our moral obligation is not to walk about as if we are morally superior to those who struggle with different sins and temptations than we do. The Marxist-Communist Democrat Party's dilutional notion that acceptance of sexual behavior or choices is in keeping with traditional Christian doctrine could not be further from the truth and signals a political weaponization of religious faith. Both the Old Testament and the New Testament cite Jesus' warning about children, saying that "whoever causes one of these little ones who believes in me to sin, it would be better for him to have a great millstone fastened around his neck and to be drowned in the depth of the sea" (Matthew 18:5-6). It strains the imagination to believe that Jesus would approve of telling children that they are *really* members of a different sex than the one to which they were born and urging them to take experimental drugs with long-term consequences, setting them on a path to removing perfectly healthy sex organs. It is hard to imagine anything crueler while at the same time implying that God made a mistake.

House Republicans, on April 11th, 2023, passed a bill that prohibits transgender women and girls from participating in female athletic programs, bringing to the forefront an issue that has thus far only been addressed at the state legislators' level and individual sports associations. Florida Republican Representative Greg Steube sponsored the "Protection of Women and Girls in Sports Act" bill. The bill passed in the House in a party-line 219-203 vote. It is the first standalone bill to restrict the rights of transgender people considered in the House. This bill would ensure that biological females compete against other biological females in women's sports operated, sponsored, or facilitated by a recipient of federal funding. Not one Republican voted against the bill, and not a single Marxist-Communist Democrat in the House of Representatives voted to protect girl's and women's sports. This is a clear indication of where the Marxist-Communist Democrat Party stands when it comes to protecting our daughters, sisters, and wives. Unfortunately, the Senate is highly unlikely to pass the bill as the Marxist-Communist Democrat Party currently controls the Senate. Should the bill somehow pass the Senate, the Marxist-Communist Democrat Party White House would veto the bill. This should have been an easily bipartisan consensus issue as both Democrats and Republicans have biological females within their families and social realm. It should not be controversial that girls deserve a chance to compete in sports against their physical peers, not boys. Across the country, girls are losing to biological males who now identify as transgender. It confirms the extent that the Marxist-Communist Democrat Party is willing to go to implement an agenda to destroy the social and moral fiber of our Nation. And yet we have American citizens who still vote Democrat despite their knowledge that these highly controversial actions are being taken against female members of their families.

Source & Additional Information: (https://www.cnn.com/2023/04/20/politics/house-transgender-sports-bill/index.html)

This morally ethical bill will amend Title IX, the Federal Civil Rights Act, to recognize sex as that which is "based solely on a person's reproductive biology and genetics at birth." It specifically calls for prohibiting recipients of federal financial assistance that operate athletic activities from allowing transgender women and girls to participate on female sports teams. It would not, however, block transgender women and girls from training or practicing in female athletic programs so long as no female is deprived of a roster spot on a team or sport, opportunity to participate in a practice or competition, scholarship, admission to an educational institution" or other benefits. However, this amendment to Title IX has failed to advance during the last three Congresses as a result of Marxist-Communist Democrat members' united opposition. *(Title IX, the Federal Civil Rights Act)*

Congress, in 1972, created Title IX to protect women's sports and enable women to have an equal playing field in athletics. In devotion to their trans idols, the Marxist-Communist Democrat Party has flipped Title IX on its head. Title IX was created for women's sports, and now the left wants to kill it. In Marxist-Communist Democrat fashion, they are giving homage to the trans movement and abandoning women all across the country. Parents do not want biological men in locker rooms or bathrooms with their daughters, nor do they believe it is equitable or fair for a male to compete against women in female athletics. It is not just parents who object; it is also the girls themselves. "A male was in our locker room when volleyball girls were trying to get changed," Blake Allen, a 14-year-old, told the Daily Signal in the fall of 2022. "And after I asked him to leave, he did not and later looked over at girls with their shirts off. And it made many people uncomfortable and feel violated. And I left as soon as I could in a panic."

But the Marxist-Communism left does not care that girls like Blake feel violated. Her feelings are irrelevant in today's Marxist-Communist political arena, so much for this being the golden era of feminism. Once again, the social system in which positions of dominance and privilege are primarily held by men is winning, even if it is now under the disguise of the transgender ideology. So much for the Marxist-Communist Democrat Party being the party of women's rights. And where are the various outspoken women political activist groups? Nowhere to be found to rally against this morally sinful action by the Marxist-Communist Democrat Party.

The doctrine of marriage as the union between a male and a female traces back throughout written history and is supported by every known religion worldwide. However, our Marxist-Communist government refuses to acknowledge this reality as a fundamental truth of the universe. On December 13, 2022, President Joe Biden signed into law the "Respect for Marriage Act," requiring the United States federal government and all states and territories to recognize the validity of same-sex civil marriages in the United States and purports to protect religious liberty, which is far from an accurate statement. The "Respect for Marriage Act" opens all religious entities and businesses to ongoing lawsuits by individuals who demand religious entities and businesses conduct activities against their religious doctrine or beliefs. This act is no more than an unconstitutional move by the Federal government to further enforce its will on the American citizenry. Like abortion decisions, marriage decrees constitutionally belong in the hands of the individual states.

Source & Additional Information: (https://www.congress.gov/117/plaws/publ228/PLAW-117publ228.pdf)

On December 8th, 2022, the House of Representatives approved Joe Biden's Respect for Marriage Act. The bill was passed 258-169. Every single Democrat voted for the legislation, as did thirty-nine Marxist-Communist Republicans. One hundred and sixty-nine Republicans voted against the measure, while one cowardly Republican voted "present," and four did not vote at all. A present vote and no vote from Republicans are votes in support of the measure. The Respect for Marriage Act has no language to protect those whose religious beliefs do not conform with this Act. The minor protections included are subjective rather than objective. They are inadequate in addressing many of the gravest risks this bill poses, particularly those threatening the tax-exempt status of religious non-profits.

Nowhere in the bill do the terms conjugal marriage, traditional marriage, biological marriage, biblical marriage, natural marriage, historical marriage, husband-wife marriage, man-woman marriage, or any other possible variation appear. The bill does not explicitly state that it will not revoke the tax-exempt status of a religious organization if that religious organization fails to comply due to its religious beliefs. As written, it gives ample opportunity for the Internal Revenue Service and any other taxing authority to do that should that taxing authority file litigation against such religious organizations.

The Act reads as follows: *"Diverse beliefs about the role of gender in marriage are held by reasonable and sincere people based on decent and honorable religious or philosophical premises. Therefore, Congress affirms that such people and their diverse beliefs are due proper respect."*

Here are the Republicans who voted for the bill: Kelly Armstrong (N.D.); Don Bacon (Neb.); Ken Calvert (Calif.); Kat Cammack (Fla.); Mike Carey (Ohio); Liz Cheney (Wyo.); John Curtis (Utah); Rodney Davis (Ill.); Tom Emmer (Minn.); Brian Fitzpatrick (Pa.); Mike Gallagher (Wisc.); Andrew Garbarino (N.Y.); Mike Garcia (Calif.); Carlos Gimenez (Fla.); Tony Gonzales (Texas); Anthony Gonzalez (Ohio); Jamie Herrera Beutler (Wash.) Ashley Hinson (Iowa); Darrell Issa (Calif.); Chris Jacobs (N.Y.); David Joyce (Ohio); John Katko (N.Y.); Nancy Mace (S.C.); Nicole Malliotakis (N.Y.); Peter Meijer (Mich.); Mariannette Miller-Meeks (Iowa); Blake Moore (Utah); Dan Newhouse (Wash.); Jay Obernolte (Calif.); Tom Rice (S.C.); Mike Simpson (Idaho); Elise Stefanik (N.Y.); Bryan Steil (Wis.); Chris Stewart (Utah); Mike Turner (Ohio); Fred Upton (Mich.); David Valadao (Calif.); Ann Wagner (Mo.); and Michael Waltz (Fla.).

Woke Insanity: "Wokism," often referred to as the "Cancel Culture," is a mind virus, an intolerant and sanctimonious ideology, which is evil, cruel, and dangerous to our Constitutional Republic. This perilous ideology is running rampant throughout the United States, demanding that their ideology be accepted, or you will be canceled. Being canceled means that an individual's life and/or business, which they spent their entire life building, will be destroyed. Strangely enough, even though those who ascribe to this "wokism" movement are a tiny fraction of our population, they have somehow managed to intimate some of America's largest corporations and well-known celebrities to bend a knee to their demands. Yet, these entities and the citizens of the United States cannot find the courage to stand up against them and say NO to their radical demands.

"Wokism" is nothing more than a politically unfounded sense of victimhood and lack of control of their actions as a result. "I'm a victim of social pressures. Therefore, I am not responsible for my actions." This false sense of victimhood denies those who fall for this ideology of true freedom. The whole point of putting freedom at the center of our Constitutional Republic is to push politics to the side. Exactly the reverse is now happening in the United States, for it is precisely in this area of personal freedom that "woke" politics demands allegiance. The term "woke" is used by both Marxist-Communist and conservatives alike to describe several radical ideologies, including critical race theory, social justice, and gender theory. The most convincing evidence for this is their insistence that we change the pronouns we use and not only change them but also start misrepresenting reality: a woman is not a "she" but a "they." Has a woman suddenly become a women? What could be more irrational and invasive to our sense of personal freedom?

"Wokism" has overtaken our country and our very heritage. People, businesses, major companies, and our government are bowing to the demands of a small fraction of mentally ill idiots in fear of being canceled out. Yet these same people, businesses, companies, and our federal government, who are all so easily brought to their knees over the fear of mere words, have no problem sending our eighteen-, nineteen-, and twenty-year-old children off to face the horrors of unwarranted wars. These young men and women sent off to war by these entities are expected to endure indescribable levels of fear and suffering for up to thirteen months while American institutions quiver in their shoes over mere words.

Republican politicians and voters alike are being attacked by the wokism movement in every aspect, from climate change policies, social responsibility, transgender rights, critical race theory, and mandatory COVID-19 vaccines to the Black Lives Matter movement. The Marxist-Communist Democrat Party administration seems more interested in woke fantasies than the complex reality Americans face in their daily life. The Marxist-Communist Democrat Party and the woke mob are dictating that we must partake in their rituals, salute their flags, and worship at the altar of their false idols. Wokism in the United States military is degrading discipline and our combat readiness, as well as challenging recruitment and retention efforts. Young men and women join the military to be warriors, not weak-kneed woke idiots.

Pride Month: June has been designated as "Pride Month," where the everyday LGBTQIA+ propaganda from our Marxist-Communist news outlets gets amplified out of all proportions. Throughout June, we can expect to be inundated with everything from store displays to commercials and parades that promote the gay, queer, and transgender agenda. On June 10th, 2023, the White House held a party as part of the month-long Pride celebration, which has increasingly turned into a promotion of trans activism and gender ideology. President Biden attended the party and spoke to activists on the South Lawn of the presidential residence. One of those activists was 27-year-old Rose Montoya, a surgically altered trans-woman from Idaho. Moments after talking to Biden, Montoya pulled down the top of her dress and played with her breasts. She then posted a video of herself and two topless trans-men activists on Instagram, with the White House visible in the background. If there was any doubt, viewers could hear whoever shot the video asking, "Are we topless at the White House?"

Marxist-Communist politicians and their woke followers believe people are born with blank minds, which the government can shape over time. The Russian/Chinese Communists and German Nazis thought they could mold children into a new type of human being who would, without descent or opposition, follow Marxist-Communist dictates and work unselfishly to protect and work for the good of their ideology. Today, the Marxist-Communist elements within the United States are molding our children to willingly participate in destroying our Constitutional Republic and Western Civilization in general. Nowhere is this clearer than in the transgender movement. Gender dysphoria is a mental illness that needs to be treated and not used to further the Marxist-Communist ideology. The Marxist-Communist Democrat Party has turned this mental illness into a weapon of war against our American culture. The Marxist-Communist Democrat Party is corrupting our children in our schools with age-inappropriate reading material, transgender and sex-altering curriculums, the teaching of Critical Race Theory, mentally and emotionally dividing our children from their parents, and enlisting these indoctrinating young minds to push their agenda to destroy our Constitutional Republic. The Marxist-Communist Democrat Party has gone a long way to normalize gender dysphoria in our future generations by exposing children to sexualized performances, pumping them full of dangerous puberty-blocking drugs, and mutilating their genitals, all to overthrow the faith, family, and freedom that underpins our society. We know that the Marxist-Communist Democrat Party is evil and corrupt to the core, but to see so many parents approve of and participate in this lunacy is total insanity. The extent of the Marxist-Communist Democrat Party's evilness can be seen in their attempts to normalize pedophilia by corrupting the word pedophilia by rebranding the term as "minor-attracted persons." The Marxist-Communist Democrat Party has caved to woke ideology and is willing to accept child molestation.

Most gays and lesbians oppose the indoctrination of our children to these adult inappropriate sexual issues in our education system and being promoted for profit by American box stores. There are groups like "Gays Against Groomers" who are actively trying to purge the transexuals and pedophiles from their ranks, but overall, the response from the gay community is restrained. Meanwhile, the Marxist-Communist Democrat Party is coordinating a full-scale assault on our children, an assault much akin to how the Communists and Nazis achieved absolute political power in their countries. The Marxist-Communist Democrat Party is using gays, lesbians, the mentally ill, greedy medical establishments, cowardly corporate executives, and naïve parents to achieve their evil agenda. This is not about tolerance; it is about satanic evil that is threatening the very foundation of our Constitutional Republic: faith, family, and freedom.

Also complicit with the indoctrination of our children in age-inappropriate marketing and selling of transgender products are family stores such as Target, which has launched its "Pride" line of clothing and merchandise for kids. The retail giant is not alone carrying woke wares for children and teens. Similar items, which have prompted the call for the "Bud Light treatment" of Target, can also be found at Walmart, Kohl's, Macy's, Old Navy, The Gap, Apple, and many more. North Face, a popular go-to for high-quality outdoor gear, has taken what some see as a profound dive into retail radicalism with its "Summer of Pride" campaign. North Face is using a drag queen, who wears excessive makeup and a poofy wig, to market their campaign. He goes by the name

Pattie Gonia. Gonia sports a mustache and introduces himself as a "real-life homosexual."

Walmart is also just as bad as Target and Bud Light. One of the more controversial items the mega retail giant offers is a "breathable" breast binder for "trans, lesbian, and tomboys." The binders, marked as a "NEW" product, are only available online. The listing for the chest binder on Walmart's website shows various pictures of a young girl modeling the breast binder. Kohl also sells LGBT merchandise for children, including an extensive range of pride merchandise, including a Baby Pride Bodysuit set. Kohl, which has long promoted itself with the slogan "The More You Know, the More You Kohl's," is also selling items like a Care Bear Pride Rug and, for early holiday shoppers, a "Gay Pride Christmas Nutcracker" complete with rainbow pants and a purple hat. Other stores with pride apparel for children include Old Navy, which sells Pride unisex swim trunks for toddlers, and Macy's, which is selling several kids' toys under its "Pride+Joy" campaign, launched around the same time as Target's Pride month.

While our Marxist-Communist government goes out of its way to promote an entire month to these insane and ridiculous movements, only one day of recognition is provided for those who gave the ultimate sacrifice in defense of our Constitutional Republic and one day for those who served in our military forces to protect our Nation and its citizens. Is this not American insanity?

Social Insanity: We slaughter the unborn in the name of freedom while our birth rate dips lower year by year; our national debt is so high that we can no longer even pretend that we will someday repay that debt, a $35-trillion monument to our federal government's corrupt squandering and cowardly refusal to confront reality; our 'entertainment' is sadistic, destructive, and as enduring as an old pair of shoes forgotten in the back of the closet; and our music is noise that spans the spectrum from annoying to repulsive. We are now living in a Nation that sees patriotism as insurrection, where treason is celebrated and perversion sanctified; we have become a Nation where a man in blue gets less respect than a man in a dress, a Nation that asks young men to fight for a nation our leaders no longer believe in; and a country which has lost its moral compass, its honor, and its integrity?

How easily it was for half of our country's population to willingly submit to the Marxist-Communist Democrat Party's corrupt control, which dictated that we wear face masks, submit to lockdowns, and accept the closing of small businesses while allowing large corporations to remain open—all with absolutely no scientific evidence that doing so would have any impact on the spreading of COVID. Many medical studies have shown the exact opposite, with no acceptance of these medical studies by our federal government, whose real intent is not to protect American lives but to control American lives. Now, we have a Globalist Administration willing to sign a treaty agreement with the World Health Organization (WHO), giving them full authority to dictate America's response and actions anytime this foreign Chinese-controlled organization determines that there is a pandemic. There are no limits to what the World Health Organization may determine to be a pandemic; it could be any issue, including but not limited to disease, overpopulation, hunger, war refugees, or anything the Chinese Communist Party determines. America's entering into such a treaty will end our Nation's sovereignty and usher in Marxist-Communist Globalism without the approval of the American citizenry. Where is the honor and integrity of our political leaders who are more than willing to abdicate our nation's sovereignty to an organization controlled by China?

Crime Epidemic: The United States is in a crisis as a result of an out-of-control crime wave. We have reached a point in our history where prosecutors are more interested in Marxist-Communist ideologies than in the rule of law. These Marxist-Communist

Democrat prosecutors are overtaking our states and communities, and they have no moral or ethical problem with sacrificing the safety and security of the residents they have taken an oath to protect and serve.

Throughout the United States, we are experiencing an increasing number of violent crimes by criminals who are being released back into society to await their trials. Many of these career criminals are receiving nothing more than slaps on the wrists in plea deals that do not hold them accountable for their criminal actions, nor do they protect our communities. This Marxist-Communist Democrat Party's push for chaos and anarchy in our communities is meant to instill fear and intimidation in citizens to break their will to resist the transformation of our Constitutional Republic into a Marxist-Communist regime. The United States of America will pay a devastating price as a result. These crime surges do not happen by accident. They are encouraged and promoted by the Marxist-Communist Democrat Party's agenda to severely transform our prosecutorial system into a two-tier justice system: one for those who ascribes to the Marxist-Communist ideology and one for the constitutional conservative citizens of the United States. The American experiment was never meant to operate in this manner.

Record levels of crimes are being committed in cities primarily governed by poor Marxist-Communist Democrat leadership. The Marxist-Communist Democrat political machine that dominates these crime-ridden cities is not interested in setting things right. According to this morally deprived political machine, the savage beating of innocent people in the street is just a "silly" indiscretion of youth. These teen looters and street thugs are not looking for jobs; they are looking to create chaos and an effortless way to obtain money for their lifestyles. This behavior is not just random youthful indiscretion; it points to a much deeper cultural problem. These young teenagers need fathers in their homes, a stable family life, and communities where crime and unruly behavior are discouraged and punished to the full extent of the law. They need safe quality schools that focus on character instead of dangerous ideologies that promote so-called social justice and cultural revolution. Teenagers committing these often-violent crimes do not get any basic needs in their homes. Instead of working to solve this problem, the Marxist-Communist Democrat Party chooses instead to lecture the country that we are "systemically racist."

Meanwhile, a demoralized police force finds it difficult, if not impossible, to do their job, as crime levels continue to climb. Decent, law-abiding citizens who have become fed up with their crime-ridden environment are forced to move to republican governed cities where a shortage of police officers and general safety are not an issue. These are Marxist-Communist Democrat Party self-inflicted wounds and a tragedy for our once beautiful and safe American cities. And our Marxist-Communist media? They pretend that there is no crime wave, and that dangerous and ugly city conditions are just a "housing" problem, which is absolute nonsense. Our cities do not have to be dangerous places filled with drug addicts passed out on the street. Instead of fabricate excuses for why things continue getting worse, the political leaders within these cities need to be identify solutions and then implement them. Failure by these Marxist-Communist Democrat Party-governed cities not by accident but is a well-thought-out choice in keeping with the Marxist-Communism playbook.

What positions of trust are equity and diversity qualifications for? If, as recently occurred, a major airline company boasted that its pilot training program is based on equity and diversity rather than on competence and ability, this should make anyone flying on that airline genuinely concerned. It certainly is not a recipe for confidence at thirty-five thousand feet in the air to know in the back of your mind that an affirmative action pilot is flying your airplane rather than a highly qualified pilot. Readers may want to google comments from qualified airline pilots regarding the near disasters caused by quota pilots. Their stories are frightening. Airline shareholders must look into the hiring criteria of the airline in which they hold shares, and if that airline is hiring pilots based on diversity and equity, demand the firing of every woke imbecile who participated in this idiotic dangerous decision, and force them to go back to hiring pilots based on ability to fly a plane. This holds equally true for any business where you place your or your family's general welfare in their hands. Diversity leads to perversity and potential injury or death! Are all of these woke ideologists brain-dead?

<u>Source & Additional Information</u>: *(https://www.prnewswire.com/news-releases/united-sets-new-diversity-goal-50-of-students-at-new-pilot-training-academy-to-be-women-and-people-of-color-301262479.html)*

<u>White Supremacy</u>: A new piece of legislation referred to the Judiciary Committee regarding "white supremacy inspired hate crime" has received widespread backlash since it was introduced on January 9th, 2023, as H.R. 61, by Marxist-Communist Democrat Party Representative Sheila Jackson Lee from Texas. The bill's stated intent is to "prevent and prosecute white supremacy inspired hate crime and conspiracy to commit white supremacy inspired hate crime." In addition, the bill intends to amend Title 18 of the United States Code to expand the scope of hate crimes. The Texas Democrat's proposal would define the conspiracy to engage in a "white supremacy-inspired hate crime" primarily as someone who has planned, developed, prepared, or perpetrated a crime inspired by white supremacy. A secondary definition of such a conspiracy is someone who has published material that supports or advances the ideology, as well as any "antagonism" based on a belief in the replacement theory. The definition also includes speech that is directed against or vilifies "any non-White person or group." The stated material would include things published on social media that have "the likelihood" of being viewed by people predisposed to or susceptible to being encouraged to engage in such a crime.

Source & Additional Information: (https://issuevoter.org/bills/4210/hr61-118-leading-against-white-supremacy-act-hr-61?)

This proposed act criminalizes posting any material that, to a "reasonable person," could "motivate actions." In this period of our history that we now find ourselves, I do not believe that there are many reasonable people left in our country, certainly not in the Marxist-Communist Democrat Party. More troubling, the definition extends to material that "was read, heard, or viewed by a person," who was then part of the planning, development, preparation, or perpetration of a white supremacy-inspired hate crime. The bill further seeks to give the DOJ the power to prosecute people found guilty of such a conspiracy, thereby tightening the government's grip of authority and power over the population. What is certain about this bill is that it was not purposed by a "reasonable person." Jackson Lee's bill would amend Section 249(a)(1) of Title 18, which deals specifically with hate crimes, adding the phrase "or because of white supremacy-based motivation against any person" after the existing wording. This would automatically place any middle-aged white male in unfounded legal jeopardy, as according to the woke Marxist-Communist Democrat Party, all middle-aged white males are born systemic racist supremacists.

Child Trafficking: It is tempting to think that child trafficking is a problem that only affects the developing world. On the contrary, the exploitation of children for forced labor or sex is alive and well in the United States. The United States is ranked as one of the worst countries in the world for human trafficking. According to a report by the State Department, the top three nations of origin for victims of human trafficking in 2018 were the United States, Mexico, and the Philippines. Similar to other countries, child trafficking in the United States is often driven by poverty. The most vulnerable children are those in our foster care system, homeless youths, or those experiencing abuse or neglect at home. There are more than 365,000 American children who go missing in our country every year. Thirty percent of those missing are being sexually trafficked. That comes out to be approximately 109,000 American children being sexually trafficked every single year.

- ➢ On average, a child enters the United States sex trade at twelve to fourteen years old. Many are runaway girls who were sexually abused as children.

- ➢ Most of the time, victims are trafficked by someone they know, such as a friend, family member, or romantic partner.

- ➢ Predators can rent a child for a single sex act for an average of ninety dollars. Often, that child is forced to have sex twenty times per day, six days a week.

- ➢ Trafficking usually occurs in hotels, motels, online websites, and at truck stops throughout the United States.

- ➢ About fifty thousand people, primarily from Mexico and the Philippines, are trafficked into the United States annually.

- ➢ According to the Federal Human Trafficking Report, "In 2018, over half (51.6%) of the criminal human trafficking cases active in the United States were sex trafficking cases involving only children."

- ➢ Traffickers use social media platforms to recruit and advertise victims of human trafficking, according to anti-trafficking advocates.

The crisis at the southern border is directly linked to an increase in child trafficking in the United States. In April of 2023, a whistleblower told Congress' House Judiciary Committee that the "United States federal government has become the 'middleman' in a multibillion-dollar human trafficking operation targeting unaccompanied minors at the southern border." In May of 2023, United States Customs and Border Protection encountered an average of four hundred and thirty-five unaccompanied minors per day. One study suggests that drug cartels and traffickers will exploit 60% of these children in prostitution, forced labor, and child pornography. To make matters worse, in June of 2023 alone, the Biden-Harris administration released three hundred and forty-four children to non-related adults in the United States, many known to have child related criminal histories and already had multiple children in their care. These children are prime targets for traffickers for sex or labor. Notably, half of United States Immigration and Customs Enforcement's "most wanted" criminals for child trafficking are from Mexico.

The United States, which was founded upon a Judeo-Christian foundation, should be the solution to this horrendous, inhumane act upon children. Instead, we are the problem. Today, we are a source of the corruption that is enslaving children. Are we going to stand up for God's children and help these defenseless young ones by demanding our federal politician take action to correct this immoral and criminal activity, do the righteous thing as envisioned by our forefathers in the creation of our Republic, or are we going to stand by and turn a blind eye towards this wicked and evil perversion infecting our Nation?

Source & Additional Information: (https://www.foxnews.com/us/human-trafficking-in-america-among-worst-in-world-report) (https://www.state.gov/reports/2018-trafficking-in-persons-report/) (https://2017-2021.state.gov/humantrafficking-about-human-trafficking/#profile)

Child trafficking is easy to find if you know where to look. For example, an exit off an interstate highway with a truck stop, an Asian massage parlor, and an adult superstore. Each of these locations separately is statistically more likely to be a location for trafficking, including the interstate itself. If they are grouped, the statistical possibilities increase dramatically. It is also not hard to figure out the types of public policies that could reduce trafficking. Legislators should focus on social media use, the porn industry, and broken families, all complex matters that demand thoughtful solutions. But one thing that can be done immediately is less complex and more direct: The Biden-Harris administration, which is complicit with this atrocity, must follow our existing laws and seal our open and unsecured southern border. Much more must be done, but that is a critical first step that could save thousands of children each year from these horrors.

If you suspect someone is a victim of trafficking, contact the National Human Trafficking Resource Center at 1-800-373-7888. This confidential hotline is open twenty-four hours a day, every day, and helps identify, protect, and serve victims of trafficking.

Chapter 21
Chinese Dominance

In China, crime is not tolerated, and the death sentence is routinely and swiftly used as punishment and deterrence measures for terrorism, murder, and drug trafficking. As a result, China has a very low crime rate. As for religion, the Chinese Communist Party does not believe that there is a God, heaven, or hell. They do not think that those who live a life of good deeds will have salvation, and those who rain down evil on the world will be subjected to eternal damnation. Chinese citizens are brainwashed not to believe in God. The Chinese Communist Party has enslaved and is killing off the indigenous Chinese Muslim population for their religious beliefs and refusal to bow to communist demands that they forsake their Muslim faith.

China has not been involved in any expensive military wars or invaded any country for the last seventy years. However, China is seriously threatening to invade Taiwan and declare the island a territory of China under Communist Chinese Party rule. China's primary weapon of choice to conquer the world is economics and finance, with countries worldwide falling fast, including the United States, which is in deep economic trouble. In the very near future, China will employ millions of American workers and dominate thousands of small communities all over the United States. Chinese acquisition of United States farmland and businesses set a new record in 2022 and is on pace to shatter that record in 2023. A further threat to the United States is the hundreds of military-age Chinese male illegal immigrants crossing our border and disappearing into the heartland of America. No one knows where they are or their intentions.

The Smithfield Foods acquisition is an excellent example of China's move to ebbed themselves into America's production of our Nation's food sources. Smithfield Foods is the largest pork producer and processor in the world. It has facilities in twenty states and employs tens of thousands of Americans. Twenty-four hundred farms are owned by anonymous Chinese citizens with direct ties with the Chinese Communist Party military, who have complete control of these companies. In 2022, a Chinese company spent $2.6 Billion to purchase AMC Entertainment, one of the largest movie theater chains in the United States. Chinese companies control more movie ticket sales than anyone else in the world. The Chinese are now the most important employer in dozens of rural communities all over America. However, China is not just relying on acquisitions to expand its economic power. China is establishing itself in the United States by acquiring businesses nationwide. A prime example is Golden Dragon Precise Copper Tube Group, Inc., which recently broke ground on a $100M plant in Thomasville, Alabama. Many of Thomasville, Alabama residents will be glad to have jobs, but it will also become yet another community that will now be heavily dependent on Communist China. China has also established Chinese police stations in Marxist-Communist Democrat governed cities to threaten and intimidate citizens of the United States of Chinese descent by threatening harm to their relatives still in China.

Chinese-owned companies are investing in American businesses and new vehicle technology and are selling everything from seat belts to shock absorbers in retail stores. They are hiring experienced American engineers and designers to soak up domestic automakers' and suppliers' talent and expertise. If you recently purchased an "American-made" vehicle, there is an excellent chance that it has many Chinese parts. Industry analysts are hard-pressed to put a number on the Chinese suppliers in the United States. China is very interested in acquiring energy resources in the United States. For example, while Biden-Harris have put the brakes on American company's ability to mine coal, the Chinese are being allowed to mine for coal in the mountains of Tennessee. Guizhou Gouchuang Energy Holdings Group spent six hundred and sixteen million dollars to acquire Triple H Coal Company in Jacksboro, Tennessee. That acquisition was never reported by the fake news outlets. Still, now a group of conservatives in Tennessee are trying to bring attention and pressure to our politicians regarding this purchase to stop the Chinese from blowing up their mountains and taking their coal. China will soon be building entire cities in the United States, just as it has been doing in other countries. Right now, China is building a city larger than Manhattan just outside Minsk, the Capital of Belarus.

When you total up all imports and exports, China is now the number one trading nation on the entire planet; overall, the United States has run a trade deficit with China for well over a decade which exceeds twenty-three trillion dollars; China has more foreign currency reserves than any other country; has the most prominent new car market in the entire world; produces more than twice as many automobiles as does the United States; and to add insult to injury, after being bailed out by American taxpayers General Motors entered into eleven joint ventures with Chinese companies. China is the number one gold miner in the world; the uniforms for the United States Olympic team are made in China; 85% of the world's artificial Christmas trees are made in China; the new World Trade Center tower in New York includes glass imported from China; China consumes more fossil-fuel energy than does the United States; China is the leading manufacturer of goods in the entire world; and China uses more cement than all the world combined.

China is the number one producer of wind and solar power, and the equipment needed for renewable energy; China produces three times as much coal and eleven times as much steel as the United States does; China produces more than ninety percent of the global supply of rare earth elements; and China is the number one supplier of components that are critical to the operation of any national defense system. As for the United States, well, the

United States is still number one in the world for the number of lawyers per capita, the highest cost of education per student, and yet the quality and outcome are among the lowest in the world and number one in growth of its National debt which has been significantly raised in the last two years under the Marxist-Communist Biden regime. For all these number ones in the world, we have the Marxist-Communist Democrat Party to blame.

Are you starting to get the picture yet? China has been on the rise for a long time while America plays political games. Unless Congress opens its eyes and sees that Rome is burning, stop playing their political fiddles and do something soon to stop this Biden-Harris Marxist-Communist from continuing to enable China's takeover of American businesses, manufacturing, production, natural resources, and American farmland, we will soon become a territory of China under the Chinese Communist Party's authoritarian rule.

It is Not Just About Balloons: China is fast overtaking the United States as the dominant power in the world. This is a result of America's culture war, which has turned our Nation from a Constitutional Republic of enforced laws to a chaotic crime and drug-infested Nation. America maintained its past world dominance, not through tyrannical mandates and total control of the population but rather by the collective willingness of our citizens to obey the laws of the land and our governing leadership's adherence to those laws and the Constitution of the United States. This willingness on the part of the American citizens gave the United States the moral strength to stand together against any foreign advisory. This is not today's America. We have become a Nation in chaos. Our streets are violent and unsafe; teenage gangs ransack businesses; and murder by and of our young is out of control.

Case in point: Chicago, a Marxist-Communist Democrat Party-run city, is rapidly descending deeper into anarchy. Rioters are destroying, looting, and burning the stores along The Magnificent

Mile. The clueless mayor-elect blames the lack of opportunity and jobs for these savage youth's behaviors. What absolute Marxist-Communist baloney. These young thugs come from life-long government-dependent households, where no adult in three or more generations has ever gotten up in the morning and gone to work. These sponges are wards of the Marxist-Communist Democrat Party, who have no work ethic. They would not know a job even if you drove them there and back in a limousine. When will Chicago and other large metropolitan city voters wake up and realize that elected Marxist-Communist Democrats are never going to protect them and their families? Today's Marxist-Communist Democrat Party leadership and their radical woke followers are criminal-loving Marxist-Communists who back criminals over police officers. These fools just vote for more crime, more anarchy, and more chaos election cycle after election cycle to keep their *freebies* coming. Just vote Marxist-Communist Democrat. It is easier than getting a job. In the most recent election for mayor of Chicago, voters have shown just how clueless they are by electing a racist, black supremacist, cop-hating, criminal-loving radical lefty as their new mayor.

More and more businesses will flee the city, and the police will assume the fetal position. How much worse does it have to get to wake up these knee-jerk Democrat voters? Democrat voters must learn and learn soon that their party's Marxist-Communist politicians are not their friends; they are not going to protect American citizens. They will not keep their campaign promises to represent you as expected by the Constitution, but rather, they will follow the dictates of their party leaders. The Marxist-Communists are destroying the Democrat party, but the fake news outlets will never report the facts but rather only what fits the Marxist-Communist elitist's narrative. Marxist-Communist elitists do not want the citizens of America to know the truth because the truth would cause American citizens to abandon Marxist-Communist candidates like a sinking ship.

Our military, once the greatest fighting force in the world, has been severely weakening, more concerned with teaching Critical Race Theory, equity, and inclusion than with being strong and ready to engage in combat with the will and training needed to win. Our education system has denigrated to that of a third-world country, and wokism and the threat of being canceled control our corporations and institutions. Americans have become complacent with their obligation and right to vote while failing to hold elected government officials accountable for their actions or lack thereof. Our government leaders no longer respect our Constitution or the will of their constituents and have been infested by sociopaths who govern only on behalf of themselves, their donors, family, and friends. Courage, honor, and integrity are in short supply among our governing officials to do the things necessary to save our Republic and maintain our position as the dominant force on earth.

China, on the other hand, has an authoritarian government that maintains tight control over its citizens through no-nonsense laws, some of which are inhumane. China's ability to challenge America as the dominant force in the world directly results from how the Chinese Communist Party controls its citizens and directly influences matters in many countries, some of which were once allies of the United States. China has:

➢ A very low tolerance for crime. The death sentence is swiftly and routinely used for terrorists, murderers, and drug traffickers.

➢ Very low tolerance for Religion, which is a direct threat to communist ideology. They do not believe there is a Magic man in the sky. In the Chinese culture, there is no such thing as a God. They systematically eliminate anyone of faith and are getting rid of the Indigenous Chinese Muslim population as fast as they can.

➢ They have not been involved in expensive wars or invaded any country for the last seventy years.

➢ Their primary weapons of choice for conquering the world are the economy and finance, and countries around the world are falling fast.

Unknown to most people worldwide is that the Chinese Communist Party (CCP) and its People's Liberation Army (PLA) have established themselves as world leaders in the development of NeuroStrike weapons. These platforms directly attack, or even control, mammalian brains (including humans) with microwave/directed energy weapons via standalone platforms (i.e., handheld guns) or the broader electromagnetic spectrum. NeuroStrike refers to the engineered targeting of military and civilian brains using distinct non-kinetic technology to impair thinking ability, reduce situational awareness, inflict long-term neurological degradation, and fog normal cognitive functions. The Chinese Communist Party views NeuroStrike and psychological warfare as a core component of its distorted warfare strategy against the United States and its Allies in the Indo-Pacific. The Chinese Communist Party's weaponization of neuroscience extends well beyond the scope and understanding of classical microwave weapons. Their new landscape of NeuroStrike development includes using massively distributed human-computer interfaces to control entire populations and a range of weapons designed to cause cognitive damage.

<u>Source & Additional Information</u>: *(https://www.washingtontimes.com/news/2023/jul/6/chinas-military-leading-world-brain-neurostrike-we/) (https://www.washingtontimes.com/news/2023/may/24/inside-ring-neuro-strike-weapons-expand-domains-wa/)*

Chinese Communist Party biological weaponry research programs are designed to be utilized over the near term and within current strategic circumstances, such as in Taiwan. Any breakthrough in this research would provide unprecedented tools for the Chinese Communist Party to forcibly establish a new world order, which has been Xi Jinping's lifelong goal. For example, these capabilities can 'fit' into the Chinese Communist Party's anti-access/area denial strategy in the Indo-Pacific. Imagine at least partially immunized People's Liberation Army troops being inserted into geography where a specific weaponized bacterial strain has been released before their entry to prepare the ground and eliminate points of resistance. Any remaining sources of resistance on the ground are then dealt with through Chinese Communist Party NeuroStrike weaponry that instills intense fear and/or other forms of cognitive incoherence, resulting in inaction.

Source & Additional Information: (https://www.airuniversity.af.edu/Wild-Blue-Yonder/Article-Display/Article/2094603/) (https://www.nbcnews.com/politics/national-security/china-has-done-human-testing-create-biologically-enhanced-super-soldiers-n1249914)

In March of 2023, BioTech, a Nevada company fronting for the Chinese Communist Party military, was caught operating an unlicensed laboratory in Reedley, California. Following a coordinated raid on the facility by the FBI, Center for Disease Control, and State and County law enforcement, this illegal operation was found to be housing experimental lab mice. More than seven hundred live mice and one hundred and seventy-five dead mice were found. All of these mice were genetically engineered to carry deadly diseases. These mice had at least twenty potentially infectious pathogens, including HIV, hepatitis, and herpes. The seizures strongly suggest China's regime was preparing to spread diseases throughout the United States in the months before the war. This deadly lab was unsecure, poorly contained, makeshift, containing dozens of deadly pathogens near a populated area. It is believed that the strategy is to inhibit our country's response to a Chinese attack in Asia. It is unknown how many of these labs operate throughout the United States. This find also strongly suggests that the deadly COVID-19 virus was, in fact, intentionally released by the Chinese military, who had operational control over the Wuhan lab.

The net result of such a scenario would be the People's Liberation Army establishing absolute control over a country such as Taiwan while simultaneously blunting any American strategic options to intervene and physically insert personnel into the theater. This would effectively negate and render immobile America's overwhelming conventional superiority with few remedies. This scenario is based on known existing Chinese Communist Party research programs, and the clear strategic aims of those programs are unclear.

Meanwhile, in the United States, a Biden-Harris Administration and a Marxist-Communist Congress provided all federal agencies a ten percent increase in their 2024 budget except for the Department of Defense which only received a three percent increase which is lower than the current rate of inflation equating to a decrease in their 2024 budget over their 2023 budget; a Secretary of Defense and a Joint Chief of Staff more concerned with critical race theory, transgender enlistment, white supremacy, and mandated unproven vaccines than in promoting initiatives which would entice young adults to enlist eliminating our military's critical shortage of warriors to defend our country; and military force with outdated and deteriorating equipment. At this point, it would be a stretch to state that American military forces would be prepared to confront China on the battlefield.

Chapter 22
Is America a Failed Experiment?

A free and independent press is crucial to a healthy constitutional republic. Without censorship, journalism functions as a watchdog of private and government action, providing information to maintain an informed citizenry of voters. From this perspective, government efforts to directly control what is published or broadcasted on both social media and news outlets, as has been occurring in America for the past several years, represents a threat to citizen's access to vital information necessary to maintain an informed public which can then act accordingly to assure the survival of our Constitutional Republic. An independent press increases political knowledge, participation, and voter turnout, essential to civic involvement. According to *Reporters Without Borders,* more than a third of the world's people live in countries without press freedom, and the United States is on the verge of becoming a part of that population. Overwhelmingly, these people live in countries where there is no system of democracy or where there are severe deficiencies in the democratic process, not unlike what is occurring in our country.

Freedom of the press is highly problematic for anti-democratic Marxist-Communist systems of government in controlling the citizenry. Anti-democratic Marxist-Communist societies must control news and social media outlets to promote their propaganda, which is critical to maintaining their political power. This form of governance must suppress dissenters through police, military, or intelligence agencies to thrive. Any attempt by news media or individual journalists to challenge the approved "government narrative" on controversial issues will lead to their demise. In such countries, journalists operating on the fringes of what is deemed to be acceptable will find themselves the subject of considerable intimidation, which can range from simple threats to their professional careers to being fired or being professionally blacklisted. In today's America, this includes being canceled by the Woke crowd. These entities' level of control or influence is becoming painfully evident with the recent release of tweets between social media management and weaponized federal government departments and agencies. Tweets confirming this activity were released by the new owner of Twitter, Elon Musk, and testimony was obtained through House oversight committees.

Marxist-Communist controlled American news outlets are continually pushing false, inaccurate, or confusing narratives that fit the narrative of America's evolving Marxist-Communist Democratic party. They publish falsehoods that an unsuspecting and uninformed American citizenry accepts without question. Unfortunately for America's Constitutional Republic, we have a large population of potential and registered voters who cannot do simple internet research to educate themselves about what is happening within the federal government or with our election processes. American citizens do not or will not read or watch opposing views on social media or news outlets to ensure they are as informed as possible to make critical decisions when election season rolls around.

America has very few remaining free press sources willing and unafraid to report news accurately with honor and integrity; news outlets such as Newsmax or OANN are still willing to tell both sides of a story so their readers and listeners can make informed decisions. Today's press core consists of individuals educated in journalism at colleges and universities by Marxist-Communist professors. To further impede the reporting of accurate news stories, journalists who would otherwise report the truth are being pressured by Marxist-Communist media owners and editors who will only allow the publication or reporting of news that fits the narrative prescribed by the new American Marxist-Communist Democrat Party.

Today's news and social media outlets are no more than propaganda arms of a corrupt Marxist-Communist Democrat

Party, refusing to report the truth about the unconstitutional actions, fraud, and criminal activities occurring within our federal government and our election system. They refused to report on the scam and unconstitutional actions taken by State election boards, State government officials, and our justice systems during the 2020 Presidential elections, preferring to consider any such reported actions as conspiracy theories. These propaganda news sources continually refuse to report on our country's transition into a Marxist-Communist nation, fulfilling Obama's promise to forever fundamentally change America; refuse to report critical news regarding Hunter Biden's laptop, which implicates the whole Biden family in corrupt payoffs by our enemies China and Russia which would have changed the outcome of the 2020 presidential election; refuse to accurately report on the out-of-control crisis on our open southern border allowing for the entry of deadly drugs, human traffickers, terrorists, Chinese military trained saboteurs, and violent criminals. Unfortunately for our Constitutional Republic, voters who could save America from these travesties and a Marxist-Communist takeover prefer to get their news from propaganda news outlets because doing a little simple research on the internet or listening to news outlets with opposing views would take too much effort.

The willingness of America's free(?) press to report news with honor and integrity destroys America from within by creating an uninformed American citizenry. Citizens are consequently left with misinformation regarding the anti-American actions of a corrupt federal government, a woke movement attacking our police forces demanding they be defunded and disbanded, leaving the general public to the mercy of criminals, unaware of our military's denigration due to reduced funding, injection of woke ideology, or the discharging of experienced warriors for refusing to accept unconstitutional mandates leaving America vulnerable to our enemies; uninformed about ongoing attacks on our religious freedoms, our children's failed education system, and attacks against both our small and large businesses by the woke crowd because the targeted business does not accept their ideology. These unethical news outlets are purposefully withholding the whole truth regarding the January 6th protest from American citizens who have a constitutional right to this information. A free press could have ensured that those politically imprisoned protesters, whose only crime was merely being present at the Capitol building, exercised their Constitutional right to assemble and protest by holding the federal government accountable for their arrests and imprisonment without their constitutional right to due process and a speedy trial. Uninformed American citizens have no idea of the consequences these unconstitutional actions, which went unreported, will have on their, their children's, and their grandchildren's lives in the future.

Because of a largely biased Marxist-Communist government influenced press, today's American citizen is not aware of universities teaching our future leaders to think and believe in Marxist-Communist ideology; they are not mindful of Marxist-Communist wokism destroying people's livelihood just because those targeted don't think or see things the way they do; they are not aware of the wokism infiltrating our entertainment industry, our institutions of learning, our military, and our corporations; unaware what the mandating of unproven vaccines can mean to their future health; or the truth about Critical Race Theory. American citizens who depend on Marxist-Communist news outlets for their news have not been fully informed as to the depth and extent of the chaos, crime, drug abuse, and human trafficking running rampant across our country. The biased Marxist-Communist government-influenced press is not reporting on the extent of harm and deaths occurring across our country because of an open border policy allowing murderers, rapists, child traffickers and molesters, and drug dealers into our country; were not told about a sitting President's attempted to buy mid-term votes for Marxist-Communist Democrat candidates by depleting our strategic oil reserves to bring down the price of fuel slightly; of President Biden's failed attempt to beg OPEC into not increasing oil production until after the midterm election; or of the extent of irrefutable evidence against the Biden family of bribery and influence peddling. The biased Marxist-Communist government-influenced press has failed to keep the general public informed as they once had. News stories that could easily propel a journalist to the level of fame of Post reporters Bob Woodward and Carl Bernstein, who uncovered information suggesting that knowledge of the Watergate break-in and attempts to cover it up, led deeply into the upper reaches of the Justice Department, FBI, CIA, and the White House. But today's mainstream media reporters and news outlets are only interested in reporting Marxist-Communist propaganda.

What the biased Marxist-Communist government-influenced press did ensure is that American citizens were well aware of President Biden's promise to forgive college student loan debts. Done in an attempt to buy those student's votes for the Marxist-Communist Democrat party. Of course, what these young, supposedly highly educated college students and graduates failed to learn in their academic studies was that President Biden is a known pathological liar. They did not learn that Biden and the Marxist-Communist federal government would never be able to follow through on their promise because doing so would be unconstitutional and would never survive a court challenge. The biased Marxist-Communist government-influenced press did enssure the reporting of the public arrest and humiliation of those opposing the Marxist-Communist Democrat Party, the unprecedented raid on the home of a former President who will be an opposing candidate against Biden in 2024, and the endless unprecedented and flimsy indictments by Marxist-Communist District Attorneys and Grand Juries of a former president of the United States.

The popular social media platforms that many Americans use to interact and exchange information regarding social and political events are censored, denying access to anyone who opposes the Marxist-Communist narrative or wishes to exercise their First Amendment right to free speech. These platforms have been exposed for their collaboration with our federal justice system to censor or eliminate any dialog, which includes anti-Marxist-Communist conversations. The FBI has been hiring private 'spies' to create false characters and use them to gain access to social media sites to learn what is happening on Reddit, Whatsapp, Discord, and other sites. This is not to protect you from terrorists but to protect the Marxist-Communist government from dissent. Social media platforms are censoring the free speech rights of conservatives, collaborating with the current Marxist-Communist Democrat Administration to block any anti-Marxist-Communist Democrat Party dialog that does not support their agenda—actions all straight out of the Marxist-Communist playbook. Patriotic Kennedy-era Democrats seem to choose to get their news from the media, which are no more than propaganda arms of the Marxist-Communist Democrat party. As a result, these Patriotic Democrats never get the full story or hear about news reports regarding the Marxist-Communist Democrat Party's failures or blatant disregard of our God-given rights under the Constitution. These Kennedy-era Democrats do not even realize that the Democrat Party their parents and grandparents believed in no longer exists.

Randi Weingarten, president of the American Federation of Teachers (AFT) and a member of the AFL–CIO, sings songs of praise for ‹LifeBrand,' a service that monitors social media posts seeking to find and mark any that are, in their opinion, 'problematic.' This is where the United States is headed. Big Tech entities already use Artificial Intelligence (AI) to monitor everything we say and do. There are somewhat effective options to limit a person's online exposure to these secretive operatives; one such option is KAMO, an application from the folks who publish CCLEANER, which periodically changes your internet address & server. So, one minute, you might be on a server in Billings, MT, and the next minute, you will be switched to a secure server in Oslo, Norway, or some other place. The idea is that frequently changing your server location minimizes these spyware attempts because they cannot track you for any extended period.

Marxist-Communist Democrat congressional member Alexandria Ocasio-Cortez (AOC), the Wicked Witch of Marxism and constitutional rights, has become the second most talked-about politician in America's free press after the President of the United States. Ocasio–Cortez regularly appears on Marxist-communist news outlets such as CNN and MSNBC, as well as other Marxist-communist broadcasting news channels. Ocasio-Cortez and her so-called "Squad" have taken over the Democrat party and are instrumental in the rapid transformation of the party into the Marxist-Communist party we see today. She is also one of the primary influencers on Capitol Hill and a supporter of purely Marxist-Communist legislation. In April of 2023, the outspoken Ocasio-Cortez appeared on MSNBC's "Inside with Jen Psaki" to discuss current affairs. During the exclusive interview on April 23rd, 2023, Ocasio-Cortez and Psaki covered various topics, from abortion laws to various Republican leaders, to climate change. When talking about conservative news media outlets, Ocasio-Cortez stated that cable news outlets such as Fox News and their most popular and highest-rated host, Tucker Carlson, do nothing more than advocate for the incitement of violence. She noted that the FOX network and similar broadcast television companies should be subject to federal laws and regulations that would limit the free speech of such conservative news media and, apparently, any other entity that speaks out against Marxist-Communism. Although Ocasio-Cortez is anti-free press, the United States Constitution and rule of law make it clear that all media companies, whether conservative or Marxist-Communist leaning, are to be safe against attacks and attempts to shut them down purely based on their ideology.

No one of influence could more eloquently express the importance of a free press and the rule of law than Professor Alan Dershowitz. Professor Dershowitz is a nationally known constitutional scholar and a socialist Democrat. Conservatives would probably not agree on most of his social issues stance. Still, when it comes to the law and the United States Constitution, nobody is more knowledgeable and dedicated to equal justice in America. Professor Dershowitz is a courageous man who puts his country above being a liberal. Sadly, this principled, honest man has lost friends because he believes in the rule of law. Hopefully, he realizes that any person who shuns him for his respect for the law and the principles of our Constitution was never a good friend in the first place.

"Solutions"

Chapter 23
Election Integrity

There is more to democracy than free and fair elections, but there can be no democracy without them. Citizen involvement and constant vigilance are required to protect this critical element of political freedom from the threats organized against it. Threats of outright fraud on election day have now been extended to days and weeks, providing additional opportunities for fraud to be committed. Threats that are real regardless of what the fake news tells you. Since the 2020 general election, there has been a national citizens' movement to learn about the election systems in our country and to understand what happened in 2020. The Marxist-Communist Democrat Party and their Marxist-Communist Republican allies do not want citizens discussing the 2020 election or questioning the process that millions of Americans believe was less than fair. We are learning more each day about how ideological advocacy groups and Marxist-Communist Democratic Party operatives and lawyers descended upon courthouses across the nation, demanding and getting changes in the duly enacted state election laws. Changes which both the United States Constitution and their State Constitutions restrict to state legislators ONLY. We are learning about judges rewriting the election rules in many cases after voting had started. We also have learned how one billionaire, Mark Zuckerberg, channeled hundreds of millions of dollars into the election system in the closing days of the general election. Zuckerberg's millions of dollars were utilized to turn election administration offices into Marxist-Communist Democrat turnout machines in targeted counties, cities, and states. These actions are hardly what Americans would think of as fair and honest elections, regardless of the media's insistence that there is 'nothing to see here' regarding the 2020 election, which is far from the truth.

The work to correct and fix our election system begins at the local level where the election offices exist. The goal is for patriotic Americans to become engaged and involved in the election process from the perspective of election operations. As many have noted, campaign engagement is crucial. Still, if the election system is hijacked by one party or candidate or partisans manipulate the outcome, the campaigns are doomed, regardless of how good the candidate or campaign may be. Election integrity is an undertaking that requires engagement and involvement year-round, year in and year out. It is not something to think about only thirty days before an election. Now is the time for all Americans to come to their country's rescue, which means becoming involved in the election process. Citizens willing to become engaged have readily available tools to help them understand what, when, and why they must act. One such tool is The Conservative Partnership Institute's Election Integrity Network, which is available to assist citizens in their efforts to build and maintain that permanent presence in every election office. You can join the Conservative Partnership Institute Election Integrity Network by signing up at www.whoscounting.us, subscribe to the "Who's Counting?" with Cleta Mitchell podcast, and help us save our country by saving our elections.

We can perform these Eight Systems of Election Integrity to keep our elections honest:

1. ***County Board of Election Liaison***: Each political party should develop a neutral relationship with the county Board of Elections employees. Political parties should then maintain ongoing contact or connection by communicating concerns or issues and obtaining any changes in election statutes and codes to ensure concerted action, cooperation, etc.

2. ***Poll Observers, poll workers, and greeters***: Recruit volunteers to serve as Poll Observers for all election sites. The role of a poll observer is critical to the ensuring of

fair and honest elections. Poll Observers are the eyes and ears of their respective political party to ensure election integrity is being conducted within the polling sites.

As a Poll Clerk/Worker you will assist the Presiding Officer/Judge to run a polling station. You will help to set up polling station equipment, assist in the issue of ballot papers to members of the public, mark the electoral register, and assist in the accurate completion of paperwork.

Poll Greeters pass out literature to voters and encourage voters to vote for their candidates. Greeters are stationed outdoors and are responsible for Reporting site issues, including voter intimidation, and directing voters to drop off absentee mail-in ballots or vote curbside. To volunteer, contact your preferred County's political party's office.

3. *__Mail Voting Processes__*: Monitors how the United States Postal Service and County Board of Election handles absentee ballots. Absentee/mail-in voting does not happen in person on Election Day but generally occurs by mail. All states allow for some form of absentee/mail-in balloting. Ballots submitted through the postal system raise concerns that ballots can too easily be compromised. Absentee/mail-in ballots are received and processed for delivery to the appropriate Board of Elections office by United States Post Offices. Post Offices should be requested to allow voting observers to tour the facility to identify the chain of custody and method of securing ballots until delivered to the County Board of Elections. During the processing of Mailed-In ballots at the County Board of Elections, there should be two observers from each party in the room, close enough to observe the ballot processing procedure.

4. ***List Maintenance:*** Our voter roll systems are not being maintained by State Board of Elections personnel to ensure that the rolls are up-to-date and accurate. As currently maintained in most states, voter rolls are hotbeds of blunders, as election officials well know. Decisions about voter list maintenance, one of state election officials' most essential bureaucratic duties, must receive intense scrutiny in every state every year. While federal law mandates a certain level of voter roll maintenance, states manage their registration databases differently. Most state officials will maintain that they are keeping voter lists clean. However, experience dictates otherwise. Inevitably, dropping voters from the rolls inspires forceful political pushback, as many voting rights activists allege that it is a form of voter suppression. They liken it to efforts to limit access, such as enacting voter ID laws, eliminating early voting, and reducing the number of polling places.

5. ***Vulnerable Voters***: Eligible voters in Nursing Home Care facilities, handicapped, and military ballots are all vulnerable to fraud. Voting is a fundamental right for every legal American citizen. Unfortunately, not all Americans can participate equally in the voting process. Many citizens find their votes are at risk of not being counted or, in the worst case, subject to fraud.

6. ***Machines & Technology***: Digital platforms are the new battleground for democracy. Shaping the flow of information on the internet is now an essential strategy for those seeking to disrupt the democratic transfer of power through elections. Incumbent political actors around the globe use both blunt and misleading methods to deter opposition movements while preserving a guise of popular legitimacy. Such internet freedom restrictions tend to escalate before and during crucial votes.

Major authoritarian powers like Russia and China have been implicated in cyberattacks and information warfare linked to elections in democratic states. Ukraine's Central Election Commission faced a wave of cyberattacks, likely emanating from Russia, before their April–May 2019 presidential election. In the run-up to the November 2018 midterm elections in the United States, Microsoft discovered that a unit associated with Russian military intelligence had created websites resembling those of the United States Senate and prominent Republican-linked think tanks to trick visitors into revealing sensitive information and passwords. Groups associated with Russia also spread disinformation across Twitter, Facebook, and YouTube during the May 2019 European Parliament elections. Such cross-border interference is meant to sow division, support favored candidates and undermine democracy.

In most countries, however, citizens of that country abused information technology to subvert the electoral process. In a review of electoral processes in thirty countries, Freedom House found three distinct forms of digital election interference: informational measures, in which online discussions are secretly manipulated in favor of the government or particular parties; technical measures, which are used to restrict access to news sources, communication tools, and in some cases the entire internet; and legal measures, which authorities apply to punish regime opponents and chill political expression.

7. ***Statutory Provisions & Compliance***: Legislative advocacy consists of engaging with legislators on either the state or federal level to influence laws and policies. A policy is a set of ideas, plans, or methods of action used to guide and determine decisions. Effective

legislative advocacy can accomplish the following: Build relationships with your legislators, educate and impact policymakers' decisions, alter existing policies, and Inspire the creation of new policies.

8. ***Audit Oversight & Development***: Advancing the best practices for auditing elections. A healthy democracy requires widespread trust in elections. In particular, people need to be sure that the official election outcomes match the will of the voters.

    ➤ Election audits that examine voted ballots provide direct evidence that the voters chose the people who take office and the ballot measures enacted.

    ➤ Audits differ from recounts in that they routinely check voting system performance in contests regardless of how close the margins of victory appear to be.

    ➤ Recounting of ballots in exceptional circumstances, such as when preliminary results show a close margin of victory. In most cases, audits require checking a small fraction of ballots, while a recount requires checking all ballots. Ideally, a post-election audit can lead to a full recount, if necessary, to correct the reported outcome. The consensus of the American population is that we should audit every election outcome. A 2018 Senate Intelligence Committee report states, "States should consider implementing more widespread, statistically sound audits of election results. Risk-limiting audits, in particular, can be a cost-effective way to ensure that votes cast are votes counted."

    ➤ The bipartisan Presidential Commission on Election Administration recommended that audits "must be conducted after each election, as part of a comprehensive audit program" and specifically endorsed risk-limiting audits.

- ➤ The National Academies of Science, Engineering, and Medicine's 2018 consensus study report on election security recommended audits that "include manual examination of statistically appropriate samples of paper ballots cast" and advocated implementing risk-limiting audits.

Republicans trying to clean up voter rolls are looking at individual names to find deceased voters, felons, and non-citizen voters. This method, while good, does not find thousands of phony voters at a time. What needs to be done is to search property addresses where blank ballots are sent. For example, if a hundred or more ballots are sent to a one-family dwelling, that is evidence of fraud. Ballots sent to commercial addresses and vacant lots are not residences, but the Party operatives will harvest those ballots. Investigators must uncover blank ballots sent to temporary addresses like hotels, hospitals, and detox centers. The persons to whom the ballots were sent do not live there anymore, or perhaps they never existed. These are called ghost voters or phantom voters. Marxist-Communist Democrat Party officials harvest these phony ballots. When they lose on election night, they determine how many votes they need to win and then dump thousands of ghost ballots into the vote-counting system.

Another unconstitutional severe infringement on our election process is the involvement of entities outside of State legislators. During the 2020 and 2022 elections, several key states' supreme courts and state secretaries injected themselves into the election process, imposing unconstitutional requirements such as extended voting periods, ballot drop boxes, and no justified absentee voting. Republican Tim Moore, the speaker of the North Carolina House of Representatives, asks the nation's highest court to recognize that state legislatures have preeminent authority under the Constitution to make the rules for presidential and congressional elections without state courts getting involved. Article I, Section 4 clearly articulates Tim Moore's accurate position on the issue of election decisions. "The Times, Places, and Manner of holding Elections for Senators and Representatives shall be prescribed in each State by the Legislature thereof;" The United States Constitution does not directly address who has the authority to make these decisions regarding the election of a President. In this situation, we must default to the Tenth Amendment: *"The powers not delegated to the United States by the Constitution, nor prohibited by it to the States, are reserved to the States respectively, or to the people."* As can be expected, the Marxist-Communist Democrat Party officials are asking the United States Supreme Court to dismiss State Representative Moore's case in which Republicans want the court to recognize state legislatures' power to regulate federal elections without interference from state courts, which they correctly state the United States Constitution requires.

Further examples of election-related misconduct and failure to follow their own State Constitution occurred in Fulton County, Georgia. Supported by over eighteen hundred pages of documented evidence of illegal voting in the 2020 general election in Georgia, the chief judge in Fulton County, Judge Chris Brasher, failed to appoint a judge eligible to hear the post-election contest, resulting in not ever hearing the testimony of experts and eyewitnesses or the presentation of evidence of the problems in Georgia's 2020 general election. A similar scenario emerged in Arizona, where the 2022 Republican nominee, Kari Lake, challenged the election results in 2022 based on substantial evidence of non-compliance with the Arizona election code by Maricopa County election officials, including problems in signature verification on absentee ballots, failure to adhere to the chain of custody laws; unequal application of election standards and protocols; and many more. Just as in Georgia, there was a pattern of election office insiders failing to administer the election correctly and then mocking the citizens and Kari Lake for raising concerns and challenging the results.

What does this mean for the American voting public? It means a dangerous reduction in confidence in our elections and an increasing loss of faith in a judicial system that allows judges to turn a blind eye to corruption and disregard election laws. How do we fix it? The most critical way we can fix our broken election process is through the participation of citizen patriots in local elections and dragging state legislatures back to exercising their constitutional duty to be decisive in election decisions, as set forth in the US Constitution.

Chapter 24
Article V - Convention of States

Our Constitution is amendable under Article V, which allows Congress to add amendments when deemed necessary for the good of the people and the Nation. However, our Founding Fathers intentionally made the process difficult to avoid abuse and the diluting of the Constitution. To add amendments to our Constitution, two-thirds of both chambers of Congress deem the addition of an amendment necessary, followed by ratification by three-fourths (thirty-eight) of the existing states.

The brilliancy of our Founding Fathers also enabled them to foresee the day when the federal government would become so bloated, power-hungry, corrupt, and inept that rather than serving the people, it would become an oppressor of the people. Our Founding Fathers further realized that to allow only Congress to make Amendments to the Constitution would give the citizens of our country no avenue to rein in an out-of-control government. The Founding Fathers unanimously voted to approve adding language to Article V, providing this country's citizens a means to circumvent a corrupt and oppressive government through their State Legislators.

The Convention of States Action movement is a national effort to call a convention under Article V of the United States Constitution. It is restricted to proposing amendments that will address fiscal irresponsibility and excessive spending by federal government, federal overreach int its power and jurisdiction, and term limits for federal officials and members of Congress. Since the Project launched in 2013, it has grown to over 4.5 million supporters nationwide, with petition signers in every state house district across America and actively working in all fifty states to pass the Convention of States application. There are hundreds of state and federal senators and representatives, governors (i.e.,

Greg Abbott and Ron DeSantis), state party leaders (Allen West), constitutional scholars, men of faith (Dr. James Dobson, Mike Huckabee), and historians (Eric Metaxas and David Barton) who have endorsed Convention of States. Thirty-four state legislatures must pass a resolution applying for a convention of states dealing with the same subject matter. The current status of the obtaining of the required thirty-four to the convening a Convention of states is as follows:

> ➤ As of July 2023, nineteen states have passed the Convention of States resolution: Georgia, Alaska, Florida, Alabama, Tennessee, Indiana, Oklahoma, Louisiana, Arizona, North Dakota, Texas, Missouri, Arkansas, Utah, Mississippi, Wisconsin, Nebraska; West Virginia; and South Carolina.

> ➤ States where the Convention of States Application has passed in one chamber but being debated in the other chamber: New Mexico, Iowa, South Dakota, Virginia, North Carolina, New Hampshire, and Wyoming.

> ➤ States considering the Convention of States Resolution in 2023: Colorado, Delaware, Hawaii, Illinois, Iowa, Kansas, Kentucky, Maine, Maryland, Massachusetts, Minnesota, Montana, New Hampshire, New Mexico, New York, North Carolina, Ohio, Pennsylvania, Rhode Island, South Dakota, Vermont, Virginia, Washington, Wyoming.

Questions and answers regarding a Convention of States under Article V of the United States Constitution:

> ➤ **Can Congress block a Convention of States?** *"No."* Once thirty-four states apply for a convention to propose amendments on the same issue, Article V of the Constitution mandates Congress to name the convention's place and time.

- **If Article V says Congress "calls" the Convention, does that mean it controls the convention and chooses the delegates?** *"No."* Once thirty-four states apply, Congress has no discretion but to call a convention and no control over the delegates. States are free to develop their own selection processes for choosing their delegates. Delegates discuss and propose amendment proposals that fit the topic framed by the thirty-four state resolutions that triggered the convention. Each state gets one vote. Thirty-eight states must ratify any proposed amendments sent back to the states by the convention.

- **How do we know that a Convention of States will work?** Interstate conventions were common during the foundation of our nation; the basic procedures and rules for such conventions were uniform. We are actually getting back to our roots. We have held two simulations of a Convention of States, the last one held in late July of 2023, with legislative delegates from all fifty states in attendance. Both simulations were total successes.

- **Is Convention of States safe?** *"Absolutely!"* Article V includes numerous safeguards that protect the United States Constitution and ensures that only widely approved amendments are adopted. The strongest safeguard? Any amendment proposed by the Convention goes through the exact same ratification process as amendments proposed by Congress. It must be approved by thirty-eight states. That means if thirteen states vote no, the answer is no. It does not get much safer than that!

- **So, what is the plan?** The goal is to call for a convention to propose amendments on particular subjects rather than a particular amendment – those subjects are (1) limiting Federal power, (2) mandating fiscal responsibility, and (3) imposing term limits. The mission is to grow the grassroots army to implement an Article V convention. We now have over 4.5 million supporters and are increasing exponentially, as well as signed petitions in 100% of legislative districts across America, so the Convention of States grassroots army is the most significant Article V movement in history.

The Convention of States Action organization is working one-on-one with state legislators nationwide to educate them regarding the critical need for calling a Convention of States and their vital role in our Constitutional Republic as the last line of defense against an oppressive and corrupt federal government.

The Convention of States Action organization believes that grassroots support is the key to successfully calling a Convention and ensuring that good amendments get ratified. The organization is building a political operation in all fifty states and recruiting at least one hundred citizens in every state legislative district in the nation.

- **Why call for an Article V Convention?** *"Simple:"* to bring power back to the states and the people where it belongs. Unelected bureaucrats in Washington, D.C., should not be allowed to make sweeping decisions that impact millions of Americans. But right now, they do. So, it all boils down to one question: Who should decide what is best for you and your family? You, or the federal government? We would vote for the American people every single time.

- **Who is behind this movement?** The American people. The Convention of States is, first and foremost, a movement of grassroots citizens fed up with business as usual in D.C. We are funded by thousands of everyday patriots who have committed their lives, fortunes, and sacred honor to protect liberty for future generations.

- **Can Delegates to the Convention propose any Amendment they want?** Once Congress has set a date and place for the convention, each state can send as many delegates as they choose, but each state is constitutionally restricted to only one vote. By the resolutions submitted to Congress, these delegates are restricted to considering only those Amendments articulated in their applications to Congress. Any deviation on the part of any delegate will subject them to being recalled, and an alternate delegate will be sent to replace them. Further, State government entities, like the federal government, are constitutionally restricted from interfering with the Convention of State process.

If you are interested in signing the petition to your state legislators, more in-depth information can be obtained at http://conventionofstates.com. They are working tirelessly to educate and inspire American citizens to actively support this desperately needed call for a Convention of States. They are working with state legislators in all fifty states to help them understand, appreciate, and recognize the need for them to draft a Resolution identical to every other State' Resolution to assure continuity and qualification of every Resolution submitted to Congress.

The text being utilized by each State in passing a Resolution calling for the convening of a Convention of States reads as follows.

APPLICATION FOR A CONVENTION OF THE STATES UNDER ARTICLE V OF THE CONSTITUTION OF THE UNITED STATES

WHEREAS the Founders of our Constitution empowered State Legislators to be guardians of liberty against future abuses of power by the federal government; and

WHEREAS the federal government has created a crushing national debt through improper and imprudent spending; and

WHEREAS the federal government has invaded the legitimate roles of the states through the manipulative process of federal mandates, most of which are unfunded to a great extent; and

WHEREAS the federal government has ceased to live under a proper interpretation of the Constitution of the United States; and

WHEREAS it is the solemn duty of the States to protect the liberty of our people— particularly for the generations to come— by proposing Amendments to the Constitution of the United States through a Convention of the States under Article V for the purpose of restraining these and related abuses of power;

BE IT THEREFORE RESOLVED BY THE LEGISLATURE OF THE STATE OF _____ THAT:

SECTION 1. The legislature of the State of _____ hereby applies to Congress, under the provisions of Article V of the Constitution of the United States, for the calling of a convention of the states limited to proposing amendments to the Constitution of the United States that impose fiscal restraints on the federal government, limit the power and jurisdiction of the federal government, and limit the terms of office for its officials and for members of Congress.

SECTION 2. The secretary of state is hereby directed to transmit copies of this application to the President and Secretary of the United States Senate and to the Speaker and Clerk of the United States House of Representatives, and copies to the members of the said Senate and House of Representatives from this State; also, to transmit copies hereof to the presiding officers of each of the legislative houses in the several States, requesting their cooperation.

SECTION 3. This application constitutes a continuing application in accordance with Article V of the Constitution of the United States until the legislatures of at least two-thirds of the several states have made applications on the same subject.

Everyone whose heads are not stuck in the sand knows our federal government is on a dangerous course. The unsustainable debt combined with crushing regulations on states and businesses is a recipe for disaster. What is less known is that the Founders gave state legislatures the power to act as a firewall between the State government and the citizens therein and the federal government. State legislators are the final check on abuses of power in Washington, DC., through Article V of the United States Constitution which authorizes the state legislatures to call a Convention to propose needed amendments to the Constitution.

The passage of just three Amendments can return our Republic to what our founding fathers intended it to be: a great nation in which we are free to choose our destiny and what is best for ourselves and our families.

> ➤ ***Term Limits***: On average, eighty-five percent of incumbents from both parties are routinely re-elected. Three hundred and ninety-seven members of the House of Representatives, in the 2022 elections, ran for reelection, and three hundred and thirty-nine won their election. The United States Senate had an almost identical rate of winning back their Senate seats. Twenty-five incumbent Senators ran for reelection, and Twenty-one won their reelection. This scenario repeats itself election after election, leaving "We the People" forgotten as these individuals accumulate seniority, influence, power, and wealth. Individuals serving in Congress who fit this situation have come to believe they are there as royalty, and "We the People" are no more than servants expected

to bend to the dictates of these Washington elites. The Washington Bureaucracy (the swamp) has become so emboldened, believing that they cannot and will not be removed from their leadership positions regardless of their competency or unwillingness to work with the sitting President to implement the changes promised during their campaigns.

The Term Limit Amendment will cause a ruling class of professional politicians, who have become increasingly controlling in their approach to the governance of the people, into a body of legislative members who are much more likely to represent their constituents than the interest of donors and lobbyists. This amendment would return our federal governing body to its original intent of being a servant of the people and not the superior of the people. Our Founding Fathers intended that citizens would serve only briefly and then return to their farms, businesses, or occupations. Service within Congress was never intended to be a lifelong career.

- ***Limit Federal Spending and Taxing:*** Congress shall develop a budget for the upcoming fiscal year no later than the First day of May of each year for submission to the President of the United States for consideration. Should Congress and the President of the United States fail to come to terms on a negotiated fiscal year budget by the First day of September of each year, then an automatic across-the-board five percent reduction in expenditures from the prior year's fiscal budget shall be imposed for the fiscal year in which a budget has not been approved and signed into law by the President. Total spending for any fiscal year shall not exceed the revenue received in the previous fiscal year.

  Congress shall not collect more than fifteen percent of a person's annual income from whatever source. Congress shall not collect taxes on the estate of a deceased citizen. The deadline for collecting taxes from any source shall be the first day of the month elections will be held. Congress shall not institute a value-added tax, national sales tax, or any other tax in kind or form.

Congress shall implement a "Gold Standard" to peg our volatile Federal Reserve notes (currency) to a fixed weight of gold bullion so that our Nation's currency can stand on a stable footing over time. Returning to a gold standard to back our currency would substantially curtail economic damage caused by inflation, runaway federal debt, and monetary system instability.

> ***Limit the Federal Bureaucracy***: All federal departments and agencies shall expire if not individually reauthorized in stand-alone reauthorization bills every ---? --- by a majority vote of the House of Representatives and the Senate. Those departments and agencies not clearly authorized by the Constitution to be within the federal government's purview shall be returned to the individual sovereign states, and each sovereign state shall determine whether or not that state desires to maintain any such department or agency.

No regulation by any department or agency shall be implemented without prior review and approval by a special congressional committee established to review any proposed regulation. The committee shall have no more than (to be determined) months from official receipt of such proposed regulations to review and issue a decision as to whether a submitted proposed regulation shall be implemented.

Congress shall make no changes or alterations to the submitted proposed regulation. Should the congressional committee fail to issue a decision within (*to be determined*) months from the date of receipt, then that regulation will be deemed denied. The legislative branch shall have no authority or power to transfer its legislative responsibility to make laws to non-elected bureaucrats.

We must push for and demand that our state legislators pass resolutions calling for the convening of an Article V Convention of States for the purpose of passing amendments to the Constitution. Just three amendments would rein in the outrageous abuse of power by the federal government, forever changing the way Washington governs. Term limits, balanced budgets, and restriction of federal jurisdiction. This can only happen if we are all willing to unite and make it happen. We are already at a point where our fight to reinstitute our Constitutional Republic will be an uphill battle. We cannot wait any longer; we must act now. In time, the Convention of States Action organizational family will be victorious and obtain the passage of the required number of State Resolutions to convene a "Convention of States" from the required thirty-four states. State legislators currently reluctant to pass our resolution will eventually come around, at the very least in states where freedom, liberty, and the Constitution are still valued. These legislators will realize that most of their constituents, "We the People," want and fully support the passage of a resolution calling for convening a Convention of States.

Convention of States Action organization leadership always knew the satanic ruling "elite" class would one day attack, but our growing success has forced them to act faster than anticipated. And you can be sure those attacks are just beginning. Today, they are coming from the radical Marxist-Communist Democrat Party officials. Still, the assaults will expand to include every person and organization in Washington, D.C., with a vested interest in keeping power in Washington. To ensure that the Convention of States Action organization responds effectively, they are focused on increasing their grassroots army to many millions of Americans. Right now, the Convention of States Action movement has well over four million supporters, but more are needed to send a strong message to all legislators of every State that the people are fed-up with the status quo that benefits only the Washington elitists and their nationwide radical Marxist-Communist Democrat followers but does nothing for "We the People." You can be a part of this historic grassroots movement by getting involved in four unique ways:

- Sign the Convention of States petition at www.conventionofstates.com. Spread the word to your friends, family members, or an elected official. Send your family members and friends to www.conventionofstates.com to sign the petition to support convening a Convention of States. Have them visit the Convention of States Action organization online for more information at any one of these internet platforms:

    - www.conventionofstates.com;
    - fb.com/conventionofstates.com;
    - instagram.com/conventionofstates;
    - twitter.com/COSProject; or,
    - call (540) 441-7227 to request a speaker for your events, group meetings, or any other venue available to you.

- Volunteering is the easiest way to get involved in the fight in your state. As a volunteer, your primary task will be contacting your state legislators and asking that they support the Convention of States resolution, spreading the word about Article V to your friends and family, and, if within a reasonable distance, attending legislative meetings at your state Capitol. You can commit as much or as little time as your schedule allows.

- Volunteer to be part of the Social Media Warriors team, which spreads the word online, or as a member of the State Follow-Up Team, which contacts recent petition signers to thank them for signing the petition and welcome them as new members of the Convention of States Action organization.

- ➢ Become a Leader: The Convention of States Action organization has leadership positions to fit any skill set. You can apply to be a: • State Director, • District Captain, • Coalition Director (e.g., Veterans, Young Americans), • State Videographer • State Communications Coordinator • Legislative Liaison • State Media Liaison • State Tech Assistant/Manager, • State Content Writer, • State Grassroots Coordinator.

Since 2013, the Convention of State Action organization has gotten nineteen states on board, leaving only fifteen states to convince them that passing a resolution is what their constituents want. A recent poll by The Trafalgar Group found that 81% of Republicans, 63% of Independents, and 50% of Democrats support a Convention of State. With this kind of support growing daily, it is only a matter of time before we achieve the thirty-four states needed to pass our Resolution to convene a convention. To save and maintain control of our constitutional republic's form of government by "We the People" will take more than just the passage of the three proposed new amendments. We must win on four critical fronts to truly win and forever change how our elected officials and unelected bureaucrats conduct themselves.

- ➢ **First**, we must achieve integrity to ensure our elections are fair and honest. Only living American citizens vote once, on one day, with voter ID and paper ballots. Without election integrity, political parties will continue to find ways to cheat and thwart the people's will. Political parties, or members thereof, have already demonstrated their contempt for and willingness to ignore our Constitution to create an elitist class and destroy our Constitutional Republic.

Every state desperately needs election poll greeters, poll workers, and poll observers. These individuals are our eyes and ears at polling sites, able to detect and report inappropriate activity. By law, each polling site is allowed two Democrats, two Republicans, and a Chief Judge. If there are not sufficient workers from one party, then those slots are allowed to be filled by workers of the opposing party. Both parties must equally represent each polling site unless all reasonable efforts have been made to fill a particular Party's slot without success; then, the Board of Elections is exempted from the two and two-rule

If we truly want honest, fraudulent, free elections, then we all need to be willing to sacrifice a small amount of our time during every election cycle by working at polling precincts in whatever capacity suits us best. Please seriously consider volunteering for these positions, and if you are inclined to serve, do not hesitate to contact your local county Republican/Democratic headquarters. For more information on election integrity, go to election-integrity.org.

- **Second**, we must work harder, ask more questions, and do more research on candidates we are considering for elected offices. Challenge their responses or positions on critical issues facing the United States. Find out if they fully support the passage of a Resolution calling for convening a Convention of States. Only vote for candidates who truly and represent your values and not solely based on name recognition or because they are members of the party for which your family has always supported, no questions asked.

If you fail to assess candidates and assure yourself of their position on the things that are important to you, or worse, do not vote, once it is over, it will do you no good to sit on your couch yelling at the TV during news broadcasts because everything is going down the tube.

- **Third**, we know from hard-earned experience that certain congressional members do not respect our Constitution and outright disregard it despite taking an oath to protect and enforce it. Without election integrity and solid conservative constitutional representatives, the passage of the proposed three amendments will only be three more amendments to be ignored, just as the current Constitution and amendments are ignored. Once we have election integrity and elected individuals who will truly protect and adhere to our constitution, our proposed amendments will have the impact we so desperately need.

- **Fourth,** Poll Workers and Poll Observers are key elements to Election Integrity. These volunteers are physically located at the polling site, which allows them to see and hear what is occurring to ensure that the voting process proceeds as dictated by State and Federal law. Election Poll Workers and Poll Observers are community-minded people who wish to be part of the election process.

  Election Poll Workers assist fellow voters at the precinct polling sites on election day. Among their duties are ensuring voters are at the correct precinct, verifying voter registration, verifying voters utilizing driver's licenses, issuing ballots, giving voting procedure instructions, operating voting equipment, and maintaining an orderly flow at the polling place. Poll Workers are paid to work at Election polling sites and are trained in voting procedures, equipment operation, and customer service. Becoming an Election Worker is an important decision that requires commitment, dedication, and the desire to be a public servant. The first steps towards becoming an election poll worker is to visit your county's Board of Elections office and apply.

An election site poll watcher, sometimes referred to as an "election observer," is an individual who observes the voter's and poll workers' interactions to ensure no inappropriate actions are conducted during the election process. Each state has its laws and procedures on when and where observers can be present and who can observe the election. Poll watchers may be members of organizations such as a political party or nonpartisan group, candidate representatives, international observers, exit polling groups, academics, or relevant federal and state agencies. Some states also allow members of the public to view election processes in person, though these rules also vary. The role of a poll watcher is to observe and monitor the election without violating voter privacy or disrupting the election.

Every county in the United States needs volunteers for these critical positions in our election process. Counties are usually short of volunteers to man every voting site within every county of every State. It is vital that patriotic, civic-minded citizens volunteer for these critical positions to ensure election integrity.

The Washington political elitists have stripped away the powers and responsibilities given to the sovereign states as articulated in our Constitution. They have established an elitist ruling class status for themselves and are determined to do whatever it takes to maintain that status and power. This alone is cause for "We The People," through our State legislators, to call for a Convention of States to bring this out-of-control, overreaching, and corrupt federal government to the bay. Term Limits are the only way to keep incompetent and corrupt Marxist-Communist Democrat Party officials and legislators from making a career out of fleecing the American people.

But it is worse than that: those same politicians have brought this country to the verge of bankruptcy, divided us through their political rhetoric for their political gain, passed laws that we are forced to comply with while exempting themselves, interjected our country into the wars of other countries which are of no direct threat to our national security at a significant loss of our young men and women. They have campaigned on promises to change the downward spiral of this nation's place in history, which is the last great hope where all citizens have the right to self-determination, the right to pursue prosperity freely, and the God-given right to liberty and justice.

They have campaigned on promises to pass legislation to help the underserved, govern under a balanced budget, restrict their overreach into the affairs of sovereign states, and reduce taxes and regulations so all Americans may obtain a life of prosperity. Then, they repeatedly break those promises, blaming the opposing party for their failures and broken promises. We must not let the federal bureaucracy destroy us as a Constitutional Republic nor divide us as a unified people, One Nation under God. I implore all of you to take the time to read the Constitution and the affixed Amendments and understand what is at stake. Take the time to learn what a "Convention of States" really means, why it is so necessary now, and why it is a safe means to bring back our Republic to the people. Then, hopefully, you will decide to no longer stand on the sidelines doing nothing and leave it up to others to do the hard work. This is not the way we will win this battle.

It will take everyone working together to make the necessary changes to bring this country back to a true Constitutional Republic. Those who have not done so get a booklet containing the Constitution and Amendments you can carry in your pocket for ready reference and review. Go to conventionofstates.com and read or reread what the movement is all about and what it will mean for our Nation. Remember, success is in the hands of "We The People" standing together and not in the hands of politicians we send to Washington, D.C., who fail us term after term.

The information I am providing is a means by which "We the People" can take back those rights from the politicians and all political parties. This battle is a State versus the Federal government issue, it is a "We The People" versus the federal bureaucracy issue. People may very well be right that in the end nothing will change, but if we do nothing then nothing will change, but we must at the very least try to bring about change before it is too late. I know that probably a majority of voters and the politicians in Washington have conveniently forgotten or were never introduced to the words of Abraham Lincoln, which states, "That government of the people, by the people, for the people, shall not perish from the earth." But with so much apathy and unwillingness of American citizens and congressional members to fight for this God-given right, "shall not perish from the earth" may soon be nothing more than a forgotten statement in our country's history. Are so many ready and willing to relinquish their right to self-governess to power-hungry bureaucrats who will and are deteriorating our God-given rights as enumerated in our Constitution?

www.ingramcontent.com/pod-product-compliance
Lightning Source LLC
Chambersburg PA
CBHW020452030426
42337CB00011B/80